Winning Investment Strategies

Using Security Analysis to Build Wealth

John B. Malloy

LIBERTY HALL
PRESS™

LIBERTY HALL PRESS books are published by LIBERTY HALL PRESS, an imprint of TAB BOOKS. Its trademark, consisting of the words "LIBERTY HALL PRESS" and the portrayal of Benjamin Franklin, is registered in the United States Patent and Trademark Office.

First Edition
First Printing

©1990 by TAB BOOKS
Printed in the United States of America

Library of Congress Cataloging-in-Publication Data

Malloy, John B.
   Winning investment strategies : using security analysis to build wealth / by John B. Malloy.
     p. cm.
   ISBN 0-8306-3509-2
   1. Stocks. 2. Bonds. 3. Taxation of bonds, securities, etc.
4. Finance, Personal. 5. Investment analysis. I. Title.
HG4661.M34 1990
332.63'2—dc20   89-77439
                                                      CIP

TAB BOOKS offers software for sale.
For information and a catalog, please contact:

TAB Software Department
Blue Ridge Summit, PA 17294-0850

Questions regarding the content of this book
should be addressed to:

Reader Inquiry Branch
TAB BOOKS
Blue Ridge Summit, PA 17294-0214

Acquisitions Editor: David Conti
Technical Editor: Lori Flaherty
Book Design: Jaclyn J. Boone
Production: Katherine Brown

Contents

Dedication

To Beth and Phil, may you profit from the ideas
in this book at a much earlier age than I did.

Acknowledgments

This book is based on 27 years of experience making economic studies of various kinds for Amoco Corporation, and for its petrochemical subsidiary, Amoco Chemicals. My ideas on economic evaluation were shaped in discussions with many of my Amoco colleagues, and I would like to thank them for their many contributions. In particular, I wish to thank Louis L. Czyzewski, who read the manuscript and offered many helpful comments.

An author's wife does not have an easy time. While he isolates himself for long hours at the computer, she does double duty. My heartfelt thanks to Nancy, who made a critical contribution to this book through her patience and understanding.

Preface

I HAVE WRITTEN THIS BOOK TO SHOW YOU THE STATE-OF-THE-ART METHODS MODERN corporations use to manage their investment programs and how you can use these same methods to manage your own program. I want to put my 27 years of hands-on experience of guiding the investment program of a major corporation at your disposal.

My experience includes economic evaluations of new industrial plants, acquisition studies, long-range investment programs, and studies of the economic environment for industry, all of which directly applies to the same problems you have managing your own investments. This background of business and science gives me an insight I would not ordinarily have if my experience were strictly as a financial analyst. The methods in this book are the same techniques corporations use to evaluate multimillion dollar investments.

For most of us, managing our affairs so that we have some money to invest after paying our bills is a struggle. That money is precious. Don't waste it by investing on hunches, tips, or trusting to luck. Know what you are doing. Invest wisely, don't gamble. Use the proven evaluation methods in this book, master them, and make them work for you. They can make your investment program pay off and help you win the investment game.

Introduction

WHY ANOTHER BOOK ON INVESTING? THE SHELVES OF YOUR LOCAL LIBRARY ALREADY groan under the weight of such books, and each year, publishers add new titles. There is no need for another book unless it can tell you something that others can't. *Winning Investment Strategies: Using Security Analysis to Build Wealth* does! It provides you with proven investment techniques that you won't find anywhere else.

Why do so many individual investors do poorly in the market, achieving only indifferent results? Because the average investor does not know how to value a stock. If he cannot value a stock, there is no way he can tell whether a stock is fairly priced, underpriced, or overpriced. More than likely, his investment program is based on hunches, luck, tips from friends and brokers, and much advice found in the financial press. Finally, he switches too frequently from one stock to another, enriching his broker in the process. It is no wonder then that he cannot possibly earn reasonable, consistent returns.

Imagine how much simpler investing would be if the financial pages of your daily newspaper listed, alongside security prices, the most you should pay for each security, and the rate of return you should earn. You could simply scan the list and choose those securities that promised the highest returns. Bargains would be easy to spot, and overpriced securities would be easy to avoid.

Unfortunately, newspapers don't publish that information, but there is a way you can value securities using proven, state-of-the-art investment techniques, and this book can show you how.

This book will show you how to evaluate investments and calculate the rate of return you should expect, as well as the most you should pay for any security. It is quantitative. You will be able to conclude that "The minimum return I should accept is 8 percent. If I invest in ABC stock, I should earn a return of 12.4 percent. I should not pay more than 58 per share for this stock. There is a 30 percent chance I will lose money." You will then be able to judge for yourself whether any investment is really attractive.

In Chapter 1, you'll learn why it is so important to have an investment program and what some of the more common investments are. In Chapter 2, you'll learn about the basic ideas behind interest rates and growth. You'll learn how much cash flows are worth today. Chapter 3 will make you an expert at discounting.

Once you understand discounting, you will be able to understand discounted cash flow analysis. Chapter 4 provides a basic understanding of the method and the tools you'll need to apply discounted cash flow analysis. In Chapter 5, you'll learn how to apply discounted cash flow analysis to fixed-interest securities such as bonds and mortgage-backed securities.

Chapter 6 shows you how to analyze a stock by understanding how corporations grow, how earnings grow, dividends are paid, and how stock prices grow.

Chapter 7 takes the mystery out of growth stocks and shows you how to allow for profitability to fall and growth to slow as these growth firms mature.

Inflation and taxes complicate security evaluations, but Chapters 8 and 9 can show you how to allow for them when analyzing a security so you know whether an investment is *really* as attractive as it first appears.

Successfully evaluating securities depends on making reasonable forecasts of future dividends and stock prices. Chapter 10 examines ways to analyze a firm's historic performance data and how to use that analysis to project future values.

By Chapter 11, you will have learned about the primary factors that affect your return when you invest in security, and you'll be able to navigate the calculation forms that take all of these factors into account.

Chapter 12 explores investment results with typical stocks. Once you've invested in a security, you'll need to know when the best time to sell is. Chapter 13 analyzes all of the factors of selling securities.

Investing in a security always carries a measure of risk. Chapter 14 shows you how to appreciate the risk involved in investing in a security using a proven method.

Chapter 15 shows you how to apply the methods developed in this book to real-life examples. Finally, Chapter 16 shows you how to target a savings plan and what it will take to realize your goals, including calculation forms that help you set up long-range savings plans such as retirement or college plans.

Once you learn the investment analysis methods in this book, the odds change greatly in your favor. You become a knowledgeable investor. You know what you are doing, and you can identify securities that promise a high return. You are independent. You no longer rely on tips, hunches, or luck. You can evaluate these tips yourself and sort out the few that might have value. You'll be able to avoid the pitfalls that snare many unwary investors. You'll make winning investments.

About This Book

This book is written for the average investor. You don't have to be a wizard to evaluate investments, and your normal skills are more than adequate. Can you add? Subtract? Multiply? Divide? Can you look up a number in a table? Can you fill out a simple form? If you can do these elementary things, you can complete the calculation forms in this book and successfully evaluate investments. The forms will lead you step-by-step with ease through all of the evaluations.

Discounted cash flow analysis is not difficult, and you don't need to be an Einstein to do the calculations yourself. You can easily do the calculation on an inexpensive hand calculator. Buy a calculator that has an e^x, a y^x, and a $\ln(x)$ key. Don't worry if these arithmetic symbols look strange. Think of them as just another key on your calculator. On the few occasions when a calculation form requires one of these values, simply enter a value from the form into your calculator and tap the e^x, y^x, or $\ln(x)$ key. A calculator that can develop averages and standard deviations automatically will also be helpful, and these features are also available on an inexpensive calculator.

Finally, I assume that most of you are not financial experts. Therefore, I've included the basic ideas behind interest rates and growth in the first few chapters and how they affect how fast your money can grow when it is invested and earns interest. Go through the book in order, beginning with Chapter 1, because all of the information builds on previous chapters.

1

Making Your
Investment Program Pay

"BUY LOW, SELL HIGH" IS THE CLASSIC ADVICE TO INVESTORS, BUT YOU CAN PROFIT FROM this advice only if you know how to tell when prices are low and when prices are high. The average investor cannot profit from this advice, simply because he does not know how to value securities. The following are some of the most frequent mistakes investors who do not know how to value securities make:

1. They invest in securities when their money could be used more effectively paying off high-interest debt.

2. They buy stocks after the market has driven stock prices far above their real value. Prices of such stocks are more likely to drop towards their real value than continue rising.

3. They pay too much for growth stocks.

4. They overestimate the performance of mutual funds. Stocks selected by throwing darts at the financial page outperform 80 percent of mutual funds.

5. They underestimate the risk involved in buying stocks and bonds.

6. They do not appreciate how increases in market interest rates cause the prices of stocks and bonds to fall.

7. They switch too often from one stock to another. Brokers reap most of the gains through commissions.

8. They lose purchasing power by investing in vehicles like bank savings accounts and certificates of deposit, where returns are often not high enough to offset taxes and inflation.

If an investor doesn't know a security's true value, there is no way he can tell whether he is buying low or selling high. If he does not know a security's true value, he cannot identify bargains or overpriced securities. His investment program is out of control. In place of sound decisions based on the real value of securities, he relies instead on tips, hunches, and luck. Tips are available in abundance. Most tips are free—a price usually indicative of their value. His broker recommends stocks. Friends offer tips. The financial press, and financial programs on television deluge him with tips. He succumbs to the euphoria of the market. When the market crashes 508 points in a single day, as it did in October 1987, and crashes again 190 points two years later, he is among the victims.

You cannot win the investment game by investing in such a haphazard, uncontrolled way. Learning how to value securities is not difficult, and you can master the procedures easily. Once you know how to value securities, the odds change greatly in your favor. You become a knowledgeable investor. You free yourself from dependence on tips. You make your own investment decisions, and you make them with confidence. You become a winner in the investment game.

Corporations have the same problems managing their investments that you do. They developed state-of-the-art methods to solve these problems. Except for size, there is no basic difference between the problems a large corporation investing millions of dollars faces and the problems an individual investor working with only several thousand dollars faces. Because the problems are the same, you can use the same methods to manage your investments.

A corporation faces serious problems managing its investment program. The corporation has limited funds, and it has more opportunities to invest than it has funds to invest. Therefore, it needs a way to evaluate each investment opportunity so it can identify the most profitable ones. It also has to know the minimum return it should accept. Otherwise, it might find itself investing money that costs 12 percent in projects that earn only 8 percent. Investments are also risky and a corporation needs to assess the risk in each potential investment and allow for that risk when it ranks investments.

You have the same problems. You have limited funds. There are many more investment opportunities available than you have money to invest in and you, too, need a way to evaluate these opportunities. You can then rank them and identify the ones that will make your money grow the fastest. You also have a minimum rate of return you should accept. You must understand what that minimum is, or you, too, might invest and lose money. Your investments are also risky. You need to measure risk, and allow for risk when you rank investment opportunities, just as a corporation does.

Solving these problems is crucial for corporations, because millions of investment dollars are at stake. Successful investments determine a corporation's future growth and profitability. Because success is so important, and so much money is at risk, corporations have developed scientific tools to help manage their investment programs.

Why Have an Investment Program?

There are many important goals you need to save for. Everyone wants a better future. You might want a comfortable retirement, a college education for your children, a home of your own, or a larger or more luxurious home. You might want a higher standard of living—perhaps a new car, a boat, or foreign travel.

All of these goals have one thing in common. They require a large sum of money, usually more than you have available. To reach those goals, you have to set money aside from current spending and save it. You need to invest that money and make it grow to whatever amount you need when the time comes to retire, to make the first tuition payment, downpayment on a home, or to meet the cost of some other goal.

You will be shocked when you calculate in Chapter 16 the amount of money you must save each month to build a fund for a college education or for retirement. How much you need to save depends on how effective your investment program is. If you make your investment program as effective as possible—if you earn the highest possible return on your investments—you will make saving for any goal much easier.

You have less time to build wealth than you think. I remember vividly the day when, fresh out of M.I.T., I went to work as a research engineer. I was telling my father about my new job and asked whether I should sign up for Amoco's pension plan. His advice was simple: "Sign up for everything they offer. You only have to go to bed and get up a few times and you'll find it's time to retire." He was right. Retirement came much faster than I expected. Each time I recall his advice, I realize how short a time there is to make an investment program pay off.

Not only is time short, but the timing of income and expenses also works against us. A young person starting a career at age 20 has 45 years of employment and income stretching before him during which he can invest and make his money grow. He could invest $1,000 at 8 percent interest, and watch it grow to $36,600 by the time he retires 45 years later. But putting aside $1,000 is extremely difficult at age 20. Paychecks are small at the beginning of a career. The expenses of starting a home and raising a family might take every penny of that paycheck, and more. Instead of saving, most of us go into debt. You might be age 50, after you have raised and educated your children, before you have a significant surplus available for savings. At age 50, $1,000 invested at 8 percent interest will only grow to $3,320 by retirement 15 years later.

INVESTING FOR RETIREMENT

Without an effective investment program, many people are going to find retirement financially trying. Two retirees out of three rely on Social Security for their primary retirement income. Social Security does not provide primary income, it supplements other income. Pensions help, but many are inadequate. Pension plans cover less than half of the workers in private industry. Only one worker in four has been in the same job long enough to be eligible for a pension. Only one retiree in five now receives a pension. Inflation compounds the problem. Many who once believed their savings adequate will find those savings are not going to stretch very far at today's prices.

Progress in medicine and technology has steadily increased the average life span. A man retiring at age 65 can look forward to 14.2 more years of life—1.4 years more than in 1950. A woman retiring at age 65 can look forward to 18.5 more years—3.5 years more. Besides living longer, more people are retiring earlier. Living longer and retiring earlier means more savings are required to provide income for those extra retirement years.

INVESTMENT POSSIBILITIES

What is the best way to invest your savings? A large variety of investments are available. Stocks, bonds, IRA accounts, mutual funds, Ginnie Maes, certificates of deposit, money market funds, and bank savings accounts are popular options. Other investments are available, but they normally require more attention than most of us are able to give. Instead, we turn our money over to a management group that has the expertise and the time to manage the investment.

When searching for ways to invest your money, don't overlook paying off high-interest loans. Paying off a loan and avoiding high interest charges is often more attractive than any other investment available to you. Many investors have charge accounts on which they are paying 18 percent interest. Prepaying a loan and avoiding 18 percent interest is obviously more attractive than investing in a certificate of deposit and earning only 8 percent.

Make your investment program effective by investing where the returns are the highest. Popular investments vary widely in yield, and the yield differences make a major difference in how fast your savings will grow. Look at how $1,000 invested in a money market fund, a certificate of deposit, and a bank savings account will grow over a 10-year period based on yields available in 1989:

	Yield, %	Savings in 10 Years
Money Market Fund	9.3	$2,535
Certificate of Deposit	8.9	2,316
Bank Super-NOW Account	5.1	1,665

Small differences in yield are important. A one percentage point difference in average yield, i.e., earning an average yield of 8 percent instead of 7 percent, will make a 57 percent difference in savings over a 45-year period. Even over as short a period as 10 years, the difference in savings is 10.5 percent.

You need some way to measure how attractive various investment opportunities are. You need a common scale you can use to rank investments and identify those that earn the highest returns. That common scale is the rate of return, the interest rate, or the yield. All mean essentially the same thing. If you know the rates of return for all of the investments you are considering, you can rank them and identify those investments that will make your savings grow the fastest.

Some investments, such as bank savings accounts and money market funds, state the rate of return directly. The true return on certificates of deposit is slightly below the stated return. Ranking these investments is straightforward. It does not take a sophisticated analyst to conclude that a money market fund paying 9.3 percent is more attractive than a certificate of deposit paying 8.9 percent, or a bank savings account paying only 5.1 percent interest.

But how do you compare a money market fund to a stock or a bond? Ranking stocks and bonds is more complicated because their rates of return are not stated directly. Knowing the rate of return a stock or a bond is likely to earn is important. Otherwise, you might pay too much for stocks and bonds, or invest in stocks and bonds when you should be investing in money market funds instead.

Stocks

There is a rate of return associated with an investment in stocks, but you won't find it listed in your daily newspaper. You have to calculate it yourself. This book will show you how. You will learn why stocks have value. You will learn how value depends on the rate of return the firm is earning, how fast it is growing, the dividends it is paying, and the amount of debt the firm carries. You will learn which of these factors is most important in determining the stock's value.

Once you have calculated the rate of return from investing in a stock, you can make straightforward comparisons of one stock with another, or with any other investment—a money market fund, a certificate of deposit, or any other security with a clearly stated interest rate. You will also be able to calculate how the value of a stock changes as market interest rates fluctuate.

You will also learn about the problems with investing in growth stocks. Growth stocks are hi tech, glamour stocks. They appear to be attractive investments. Business publications and analysts' reports emphasize the high-tech nature of their business and the prospects for growth, but they say little about whether the stock is reasonably priced. The problem with growth stocks is that investors have already recognized the growth potential of these stocks, and bid their prices up to very high levels. I will show you how to calculate whether these stocks are overpriced. You cannot realistically expect growth firms to continue growing rapidly forever. Growth will slow as these firms mature. I will show you how to allow for slowing growth so that your evaluations of growth stocks will be realistic.

Many analysts advocate buying stocks that sell at low price/earnings ratios. These stocks appear to be bargains. You will be able to calculate whether these stocks really are bargains, or whether there is good reason for their low prices. Most companies plod along from year-to-year, making unspectacular profits. The investment community does not value these stocks highly. You will be able to calculate whether the low prices asked for these stocks provide a good return on investment.

You can earn above-average returns in the stock market. To do so, you will have to stand aside from the barrage of tips, and learn to make your own evaluation of stocks. Learning how to evaluate stocks is well within your ability. This book will help you understand why a stock has value, and show you how to translate that value into a rate of return you should expect and the maximum price you should pay for any stock.

Bonds

A bond bears a stated interest rate, but you are not likely to earn that stated rate. The price you pay for a bond, and the price you will receive if you sell the bond before it matures, fluctuate with market interest rates. These fluctuations make the rate of return different from the bond's stated interest rate. If interest rates rise after you have invested in a bond, the bond will drop in value. I will show you how to account for these price fluctuations, and how to calculate the rate of return from investing in bonds and the maximum price you should pay in Chapter 5.

Discounted Cash Flow Analysis

You will learn a sophisticated technique called discounted cash flow analysis. Don't be awed by an imposing name. The basic idea of discounted cash flow analysis is simple and easy to understand. You do not have to be a wizard to use it.

I will also show you two ways to evaluate any investment. The first will enable you to calculate the rate of return you can earn. The second recognizes that you have alternative investments available. You might, for example, be able to earn 8 percent interest from a certificate of deposit or you might be able to pay off a loan on which you are paying 15 percent interest. I will show you how to analyze an investment and conclude, "If I have an alternative investment that will earn a 15 percent return, the most I should pay for XYZ stock is $43 per share. IF XYZ stock costs more than $43 per share, I should choose the alternative investment. If XYZ stock costs less, I should buy the stock.''

You'll soon learn how to tune the analysis to your own particular financial situation.

Discounted cash flow analysis is not restricted to security analysis. It is a general way to analyze any problem involving cash flows and you will find several valuable ways to use it. It will help you set up a savings plan to meet a savings target. One estimate you should make is how much you will have to save each month to build a fund for a college education or retirement. Discounted cash flow analysis will help you make that estimate. You will also find discounted cash flow analysis helpful in figuring mortgage and bank loan payments for any combination of interest rates and loan periods, and for calculating the true interest rate on consumer loans.

Risk

Securities are risky. Junk bonds and the stock of fledgling companies with no track record are very risky. Stocks and bonds of mature companies are less risky. Government bonds and federal-insured securities are essentially risk-free.

Risk complicates security analysis. You cannot simply analyze securities and invest in those that promise the highest returns. If you do, you will build a portfolio of risky securities. Besides a rate-of-return scale for ranking securities, you also need a way to measure risk, then you can limit your investments to securities whose risk you are willing to accept.

Some risk is predictable. Most firms have a track record. You know how fast their earnings, dividends, and stock prices have grown in the past. You can relate this growth to the growth of the national economy and predict how the firm is likely to grow in the future. Growth depends on a few basic factors such as the rate of return the firm earns, how much of its earnings the firm pays out as dividends and how much it reinvests, and how much new debt the firm takes on. For many firms, these basic factors follow reasonably stable patterns from which you can forecast future growth and likely stock prices.

Other risk is unpredictable. The government might ban the firm's product or a competitor might bring out a superior product. The firm might lose a major customer, or a key employee. Fire or explosion could destroy the firm's manufacturing facilities. Lower cost imports might take away the firm's market. These and a host of other misfortunes could suddenly reduce a firm's earning potential. There is no way to allow for such events. They are what makes investing risky.

In Chapter 14 you'll learn about a sophisticated technique called Monte Carlo analysis to measure risk. The basic idea is simple. Analyze a security many times, each time choosing random values of the critical factors from the likely range of values those factors might have. Each analysis provides one possible outcome for that investment. By analyzing many such outcomes, you can estimate the most likely return from the investment, and the probability of reaching any other return. Most analysts use a computer to analyze, say, a thousand random outcomes. But you can get surprisingly good results evaluating just a few random outcomes by hand.

Doing the Analysis

I am going to show you how to make a sophisticated analysis and get quantitative results. Don't worry about getting lost in complicated calculations. I have developed calculation forms that make each calculation easy. You will begin by entering the basic information for the security you are evaluating. The calculation form will then lead you step-by-step through the analysis. Each step will involve nothing more complicated than elementary arithmetic. There are also examples to guide you through each calculation form as well as tables of the discount and growth factors needed for these calculations. With the help of the calculation forms and these tables, analyzing a security will be no more complicated than looking up a number in the phone book, filling out a form, and doing some simple arithmetic.

SUMMARY

☐ You can use the same state-of-the-art tools modern corporations use to manage your investment program and make your investment dollars grow faster.

☐ You must calculate the rate of return for any investment in order to rank them and choose those with the highest returns consistent with the level of risk you are willing to accept. These are the investments that make your savings grow the fastest. You must also calculate the minimum return you should accept, and the maximum price you should pay for any security.

☐ Discounted cash flow analysis has many applications beyond analyzing securities. It allows you to analyze any problem involving cash flows. You will be able to calculate the savings you will need for a college education, retirement, or any other goal, and how much you will have to save each month to reach those targets.

☐ Growth stocks do not follow the steady-state analysis, which assumes that all cash flows connected with a stock grow at steady rates. You must make realistic allowances for gradual changes in profitability and growth as these firms mature.

☐ Evaluating an investment requires forecasting how fast the firms you invest in will grow in the future. You must also correlate the growth of any company with the growth of the national economy and make reasonable forecasts of future growth.

☐ You must allow for risk when evaluating securities. If you simply choose securities that promise the highest returns, you will build a portfolio of risky securities. You must measure risk and adjust your choice of securities to the level of risk you are willing to accept.

☐ Calculation forms keep analysis investments in securities simple. These forms lead you step-by-step through the analysis. No step involves anything more complicated than elementary arithmetic. After completing the form, you will know the rate of return you should expect and the maximum price you should pay for that security.

2

Making Money Grow

Interest rates play a crucial role in regulating the nation's financial activities. Like setting a thermostat to call for more or less heat, financial markets set interest rates to call for more or less savings. Interest rates are critically important signals to investors. Changes in interest rates signal turning points in security prices. When interest rates rise, the market price of securities such as stocks and bonds fall. When interest rates fall, the market price of these securities rise.

You will use interest rates to rank alternative investment opportunities, so you can invest where your money will grow the fastest. You will also use interest rates to find the maximum price you should pay for any security. In this chapter, you will examine how the market uses interest rates to regulate savings and investment, and thereby changes the returns available to you. You will then learn how to calculate how fast your money will grow when you invest it and earn interest.

REGULATING FINANCIAL ACTIVITY

Our society covers a wide range of economic activity. A host of organizations, large and small, supply all of the goods and services we regard as essential. Often these organizations need more money for their business than they now have available. At the same time, other sectors of society have more money available than they now need. The financial market brings these two groups together. It raises money from those who have more than they need and lends it to those who need more money than they have.

The federal government lies at one extreme of the economic spectrum. It intrudes in almost every facet of economic life. The federal government provides 23 percent of all the goods and services produced in the entire economy. Normally, the government does not take in enough taxes to pay for this activity. It borrows the rest by selling treasury notes and bonds.

Major corporations are also major borrowers. They supply us with automobiles, oil and gas, food, appliances, computers, steel, communications, entertainment, and a host of other goods. These firms continually struggle to develop new products and improve existing products and services. They require a great deal of money to finance growth and product improvements—often more than they can supply out of current earnings. These firms turn to financial markets and sell stocks and bonds to raise the money they need.

Our economy also includes a host of smaller firms who supply a myriad of services to other firms and to consumers. Small businesses, like contractors, build our houses, factories, schools, and roads. Retailers supply us with hardware, clothing, food, appliances, gasoline, lumber, and many other goods. Professionals such as doctors, dentists, lawyers, and accountants, supply essential services. These groups also need money to carry their inventories and expand their businesses. They often turn to their local banks for financing.

Consumers are at the other end of the spectrum. Their daily needs are financed primarily from wages. From time to time, a major need, such as a house, a new car, a major appliance, or college tuition, requires more money than consumers have available. Consumers then turn to banks, savings and loan associations, or buy on credit from retailers.

Where does all of this borrowed money come from? It comes from those in the economy who have enough money left over after meeting their needs to save some. They are willing to lend it in return for interest payments. The government, business firms, consumers who need the money are willing to pay the interest to use this money.

Financial markets act as intermediaries between borrowers and savers. Banks, savings and loan associations, and financial markets raise money from those who have money to lend, and make the money available to those who need to borrow. They match the needs of savers, who want to earn interest on their savings, with the needs of borrowers, who believe they can earn more using the borrowed money than the money costs.

How are financial markets arranged so that they have just enough money available to satisfy the demands of all those who want to borrow? Interest rates do the job. Interest rates are the adjusting mechanism that makes the amount of money savers make available just match the amount borrowers want to borrow. If there is not enough money available to lend at any point in time, financial markets raise the interest rate they offer savers. Higher interest rates make two things happen. First, savers respond to the higher rates and make more savings available. The supply of savings then expands. Second, financial markets raise the interest rate they charge on loans to cover the higher rate they now pay savers. Faced with higher interest rates, borrowers with the least need to borrow decide that money now costs too much, and postpone their borrowing. This makes the demand for loans contract. Both responses, the increased supply of savings, and the reduced demand for loans, bring the amount of savings available, and the amount borrowers demand, into balance at the higher interest rate.

If more money is available than borrowers need, the reverse happens. Financial markets lower the interest rates they pay savers. Lower interest rates cause savers to save less, and the supply of savings contracts. At the same time, lower interest rates cause borrowers to demand more, and the demand for loans expands. The supply of savings and the demand for loans readjusts, and the market comes to a new balance at the lower interest rate.

In addition to these normal pressures on interest rates, the Federal Reserve Board also intervenes. It adjusts interest rates to control the economy. If the economy grows too fast, inflation will be too high. The Fed then intervenes by raising interest rates to slow the economy and keep inflation under control. The Fed also intervenes if the economy is too sluggish. It lowers interest rates to make the economy grow faster.

Interest rates adjust continuously to keep the amount of money available from savers just equal to the amount of money demanded by borrowers. These continual fluctuations in interest rates causes continual fluctuations in the value of the securities you are likely to invest in. Market prices of stocks, bonds, and mutual funds all fluctuate with interest rates.

As Fig. 2-1 shows, interest rates can fluctuate widely. The upper curve shows monthly variations in the Federal Funds rate over the past 20 years. The Federal Funds rate is the interest rate banks charge each other for overnight loans, and is a good index of the general level of interest rates. The Federal Funds rate varied from a low of 3 percent in 1972 to a peak of 19 percent in 1981, with many peaks and valleys in between. Interest rates have dropped substantially from the 1981 peak, and in 1989, the Federal Funds rate was down to 9 percent.

Interest rates are made up of a real component and an inflation component. The lower curve in Fig. 2-1 shows the Federal Funds rate adjusted to remove the inflation component. Interest rates adjusted to remove inflation are known as real interest rates. Real interest rates measure real gains in purchasing power. Real interest rates fluctuated around a rate of zero through most of the 1970s. Real interest rates were often negative—those who lent money at negative real interest rates did not collect enough in interest to offset inflation. Consequently, they lost purchasing power even though they collected interest and had their loans repaid in full. Real interest rates rose in the 1980s and peaked at nearly 12 percent in 1981. By 1989, the real interest rate had fallen to 5 percent.

Fig. 2-1

INTEREST RATES

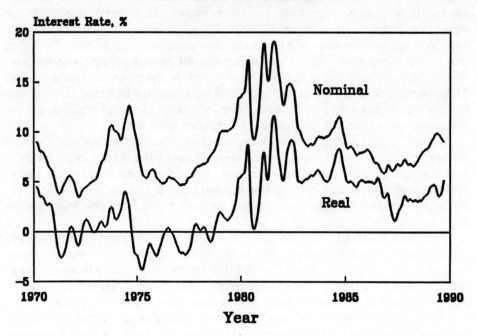

WORKING WITH INTEREST RATES

Interest rates are the key to managing your investment program. The interest rate determines how attractive any investment is, regardless of how complicated that investment might be. Interest rates are also called yields and rates of return, which essentially mean the same thing. Interest rates are the tool that lets you rank investments, compare one investment with another, and identify the most profitable ones. All of the evaluations you will do involve interest rates in one way or another. Therefore, you must have a good understanding of interest rates to manage your investment program effectively. The arithmetic of interest rates is not difficult. I have provided the appropriate calculation forms and interest rate tables to make it even easier. Any calculations you are likely to make will involve nothing more complicated than looking up a number in a table, filing out a form, and doing some elementary arithmetic.

How to Calculate Interest

The amount of interest any investment earns depends on the amount of money invested, the interest rate, and the length of time you invest the money. The basic calculation is simple: the amount of interest is equal to the amount invested, multiplied by the interest rate (in decimal form), and by the time period. If you invest $1,000 for one year at 8 percent interest, you will earn $80 in interest. The $80 is the product of the $1,000 invested, an interest rate of 0.08, and one year. Your investment will grow to $1,080. You can also express the future value as the initial investment multiplied by a growth factor. In this example, the growth factor is 1.08.

Compounding

Interest is normally compounded and added to your account periodically. Interest payments are based on your total investment (the amount you invested initially, plus all prior interest payments that have accumulated in your account.) Interest can be credited to your account annually, semiannually, quarterly, monthly, daily, and even continuously. The more often interest is credited, the faster your savings will grow.

Compounding Frequency

The amount of interest you will earn increases as interest compounds more frequently during the year. Figure 2-2 shows how the growth factor for one-year investment periods increases as payment frequency increases from one payment per year to continuous payments. Differences between compounding frequencies are small at interest rates below about 10 percent. Above 10 percent, the growth factors for annual and semiannual payments are significantly lower than the growth factors for more frequent compounding. There is little difference between growth factors when compounding more often than quarterly except for much higher interest rates. Interest rates have to reach 30 percent before the growth factor for continuous compounding exceeds the growth factor for quarterly compounding by as much as 1 percent.

Equivalent Interest Rates

You can draw a horizontal line cutting across the curves in Fig. 2-2 to locate the interest rates that are equivalent, that is, interest rates that produce the same growth factors. A

Fig. 2–2
EQUIVALENT INTEREST RATES

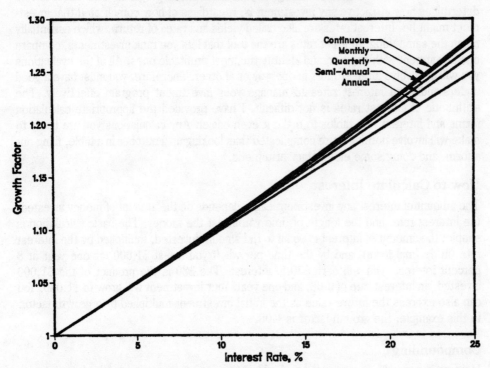

continuous interest rate of 15 percent yields an annual growth factor of 1.1618. The equivalent annual interest rate is 16.18 percent—an interest rate of 16.18 percent produces the same growth factor when interest compounds only once per year. If interest compounds twice per year, the rate equivalent to 15 percent continuous interest drops to 15.58 percent. If interest compounds quarterly, the equivalent rate drops to 15.28 percent. Monthly compounding brings the equivalent interest rate to 15.09 percent, daily compounding to 15.003 percent. The more frequent the compounding, the closer the interest rate approaches the continuous interest rate.

A vertical line through the curves in Fig. 2-2 would show how the growth factor increases at a constant interest rate when compounding frequency increases. When interest is compounded annually, a 15 percent interest rate produces a one-year growth factor of 1.150. If compounding is semiannual, the growth factor increases to 1.156. Quarterly compounding brings the growth factor to 1.159. Continuous compounding raises the growth factor to 1.162.

Banks and savings and loan associations normally pay interest daily, monthly, or quarterly, and quote this periodic rate in their advertising. They also quote an equivalent annual interest rate so that savers can compare interest rates without being confused by different compounding frequencies. The equivalent annual rate is called the yield.

The calculation form in Table 2-1 makes it easy to find equivalent interest rates—the interest rate at one compounding frequency that produces the same growth factor as an interest rate at any other frequency.

TABLE 2-1
Calculation Form—Equivalent Interest Rates

1. Divide Base Interest Rate (%) by 100 _____

2. Base Payment Frequency, times per year _____

3. New Payment Frequency, times per year _____

A. Both Interest Rates Periodic

4. Divide Line 1 by Line 2; Add 1.0 to the result _____

5. Divide Line 2 by Line 3 _____

6. Use your calculator's y^x key to raise y (Line 4) to the x (Line 5) power* _____

7. Equivalent Interest Rate: Subtract 1.0 from Line 6, then Multiply by 100 and by Line 3 _____

B. Base Rate Periodic, Equivalent Rate Continuous

8. Divide Line 1 by Line 2; Add 1.0 to the result _____

9. Enter Line 8 into your calculator and tap the ln(x) key* _____

10. Equivalent Interest Rate: Multiply Line 9 by 100 and by Line 2 _____

C. Base Rate Continuous, Equivalent Rate Periodic

11. Divide Line 1 by Line 3 _____

12. Enter Line 11 in your calculator and tap the e^x key* _____

13. Equivalent Interest Rate: Subtract 1.0 from Line 12, then Multiply by 100 and Line 3 _____

---
*Check your calculator's directions for using the y^x, ln(x), and e^x keys.

Example 2-1. A bank quotes an interest rate of 7.25 percent with interest paid monthly, and a yield of 7.496 percent. Use the calculation form in Table 2-1 to confirm that the yield corresponds to the quoted monthly rate. Table 2-2 shows the calculation. Enter the base interest rate of 7.25 percent on line 1 and the base compounding frequency of 12 times per year on line 2. The yield is the equivalent rate when interest is paid only once per year. Enter 1 in line 3. Use Part A of Table 2-2 because both interest rates are periodic. Follow the step-by-step directions and calculate a yield of 7.496 percent on line 7.

Continuous Compounding

You want to think of your investment earning interest every instant. Therefore, I will use continuous compounding throughout this book. Continuous compounding also makes the arithmetic of security analysis much easier. When interest is compounded continuously, the amount an initial investment grows to at any future time is determined by this simple calculation:

$$A_T = (A_o)(Gi_{R,T})$$

TABLE 2-2
Equivalent Interest Rates—Example 2-1

1. Divide Base Interest Rate (%) by 100	0.0725
2. Base Payment Frequency, times per year	12
3. New Payment Frequency, times per year	1

A. Both Interest Rates Periodic

4. Divide Line 1 by Line 2; Add 1.0 to the result	1.00604
5. Divide Line 2 by Line 3	12
6. Use your calculator's y^x key to raise y (Line 4) to the x (Line 5) power*	1.07496
7. Equivalent Interest Rate: Subtract 1.0 from Line 6, then Multiply by 100 and by Line 3	7.496

B. Base Rate Periodic, Equivalent Rate Continuous

8. Divide Line 1 by Line 2; Add 1.0 to the result	
9. Enter Line 8 into your calculator and tap the ln(x) key*	
10. Equivalent Interest Rate: Multiply Line 9 by 100 and by Line 2	

C. Base Rate Continuous, Equivalent Rate Periodic

11. Divide Line 1 by Line 3	
12. Enter Line 11 in your calculator and tap the e^x key*	
13. Equivalent Interest Rate: Subtract 1.0 from Line 12, then Multiply by 100 and Line 3	

---

*Check your calculator's directions for using the y^x, ln(x), and e^x keys.

Find A_T, the amount at any future time, by multiplying A_o, the amount you invest initially, by the growth factor $Gi_{R,T}$. The R in the subscript R,T refers to the interest rate, T refers to the length of time you invest the money.

You will use this rule often, and Appendix Table A1 provides any growth factor you are likely to need. Multiply the interest rate R, expressed as a percentage, by the time period in years. Enter Table A1 at this value of RT and read the growth factor. If you invest money at 9 percent interest for five years, for example, RT would be 9 percent times five years, or 45. Run your finger down the extreme left hand column of Appendix Table A1 until you reach the row labeled "40." Then read across that row to the column headed "5," the growth factor will be 1.5683. At 9 percent continuous interest, the amount you will have five years from now is 1.5683 times the amount you invest today.

The growth factor from Appendix Table A1 is the Gi growth factor. The G stands for growth; the i means that the growth factor applies to money invested at an instant in time. Identify a particular growth factor by the subscript R,T, where R means the interest rate and T the time period for which you invest the money. The growth factor of 1.5683 in the preceding paragraph, for example, will be called $Gi_{9,5}$, where the 9 refers to the 9 percent interest rate and the 5 refers to the five-year investment period. Appendix

Table A1 reduces this interest calculation to a simple multiplication of the initial investment by a growth factor.

Example 2-2. How much money will you have if you invest $1,000 at 8 percent interest and let the investment compound continuously for seven years? The RT product is 8 percent times seven years, or 56. Enter Appendix Table A1 at an RT product of 56 and read a growth factor of 1.7507. Consequently, $1,000 invested for seven years at 8 percent continuous interest will grow to:

$$A_7 = (\$1,000)\ (1.7507) = \$1,750.70$$

You might prefer to calculate growth factors rather than look them up in Appendix Table A1. Calculating growth factors on a hand calculator saves you from interpolating between entries in the table, and gives you more significant digits. A hand calculator also allows you to calculate growth factors beyond the range of the table. The calculation form in Table 2-3 makes growth factors easy to calculate. The lower half of Table 2-3 shows how to calculate the Gi growth factor used in Example 2-2.

Doubling Time

Your initial investment will double when the growth factor is two. Appendix Table A1 shows that the growth factor reaches two at an RT product of 69.3. Therefore, the time

TABLE 2-3
Calculation Form—Growth Factors

1. Divide Interest Rate (%) by 100	_____
2. Time Period, years	_____
3. Multiply Line 1 by Line 2	_____

A. Gi Growth Factor for Instantaneous Investments

4. $Gi_{R,T}$: Enter Line 3 in your calculator and tap the e^X key* _____

B. Gc Growth Factor for Continuous Investments

5. Subtract 1.0 from Line 4, then Divide by Line 3 _____

Example—Gi and Gc Growth Factors for Examples 2-2 and 2-3

1. Divide Interest Rate (%) by 100	0.08
2. Time Period, years	7
3. Multiply Line 1 by Line 2	0.56

A. Gi Growth Factor for Instantaneous Investments

4. $Gi_{R,T}$: Enter Line 3 in your calculator and tap the e^X key* 1.7507

B. Gc Growth Factor for Continuous Investments

5. Subtract 1.0 from Line 4, then Divide by Line 3 1.3405

---

*Check your calculator's directions for using the e^X key.

it takes for your investment to double is very nearly 70, divided by the interest rate. If you invest in a bank savings account paying 5.1 percent interest, your investment will double in 70 divided by 5.1, or 13.7 years. If your investment program is more effective, and you average 10 percent interest, your savings will double in only seven years. If you continue this program for 28 years your savings will double four times, and your savings will have grown to 16 times the amount you originally invested. This example illustrates the power of compound interest.

CONTINUOUS INVESTING

The Gi growth factor tells you how a lump sum of money invested now will grow at any future time. Sometimes you want to invest a steady flow of cash, such as $100 per month, instead of a lump sum. How will this steady flow of cash grow? The solution for a steady cash flow involves a new growth factor, Gc:

$$A_T = (C)\ (T)\ (Gc_{R,T})$$

Find A_T, the amount you will have in the future, by multiplying the steady cash flow of C dollars per year by T, the investment period in years, and by $Gc_{R,T}$, the growth factor that applies to continuous cash flows. This growth factor is Gc, where the c refers to continuous cash flows, and distinguishes the Gc factor from the Gi factor for instantaneous cash flows.

You will use continuous growth factors often. Appendix Table A2 provides any Gc growth factor you are likely to need. Use Appendix Table A2 just like Appendix Table A1—enter the table at the appropriate value of RT, and read the growth factor. Then multiply the initial cash flow by the time period and by the growth factor. Note that the cash flow must be in dollars per year. Appendix Table A2 reduces this problem to a simple multiplication of the cash flow by the time period and by a Gc growth factor.

Example 2-3. Suppose you invest $100 per month in a fund paying 8 percent interest for seven years. How much money will you have at the end of that period? Enter Appendix Table A2 at an RT product of 8 percent times seven years, or 56, and read a growth factor of 1.3405. The calculation requires cash flows in dollars per year, not dollars per month. The steady cash flow of $100 per month is $1,200 per year. The amount in the fund at year seven is:

$$(1,200\ \$/yr.)\ (7\ yrs.)\ (1.3405) = \$11,260$$

You might prefer to calculate Gc growth factors rather than look them up. The calculation form in Table 2-3 shows you how to calculate Gc as well as Gi growth factors. The lower half of Table 2-3 shows how to calculate the growth factor for Example 2-3. With a little practice, you might find that calculating Gc factors is easier than looking them up in Appendix Table A2.

Continuous Cash Flows that Grow with Time

The steady flow of cash does not have to be a constant amount. You can increase the cash flow and make it grow steadily at some constant percentage rate. You can use the growth factors from Appendix Tables A1 and A2 find the amount of money that this investment pattern grows to. To do this, multiply the initial rate of investment (in dollars per year) by the investment period in years and by the growth factor $Gi_{R,T}$ from Appendix Table A1. If the growth rate is greater than the interest rate, also multiply by the growth factor $Gc_{(g-R),T}$. Evaluate this growth factor at $(g-R)$, the difference between the growth rate and the interest rate.

If the interest rate is greater than the growth rate, multiply by the discount factor $Dc_{(R-g),T}$ instead of the growth factor $Gc_{(g-R),T}$. Discount factors are discussed in the next chapter. Dc factors are listed in Appendix Table A4, which is similar to Appendix Table A2 for Gc factors. Evaluate the discount factor at $(R-g)$, the difference between the growth rate and the interest rate. Enter Table A4 at the appropriate value of the $(R-g)T$ product, and read the corresponding discount factor.

When the growth rate and the interest rate are equal, the Gc and Dc factors become 1.0, and you use only the $Gi_{R,T}$ growth factor. The calculation form in Table 2-4 simplifies this calculation. Fill the appropriate values in the blanks; the form will direct you to the correct growth or discount factors.

Example 2-4a. Suppose you expect to increase the $100 per month you are investing in Example 2-3 at the rate of 5 percent per year. How much will this investment pattern grow to in 10 years at 8 percent interest?

Use the calculation form in Table 2-4 to find the result. Table 2-5 shows the calculations. Ignore lines 10 and 11 for the moment. The initial investment rate of $1,200 per year is multiplied by the 10-year time period and by the $Gi_{8,10}$ growth factor in line 6. The Gi factor from Appendix Table A1 for an 8 percent interest rate and a 10-year time period is 2.2255. This result is also multiplied by the $Dc_{(8-5),10}$ discount factor in line 9 because the 8 percent interest rate is greater than the 5 percent per year growth rate. The Dc discount factor in Appendix Table A4 at an $(R-g)T$ product of $(8-5)$ times 10, or 30, is 0.8639. The calculation form in line 8 shows that you will have $23,071 in 10 years.

b. Suppose you can make the initial $1,200 per year investment grow 10 percent per year instead of 5 percent per year. Table 2-6 shows the calculations. The growth rate is greater than the interest rate, so use a $Gc_{(g-R),T}$ growth factor in place of the $Dc_{(R-g),T}$ discount factor. Ignore lines 14 and 15 for now. The Gi factor is still 2.2255. The Gc factor at a $(g-R)T$ product of $(10-8)$ times 10, or 20, is 1.1070. The calculation form in line 12 shows that you will have $29,563 in 10 years.

c. If the initial cash investment grew 8 percent per year, the same as the interest rate, the calculation would end at line 6. The initial investment of $1,200 per year is multiplied by the 10-year time period and by the growth factor $Gi_{R,T}$. Line 6 shows that you will have $26,706 in 10 years.

The calculation form can also be used if the investment rate falls off instead of grows with time. If the investment rate falls off with time, discount at the sum of the interest rate and the decay rate.

Continuous vs. Periodic Investments

Continuous compounding is used throughout this book because the arithmetic is simpler and easier to understand, but the actual cash flows might be periodic rather than continuous. Cash flows might occur monthly or quarterly, for example. In most cases, any

TABLE 2-4
Calculation Form
Future Value of Investments that Grow at Constant Percentage Rates

1. Initial Investment Rate, $/yr.   _____

2. Investment Period, years   _____

3. Growth Rate of Investment, %/yr.   _____

4. Interest Rate, %/yr.   _____

5. $Gi_{R,T}$ Growth Factor from Appendix Table A1 at RT equal to Line 4 times Line 2   _____

A. If Growth and Interest Rates Are Equal

6. Multiply Line 1 by Lines 2 and 5   _____

B. If Interest Rate Is Greater than Growth Rate

7. $Dc_{(R-g),T}$ Discount Factor from Appendix Table A4   _____

8. Future Value: Multiply Line 6 by Line 7   _____

If you wish to allow for periodic instead of continuous investment, complete Lines 9 and 10.

9. $Dc_{(R-g),p}$ Discount Factor from Appendix Table A4*   _____

10. Future Value: Divide Line 8 by Line 9   _____

C. If Growth Rate Is Greater than Interest Rate

11. $Gc_{(g-R),T}$ Growth Factor from Appendix Table A2   _____

12. Future Value: Multiply Line 6 by Line 11   _____

If you wish to allow for periodic instead of continuous investment, complete Lines 13 and 14.

13. $Gc_{(g-R),p}$ Growth Factor from Appendix Table A2   _____

14. Future Value: Divide Line 12 by Line 13   _____

---

*p is the time period between periodic investments in years.

---

errors caused by treating monthly or quarterly cash flows as though they were continuous is negligible. If the cash flows occur semiannually or for longer periods, the error might be larger than you are willing to tolerate.

Lines 9 and 13 in Table 2-4 show you how to adjust for periodic investments. If the growth rate of the growing stream of investments is greater than the interest rate, divide by the continuous growth factor $Gc_{(g-R),p}$ in line 14. The time period p in this growth factor is the time period between investments. If you invest cash quarterly, p is 0.25 years; if you invest cash monthly p is $1/12$, or 0.0833 years. Note that, as the investments become more frequent, p comes closer to zero. The growth factor $Gc_{(g-R),p}$ then comes closer to 1.0, and the correction for periodic investments become negligible.

If the interest rate is greater than the growth rate, adjust for periodic payments by dividing by the continuous discount factor $Dc_{(R-g),p}$ in line 10. If the interest rate and growth rate are equal, the Gc and Dc factors involving net rates of $(g-R)$ or $(R-g)$ all become 1.0. The adjustment then disappears. The adjustment for semiannual invest-

TABLE 2-5
Calculation Form
Steadily Growing Cash Flows—Example 2-4A

1. Initial Investment Rate, $/yr. — 1,200
2. Investment Period, years — 10
3. Growth Rate of Investment, %/yr. — 5
4. Interest Rate, %/yr. — 8
5. $Gi_{R,T}$ Growth Factor from Appendix Table A1 at RT equal to Line 4 times Line 2 — 2.2255

A. If Growth and Interest Rates Are Equal
6. Multiply Line 1 by Lines 2 and 5 — $26,706

B. If Interest Rate Is Greater than Growth Rate
7. $Dc_{(R-g),T}$ Discount Factor from Appendix Table A4 — 0.8639
8. Future Value: Multiply Line 6 by Line 7 — $23,071

If you wish to allow for periodic instead of continuous investment, complete Lines 9 and 10.

9. $Dc_{(R-g),p}$ Discount Factor from Appendix Table A4* — 0.9925
10. Future Value: Divide Line 8 by Line 9 — $23,244

C. If Growth Rate Is Greater than Interest Rate
11. $Gc_{(g-R),T}$ Growth Factor from Appendix Table A2 —
12. Future Value: Multiply Line 6 by Line 11 —

If you wish to allow for periodic instead of continuous investment, complete Lines 13 and 14.

13. $Gc_{(g-R),p}$ Growth Factor from Appendix Table A2 —
14. Future Value: Divide Line 12 by Line 13 —

*p is the time period between periodic investments in years.

Investments	p, years	$Gi_{8,10}$	$Dc_{3,10}$	$Dc_{3,p}$	Future Value
Continuous	0	2.2255	0.8639	1.000	$19,226
Monthly	0.083	2.2255	0.8639	0.9988	19,249
Quarterly	0.25	2.2255	0.8639	0.9963	19,297
Semiannually	0.5	2.2255	0.8639	0.9925	19,371
Annually	1.0	2.2255	0.8639	0.9851	19,517

ments is normally negligible, as shown in Example 2-4, which is worked out in Tables 2-5 and 2-6.

Example 2-5. Suppose you invest a stream of cash beginning at $1,000 per year and growing 5 percent per year for 10 years. The interest rate is 8 percent. What will the future value be if you invest the money continuously, monthly, quarterly, semiannually, or annually? Follow the directions of Table 2-4, and multiply the initial investment rate of $1,000 per year by the 10-year investment period and by the growth factor $Gi_{8,10}$ in line 6, and by the discount factor $Dc_{(8-5),10}$ in line 8. Allow for periodic investment by dividing by the discount factor $Dc_{(8-5),p}$ in line 10:

Annual investments grow to a larger sum in this example because you invest at the beginning of each year. The other investments are spread over the year, and do not earn interest for the full year.

The Arithmetic of Growth

When any quantity grows at a constant percentage rate, calculate future values from:

$$A_T = (A_o)(Gi_{g,T})$$

_____TABLE 2-6_____
Steadily Growing Cash Flows—Example 2-4B

1. Initial Investment Rate, $/yr.	1,200
2. Investment Period, years	10
3. Growth Rate of Investment, %/yr.	10
4. Interest Rate, %/yr.	8
5. $Gi_{R,T}$ Growth Factor from Appendix Table A1 at RT equal to Line 4 times Line 2	2.2255

A. If Growth and Interest Rates Are Equal

6. Multiply Line 1 by Lines 2 and 5	$26,706

B. If Interest Rate Is Greater than Growth Rate

7. $Dc_{(R-g),T}$ Discount Factor from Appendix Table A4	_____
8. Future Value: Multiply Line 6 by Line 7	_____

If you wish to allow for periodic instead of continuous investment, complete Lines 9 and 10.

9. $Dc_{(R-g),p}$ Discount Factor from Appendix Table A4*	_____
10. Future Value: Divide Line 8 by Line 9	_____

C. If Growth Rate Is Greater than Interest Rate

11. $Gc_{(g-R),T}$ Growth Factor from Appendix Table A2	1.1070
12. Future Value: Multiply Line 6 by Line 11	$29,563

If you wish to allow for periodic instead of continuous investment, complete Lines 13 and 14.

13. $Gc_{(g-R),p}$ Growth Factor from Appendix Table A2	1.0050
14. Future Value: Divide Line 12 by Line 13	$29,416

_____

*p is the time period between periodic investments in years.

where g is the percentage growth rate. This equation is a general equation for growth at a constant percentage growth rate and has broad application. The equation is identical to the equation used to show how money grows with time when you invest it at continuous interest. The only difference is terminology. When calculating how money grows at interest, the growth rate is called an interest rate. An identical equation uses an inflation rate as the growth rate, which describes how the price of an item grows because of inflation. In the next chapter, you will use a variation of this equation for discounting. The growth rate is then negative and is called a discount rate.

Remember, interest rates, growth rates, inflation rates, and discount rates are simply different names for the same basic quantity—the growth rate in the equation above. Mathematically, they are identical, and they all act the same way. Therefore, the growth factors in Appendix Tables A1 and A3 are not restricted to interest rates. They can be applied to growth problems in general, as Examples 2-7 and 2-8 show.

Example 2-7. A company earns $4 per share. If you expect earnings to grow at 8 percent per year, how high will earnings be in five years? Use Appendix Table A1 because the $4 per share is a value at this instant. Enter Appendix Table A1 at an RT product of 8 percent times five years, or 40, and read a growth factor of 1.4918. Multiply current earnings by the growth factor:

$$E_5 = (4 \text{ \$/share}) (1.4918) = 5.97 \text{ \$/share}$$

Example 2-8. A four-door Chevrolet Caprice cost $12,173 in 1989. If you expect inflation to average 6 percent per year, what will the equivalent car cost in 10 years? Enter Appendix Table A1 at an RT product of 6 percent times 10 years, or 60, and read a growth factor of 1.8221. Therefore, an equivalent car in 1999 will cost:

$$C_{10} = (\$12,173) (1.8221) = \$22,180$$

You will find growth factors extremely useful for projecting how fast a firm is likely to grow, and what earnings, dividends, and stock prices are likely to be at any future time.

SUMMARY

☐ Interest rates fluctuate continually to balance the supply of savings against the demand for loans. The continual fluctuation in interest rates results in a continual fluctuation in the prices of any securities you own, and in interest rates you can earn.

☐ Interest normally compounds. Compounding frequency can vary from once per year to every instant. Continuous compounding is used throughout this book. You want to think of your investments as compounding every instant. Continuous compounding also simplifies the arithmetic of security analysis and makes the analysis easier to understand.

☐ The future value of money invested at an instant in time is: $A_T = (A_o) (Gi_{R,T})$.

☐ Appendix Table A1 lists the growth factor $Gi_{R,T}$. The future value of money invested continuously for T years is: $A_T = (C) (T) (Gc_{R,T})$.

☐ Appendix Table A2 lists the continuous growth factor $Gc_{R,T}$.

☐ The calculation form in Table 2-4 gives the future value of continuous cash investments that grow at a constant percentage rate. The calculation form also contains adjustment factors to use if the investment is periodic rather than continuous.

3

What is Cash in the Future Worth Today?

IN THE LAST CHAPTER, YOU LEARNED HOW MONEY GROWS WHEN YOU INVEST IT AND EARN interest. The basic rule for calculating how money grows is to multiply the money you invest today by a growth factor. When you evaluate securities, you find the opposite problem. Instead of beginning with a sum of money today, you begin with money you expect that investment to generate in the future and ask how much that money is worth today. It will be worth less because you can invest some smaller amount today that will earn interest and grow to that future sum. The rule for finding how much that future sum of money is worth today is:

$$A_o = (A_T) (Di_{R,T})$$

Find the present value, A_o, by multiplying the future value, A_T, by the discount factor, $Di_{R,T}$. The discount factor determines how much less a future sum of money is worth today because the lesser amount can be invested at interest and grow to the future sum. The rule is just like the rule for growth at interest except that you use the discount factor $Di_{R,T}$ in place of the growth factor $Gi_{R,T}$.

INSTANTANEOUS CASH FLOWS

The previous equation is the basic equation of discounting and is fundamental to security analysis. Because you will use this discount factor often, I have provided all of the discount factors you are likely to need in Appendix Table A3. These discount factors are Di factors. The D means discounting and the i means that the discount factor applies to cash that flows at some future instant in time. Use the subscript R,T to identify the discount rate and the time period. $Di_{6,8}$ means a discount factor at a 6 percent discount rate for an instantaneous cash flow that occurs eight years from now. Use Appendix Table A3 just like you used Appendix Table A1 in Chapter 2. Enter the table at the product of the discount rate in percent and the time in years, and read the discount factor. Then multiply the future sum of money by the discount factor to determine the present value of that future sum.

Example 3-1. Suppose you expect to receive $1,000 five years from now. How much is that money worth today if you can earn 12 percent interest in the meantime? The RT product is 12 percent times five years, or 60. Enter Appendix Table A3 at an RT product of 60 and read a discount factor of 0.5488. The present value is:

Present Value = ($1,000) (0.5488) = $548.80

Check this answer by showing that $548.80 will grow to $1,000 in five years when invested at 12 percent interest. To do this, multiply $548.80 by a growth factor from Appendix Table A1. Enter Appendix Table A1 at an RT product of 60 and read a growth factor of 1.8221. The future value is:

Future Value = ($548.80) (1.8221) = $1,000

The discount factor in Appendix Table A3 and the growth factor from Appendix Table A1 are simply related. One is the reciprocal of the other. The reciprocal of the 0.5488 discount factor from Appendix Table A3 in the example above is 1/0.5488, or 1.8221, the growth factor from Appendix Table A1. The reciprocal of the 1.8221 growth factor from Appendix Table A1 is 1/1.8221, or 0.5488, the discount factor from Appendix Table A3.

The Gi growth factor begins at 1.0 when the RT product is zero and increases as the RT product increases. The Di discount factor also begins at 1.0 when the RT product is zero but decreases towards zero as the RT product increases.

The calculation form in Table 3-1 makes calculating discount factors easy. This form is identical to the form used to calculate growth factors, except that the RT product is

---
TABLE 3-1
Calculation Form—Discount Factors

1. Divide the Discount Rate (%) by 100	————
2. Time Period, years	————
3. Multiply Line 1 by Line 2	————

A. Instantaneous Cash Flows

4. Di Discount Factor: Enter Line 3 in your calculator, tap the change sign key to make the entry negative, then tap the e^X key*	————

B. Continuous Cash Flows

5. Subtract Line 4 from 1.0	————
6. Dc Discount Factor: Divide Line 5 by Line 3	————

Examples 3-1 and 3-2

1. Divide the Discount Rate (%) by 100	0.12
2. Time Period, years	5
3. Multiply Line 1 by Line 2	0.60

A. Instantaneous Cash Flows

4. Di Discount Factor: Enter Line 3 in your calculator, tap the change sign key to make the entry negative, then tap the e^X key*	0.5488

B. Continuous Cash Flows

5. Subtract Line 4 from 1.0	0.4512
6. Dc Discount Factor: Divide Line 5 by Line 3	0.7520

---
*Check your calculator's directions for using the e^X key.

made negative in line 4 before tapping the e^x key. The lower part of Table 3-1 shows how to calculate the discount factor for Example 3-1.

You might find that calculating discount factors is easier than reading them from the table. Calculating discount factors on a hand calculator avoids interpolating between entries in the table, and provides more significant figures. You can also calculate discount factors beyond the range shown in the table.

I have plotted the discount factor against the RT product in Fig. 3-1 to help you understand how discount factors behave. The Di discount factor applies to cash that flows at an instant in the future and is the lower curve in Fig. 3-1. The discount factor begins at a value of 1.0 when the RT product is zero, and approaches (but never reaches) zero as the RT product increases.

Money you have in your hand today is money at time zero. Zero time makes the RT product zero and the discount factor 1.0. Therefore, money in hand is worth face value. If the interest rate is zero, the RT product is also zero, and the discount factor is 1.0. At a zero discount rate, there is also no discounting. The present value is equal to the future value regardless of how far out in time you receive the money. As the discount rate increases, or as you have to wait longer to get your hands on the money, or both, the RT product builds up. The discount factor then drops below 1.0. The higher the RT product, the closer the discount factor approaches zero.

Suppose you can earn 10 percent interest. You expect to receive $1,000 one year from now. The discount factor from Appendix Table A3 at an RT product of 10 percent

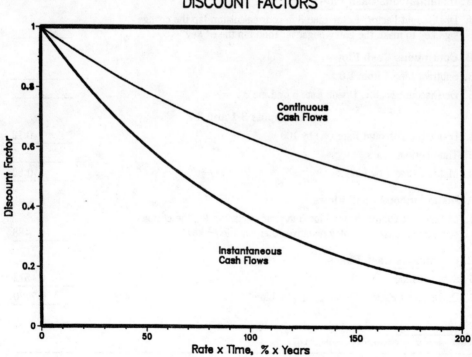

Fig. 3–1
DISCOUNT FACTORS

times one year is 0.9048. Therefore, that $1,000 will be worth only $904.80 today. If you have to wait five years, the thousand dollars will be worth only $606.53. If you have to wait ten years, the thousand dollars will be worth only $367.90. And if you have to wait 50 years, the $1,000 will be worth only $6.74. The $1,000 is worth these lower values because these lower values are all you have to invest at 10 percent interest today to grow to $1,000 in one, five, 10, or 50 years.

Study this example carefully. Once you understand it, you understand the basic idea of discounting, discounted cash flow analysis, and the time value of money. The basic idea is simply that a dollar you won't receive until some time in the future is worth less than a dollar in your hands today. How much less depends on how long you have to wait until you get the money, and on the interest you can earn in the meantime.

CONTINUOUS CASH FLOWS

The Di discount factor from Appendix Table A3 applies to cash that flows at an instant in time. Another cash flow you'll often encounter is cash that flows continually over a period of time. A flow of interest payments over the period you own a bond or dividend payments over the period you own a stock are examples. The present value of a cash stream of C dollars per year, flowing for T years is:

$$\text{Present Value} = (C)\ (T)\ (Dc_{R,T})$$

Find the present value by multiplying the cash flow steam C (in dollars per year) by the time period, T (in years), and by a new discount factor, $Dc_{R,T}$. $Dc_{R,T}$ is the discount factor that applies to cash that flows continuously during a period of time. To make this discount factor easy to use, I've listed it in Appendix Table A4. This discount factor is the Dc discount factor. The c refers to continuous cash flows and distinguishes Dc from the Di discount factor, which applies to instantaneous cash flows. Multiplying by the Dc discount factor is equivalent to multiplying the cash flowing in each instant of time by a Di discount factor and adding up the discounted cash flows for all the instants of time.

Example 3-2. Suppose you expect to receive a continuous flow of $100 per year for five years. How much is this stream of cash worth discounted at 12 percent? Look up the Dc discount factor in Appendix Table A4 at an RT product of 12 percent times five years, or 60, and read a Dc discount factor of 0.7520. The present value of this flow of cash is:

$$\text{Present Value} = (100\ \$/yr.)\ (5\ yrs.)\ (0.7520) = \$376.00$$

Note that the Dc factor multiplies the total cash that flows during the five-year period.

I have plotted the Dc discount factor as the upper curve in Fig. 3-1 to help you understand how this discount factor behaves. The continuous discount factor also begins at 1.0 when the RT product is zero, and gradually approaches zero as the RT product increases. The Dc discount factor for continuous cash flows is always larger than the Di factor for instantaneous cash flows.

The calculation form in Table 3-1 also gives the Dc discount factor. The lower part of the Table shows how to calculate the discount factor from Example 3-2. With a little practice, you might find that calculating Dc factors are easier than looking them up in the table.

INFINITE STREAM OF CASH FLOWS

You can also discount a stream of cash that flows for an infinite period of time. The present value for infinite cash flows is provided using this simple method:

$$\text{Present Value} = C/R$$

Divide the cash flow C, in dollars per year, by the discount rate R (in decimal form).

Example 3-3. What is the present value of the $100 per year of Example 3-2 if the cash flow continues for an infinite period?

$$\text{Present Value} = (100 \text{ \$/yr.})/(0.12) = \$833.33$$

COMBINING DISCOUNT FACTORS

Sometimes, you need both discount factors together. You might, for example, have a stream of cash that flows for 10 years, with the 10-year period beginning five years from now. Apply a Dc discount factor to the cash that flows during the 10-year period. The Dc factor converts that cash to an equivalent lump sum in year five—the beginning of the 10-year period. This lump sum is an instantaneous cash flow at year five. Multiply this lump sum by a Di discount factor to convert the lump sum at year five to the equivalent lump sum at year zero.

Example 3-4. Suppose that the cash stream of $100 per year for five years you expect in Example 3-2 doesn't begin until year four. What is the present value of this cash stream discounted at 12 percent? Look up a Dc factor from Appendix Table A4 at an RT product of 12 percent times five years, or 60. The Dc factor is 0.7520. This Dc factor converts the cash stream into an equivalent lump sum at year four, the beginning of the cash flow period. Now apply a Di discount factor from Appendix Table A3 at an RT product of 12 percent times four years, or 48. The Di factor is 0.6188. It converts the lump sum at year four to a lump sum at time zero. The present value is:

$$\text{Present Value} = (100 \text{ \$/yr.}) (5 \text{ yrs.}) (0.7520) (0.6188) = \$232.67$$

THE DISCOUNT AND GROWTH FACTOR RELATIONSHIP

The two discount factors for instantaneous and continuous cash flows in Appendix Tables A3 and A4 are related to the corresponding growth factors in Appendix Tables A1 and A2. If you extend the two discount factor curves of Fig. 3-1 to the left of the zero RT axis, both curves will increase above a value of 1.0. The curve for instantaneous discount factors becomes a curve for the instantaneous growth factors of Appendix Table A1. The curve for continuous discount factors becomes a curve for the continuous growth factors of Appendix Table A2.

GROWING OR DECAYING CASH FLOWS

Often, the continuous cash flow streams you encounter in security analysis either grow or decay at constant percentage rates. A growing stream of dividends is an example. The growing dividends reflect the underlying growth of the company. You will need to discount this growing stream of dividends to evaluate the stock.

To do this, discount with either a discount factor or a growth factor, depending on whether the discount rate is larger or smaller than the growth rate. Discount rates and growth rates pull present value in opposite directions. Discounting lowers present value, growth raises present value. The net effect depends on which rate is larger. If the discount rate is larger than the growth rate, the net rate is a discount rate. Use a Dc discount factor to calculate present value. Read the Dc factor from Appendix Table A4 at the difference between the discount rate and the growth rate:

$$\text{Present Value} = (C_o) \ (T) \ (Dc_{(R-g),T})$$

Note that C_o in this equation is the initial cash flow rate. Discounting at a net rate of $(R-g)$ allows for the steady growth of this initial cash flow. If the growth rate is greater than the discount rate, the net rate is a growth rate. In that case, use a Gc growth factor in place of the Dc discount factor:

$$\text{Present Value} = (C_o) \ (T) \ (Gc_{(g-R),T})$$

Read the Gc growth factor at the difference between the growth rate and the discount rate. If the stream of cash declines instead of grows, the growth rate is negative. In that case, discount at the sum of the discount and growth rates:

$$\text{Present Value} = (C_o) \ (T) \ (Dc_{(R+g),T})$$

The calculation form in Table 3-2 simplifies discounting cash flows that grow or decay at constant percentage rates. Use Part A, B, or C of the table depending on whether the discount rate is equal to, greater than, or less than the growth rate. When the discount and growth rates are equal, the net rates $(R-g)$ and $(g-R)$ are zero, and the discount and growth factors are 1.0. Present value is then the product of the initial cash flow rate and the time period, as shown in line 5 on Table 3-2. Fill the appropriate values in the blanks; the form will direct you to the correct discount and growth factors.

Example 3-5. Suppose you invest in a stock and begin receiving dividends at the rate of $100 per year. You expect those dividends to grow at 5 percent per year. What is the present value of this stream of dividends over an eight-year period, discounted at 12 percent? Use the calculation form in Table 3-2. Table 3-3 shows you how to do the calculation. The net rate is the difference between the 5 percent growth rate and the 12 percent discount rate, or 7 percent. The net rate is a discount rate because the 12 percent discount rate is larger than the 5 percent growth rate. Look up a Dc discount factor in Appendix Table A4 at an RT product equal to the 7 percent net discount rate times eight years, or 56, and read a value of 0.7657. The present value is:

$$\text{Present Value} = (100 \ \$/\text{yr.}) \ (8 \ \text{yrs.}) \ (0.7657) = \$612.56$$

Example 3-6. Suppose dividends in the previous example grew 15 percent per year instead of 5 percent per year. Table 3-4 shows how to do the calculation. The 15 percent per year growth rate is now larger than the 12 percent discount rate, and the net rate of $15 - 12$ percent, or 3 percent, is a growth rate. Look up a growth factor for continuous cash flows from Appendix Table A2 at a net growth rate of 3 percent and a time period of eight years, and read a growth factor of 1.1302. The present value is:

$$\text{Present Value} = (100 \ \$/\text{yr.}) \ (8 \ \text{yrs.}) \ (1.1302) = \$904.16$$

TABLE 3-2
Calculation Form
Discounting Cash Flows that Grow at Constant Percentage Rates
---

1. Initial Cash Flow, $/yr.   _____
2. Investment Period, years   _____
3. Growth Rate of Cash Flow, %/yr.   _____
4. Discount Rate, %   _____

A. Discount Rate and Growth Rate Equal

5. Present Value: Multiply Line 1 by Line 2   _____

B. Discount Rate Greater than Growth Rate

6. $Dc_{(R-g),T}$ from Appendix Table A4*   _____
7. Present Value: Multiply Line 5 by Line 6   _____

If you wish to allow for periodic instead of continuous cash flows, complete Lines 8 and 9.

8. $Gc_{(R-g),p}$ from Appendix Table A2**   _____
9. Present Value: Divide Line 7 by Line 8   _____

C. Growth Rate Greater than Discount Rate

10. $Gc_{(g-R),T}$ from Appendix Table A2   _____
11. Present Value: Multiply Line 5 by Line 10   _____

If you wish to allow for periodic instead of continuous cash flows, complete Lines 12 and 13.

12. $Dc_{(g-R),p}$ from Appendix Table A4**   _____
13. Present Value: Divide Line 11 by Line 12   _____

---
*Discount at the sum (R + g) if the growth rate is negative.

**p is the period between cash flows in years.

In a later chapter, you will be allowing for growth in the number of shares of stock outstanding and inflation. The net rate will involve the growth rate of dividends, the growth rate of the number of shares outstanding, an inflation rate, and a discount rate. Add the rates, and test whether the net rate is a growth rate or a discount rate. If the net rate is a growth rate, use a growth factor. If the net rate is a discount rate, use a discount factor.

CONTINUOUS VS. PERIODIC CASH FLOWS

You can treat periodic cash flows like stock dividends and bond interest payments as though they were continuous. Discount them using continuous Dc discount factors from Appendix Table A4. The error introduced by this simplified assumption is small for monthly and quarterly cash flows. For semiannual or longer periods, the error might be more than you are willing to tolerate.

TABLE 3-3

Discounting Cash Flows that Grow at Constant Percentage Rates
Example 3-5

1. Initial Cash Flow, $/yr.	100
2. Investment Period, years	8
3. Growth Rate of Cash Flow, %/yr.	5
4. Discount Rate, %	12

A. Discount Rate and Growth Rate Equal

5. Present Value: Multiply Line 1 by Line 2	$800

B. Discount Rate Greater than Growth Rate

6. $Dc_{(R-g),T}$ from Appendix Table A4*	0.7657
7. Present Value: Multiply Line 5 by Line 6	$612.56

If you wish to allow for periodic instead of continuous cash flows, complete Lines 8 and 9.

8. $Gc_{(R-g),p}$ from Appendix Table A2**	1.0088
9. Present Value: Divide Line 7 by Line 8	$607.22

C. Growth Rate Greater than Discount Rate

10. $Gc_{(g-R),T}$ from Appendix Table A2	
11. Present Value: Multiply Line 5 by Line 10	

If you wish to allow for periodic instead of continuous cash flows, complete Lines 12 and 13.

12. $Dc_{(g-R),p}$ from Appendix Table A4**	
13. Present Value: Divide Line 11 by Line 12	

---

*Discount at the sum $(R+g)$ if the growth rate is negative.

**p is the period between cash flows in years.

The calculation form in Table 3-2 adjusts for periodic discounting instead of continuous discounting.

If the discount rate is greater than the growth rate, proceed to lines 8 and 9 and divide the result for continuous discounting by the growth factor $Gc_{(R-g),p}$. The time p is the period between cash flows. For quarterly dividend payments, p is 0.25 years. For semiannual bond interest payments, p is 0.5 years. This adjustment allows for a series of cash flows p years apart, with the first cash flow p years after making the investment. If the growth rate is greater than the discount rate, proceed to lines 12 and 13 and divide the result from continuous discounting by $DC_{(g-R),p}$.

Example 3-7. Repeat Example 3-5 using quarterly discounting in place of continuous discounting. Make the adjustment for quarterly discounting in lines 8 and 9 in Table 3-3. The stock pays dividends quarterly, so that p is 0.25 years. Allowing for quarterly discounting instead of continuous discounting, reduces the present value of dividends from

TABLE 3-4

Discounting Cash Flows that Grow at Constant Percentage Rates
Example 3-6

1. Initial Cash Flow, $/yr.	100
2. Investment Period, years	8
3. Growth Rate of Cash Flow, %/yr.	15
4. Discount Rate, %	12

A. Discount Rate and Growth Rate Equal

5. Present Value: Multiply Line 1 by Line 2	800

B. Discount Rate Greater than Growth Rate

6. $Dc_{(R-g),T}$ from Appendix Table A4*	
7. Present Value: Multiply Line 5 by Line 6	

If you wish to allow for periodic instead of continuous cash flows, complete Lines 8 and 9.

8. $Gc_{(R-g),p}$ from Appendix Table A2**	
9. Present Value: Divide Line 7 by Line 8	

C. Growth Rate Greater than Discount Rate

10. $Gc_{(g-R),T}$ from Appendix Table A2	1.1302
11. Present Value: Multiply Line 5 by Line 10	$904.16

If you wish to allow for periodic instead of continuous cash flows, complete Lines 12 and 13.

12. $Dc_{(g-R),p}$ from Appendix Table A4**	0.9963
13. Present Value: Divide Line 11 by Line 12	$907.52

---

*Discount at the sum (R+g) if the growth rate is negative.

**p is the period between cash flows in years.

---

only $612.56 to $607.22. In this example, the assumption of continuous dividends introduces an error of only 0.9 percent.

LOAN PAYMENTS

Although this book concentrates on using discounting to analyze investments, discounting has other applications. One application you will find useful is calculating a schedule of monthly payments for a loan or a mortgage. The required monthly payment is equal to the amount of the loan or mortgage divided by the term of the loan in months and by the discount factor $Dc_{R,T}$. The discount rate is the interest rate you are paying on the loan. The calculation form in Table 3-5 simplifies the calculation.

Example 3-8. What is the monthly mortgage payment per $1,000 of mortgage if the interest rate is 12 percent and the mortgage runs 20 years? Use the calculation form in Table 3-5. Table 3-6 shows how to do the calculation. The calculation requires a Dc dis-

---
TABLE 3-5
Calculation Form—Monthly Payments for Loans and Mortgages

1. Amount of Loan or Mortgage $ _____
2. Term, years   _____
3. Interest Rate, %   _____
4. $Dc_{R,T}$ from Appendix Table A4 at RT equal to Line 2 times Line 3 _____
5. Monthly Payment: Divide Line 1 by 12, and by Lines 2 and 4   _____

If you wish to allow for monthly instead of continuous discounting, complete Lines 6 and 7.

6. $Gc_{R,0.0833}$ from Appendix Table A2   _____
7. Monthly Payment: Multiply Line 5 by Line 6   _____

TABLE 3-6
Monthly Payments for Loans and Mortgages—Example 3-8

1. Amount of Loan or Mortgage $ $1,000
2. Term, years   20
3. Interest Rate, %   12
4. $Dc_{R,T}$ from Appendix Table A4 at RT equal to Line 2 times Line 3 0.3789
5. Monthly Payment: Divide Line 1 by 12, and by Lines 2 and 4 $11.00

If you wish to allow for monthly instead of continuous discounting, complete Lines 6 and 7.

6. $Gc_{R,0.0833}$ from Appendix Table A2   1.0050
7. Monthly Payment: Multiply Line 5 by Line 6 $11.06

---

count factor from Appendix Table A4 at an RT product of 12 percent times 20 years, or 240. The discount factor is 0.3789. Line 5 shows a monthly payment of $11 per $1,000 of mortgage. How much can you reduce the monthly payment by extending the mortgage to 40 years? The Dc factor for 12 percent interest and 40 years is 0.2066. The longer time period reduces the monthly payment only a small amount:

$$P = \$1,000/[(12)\ (40)\ (0.2066)] = \$10.08 \text{ per month}$$

The equation for the monthly payment can also be written:

$$P = (Loan)\ (R)/[(12)\ (1 - Di_{R,T})]$$

As you extend the mortgage, the Di discount factor gets smaller, which makes the divisor $(1 - Di)$ become larger. The larger divisor reduces the monthly payment. Di, however, cannot get any smaller than zero, which means that the divisor $(1 - Di)$ cannot get any larger than 1.0. As the divisor $(1 - Di)$ approaches 1.0, further extensions of the mortgage term become ineffective for reducing monthly payments. A mortgage for an infinite time period would still require monthly payments for $10 per 1,000 of mortgage. All of the payment would go towards paying interest, and there would be nothing left to reduce the mortgage.

SUMMARY

☐ Discounting is a way to calculate what future cash payments are worth today. Present value is smaller than the future value because the smaller sum can be invested, earn interest, and grow to the future sum.

☐ The present value of an instantaneous cash flow at some future time is: $A_o = (A_T)(Di_{R,T})$. Di is the discount factor for instantaneous cash flows. Appendix A3 lists values of Di discount factors. Di discount factors are the reciprocal of the Gi growth factors in Appendix Table A1.

☐ The present value of cash, which flows continuously is: $A_o = (C)(T)(Dc_{R,T})$. C is the cash flow rate, T is the time, and Dc is the discount factor for continuous cash flows. Appendix Table A4 lists values of the Dc discount factor.

☐ If the continuous cash flow grows or decays at some constant percentage rate, discount at the difference between the growth rate and the discount rate. If the discount rate is larger than the growth rate, the net rate is a discount rate. Use Dc discount factors from Appendix Table A4. If the growth rate is larger than the discount rate, the net rate is a growth rate. In that case, use Gc growth factors from Appendix Table A2. If the continuous cash flow does not begin at time zero, use a Dc discount factor to convert the continuous cash flow to a lump sum at the start of the cash flow period. Then, use a Di discount factor to convert this lump sum to a present value at time zero. In addition to evaluating investments, you can also use discounting to calculate monthly payments for loans and mortgages.

4

Ranking Investments by Rate of Return

DISCOUNTED CASH FLOW ANALYSIS IS A SOPHISTICATED WAY TO ANALYZE ANY INVESTMENT and measure quantitatively how attractive that opportunity is. It helps you determine which of your investment opportunities will prove the most fruitful.

DISCOUNTED CASH FLOW ANALYSIS

Discounted cash flow analysis translates the cash flows you expect any investment to generate into the rate of return you earn on that investment. You can compare this rate of return directly to the rate of return you can earn from any other investment.

A discounted cash flow analysis of a particular stock, for example, might tell you that the stock should earn a return of 9 percent. If you have alternative investment opportunities, such as a money market fund yielding 10 percent or a certificate of deposit yielding 8 percent, you can correctly conclude that investing in the stock is more profitable than investing in the certificate of deposit, but not as profitable as investing in the money market fund.

Discounted cash flow analysis also tells you the most you should pay for any security. The most you should pay is the present value of the future stream of cash flows you expect that security to generate.

Suppose you consider investing in a stock, but you also have the alternative of investing in a money market fund that is paying 10 percent interest. Obviously, you should not invest in the stock unless you expect the stock to earn more than a 10 percent return. Discount the cash flows you expect the stock to generate at a 10 percent discount rate. The result is the most you can afford to pay and still earn at least a 10 percent return. If the stock costs less than this maximum, the stock will earn more than a 10 percent return, and it is a better investment than the money market fund. If the stock costs more than discounted cash flow analysis says you should pay, then the stock will earn less than a 10 percent return, and the money market fund is the better investment. The mechanics of discounted cash flow analysis is simple:

1. Define the amount and the timing of all the cash flows involved in the investment. Normally, there are three cash flows. The first is a cash outflow when you invest in the security. The second is the stream of interest or dividends you receive for as long as you hold the security. The third is a cash inflow when you eventually sell the security.

2. Discount these cash flows over a range of discount rates. Use the methods demonstrated in Chapter 3 to do the discounting. The present value at any discount rate is the sum of the discounted cash flows at that discount rate.

3. The rate of return the investment earns is the discount rate that makes the present value equal to zero.

Count only actual cash flows. The amount you pay for a stock, together with the broker's commission, is a cash flow. Interest payments and cash dividends are cash flows. Taxes are cash flows. The cash you receive when you sell your stock is a cash flow. Stock dividends—those paid in stock instead of cash—are not cash flows. Count cash inflows as positive and cash outflows as negative.

Recognize the timing of the cash flow as the time you gain or lose control of the money. Interest earned from a certificate of deposit might be credited to your account quarterly, for example, but you cannot withdraw the interest without penalty until the certificate matures. Count the interest at maturity, when you gain the use of the money, not when the interest is credited to your account.

Take a simple example with a known result to illustrate how simple discounted cash flow analysis is. Consider a $1,000 investment that pays 12 percent interest for 10 years. Discounted cash flow analysis should show a 12 percent return for this investment.

The first step of the analysis is to define all of the cash flows involved in the investment and the timing of each cash flow. A cash flow diagram is extremely helpful for keeping track of the cash flows. The cash flow diagram is a simple diagram that locates cash flows on a time scale and shows whether they are inflows or outflows. Draw a horizontal line to serve as a time scale and as a zero reference line for cash flows. A cash outflow is negative; represent it by a vertical arrow extending down from the baseline. A cash inflow is positive; represent it by a vertical arrow extending up. Make these lines roughly proportional to the size of the cash flows.

Figure 4-1 shows the cash flows involved in this investment. The first cash flow is the $1,000 you invest at time zero. This is a cash outflow; represent this flow by a down-

Fig. 4-1
CASH FLOW DIAGRAM

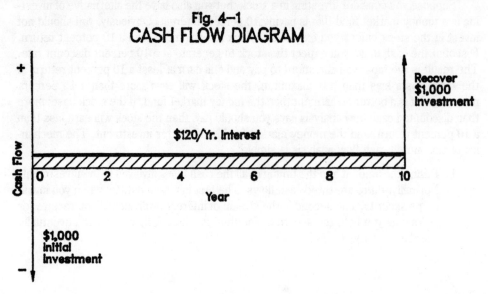

ward-pointing arrow at time zero. The second cash flow is the interest payment of $1,000 times 12 percent, or $120 per year. Interest is a cash inflow. Assume that the security pays interest continuously. Represent the interest by a rectangle $120 per year high and ten years long lying on top of the zero baseline. The final payment is a $1,000 cash inflow when you recover the investment at year 10. Represent this cash inflow by an arrow pointing up at year 10.

The second step of the analysis is to discount these cash flows over a range of discount rates. The calculation form in Table 4-1 simplifies the calculation. Identify the cash flows in the first column of the table; list the dollar amounts in the second column, and their timing in the third column. Remember that cash outflows are negative numbers and cash inflows are positive. Choose a trial discount rate, and multiply the times in column three by the discount rate. Write the result—the RT product—in the fourth column. Look up the appropriate discount factors from Appendix Tables A3 and A4 at those RT products and list them in column five. Now convert each cash flow in column two to its present value. Multiply each cash flow by the discount factor in column five and write the resulting present value in the last column. Total the present value column.

To calculate the rate of return for this investment, you need to find the discount rate that makes all the discounted cash flows add up to zero. Finding this discount rate is normally a trial-and-error process. Begin with a trial discount rate of 6 percent. Table 4-2 develops the calculations.

The three cash flows are the initial investment, the interest payments, and the final recovery of the investment. Label these three flows in column one. The initial cash flow is – $1,000. It is negative because it is a cash outflow. Enter – $1,000 in column two and 0 years in column three. Total interest payments are $120 per year times 10 years, or $1,200. Enter $1,200 in column two, and 10 years in column three. Remember that the continuous discount factor for discounting interest payments applies to the total cash flow. The total cash flow is the product of the $120 per year interest payment and the 10-year time period. The final cash inflow of $1,000 occurs in year 10; enter $1,000 in column two and 10 in column three.

TABLE 4-1

Calculation Form—Discounted Cash Flow Analysis

Trial Discount Rate (%): _____

Cash Flow	Amount	Year	RT	Discount Factor	Present Value
_____	_____	___	__	_____	_____
_____	_____	___	__	_____	_____
_____	_____	___	__	_____	_____
_____	_____	___	__	_____	_____
_____	_____	___	__	_____	_____
_____	_____	___	__	_____	_____
				Total Present Value	_____

TABLE 4-2
Discounted Cash Flow Example

Trial Discount Rate: 6%

Cash Flow	Amount	Year	RT	Discount Factor	Present Value
Initial Investment	−$1,000	0	0	D_i = 1.0000	−$1,000.00
Interest Payments	1,200	0–10	60	D_c = 0.7520	902.38
Recover Investment	1,000	10	60	D_i = 0.5488	548.80
				Total Present Value	$451.18

The RT products at a trial discount rate of 6 percent are zero for the initial cash investment, and 60 for the interest payments and the final cash inflow. Enter these RT products in column four. The first and final cash flows occur at points in time. Discount them with D_i discount factors for instantaneous cash flows from Appendix Table A3. The D_i factor at year zero is 1.000. The D_i factor at year 10 is 0.5488. Enter these values in column five. Interest payments are a continuous cash flow. Discount them with a D_c discount factor from Appendix Table A4. The D_c factor is 0.7520, so enter this discount factor in column five.

Multiply each cash flow in column two by its discount factor in column five and write the resulting present value in the last column. Total the present values. In this example, a trial discount rate of 6 percent gives a present value of $451.18. The rate of return is the discount factor, which makes present value zero. The 6 percent trial discount rate is obviously not high enough because the net present value is greater than zero. You will have to repeat the calculation with higher discount rates. A higher discount rate will make the discount factors and present values smaller, and bring the net present value closer to zero.

Repeating the calculation for discount rates of 8, 10, and 12 percent gives the following present values:

Discount Rate, %	Present Value
6	$451.18
8	275.34
10	126.42
12	0.00

These trial-and-error solutions show that a 12 percent discount rate makes the total present value zero. Consequently, discounted cash flow analysis gives the correct interest rate of 12 percent.

Normally, you will not be so fortunate as to pick a discount rate that gives a present value of exactly zero. If the first trial discount rate gives a positive present value, you have not discounted at a high enough rate. Choose a higher discount rate for the next trial. If the first trial discount rate gives a negative present value, you have discounted at too high a rate. Choose a lower discount rate for the next trial. Repeat these calculations until the calculated present value comes reasonably close to zero.

The calculation form in Table 4-3 speeds the trial-and-error solution for rate of return. Choose a trial discount rate you think approximates the rate of return from the investment and calculate present value. If the present value is positive, you need a higher discount rate. Choose a new discount rate five percentage points higher. If present value is negative, you need a lower discount rate. Choose a new discount rate five percentage points lower. Recalculate present value. Enter the two discount rates and the corresponding present values in Table 4-3. Use Part A of the table if both present values are positive. Use Part B if one present value is positive and the other is negative. Use Part C if both present values are negative.

Table 4-4 illustrates the procedure for the previous example. A trial discount rate of 6 percent gives a positive present value of $451.18. Enter this discount rate and present

TABLE 4-3
Trial-and-Error Solution for Rate of Return

	First Estimate	Second Estimate
1. Low Discount Rate, %	_____	_____
2. Present Value at Low Discount Rate	_____	_____
3. High Discount Rate, %	_____	_____
4. Present Value at High Discount Rate	_____	_____
5. Subtract Line 1 from Line 3	_____	_____
A. Both Present Values Positive		
6. Subtract Line 4 from Line 2	_____	_____
7. Divide Line 5 by Line 6, then Multiply by Line 4	_____	_____
8. Estimated Return: Add Lines 3 and 7	_____	_____
B. One Present Value Positive and One Negative		
9. Make Lines 2 and 4 positive, and Add them together	_____	_____
10. Divide Line 5 by Line 9, then Multiply by Line 2	_____	_____
11. Estimated Return: Add Lines 1 and 10	_____	_____
C. Both Present Values Negative		
12. Make Lines 2 and 4 positive, and Subtract one from the other	_____	_____
13. Divide Line 5 by Line 12, then Multiply by Line 2	_____	_____
14. Estimated Return: Treat Line 13 as positive, and Subtract it from Line 1	_____	_____

For a more accurate estimate, calculate present value at the estimated return. Then use this form again using the estimated return and Line 1 or Line 3, whichever is closer to the estimated return. Continue until successive estimates are essentially identical.

_____*TABLE 4-4*_____
Trial-and-Error Solution for 12% Return Example

	First Estimate	Second Estimate
1. Low Discount Rate, %	6	11
2. Present Value at Low Discount Rate	$451.18	$60.65
3. High Discount Rate, %	11	11.78
4. Present Value at High Discount Rate	$60.65	$12.93
5. Subtract Line 1 from Line 3	5	0.78
A. Both Present Values Positive		
6. Subtract Line 4 from Line 2	$390.53	$47.72
7. Divide Line 5 by Line 6, then Multiply Line 4	0.78	0.21
8. Estimated Return: Add Lines 3 and 7	11.78	11.99
B. One Present Value Positive and One Negative		
9. Make Lines 2 and 4 positive, and Add them together		
10. Divide Line 5 by Line 9, then Multiply by Line 2		
11. Estimated Return: Add Lines 1 and 10		
C. Both Present Values Negative		
12. Make Lines 2 and 4 positive, and Subtract one from the other		
13. Divide Line 5 by Line 12, then Multiply by Line 2		
14. Estimated Return: Treat Line 13 as positive, and Subtract it from Line 1		

For a more accurate estimate, calculate present value at the estimated return. Then use this form again using the estimated return and Line 1 or Line 3, whichever is closer to the estimated return. Continue until successive estimates are essentially identical.

_____

value in lines 1 and 2 of the column headed "First Estimate" in Table 4-3. Choose 11 percent as the new trial discount rate, and calculate a present value of $60.65. Enter this discount rate and present value in lines 3 and 4. Use Part A of Table 4-3 because both present values are positive. Part A of the table gives an estimated rate of return of 11.78 percent in line 8—reasonably close to the true value of 12 percent.

The first pass through Table 4-3 will give you a good estimate of the rate of return you should expect from any security. You can refine that estimate by using it as a new trial discount rate. Recalculate a new present value at that discount rate and use the new discount rate and present value to make another pass through Table 4-3.

The second pass is shown in the last column of Table 4-4. Discounting at a discount rate of 11.78 percent gives a present value of $12.93. Use the estimated return of 11.78 percent and present value of $12.93 as the new high estimate, and the previous trial discount rate of 11 percent as the new low estimate. This pass gives a new estimate of 11.99 percent for the rate of return, essentially equal to the true return of 12 percent.

Suppose you have an alternative investment that earns 10 percent interest. Discounting the cash flows in the previous example at a 10 percent discount rate gives a present value of $126.42. That present value means that you can earn the same 10 percent return as you can with the alternative investment and an extra $126.42 as well.

The assumption of continuous cash flow for the monthly interest payments in the previous calculation is normally a very good approximation and gives acceptable results. The errors introduced by using continuous discount factors for monthly or quarterly interest and dividend payments are normally trivial. The errors in estimating future cash flows from investments in securities are much more important. If cash flows are less frequent, or if you need a more precise calculation, use the methods in Chapter 3 to discount periodic interest and dividend payments.

OPPORTUNITY COSTS

A cost is whatever you give up in return for what you get. When you invest in a security, you give up alternate uses for that money. Your opportunity cost is the return you could have earned on the next best use of that money.

Opportunity cost is a critical yardstick for managing your investment program. Suppose you are using money that costs 10 percent, i.e., money that could earn a 10 percent return from some other investment. You certainly don't want to invest that money in a security that earns only 8 percent. Opportunity cost sets a floor under the returns you should consider for all of the investments available to you. The prospective rate of return must be above your opportunity cost, otherwise you will lose money on the investment, or you will not earn as much as you could have earned from the alternative investment.

Determine your opportunity cost by listing all of the investments you might make that have a clearly stated rate of return. Federal-insured certificates of deposit belong on your list. So do money market funds. Don't overlook paying off debt on which you are paying interest. Paying off credit card debt and prepaying mortgages are examples. The highest rate of return on that list is your next best investment opportunity. The rate of return you could earn from that investment becomes your opportunity cost. Any other investment you consider must promise a return greater than your opportunity cost to be attractive.

Suppose your next best use of that money is investing in a certificate of deposit that is paying 10 percent interest. Your opportunity cost is then 10 percent. You should not invest in a stock or in any other security unless it promises a return greater than 10 percent.

Perhaps you have the opportunity to pay off debt and avoid interest costs. Avoiding payments at 10 percent interest is just as profitable to you as earning 10 percent interest on some investment. You might have charge account debt on which you are paying 18 percent interest. Your opportunity cost is then 18 percent. You should not invest in any security unless that security promises a return greater than 18 percent. If no such investments are available, use the money to pay off the 18 percent debt. After you pay that debt, you might have a mortgage on which you are paying 12 percent interest. If paying off the mortgage is the next best thing to do, your opportunity cost then drops to 12 percent. Paying off high-interest debt will often be more attractive than investing in securities.

Understanding Discounted Cash Flow Analysis

Discounted cash flow analysis is the core idea of this book. You will want to go beyond the mechanics of the analysis and develop a thorough understanding of what the analysis means. Then you will feel confident when you apply the analysis to actual investments. Figure 4-2 illustrates the basic idea of discounted cash flow analysis. The diagram is a plot of present value over a range of discount rates. Consider the $1,000 investment that pays 12 percent interest for 10 years. The cash flows involved in this investment before discounting are:

Initial Investment	−$1,000
Interest Payments	
($120 per year for 10 years)	1,200
Recover Investment	1,000
Total Cash Flow	$1,200

The horizontal dashed line across the top of Fig. 4-2 represents the total undiscounted cash flow of $1,200. The curved line is the present worth you get by discounting this cash flow at various discount rates. At a discount rate of 0 percent all the discount factors are 1.0, and the present value is the same as the undiscounted cash flow. The curved line therefore begins at the dashed horizontal line when the discount rate is 0 percent. As the discount rate increases, the discount factors drop below 1.0, and the

Fig. 4–2
DISCOUNTED CASH FLOW

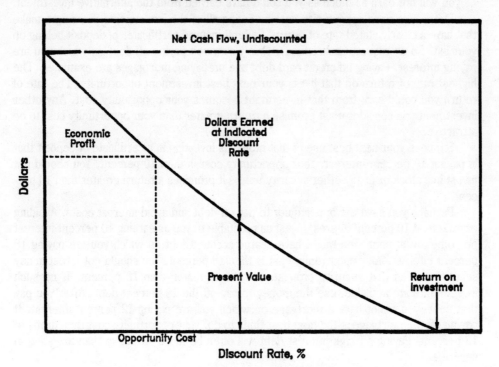

curved line falls below the undiscounted cash flow line and moves towards the horizontal zero line. Eventually, the discount factors become small enough that the curved line crosses the zero baseline and drops below. Present values then turn negative.

Now, consider any vertical distance between the dashed horizontal line representing the undiscounted cash flow of $1,200 and the zero baseline. The curve passing through Fig. 4-2 divides this vertical distance into two segments. The top segment represents a sum of money earned on that investment at the indicated discount rate. When the interest rate is zero, you earn no interest on the investment and the top segment disappears. As the discount rate increases, the money earned as interest also increases. The top segment therefore becomes larger as the discount rate increases.

The point where the curve crosses the zero baseline is critical. At this point, the top segment accounts for all the cash flow and the bottom segment disappears. Consequently, all of the cash flow at this point represents interest earned on the investment at that discount rate. The discount rate that makes the curve cross the zero line (the discount rate which makes present value zero) is, therefore, the rate of return on that investment.

The vertical distance below the curve is the present value at any discount rate. This distance is the sum remaining from the net cash flow after paying interest at that discount rate on the money invested in the security. At zero interest rate, there is no interest cost, and the vertical distance below the curve is equal to the net cash flow from the investment. As the discount rate increases, more money is diverted to paying interest on the money used for the investment, and the present value falls below the undiscounted net cash flow.

A second critical point is the present value when you discount cash flows at your opportunity cost. The vertical distance above the curve at this point represents a sum of money just sufficient to pay the cost of the money you invested. The vertical distance below the curve represents the economic profit from the investment. Economic profit is what's left of the net cash flow after deducting all outlays, including the cost of the money you invested. Think of the economic profit as the extra profit you make beyond the profit you would have made from whatever investment determines your opportunity cost.

If the present value curve for a security crosses the horizontal zero axis at a discount rate below your opportunity cost, the rate of return will be less than your opportunity cost. Present value will be negative, and you will lose money on that investment.

THE IMPORTANCE OF TIMING CASH FLOWS

How attractive an investment is depends not only on how much money you make, but also on how soon you make that money. The timing of cash flows determines the shape of the present value curve, as Fig. 4-3 shows. If an investment returns your money quickly, time will be short. Shorter times take higher discount rates to make RT products high enough, and discount factors small enough, to make the curve cross the zero axis. Therefore, the return on investment will be high. If you have to wait a long time before receiving your money, smaller discount rates will generate the high RT products and small discount factors needed to make the curve cross the zero axis. The return on investment is then less.

Fig. 4-3.
Effect of Cash Timing

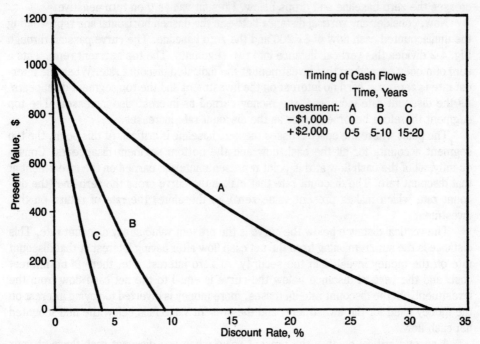

Timing of Cash Flows			
	Time, Years		
Investment:	A	B	C
− $1,000	0	0	0
+ $2,000	0-5	5-10	15-20

Suppose you invest $1,000 in a security that returns $2,000 over a five-year period. In one case, the five-year period begins immediately. In a second case, the five-year period begins in year five, and in a third case, in year 10. Figure 4-3 shows how this difference in timing affects the shape of the present value curves and the rates of return. In the first case, the cash flow occurs between years zero and five. It takes high discount rates to offset these short times, make discount factors small, and make the curve cross the zero axis. The rate of return is 31.9 percent. Cash returns in the second and third cases don't occur until years five to 10, and 10 to 15, respectively. Because the times are longer, smaller discount rates make the discount factors small enough to make these curves cross the zero axis. Rates of return for the second and third cases are 9.4 and 3.9 percent, respectively.

The Significance of Setting Present Value Equal to Zero

Solving for rate of return involves setting the net present value for all the cash flows involved in the investment equal to zero. When you set present value equal to zero, you are specifying the conditions required to make the present value curve in Fig. 4-2 cross the zero axis.

If you specify all of the cash flows, the discount rate is the only remaining unknown, and you solve for it. This is the procedure for finding the rate of return for any investment. Alternately, you might specify the discount rate. You might, for example, specify an opportunity cost as the discount rate. Setting present value equal to zero then forces that opportunity cost to be the rate of return. Some other variable will then be the unknown, perhaps the money required for the investment. Setting present value equal to zero at a discount rate equal to your opportunity cost is the way to calculate the most you can afford to pay and still earn your opportunity cost.

THE MAXIMUM ALLOWABLE PRICE

When you invest in a security, you expect to receive a stream of interest or divided payments, and, at some future time, recover your investment. The more you pay for the security, the lower your rate of return will be. The most you should pay for a security is the price that reduces the rate of return from the security to your opportunity cost. The maximum allowable price is therefore the present value of this future stream of interest or dividends and the final recovery of the investment discounted at your opportunity cost. If you pay more, your rate of return will be less than your opportunity cost.

You can also use the calculation form in Table 4-1 to calculate your maximum allowable price. Leave the initial investment in line 1 blank for the moment, discount at your opportunity cost, and complete the rest of the table. The total of the present value column is the maximum allowable price for the security. This value will be a positive number—the sum of discounted interest or dividend payments, and the final recovery of the investment. If you enter that number in line 1 with a negative sign, the present value column will then total exactly zero. Paying the maximum allowable price for that stream of interest or dividend payments and the final recovery of the investment earns a return just equal to your opportunity cost.

Suppose your opportunity cost were 8 percent. Table 4-5 shows how the maximum allowable cost would be calculated for the $1,000 investment paying 12 percent interest. Maximum allowable price is $1,275.34. At this price, total present value is zero, and you would just earn your 8 percent opportunity cost.

TABLE 4-5
Maximum Allowable Price

Opportunity Cost, (%): 8

Cash Flow	Amount	Year	RT	Discount Factor	Present Value
Initial Investment	—	0	0	Di = 1.0000	
Interest Payments	$1,200	0–10	80	Dc = 0.6883	$826.01
Recover Investment	1,000	10	80	Di = 0.4493	449.33
				Maximum Allowable Price	$1,275.34

Note that if −$1,275.34 is entered as the initial investment in Line 1, the net present value will be exactly zero, and the return will be the 8 percent opportunity cost.

UNDERSTANDING RATE OF RETURN

A high rate of return does not necessarily mean that you will earn a lot of money from an investment. Dollar returns will not be high unless the dollars invested are also high, regardless of the rate of return. Rate of return measures how efficiently you invest each dollar. And efficiency is a combination of high dollar earnings per dollar invested, and receiving those earnings early. Rate of return does not depend on the size of the investment.

Figure 4-4 illustrates what rate of return means. It shows the present value curves of four investments that all have the same rate of return—the present value curves all cross the zero axis at the same point. The economic profits (the present values at the investor's opportunity cost), however, differ widely. Investment A is a large investment and earns a large profit. Investment D is a trivial investment—investing in a two-year magazine subscription instead of two, one-year subscriptions, for example. It has a trivial profit. Rate of return measures efficiency—dollar returns per dollar invested—and timing. Rate of return does not measure total dollars earned.

Because you want to invest your money as efficiently as possible, the rate-of-return scale is the correct scale to use for ranking investments. Discounted cash flow analysis allows you to analyze the cash flow pattern of any investment and calculate a rate of return for that investment. You can then locate that investment on a rate-of-return scale and rank that investment against all of the other investments you are considering.

Fig. 4–4
RATE OF RETURN

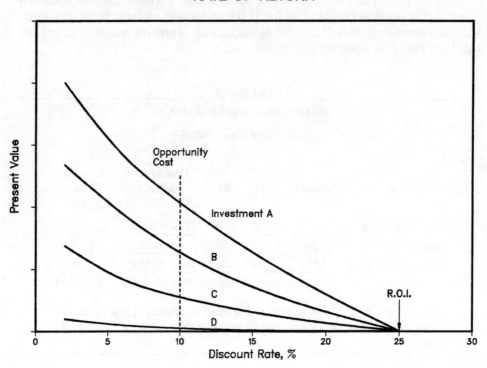

Fig. 4–5
PRESENT VALUE

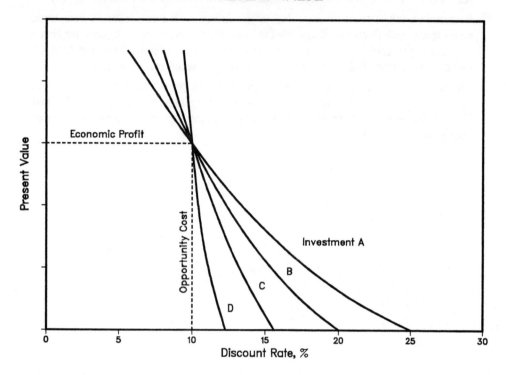

UNDERSTANDING PRESENT VALUE

Present value measures dollars earned, but says nothing about how efficiently you invest those dollars. Figure 4-5 illustrates what present value means. It shows present value curves for four investments, which all have the same present value (the curves all cross at the same point at the investor's opportunity cost). These investments differ widely, however, in rate of return (the four curves cross the zero line at widely different points). Investment A not only has a large present value, it is also efficient, because it earns a high rate of return. Therefore, Investment A will not take as many investment dollars to earn that present value as the other investments will. Investment D is not efficient, because it earns a low rate of return. It would take a much larger investment to earn the same present value as the other investments.

SUMMARY

☐ Discounted cash flow is a method you can use to analyze the cash flow patterns of any investment and express the economic attractiveness as a rate of return. The analysis accounts not only for the cash flows involved, but also the timing of those cash flows.

☐ Rate of return is the discount rate that makes present value go to zero. Rate of return measures efficiency—a combination of the dollar return per dollar invested and how soon you receive those dollars. Rate of return does not depend on the size of the investment. Because you want to invest each dollar as efficiently as you can, rate of return is the correct scale to use to rank all of the investments available to you.

☐ Economic profit is the present value of the future cash flows from an investment when those cash flows are discounted at your opportunity cost. Opportunity cost is the return you could earn on the next best use of your money. The next best use might be paying off a high-cost debt, or investing in some other security.

☐ The maximum allowable price for any security is the present value of all the future cash flows you expect that security to generate, discounted at your opportunity cost. The maximum allowable price is the most you can pay for any security and still earn your opportunity cost.

5

Evaluating Fixed-Interest Securities

You NOW KNOW EVERYTHING YOU NEED TO KNOW TO ANALYZE ANY INVESTMENT. LET'S begin applying discounted cash flow analysis by using it to evaluate securities that pay a fixed interest rate. This chapter covers securities like bank savings accounts, certificates of deposit, bonds, and mortgage-backed securities. In return for your investment, these securities promise interest at a stated rate, and paid at a stated time. With some investments, such as bank savings accounts, money market funds, and bonds, you are free to recover your investment whenever you like. With others, such as certificates of deposit, you agree to leave your money invested for a stated period of time. You can withdraw your money before the certificate matures, but you will pay a penalty if you do.

INVESTING IN FIXED-INTEREST SECURITIES

Investing in fixed-interest securities involves three cash flows, as shown in Fig. 5-1. There is an initial cash outflow when you buy the security. There is a stream of interest payments that continue as long as your investment continues. There is a final cash inflow when you eventually sell the security. These are the cash flows you will be discounting to calculate rates of return and the maximum price you should pay for fixed-interest securities.

Ignore taxes and inflation for the moment. Taxes and inflation are important, but ignoring them simplifies the analysis. You will find the basic economics of fixed-interest securities easier to understand without these complications. Before applying the analysis to an actual investment, however, read how inflation and taxes affect your investment in Chapters 8 and 9.

Bank Savings Accounts

Banks encourage savings accounts as a source of funds they can lend to others. Banks pay one interest rate to attract savings, then lend these savings at higher rates. Banks profit from the spread between the interest rate they pay for savings and the interest rate they charge for loans.

Bank Super-NOW accounts paid 5.1 percent interest in 1989, often compounded daily. Daily compounding is so close to continuous compounding that the bank's rate can be compared directly to the rates you will be calculating for other investments.

Be aware of how your bank calculates interest. Some banks pay interest only on the smallest balance in your account for the full interest period. Also be aware of penalties.

47

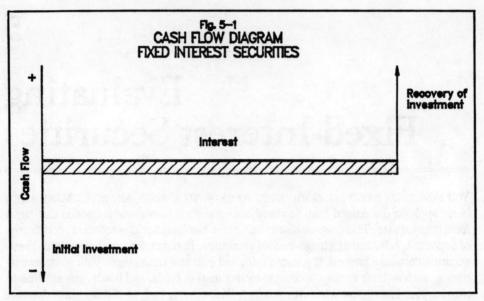

Fig. 5-1
CASH FLOW DIAGRAM
FIXED INTEREST SECURITIES

Some banks charge a penalty if your balance falls below some minimum. These practices will lower your rate of return, or could even make your return negative.

Money Market Funds

Federal regulations formerly limited the interest rate banks could pay small savers to 5.5 percent. These regulations did not apply to institutions which invest large sums of money. These institutions could earn much higher returns on money market instruments—Treasury bills, corporate commercial paper, bank certificates of deposit, and international securities—where yields are not regulated.

In 1971, an investment company made these high returns available to small savers by developing a money market mutual fund. By pooling the savings of many small investors, the fund was able to invest in these unregulated, higher-yielding securities.

Money market funds state rates of return directly and interest is compounded daily. Daily interest is so close to continuous compounding that yields on money market funds can be compared directly to the rates of return you will calculate for other investments. The financial pages of your daily newspaper list the rates money market funds pay. In 1989, money market funds paid a 9.3 percent return, and savers had invested over 300 billion dollars in them.

Certificates of Deposit

The major difference between certificates of deposit and other fixed-interest securities is that you commit your money until the certificate matures. The interest, even though compounded and credited to your account daily, monthly, quarterly, or annually, does not pass into your hands until the certificate matures. Your rate of return is less than the certificate's stated return because you do not collect the interest until the certificate matures.

Banks and Savings and Loans report the interest they pay on certificates of deposit, the compounding frequency, and the yield. The yield is simply the equivalent interest rate if the bank compounded interest annually. Certificates of deposit involve only two cash flows. One is the initial investment; the second is the final recovery of the investment and interest when the certificate matures. Remember, in discounted cash flow analysis, you count money only when it comes into your hands. Count the interest from a certificate of deposit when the certificate matures and you take possession of the money, not when the bank credits interest to your account.

Your rate of return depends on the return the certificate promises and the number of times per year the bank compounds the interest. The length of time you invest your money does not affect your rate of return. Table 5-1 shows how to calculate the true rate of return for certificates of deposit. Divide the certificate's interest rate by 100 and enter the result in line 1. Enter the number of times per year the certificate pays interest in line 2, and follow the directions on the form.

Example 5-1. What is the true rate of return on a certificate of deposit that pays 12 percent interest compounded quarterly. Table 5-2 illustrates the calculation. Interest compounds quarterly, so that the value in line 2 is 4. The true rate of return is 11.82 percent. The true interest rate of 11.82 percent is slightly less than the advertised rate of 12 percent because you receive interest at the end of the term rather than continuously during the term.

BONDS

Government bodies and corporations raise money by selling bonds. Bonds are loans for a stated period of time, usually in units of $1,000, carry a fixed interest rate, and are usually payable semiannually.

Bond prices fluctuate with market interest rates. If you invest in a bond, you assume an interest rate risk—the risk that the bond's price will drop if market interest rates rise.

TABLE 5-1
Calculation Form—Certificates of Deposit

1. Divide the Certificate's Interest Rate (%) by 100 _____
2. Enter the number of times per year the certificate pays interest _____
3. Divide Line 1 by Line 2 and Add 1.0 _____
4. Enter Line 3 on your calculator and tap the ln(x) key. Enter the result: _____
5. Rate of Return, %: Multiply Line 4 by 100 and by Line 2: _____

Example 5-1

1. Divide the Certificate's Interest Rate by 100 — 0.12
2. Enter the number of times per year the certificate pays interest — 4
3. Divide Line 1 by Line 2 and Add 1.0 — 1.03
4. Enter Line 3 on your calculator and tap the ln(x) key. Enter the result: — 0.0296
5. Rate of Return, %: Multiply Line 4 by 100 and by Line 2: — 11.82

TABLE 5-2
Calculation Form—Bonds

A. The Bond

1. Bond Price (Par = 100)   _____
2. Bond Interest Rate, %   _____
3. Years to Maturity   _____

B. The Investor

4. Investment Period, years   _____

C. Future Cash Flows

If the bond is redeemed at maturity, skip to Line 11 and enter 100. If the bond is called, skip to Line 11 and enter the call price. Adjust Line 4 to reflect the timing of the call.

5. Subtract Line 4 from Line 3   _____
6. Future Market Interest Rate, %   _____
7. Di Factor at RT = Line 5 times Line 6   _____
8. Dc Factor at RT = Line 5 times Line 6   _____
9. Multiply Line 2 by Lines 5 and 8   _____
10. Multiply Line 7 by 100   _____
11. Future Price: Add Lines 9 and 10   _____

D. Discounting

12. Trial Discount Rate, %   _____
13. Di Factor at RT = Line 4 times Line 12   _____
14. Dc Factor at RT = Line 4 times Line 12   _____
15. Gc Factor at RT = Line 12 times 0.5   _____
16. Present Value of Interest: Multiply Line 2 by Lines 4 and 14, then Divide by Line 15   _____
17. Present Value at Redemption: Multiply Line 11 by Line 13   _____
18. Present Value: Add Lines 16 and 17, then Subtract Line 1   _____

If the present value in Line 18 is positive, try a new discount rate 5 percentage points higher. If Line 18 is negative, try a new discount rate 5 percentage points lower. Use Table 4-3 to speed the solution for rate of return.

E. Maximum Allowable Price

Enter your opportunity cost as the discount rate in Line 12, and complete Lines 13 through 17.

19. Maximum Allowable Price: Add Lines 16 and 17   _____

Suppose you buy a bond with an 8 percent interest rate, and market interest rates later rise to 10 percent. You might keep the bond until it matures and collect the face value of $1,000, but if you choose to sell, no investor is going to buy your 8 percent bond if he can earn 10 percent from some other investment. The only way you can sell your 8 percent bond is to lower its price. You need to lower the price enough so that a buyer can earn the market interest rate of 10 percent. Increases in market interest rates can make bond prices drop sharply.

If market interest rates fall to, say, 6 percent, the bond's price will rise. No owner will sell an 8 percent bond to another investor whose only alternative is an investment that earns only 6 percent. The owner will raise the price of the bond until a buyer earns only the market interest rate of 6 percent. Therefore, fluctuating market interest rates cause the value of bonds and the rates of return from investing in bonds to fluctuate.

The more you pay for a security, the lower your rate of return. The most you should pay is the price that lowers the rate of return to your opportunity cost. Calculate the maximum allowable price by discounting the future cash flows you expect to receive from that security. Discount at your opportunity cost. The future cash flows from a bond are interest payments and the final cash receipt when you sell or redeem the bond.

Consider three cases. In the simplest case, you buy a bond at its $1,000 face value when the bond is issued, hold it until it matures, and then redeem it for $1,000. In the second case, you buy an existing bond. The purchase price is different from the $1,000 face value because interest rates have changed since the bond was issued. You hold the bond to maturity and then redeem it for $1,000. In the last case, you buy the bond after it was issued and sell it before it matures. Both the purchase and redemption price are different from the bond's $1,000 face value.

The calculation form in Table 5-2 makes it easy to evaluate bonds. The form contains five sections. Part A records basic data about the bond. Part B records information about the investor. Part C develops the future cash flows the bond will generate. Part D discounts the cash flows. Part E develops the maximum price you should pay for the bond.

Enter the basic information about the bond; its cost, interest rate, and the years to maturity, in lines 1 through 3. The calculation form is based on a par value of 100. This is the basis the financial press uses to report bond prices. Enter the number of years you expect to hold the bond in line 4. If you sell the bond before it matures, you will have to estimate the future selling price. Enter the market interest rate you expect when you sell the bond in line 6. Lines 5 through 11 show how the buyer will value your bond. The future price in line 11 is the present value the buyer will calculate for interest payments and the eventual redemption price.

If you hold the bond until it matures, skip to line 11 and enter the maturity value of 100. If you expect the bond to be called, skip to line 11 and enter the call price. Adjust the investment period in line 4 to match the timing of the call.

Discount cash flows in Part D of the form allows for semiannual interest payments instead of continuous interest payments. It discounts bond interest using the Dc/Gc discount factor suggested in Chapter 3. Read the Gc factor from Appendix Table A2 at each trial discount rate and, for semiannual interest payments, a time period of 0.5 years.

The quickest way to use the form is to begin with your opportunity cost as the trial discount rate in line 12. If you find a negative present value in line 18, the bond is not attractive. You can end the evaluation at that point. If the present value is positive, the bond might be attractive. Choose a new discount rate 5 percentage points higher and repeat Part D. You will then have present values at each of the two discount rates. Enter the pair of present values and discount rates in Table 4-3, and estimate the rate of return.

Part E of the form develops the maximum price you should pay for the bond. Enter your opportunity cost as the discount rate in line 12, and calculate the present values of interest payments and the redemption value in lines 16 and 17. The maximum allowable price in line 19 is the sum of these two values.

Full-Term Bonds

The simplest bond to evaluate is one you buy at its $1,000 face value when the bond issues, and later redeem for $1,000 when the bond matures.

Example 5-2. You buy a bond paying 9 percent interest when it issues and sell the bond when it matures 10 years later. What rate of return will you earn? Use Table 5-2 to evaluate the bond. Table 5-3 illustrates the calculation. Your rate of return should be close to the bond's interest rate. Begin with the bond's 9 percent interest rate as the trial discount rate. The Gc growth factor in line 15 allows for periodic interest payments at six-month intervals. Discounting at a 9 percent discount rate yields a negative present value of −$1.32.

The negative present value shows that a 9 percent discount rate is too high. Choose 8 percent as the second trial discount rate. Discounting at 8 percent gives a positive present value of $5.64. These positive and negative present values bracket the rate of return as some value between 8 and 9 percent. Use Table 4-3 to pinpoint the rate of return. Table 4-3 will show a return of 8.81 percent from this bond.

Your rate of return is less than the bond's coupon rate because you are using continuous interest rates to evaluate investments. The bond pays interest semiannually, not continuously. If the bond paid interest continuously, the Gc growth factor in line 15 would drop to 1.0, and the analysis would show a true return of 9 percent.

Existing Bonds

You will rarely buy a bond for its face amount. Normally, market interest rates will have changed since the bond issued, and the price of the bond will have changed as a result. The financial pages of your daily newspaper list bond prices. Discounted cash flow analysis is straightforward because all of the cash flows (the purchase and redemption price and the interest payments) are known.

Example 5-3. The Philadelphia Electric Company has bonds due in 1994 that bear 4.5 percent interest. Because market interest rates in early 1985 were about 10 percent, this bond sold for $540—a substantial drop from its original $1,000 price. If you buy this bond and hold it until it matures in nine years, you can redeem it for $1,000. You will also collect $45 in interest each year, for a total of $405 over the nine years to maturity. What rate of return could you earn from this investment?

Table 5-4 shows how to evaluate this bond. Enter a price of $54 in line 1 because the form is based on a face value of $100, not $1,000. A trial discount rate of 11 percent is too low—it gives a positive present value of $8.17. A second trial discount rate of 15 percent is too high—it gives a negative present value of −$6.68. Enter these two results into Table 4-3 and find an estimated return of 13.28 percent.

You can refine this estimate by repeating Part D using 13.28 percent as the trial discount rate. Discounting at 13.28 percent gives a present value of −$0.88. Enter the present values at discount rates of 13.28 and 15 percent in Table 4-3, and find a better estimate of 13.02 percent for your rate of return. The 13 percent return is known as the

TABLE 5-3
Bonds—Example 5-2

A. The Bond
1. Bond Price (Par = 100) — 100
2. Bond Interest Rate, % — 9
3. Years to Maturity — 10

B. The Investor
4. Investment Period, years — 10

C. Future Cash Flows
If the bond is redeemed at maturity, skip to Line 11 and enter 100. If the bond is called, skip to Line 11 and enter the call price. Adjust Line 4 to reflect the timing of the call.

5. Subtract Line 4 from Line 3
6. Future Market Interest Rate, %
7. Di Factor at RT = Line 5 times Line 6
8. Dc Factor at RT = Line 5 times Line 6
9. Multiply Line 2 by Lines 5 and 8
10. Multiply Line 7 by 100
11. Future Price: Add Lines 9 and 10 — 100

D. Discounting

12. Trial Discount Rate, %	9	8
13. Di Factor at RT = Line 4 times Line 12	0.4066	0.4493
14. Dc Factor at RT = Line 4 times Line 12	0.6594	0.6883
15. Gc Factor at RT = Line 12 times 0.5	1.0228	1.0203
16. Present Value of Interest: Multiply Line 2 by Lines 4 and 14, then Divide by Line 15	58.02	60.71
17. Present Value at Redemption: Multiply Line 11 by Line 13	40.66	44.93
18. Present Value: Add Lines 16 and 17, then Subtract Line 1	-1.32	5.64

If the present value in Line 18 is positive, try a new discount rate 5 percentage points higher. If Line 18 is negative, try a new discount rate 5 percentage points lower. Use Table 4-3 to speed the solution for rate of return.

E. Maximum Allowable Price
Enter your opportunity cost as the discount rate in Line 12, and complete Lines 13 through 17.

19. Maximum Allowable Price: Add Lines 16 and 17

yield to maturity. The most you should pay for a bond is the present value of future cash flows discounted at your opportunity cost.

Example 5-4. The cash flows you expect in Example 5-3 are interest payments of $45 per year for the next nine years, and a final payment of $1,000 when the bond

_____*TABLE 5-4*_____
Bonds—Example 5-3

A. The Bond

1. Bond Price (Par = 100)	54
2. Bond Interest Rate, %	4.5
3. Years to Maturity	9

B. The Investor

4. Investment Period, years	9

C. Future Cash Flows

If the bond is redeemed at maturity, skip to Line 11 and enter 100. If the bond is called, skip to Line 11 and enter the call price. Adjust Line 4 to reflect the timing of the call.

5. Subtract Line 4 from Line 3	
6. Future Market Interest Rate, %	
7. Di Factor at RT = Line 5 times Line 6	
8. Dc Factor at RT = Line 5 times Line 6	
9. Multiply Line 2 by Lines 5 and 8	
10. Multiply Line 7 by 100	
11. Future Price: Add Lines 9 and 10	100

D. Discounting

12. Trial Discount Rate, %	11	15
13. Di Factor at RT = Line 4 times Line 12	0.3716	0.2592
14. Dc Factor at RT = Line 4 times Line 12	0.6348	0.5487
15. Gc Factor at RT = Line 12 times 0.5	1.0280	1.0385
16. Present Value of Interest: Multiply Line 2 by Lines 4 and 14, then Divide by Line 15	25.01	21.40
17. Present Value at Redemption: Multiply Line 11 by Line 13	37.16	25.92
18. Present Value: Add Lines 16 and 17, then Subtract Line 1	8.17	−6.68

If the present value in Line 18 is positive, try a new discount rate 5 percentage points higher. If Line 18 is negative, try a new discount rate 5 percentage points lower. Use Table 4-3 to speed the solution for rate of return.

E. Maximum Allowable Price

Enter your opportunity cost as the discount rate in Line 12, and complete Lines 13 through 17.

19. Maximum Allowable Price: Add Lines 16 and 17	$62.17	$47.32

matures in year nine. Suppose the next best thing you can do with your money is to pay off a debt on which you are paying 15 percent interest. Your opportunity cost is then 15 percent. What is the most you should pay for this bond?

Part E of Table 5-4 shows how to calculate the maximum allowable price. The present value of future interest payments at a 15 percent discount rate is $21.40 in line 16. The present value for recovering the bond's face value at maturity is $25.92 in line 17. The most you should pay for this bond is the sum of these two present values, or $47.32. If you pay more than $47.32 for the bond, your return will be less than your 15 percent opportunity cost. In this example, the bond at $54 costs more than this maximum. For the highest return, you should use the money to pay off the debt. Save 15 percent interest. Don't buy the bond and earn only 13 percent.

Suppose the next best way to use your money is to invest in a certificate of deposit earning 11 percent interest. Table 5-4 shows that the maximum allowable price rises to $62.17 at an opportunity cost of 11 percent. At a price of $54, the bond is cheaper than this maximum. For the highest return, buy the bond instead of the certificate of deposit. The bond's 13 percent return is greater than the 11 percent return you could earn on the certificate of deposit.

Bonds Sold Before Maturity

Analyzing an investment in a bond is straightforward if the bond is held to maturity. You know all of the factors that determine your rate of return. These factors are the bond's cost, interest rate, years to maturity, and redemption price, but you might not want to hold the bond that long. The analysis then becomes more uncertain, because you don't know the price you will be able to sell the bond for. The future price depends on market interest rates at the time you sell. Therefore, evaluating the economics of a typical bond investment requires estimating future interest rates and bond prices.

In Table 5-5, lines 5 through 11 of the calculation form develop the future price of the bond. Assume that the future buyer of your bond will hold the bond to maturity. He will price your bond so that he can earn the same return similar bonds offer at that time. Put yourself in his place, and estimate how he will value your bond. Estimate the interest rate similar bonds will pay when you plan to sell. Enter that rate in line 6, and use it to calculate how the buyer will value his interest payments in line 9 and the redemption value in line 10. The sum of these two values is the price a buyer should pay for your bond. At that price, the buyer of your bond will then earn the same rate similar bonds pay at that time. You will then have all the information you need to calculate your rate of return from Table 5-2.

Example 5-5. You want to evaluate a bond bearing 6 percent interest and maturing in 11 years. The bond sells for $81. Suppose you expect to sell the bond after five years. You estimate that interest rates will be 7 percent by the time you sell the bond. The buyer of your bond can earn only 7 percent from similar bonds, and will have to wait six years until the bond matures. Table 5-5 shows how a future buyer would evaluate your bond. At a future interest rate of 7 percent, line 11 shows he should be willing to pay $95.10. Once you know the future selling price, you have all of the information you need to evaluate this bond. Table 5-6 shows the evaluation at a discount rate of 12 percent.

TABLE 5-5
Bonds—Example 5-5

A. The Bond

1. Bond Price (Par = 100)	81
2. Bond Interest Rate, %	6
3. Years to Maturity	11

B. The Investor

4. Investment Period, years	5

C. Future Cash Flows

If the bond is redeemed at maturity, skip to Line 11 and enter 100. If the bond is called, skip to Line 11 and enter the call price. Adjust Line 4 to reflect the timing of the call.

5. Subtract Line 4 from Line 3	6
6. Future Market Interest Rate, %	7
7. Di Factor at RT = Line 5 times Line 6	0.6570
8. Dc Factor at RT = Line 5 times Line 6	0.8166
9. Multiply Line 2 by Lines 5 and 8	29.40
10. Multiply Line 7 by 100	65.70
11. Future Price: Add Lines 9 and 10	95.10

D. Discounting

12. Trial Discount Rate, %	12
13. Di Factor at RT = Line 4 times Line 12	0.5488
14. Dc Factor at RT = Line 4 times Line 12	0.7520
15. Gc Factor at RT = Line 12 times 0.5	1.0306
16. Present Value of Interest: Multiply Line 2 by Lines 4 and 14, then Divide by Line 15	21.89
17. Present Value at Redemption: Multiply Line 11 by Line 13	52.19
18. Present Value: Add Lines 16 and 17, then Subtract Line 1	−$6.92

If the present value in Line 18 is positive, try a new discount rate 5 percentage points higher. If Line 18 is negative, try a new discount rate 5 percentage points lower. Use Table 4-3 to speed the solution for rate of return.

E. Maximum Allowable Price

Enter your opportunity cost as the discount rate in Line 12, and complete Lines 13 through 17.

19. Maximum Allowable Price: Add Lines 16 and 17	$74.08

One pass through Table 4-3 using discount rates of 7 and 12 percent gives an estimated return of 10.06 percent. A second pass using discount rates of 10.06 and 12 percent gives a more refined estimate of 9.90 percent.

Interest rates are difficult to predict. The rate of return in the example above depends largely on the estimate that interest rates will be 7 percent five years from now. You will get a better feel for the investment by repeating the analysis over a range of likely future interest rates. This calculation has been done for future interest rates ranging from 6 to 12 percent with the following results:

Future Interest Rate, %	Future Bond Price, $	Rate of Return, %
6	1,000	10.8
7	951	9.9
8	905	9.1
9	861	8.3
10	820	7.5
11	780	6.7
12	743	5.9

This analysis shows that, if your opportunity cost were 10 percent, you would earn at least your opportunity cost if future interest rates were 7 percent or less.

Falling Interest Rates

If interest rates fall instead of rise after a bond issues, the price of the bond will go up.

Example 5-6. Suppose a bond issues with a 12 percent interest rate and market interest rates later fall to 6 percent. How much will this bond be worth if it is 10 years from maturity? When market interest rates fall to 6 percent, comparable bonds will yield a return of only 6 percent. The bond will then be worth the present value of the future interest payments and redemption value discounted at 6 percent.

	Cash Flow	Discount Factor	Present Value
Dividends	(100) (0.12) (10 yrs) = $120	0.7520/1.0152	88.89
Redemption	$100	0.5488	54.88
Total			$143.77

Although the bond will be redeemed for only $100 in ten years, it is worth $143.77 now because it pays 12 percent interest when alternative investments pay only 6 percent.

Callable Bonds

In the previous example, the issuer of the bond will not be happy paying 12 percent interest after market interest rates have fallen to 6 percent. Institutions protect themselves by making their bonds callable at a stated price schedule over a stated period of time. If interest rates later fall, the institution can sell new debt at the lower rate and use the proceeds to retire the older, high-interest bonds. Moody's Industrial and Utility Manuals list the call schedule for outstanding bonds. Analysis of callable bonds is similar to the analysis of bonds held to maturity, except that you redeem the bond at the call price and on the call date rather than when the bond matures. A callable bond is one of the examples analyzed in Chapter 15.

The call feature protects the borrower, and puts the interest rate risk on your shoulders. If interest rates rise, bond prices will fall, and you will lose. If interest rates rise, however, the borrower will call the bond, and you will not enjoy the rise in the bond's price that would otherwise have occurred.

Zero Coupon Bonds

Zero coupon bonds pay no interest. They sell at a deep discount from face value instead. You profit from these bonds by redeeming them at face value at maturity.

You can use Table 5-2 to evaluate zero coupon bonds by setting the interest rate equal to zero, but there is an easier way. Zero coupon bonds have only two cash flows—the initial purchase and the final redemption. Calculate the rate of return by dividing the purchase price by the eventual selling price. The eventual price is $1,000 if you hold the bond to maturity. The result is a Di discount factor. Look that factor up in Appendix Table A3 and read the corresponding RT product. Divide the RT product by the investment period to obtain the rate of return.

Example 5-7. A zero coupon bond with a 15-year term sells for $175. What is the rate of return from investing in this bond? The Di factor is 175/1,000, or 0.175. Look up a Di factor of 0.175 in Appendix Table A3 and read that it corresponds to an RT product of 174.3. Divide the RT product by the 15-year term of the bond:

$$\text{Rate of Return} = 174.3/15 = 11.6\%$$

The maximum allowable price is the $1,000 maturity value multiplied by a Di discount factor. Read the discount factor from Appendix Table A3 at the product of your opportunity cost and the investment period.

Example 5-8. If your opportunity cost is 8 percent, what is the most you should pay for the bond in Example 5-7? The Di discount factor at an 8 percent opportunity cost and a 15-year investment period is 0.3012. The most you should pay is:

$$\text{Maximum Allowable Price} = (\$1,000)(0.3012) = \$301.20$$

Evaluate zero coupon bonds sold before maturity the same way you evaluated interest-bearing bonds in Example 5-5. Use lines 5 through 11 of Table 5-2 to calculate what your bond will be worth to an eventual buyer. Use this price as your eventual selling price, and calculate the rate of return as in Example 5-7. The Di discount factor for this calculation is the purchase price divided by the selling price.

Graphical Solution

The economics of investing in bonds can also be shown graphically. The graphical solution is useful because it provides better insight on how market factors affect the economics of investing in bonds. Figure 5-2 illustrates the graphical solution. The bond's current market price, Po, is divided by the $1,000 face value and plotted on the vertical axis. The Di discount factor at an RT product corresponding to a discount rate, and the investment period, is plotted on the horizontal axis. Straight lines fan out from a point on the extreme right side of the graph. The elevation of that point is the bond's final price, P_f, divided by 1,000. Figure 5-2 illustrates a bond held to maturity. The final price is $1,000, and the lines fan out from a $P_f/1,000$ value of 1.0. Each line ends at the extreme left side of the graph at a value of Po/1000 equal to i/RGc, where i is the bond's interest rate, R is a discount rate, and Gc is a growth factor evaluated at that discount rate, and an interest period of 0.5 years. A series of lines are shown for a range of values of the i/RGc ratio.

The critical points in this diagram are points where corresponding vertical and slanting lines cross. Draw vertical lines through the appropriate Di factor on the horizontal axis. Draw the slanting line at the corresponding i/RGc value. These crossing points locate solutions to the bond-evaluation problem. Read the crossing points in either of two ways. Read the Po/1000 value as the maximum allowable price you can pay when the discount rate is your opportunity cost, or read the discount rate at the crossing point as the rate of return you earn when you buy the bond for that value of Po/1000. These two interpretations permit calculating the rate of return you can earn on the bond and the maximum price you should pay.

Maximum Allowable Price

You previously calculated that the maximum price an investor with an 11 percent opportunity cost should pay for the Philadelphia Electric bond was $621.70. Figure 5-2 illustrates the graphical solution for maximum allowable price. Read a Di factor of 0.3716 from Appendix Table A3 at an opportunity cost of 11 percent and nine years to maturity. Locate this value on the horizontal Di axis and draw a vertical line through it. For a bond with a 4.5 percent coupon rate, i/RGc at an 11 percent opportunity cost is (4.5)/[(11)

Fig. 5–2
MAXIMUM ALLOWABLE PRICE FOR BONDS

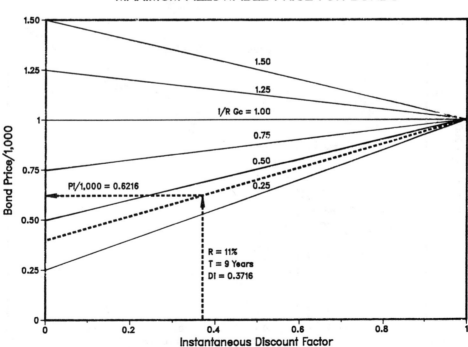

(1.0280)], or 0.3979. Draw a slanting line passing through the points $P_f/1000 = 1.0$ at the extreme right side of the graph, and $Po/1000 = 0.3979$ at the extreme left side. Read the maximum allowable price at the point where these vertical and slanting lines cross. In this example, the lines cross at a $P/1,000$ value of 0.6216. Therefore, the maximum price you should pay for this bond is $621.60, a price which agrees with the previous calculation.

Rate of Return

Figure 5-3 illustrates the graphical method for calculating the rate of return earned on a bond. Choose a number of trial discount rates. Draw vertical lines through the Di factors on the horizontal scale at each discount rate. Draw slanting lines for the corresponding i/RGc ratios. Mark the points where the vertical Di lines cross the slanting i/RGc lines at each discount rate, and connect these crossing points by a smooth curve. The smooth curve is the solution curve. The solution to the problem lies on this curve.

Solve for rate of return by dividing the bond's current market price by 1,000. Enter that value on the vertical axis. Draw a horizontal line at that $Po/1,000$ value and extend it until it crosses the solution curve. Now, draw a vertical line from this crossing point down to the horizontal axis and read a value for the Di discount factor. Look up that Di factor in Appendix Table A3, and read the RT product it corresponds to. The rate of return for the bond is that RT product divided by the investment period.

Fig. 5–3
RATE OF RETURN FOR BONDS

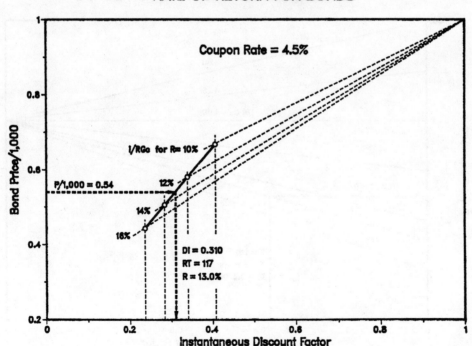

For example, choose a trial discount rate of 10 percent. The Di factor for an RT product of 10 percent times nine years is 0.4066. Draw a vertical line in Fig. 5-3 through a Di factor of 0.4066 on the horizontal axis. The Gc factor at a 10 percent discount rate and 0.5 years is 1.0254. At the bond's coupon rate of 4.5 percent and a 10 percent discount rate, i/RGc is (4.5)/[(10) (1.0254)], or 0.4388. Draw a slanting line through the points P_f/1000 = 1.0 at the extreme right side of the graph and Po/1000 = 0.4388 at the extreme left side. Mark the point where this slanting line crosses the vertical line. Repeat the process for several other discount rates. Mark the points where the vertical and slanting lines cross, then connect these crossing points by the smooth solution curve.

The Philadelphia Electric bond costs $540. Draw a horizontal line at a Po/1,000 value of 540/1,000, or 0.54. The horizontal line crosses the solution curve at a Di value of 0.310. The rate of return corresponds to this Di value. Read an RT product of 117 for this Di discount factor from Appendix Table A3. Divide the RT product of 117 by the nine-year investment period. The rate of return is 13.0 percent, which agrees with the return calculated earlier in Table 5-4. Once you have plotted the solution line, changes in the rate of return for this bond can be read from the diagram as the daily market price fluctuates.

Effect of Market Interest Rate

Bond prices fluctuate inversely with market interest rates. Investors continually adjust the price they will pay for bonds so that the return from any bond is the same as the return from similar bonds. The value of a bond depends primarily on the ratio of the bond's coupon rate to the market interest rate, i/R, and the number of years until the bond matures. Figure 5-4 shows how these factors combine to determine the value of a bond.

Figure 5-4 contains several solution curves for a bond with a 4.5 percent coupon rate and 5, 10, 15, and 20 years to maturity. Points are marked along the solution curves where i/RGc curves cross at discount rates of 4, 6, 8, 10, and 15 percent. Years to maturity and market interest rate determines the location of the solution curves. If the bond is a long way from maturity, or if market interest rate is high, the RT product will be high. High RT products make the Di discount factor small. Therefore, the solution curve will be on the left side of Fig. 5-4. If the bond is near maturity, or if market interest rate is low, the Di discount factor will be closer to 1.0. The solution curve will then be on the right side of Fig. 5-4.

The value of a bond is more sensitive to changes in interest rates when the bond is far from maturity. The solution curve then lies on the left side of the graph, where the slanting i/RGc lines spread far apart. As a result of this wide spread, a given change in market interest rates moves the solution point a greater distance along the solution curve. The result is a greater change in the bond's value. If the bond is closer to maturity, the solution curve lies closer to the right side of the graph, where the i/RGc curves are closer together. Because the curves are closer, the same change in market interest rates causes the solution point to move a shorter distance along the solution curve. The result is a smaller change in the bond's value. The extreme case is one where the bond matures tomorrow. The bond is then worth the $1,000 the issuer is about to redeem the bond for, regardless of the market interest rate.

Fig. 5–4
EFFECT OF MARKET CONDITIONS
4.5% Coupon Rate

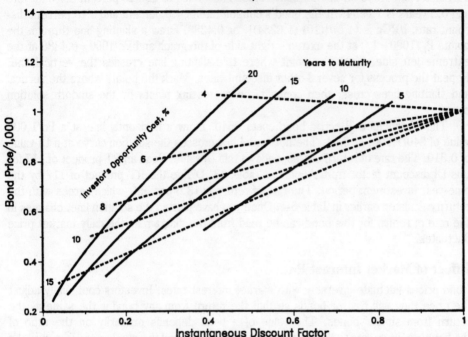

Suppose you buy this bond when it is 20 years from maturity and market interest rates are 6 percent. The bond will cost $818, as read from the point where the 6 percent interest rate line crosses the 20-year solution curve in Fig. 5-4. Now suppose market interest rates rise to 15 percent. The value of your bond will fall to $324, the point where the i/RGc line for 15 percent interest crosses the solution curve. Your bond will have lost 60 percent of its value. Suppose you bought this bond when it was only five years from maturity. The five-year solution curve shows that its value would have dropped only 33 percent—from $932 when purchased at a market interest rate of 6 percent to $625 when the market interest rate later rose to 15 percent.

Note how the solution lines crowd together on the left side of the diagram. Only when the bond approaches maturity and the Di discount factor approaches 1.0 does the solution line move towards the right side. If you bond drops in value because of a rise in market interest rates, you can hold the bond until it matures and recover its face value of $1,000. The recovery in value will be slow, however, until the bond gets close to maturity and the solution curves move to the right side of the graph. Suppose you buy the bond in the example above. Market interest rates rise from 6 percent to 15 percent, and the price of the bond falls from $818 to $324. You decide to hold the bond to maturity.

The following table shows how the bond's value will increase across five-year periods as you move closer to maturity:

Years to Maturity	Bond Price, $	Gain in Value, $
20	324	–
15	364	40
10	448	84
5	625	177
0	1,000	375

Read these values from Fig. 5-4 at points where the slanting line at 15 percent interest rate crosses the group of solution curves. Your bond eventually recovers to its $1,000 face value, but recovery is slow until the bond gets close to maturity. Recovery would be faster if market interest rates dropped and moved the bond's price up along one of the solution curves.

Interest Rates Sensitivity

The calculation form in Table 5-6 allows you to estimate how much a bond's value changes as the result of a 1 percentage point change in market interest rates. The change in value depends primarily on the years to maturity, the bond's interest rate, and the market interest rate. The calculation form is most accurate for small changes in market interest rates.

Example 5-9. The Philadelphia Electric bond pays 4.5 percent interest and matures in nine years. Suppose the market interest rate is now 8 percent. How much is the value of this bond likely to change if market interest rates change by 1 percentage point? Use the calculation form in Table 5-6. The lower half of Table 5-6 shows the calculation. Enter the years to maturity, the bond's interest rate, and the market interest rate in lines 1 through 3. Enter Di and Dc discount factors in lines 4 and 5. Follow the instructions in lines 6 through 8 and calculate a change in value of $55.25 in line 10. This Philadelphia Electric bond should gain approximately $55 if market interest rates drop by one percentage point, or lose approximately $55 if market interest rates rise one percentage point.

You can minimize interest rate risk by investing in short-term bonds. Note that bonds that bear lower interest rates will have a smaller value in line 7 of the calculation form, and therefore, will change less in value. Investing in low-interest rate bonds (at a corresponding discount from face value) is another way to minimize interest rate risk. Changes in bond prices will also be less when market interest rates are high.

Bond Safety

The safety of bonds depends on the issuer's ability to meet interest payments and to redeem the bonds when they mature. The number of times the issuer's cash flow covers his interest costs is a good index of safety. Moodys and Standard and Poor's are the major organizations that evaluate bonds and issue safety ratings.

TABLE 5-6

Sensitivity of Bond Prices to Interest Rates

Basis: $1,000 Face Value

1. Bond Interest Rate, %	_____
2. Years to Maturity	_____
3. Market Interest Rate, %	_____
4. Di Discount Factor at RT = Line 2 times Line 3	_____
5. Dc Discount Factor at RT = Line 2 times Line 3	_____
6. Subtract Line 1 from Line 3. Multiply the result by Line 4	_____
7. Multiply Line 1 by Line 5	_____
8. Price Change for a 1.0 Percentage Point Change in Market Interest Rate: Add Lines 6 and 7. Multiply the result by 10, and by Line 2. Divide that result by Line 3	_____

Example 5-9

Basis: $1,000 Face Value

1. Bond Interest Rate, %	4.5
2. Years to Maturity	9
3. Market Interest Rate, %	8
4. Di Discount Factor at RT = Line 2 times Line 3	0.4868
5. Dc Discount Factor at RT = Line 2 times Line 3	0.7128
6. Subtract Line 1 from Line 3. Multiply the result by Line 4	1.7038
7. Multiply Line 1 by Line 5	3.2076
8. Price Change for a 1.0 Percentage Point Change in Market Interest Rate: Add Lines 6 and 7. Multiply the result by 10, and by Line 2. Divide that result by Line 3.	$55.25

The safest corporate bonds are those of healthy firms who have only a small amount of debt. Such firms have high cash flow, low interest costs, and a high ratio of cash flow to interest cost. Until recently, the market judged bonds of most major corporations to be "investment grade." But the wave of leveraged buyouts during the 1980s brought the safety of corporate bonds into question.

Managements often finance buyouts by issuing a large amount of junk bonds. Existing bondholders might think their bonds are investment grade because of the firm's high ratio of cash flow to interest cost. Suddenly, they find the firm taking on a huge new interest cost obligation. The firm's interest costs jump, and the ratio of cash flow to interest cost plummets. Their quality bonds turn to junk overnight.

The $25 billion leveraged buyout of RJR Nabisco in late 1988 highlighted this problem. Investors saw their RJR Nabisco bonds drop nearly 20 percent within a week after RJR Nabisco announced the buyout. The bonds fell from investment grade to junk. The RJR Nabisco buyout shocked investors because they believed firms of RJR Nabisco's size were too large for leveraged buyouts. Now investors realize that none but the very largest firms are immune. The problem can be minimized by investing only in short-term corporate bonds, or by avoiding corporate bonds entirely and investing in government securities instead.

MORTGAGE-BACKED SECURITIES

Congress established the Government National Mortgage Association (GNMA) in 1968 to make more money available for mortgages. GNMA is part of the Department of Housing and Urban Development. It makes lending money for mortgages attractive by guaranteeing investors full payment of principal and interest. Private mortgage lenders establish pools of mortgages, obtain GNMA approval, and then sell certificates representing shares of these mortgage pools. Private lenders receive a servicing fee of 0.5 percent. The fee makes the interest rate on the certificate 0.5 percentage points lower than the interest rate on the underlying mortgages. Monthly payments on the pool of mortgages pass through to the holders of these certificates. Popularly known as "Ginnie Maes," these certificates are available for a minimum investment of $25,000. Unit investment trusts make these certificates even more available by buying GNMA certificates and selling shares in the trust for $1,000.

As an investor in mortgage-backed securities, you are lending money on mortgages. You receive monthly payments of principal and interest. The government guarantees payment. You might receive additional sums as mortgagees pay their mortgages early. You recover your investment gradually as mortgagees pay off their mortgages. You recover your investment fully at the end of the mortgage, and the certificate has no further value. Although the standard mortgage term is 30 years, most mortgagees pay their mortgages off earlier. The actual mortgage term averages about 12 years.

Table 5-7 shows how to evaluate GNMA securities. The financial pages quote prices on a $100 face value basis. Table 5-7 is consistent with this basis. Enter the basic information, the current price, the certificate's interest rate, and the nominal and actual term, in lines 1 through 5 of Table 5-7. Read the appropriate discount factors in lines 6 through 8. The discount factor in line 8 depends on a time difference between the nominal and actual term of the mortgage. Calculate the annual mortgage payments in line 9, and the final amount that pays off the mortgage in line 11.

Choose a trial discount rate in line 13 of Table 5-7. Read Di and Dc discount factors and a Gc growth factor in lines 14 through 17. If the discount rate is greater than the total of the mortgage interest rate and the service fee in line 3 of Table 5-7, use a Dc discount factor instead of a Gc growth factor in line 17. Use the discount factors to discount the monthly mortgage payments in line 18 and the final payment in line 19. Find the present value of the servicing fee in line 22. Calculate net present value in line 23. Calculate the maximum price you should pay for this mortgage by discounting at your opportunity cost. Find the maximum price in line 24 by adding the present values of the monthly payments and the final payment, and deducting the present value of the servicing fee.

Example 5-10. You could buy a Ginnie Mae 8 percent certificate for $93 in 1989. The underlying mortgages have a 30-year term. Assume the average life will be 12 years. What rate of return would you earn? If your opportunity cost were 12 percent, what is the most you should pay for this certificate? Use Table 5-7 to evaluate the certificate. Table 5-8 shows the calculation. Enter the basic data about the Ginnie Mae in lines 1

TABLE 5-7
Calculation Form—Ginnie Maes

A. The Ginnie Mae

1. Price _____
2. GNMA Interest Rate, % _____
3. Add 0.5 to Line 2 _____
4. Mortgage Term, years _____
5. Expected Life, years _____

B. Future Cash Flows

6. Gc Factor at RT = Line 3 times Line 4 _____
7. Dc Factor at RT = Line 3 times Line 4 _____
8. Dc Factor at RT = Line 3 times the difference between Lines 4 and 5 _____
9. Mortgage Payments, $/yr.: Divide 100 by Lines 4 and 7 _____
10. Divide Line 5 by Line 4; Subtract the result from 1.0 _____
11. Investment Recovered When Mortgage Repaid: Multiply Line 10 by 100 and by Line 8. Divide the result by Line 7 _____
12. Divide 0.5 by Line 3 _____

C. Discounting

13. Trial Discount Rate, % _____
14. Di Factor at RT = Line 5 times Line 13 _____
15. Dc Factor at RT = Line 5 times Line 13 _____
16. RT: Multiply the difference between Lines 3 and 13 by Line 5 _____
17. Gc Factor at RT = Line 16. If Line 13 is greater than Line 3, use a Dc Factor instead _____
18. Present Value of Mortgage Payments: Multiply Line 9 by Lines 5 and 15 _____
19. Present Value of Recovered Investment: Multiply Line 11 by Line 14 _____
20. Divide Line 17 by Line 6 _____
21. Divide Line 15 by Line 7, then Subtract Line 20 _____
22. Present Value of Service Fee: Multiply 100 by Lines 5, 12, and 21. Then Divide by Line 4 _____
23. Present Value: Add Lines 18 and 19; Subtract Lines 1 and 22 _____

If Line 23 is positive, choose a new discount rate 3 percentage points higher. If Line 23 is negative, choose a new discount rate 3 percentage points lower. Use Table 4-3 to complete the calculation for rate of return.

D. Maximum Allowable Price

Use your opportunity cost as the trial discount rate in Line 13, and complete Lines 14 through 22.

24. Maximum Allowable Price: Add Lines 18 and 19, then Subtract Line 22 _____

TABLE 5-8
Ginnie Maes—Example 5-10

A. The Ginnie Mae

1. Price	93
2. GNMA Interest Rate, %	8
3. Add 0.5 to Line 2	8.5
4. Mortgage Term, years	30
5. Expected Life, years	12

B. Future Cash Flows

6. Gc Factor at RT = Line 3 times Line 4	4.6302
7. Dc Factor at RT = Line 3 times Line 4	0.3615
8. Dc Factor at RT = Line 3 times the difference between Lines 4 and 5	0.5121
9. Mortgage Payments, $/yr.: Divide 100 by Lines 4 and 7	9.22
10. Divide Line 5 by Line 4; Subtract the result from 1.0.	0.6
11. Investment Recovered When Mortgage Repaid: Multiply Line 10 by 100 and by Line 8. Divide the result by Line 7.	85.00
12. Divide 0.5 by Line 3	0.0588

C. Discounting

13. Trial Discount Rate, %	12
14. Di Factor at RT = Line 5 times Line 13	0.2369
15. Dc Factor at RT = Line 5 times Line 13	0.5299
16. RT: Multiply the difference between Lines 3 and 13 by Line 5	42
17. Gc Factor at RT = Line 16. If Line 13 is greater than Line 3, use a Dc Factor instead	0.8166
18. Present Value of Mortgage Payments: Multiply Line 9 by Lines 5 and 15	58.63
19. Present Value of Recovered Investment: Multiply Line 11 by Line 14	20.14
20. Divide Line 17 by Line 6	0.1764
21. Divide Line 15 by Line 7, then Subtract Line 20	1.2894
22. Present Value of Service Fee: Multiply 100 by Lines 5, 12, and 21. Then Divide by Line 4	3.03
23. Present Value: Add Lines 18 and 19; Subtract Lines 1 and 22	−$17.26

If Line 23 is positive, choose a new discount rate 3 percentage points higher. If Line 23 is negative, choose a new discount rate 3 percentage points lower. Use Table 4-3 to complete the calculation for rate of return.

D. Maximum Allowable Price

Use your opportunity cost as the trial discount rate in Line 13, and complete Lines 14 through 22.

24. Maximum Allowable Price: Add Lines 18 and 19, then Subtract Line 22	$75.74

through 5. Line 9 shows that mortgagees will pay $9.22 per year per $100 of mortgage to cover principal and interest. Line 11 shows that you will recover $85 when the mortgage is paid in year 12.

Begin discounting at your 12 percent opportunity cost in line 13. You can then find whether the certificate costs more than you should pay in one pass through the form. Line 18 shows that the mortgage payments during the 12-year average life have a present value of $58.63. This value includes the service fee. Line 22 shows a $3.03 present value for the service fee. Line 19 gives a present value of $20.14 for the balance of your investment you recover in year 12. Net present value in line 23 is −$17.26.

The negative present value shows that this Ginnie Mae is not attractive. Line 24 shows a maximum allowable price of $75.74. The current price of $93 is 23 percent more than you should pay. If you continue the analysis, you will find a rate of return of 9.0 percent.

If mortgage interest rates fall significantly, mortgagees will refinance their high-interest mortgages. The average life of the mortgage pool will then drop below the 12-year normal life. The shorter life has a small effect on your rate of return. For the GNMA certificate in Example 5-10:

Average Life, yrs.	Rate of Return, %
6	9.30
8	9.83
10	10.14
12	10.35

Your rate of return drops a small amount as the average mortgage life shortens. The disadvantage is that you recover your money sooner than you wanted. You then have to reinvest when interest rates are low.

Like callable bonds, GNMA certificates have an asymmetrical interest rate risk. If interest rates rise, the value of your certificates will fall. If interest rates fall, however, mortgagees refinance their mortgages. You then have to reinvest when interest rates are low.

SUMMARY

☐ There are three cash flows involved when investing in a fixed-interest security—an initial investment, a stream of interest payments for as long as you invest the money, and a final cash return when you redeem the investment. These are the cash flows you will discount to evaluate fixed-interest securities.

☐ The yields reported for bank savings accounts and for money market funds are close to the continuous compounding used to evaluate other investments. These yields can be compared directly with the rates of return calculated for other investments.

☐ Rates of return for certificates of deposit are slightly less than advertised, because interest does not pass into your hands until the certificate matures.

☐ Table 5-2 simplifies the evaluation of bonds. The evaluation is straightforward if you redeem the bond at maturity. All of the factors that determine the bond's attractiveness—the purchase and redemption price, your opportunity cost, the bond's coupon rate, and the years to maturity are known.

☐ The analysis is more difficult if you sell the bond before maturity because the future selling price of the bond is not known. Estimate the future selling price by putting yourself in the place of the investor who buys your bond and holds the bond until it matures. Once you project the market interest rate at the time you sell your bond, all of the factors that determine how attractive your bond is to that investor are known, and you can calculate the price he should be willing to pay. That estimate of the future selling price allows you to calculate the rate of return for investing in the bond.

☐ The most you should pay for a bond is the present value of future interest payments and the redemption value of the bond, discounted at your opportunity cost.

☐ Bondholders assume the risk of fluctuating bond prices. Bond prices fluctuate in response to changes in market interest rates. If interest rates rise, the price of the bond will fall. If interest rates drop, the bond's price will rise. If the bond is callable, you will not be able to enjoy this rise in price.

☐ The further a bond is from maturity, the more sensitive its price becomes to interest rate fluctuations. Bonds with low interest rates are less sensitive to interest rate changes than bonds with higher interest rates. You can minimize the risk of a serious drop in bond value by investing in short-term bonds and in bonds with low interest rates.

☐ The graphical solution for the economics of investing in a bond helps to understand how market conditions affect your investment. The graphical solution vividly illustrates why bonds far from maturity are more sensitive to interest rate fluctuations. Graphical analysis also shows why recovery in bond prices is slow until the bond comes close to maturity or until interest rates fall.

☐ Table 5-7 shows how to evaluate Ginnie Mae certificates. Ginnie Maes are like callable bonds. If interest rates rise, the value of the security falls. If interest rates drop, however, you still do not enjoy a rise in price. Mortgagees refinance their mortgages, and you have to reinvest when interest rates are low.

☐ Taxes and inflation were ignored in this chapter to make the economics of fixed-interest securities easier to understand. Inflation and taxes are important, however. Before you apply the analysis of this chapter to an actual investment, read how taxes and inflation affect the economics of an investment in Chapters 8 and 9. Inflation and taxes should always be a part of your evaluation.

6

Evaluating Stocks

A SHARE OF STOCK IS A SHARE OF OWNERSHIP IN A COMPANY AND A CLAIM ON THAT company's earnings. The relationship between price and the earnings you have a claim to is a critical one. Security analysts relate price to earnings by the price/earnings ratio. The price/earnings ratio is simply the price you must pay for a share of stock divided by the earnings per share of that stock. A stock that sells for $50 per share and earns $5 per share has a price/earnings ratio of 50 divided by five, or 10. For $10, you buy a claim to one dollar of earnings per year, extending an indefinite time into the future. Major newspapers list price/earnings ratios in their financial pages.

PRICE/EARNINGS RATIOS

You can buy stocks over a wide range of price/earnings ratios. The average price/earnings ratio was 13 in 1989. Some stocks had price/earnings ratios as low as 0.6; others had ratios as high as 60. Stocks selling at extremely low and extremely high price/earnings ratios in 1989 were:

Low Price/Earnings Ratios	Price/Earnings Ratio
LTV Corp.	0.6
Chase Manhattan	2.6
Eagle-Picher	2.7
High Price/Earnings Ratios	
Hudson's Bay Co.	59
NEC	56
First Fidelity	52

Why do some stocks sell at price/earnings ratios of only 0.6 when the average stock sold for a price/earnings ratio of 13? Are these stocks bargains? Or is there good reason these stocks are so cheap? Why do other stocks sell for price/earnings ratios of 50 or more? Are these stocks overpriced? Or are future earnings high enough to justify such high prices? In this chapter, you learn how to calculate whether there are any bargains among low price/earnings ratio stocks and whether there are any good buys among the high price/earnings ratio stocks.

High Price/Earnings Ratio Stocks

Investors willing to pay price/earnings ratios of 50—four times the price/earnings ratio of the average stock—are paying for faster growth. They are investing in glamour stocks, or stocks with high growth potential. These types of stocks are likely to be in hi-tech firms, such as those connected with computers and biotechnology. These firms might be growing 20 percent per year or more. They are in the early stages of their life cycle, and their products are in great demand. Most of their growth stretches before them. Investors already recognize the potential of these firms and have bid the price of their stock up to very high levels. Investors believe that, although prices are high compared to earnings now, they are reasonable compared to earnings they expect in the future. These firms do have high growth potential, but the high price for that growth might prevent you from earning a reasonable return.

Fast growth cannot continue forever. Fast growth is likely only in the early stages of a firm's life cycle, when there is a high demand for the firm's product. As the firm gradually satisfies demand, however, growth slows. In time, all markets become saturated, and growth falls to the growth rate of the national economy. Chapter 7 discusses how to allow for declining growth and how to calculate the maximum price you should pay for a growth stock. Price/earnings ratios can sometimes exceed 500. Such high ratios reflect unusually low earnings in the previous year. Investors are paying for future earnings, not last year's earnings.

Average Price/Earnings Ratios

Most firms are not exciting. They are mature and their period of rapid growth is over. They struggle in mature markets. There is little possibility of rapid growth and they have many competitors. Such firms plod along each year, making moderate, not outstanding, profits. Investors recognize that these firms are mature and going to grow slowly. Consequently, they offer only an average price for the stock, but these lower stock prices might offer a good return on your investment. You will learn how to tell whether there are any good investment possibilities in stocks with average price/earnings ratios.

Low Price/Earnings Ratios

Investors willing to pay only 0.6 times earnings—5 percent of the price/earnings ratio for an average stock—are seriously concerned about the future of those firms. They are uncertain about future sales, earnings, dividends, and stock price. To compensate for poor future performance, investors lower the price they are willing to pay.

On the other hand, some firms have had recent losses or serious drops in earnings, yet their stock still commands a price. Investors aren't paying for a stream of losses or depressed earnings. They expect those firms to recover and once again make reasonable earnings. They are offering what they believe is a reasonable price based on the earnings they expect when the firm recovers.

EVALUATING STOCKS

Evaluating stocks is no different from evaluating any other security. Project the cash flows you expect that stock to generate. Then use discounted cash flow analysis to determine the rate of return that stock offers, and the maximum price you should pay for it.

To make learning how to evaluate stocks much easier, begin the analysis by making some simplifying assumptions. Assume that the firm whose stock you are evaluating is mature and operates under steady-state conditions. It grows at a constant percentage rate. The factors that determine growth—the rate of return the firm earns, the fraction of earnings it pays out as dividends and the fraction it reinvests, and the proportions of debt and equity capital in its capital pool—stay constant at steady-state values. The price/earnings ratio reflects these steady conditions, and stays constant as well. Steady-state conditions make the size of the firm, its earnings, dividends, and the price of its stock all grow at the same percentage growth rate. Inflation, taxes, and broker's commissions complicate the analysis, so we will ignore them until a later chapter.

The great advantage of the steady-state assumption is that it makes the evaluation process much easier to understand. You will find it much easier to appreciate the cash flows a firm generates, and how those flows determine the value of their stock. You will want to go beyond these simplifying assumptions, however, before you attempt to analyze a particular stock, and bring inflation, taxes, and broker's commissions into the analysis. Chapters 8 and 9 will show how to allow for inflation and taxes. You will resume your evaluation of mature stocks in Chapter 11, when you can make realistic evaluations that include inflation, taxes, and commissions.

The steady-state assumption is reasonable for mature firms, whose growth rates, rates of return, dividends, and capital structures tend to fluctuate in a narrow band around some average value. The steady-state assumption is not reasonable for rapidly growing firms, because you cannot reasonably expect rapid growth to continue unchanged forever. Growth slows as these firms mature. Learn how to allow for this slowing growth in Chapter 7 before attempting to analyze growth stocks.

Discounted Cash Flow Solution

Stock market analysts point to several factors that determine a stock's value. They cite how fast the firm is growing, the earnings, dividends, and cash flow the firm is generat-

Fig. 6-1
Cash Flows for Investing in Stock

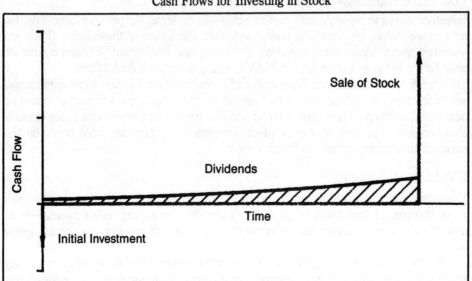

ing, the stock's price/earnings ratio, and the firm's book value per share. You already know from discounted cash flow analysis that these factors cannot be the critical ones. The critical factors are the cash flows you will either spend or receive because of investing in a stock.

There are three cash flows: the cash you pay when you buy the stock, and dividends you receive as long as you hold the stock, and the cash you recover when you finally sell the stock. Growth, earnings, dividends, cash flow, and book value are important only insofar as they affect these cash flows. Therefore, analyzing stock investments will concentrate on those cash flows you will either spend or receive because of your investment.

Figure 6-1 shows the cash flow diagram for investing in a stock. The diagram is similar to the cash flow diagram for a fixed-interest security such as a bond. The difference is that the stream of dividends and the price of the stock grow with time as the company grows.

Your return for investing in a mature firm operating under steady-state conditions depends on the current price of the stock, the current dividend, and how fast you project the stock price and dividends to grow. The simplified calculation form in Table 6-1 explains the basic evaluation. Enter the current price of the stock in line 1, current divi-

---
TABLE 6-1
Calculation Form—Stocks

A. The Firm
1. Stock Price, $/share   _____
2. Dividends, $/share   _____
3. Investment Period, years   _____
4. Growth Rate, %/yr.   _____
5. Gi Growth Factor at RT = Line 3 times Line 4   _____
6. Future Stock Price: Multiply Line 1 by Line 5   _____

B. Discounting
7. Trial Discount Rate, %   _____
8. Di Discount Factor at RT = Line 3 times Line 7 _____
9. RT: Subtract Line 4 from Line 7. Multiply the result by Line 3 _____
10. If Line 7 is greater than Line 4, enter a Dc Discount Factor at RT = Line 9. If Line 4 is greater, enter a Gc Growth Factor instead. _____
11. Present Value of Stock Sale: Multiply Line 6 by Line 8 _____
12. Present Value of Dividends: Multiply Line 2 by Lines 3 and 10 _____
13. Present Value: Add Lines 11 and 12, then Subtract Line 1 _____

If Line 13 is positive, try a new discount rate 5 percentage points higher. If Line 13 is negative, try a new discount rate 5 percentage points lower. Use Table 4-3 to complete the solution for rate of return.

C. Maximum Allowable Price
Discount at your opportunity cost, and complete Lines 8 through 12. Continue below.
14. Maximum Allowable Price: Add Lines 11 and 2 _____

dends in line 2, and the time you plan to hold the stock in line 3. The basic projection you must make is how fast you expect the firm to grow. Project future growth in line 4. Working from these basic numbers, the calculation form develops the future price of the stock in line 6.

Discount cash flows in Part B of Table 6-1. Choose a trial discount rate in line 7. Enter a Gc growth factor or a Dc discount factor in line 11. If the discount rate is greater than the growth rate, use a discount factor. If the growth rate is greater, use a growth factor. Read the discount or growth factor at the difference between the discount rate and the growth rate. Calculate the present value of the proceeds from the eventual sale of the stock in line 11 and the present value of dividends in line 12. Calculate the total present value in line 13, then use Table 4-3 to find your rate of return. The maximum price you should pay for this stock is the present value of future dividends and the proceeds from the eventual sale of the stock, discounted at your opportunity cost. Part C of Table 6-1 shows how to calculate maximum allowable price.

Example 6-1. You are considering a stock that sells for $50 per share and earns $5 per share. The company pays half its earnings, or $2.50 per share, as dividends. You expect the firm to grow 8 percent per year, and, based on the steady-state assumption, that its dividends and stock price will grow 8 percent per year as well. What will your rate of return be for investing in this stock if you hold the stock 10 years? What is the most you should pay if your opportunity cost is 10 percent?

Table 6-2 shows how to evaluate this stock. The expected price of the stock when you sell it 10 years from now is the current price multiplied by a Gi growth factor from Appendix Table A1. Read Gi at a growth rate of 8 percent per year and a 10-year time period. The growth factor is 2.2255; line 8 shows the expected price is $111.28.

Begin with your 10 percent opportunity cost as the trial discount rate in line 7. The present value of the proceeds when you eventually sell the stock is the projected future price of $111.28 multiplied by a Di discount factor of 0.3679. The present value is $40.94, which is shown in line 11. You expect dividends to grow 8 percent per year. At a discount rate of 10 percent, the net rate—the difference between the 10 percent discount rate and the 8 percent growth rate—is a discount rate of 2 percent. Use a Dc discount factor of 0.9063 in line 10. Dividends have a present value of $22.66, as line 12 shows.

The net present value of $13.60 is positive. A discount factor of 10 percent is not high enough. Choose a second discount rate 5 percentage points higher, and repeat the calculation. Table 6-2 shows that discounting at a 15 percent discount rate gives a present value of −$7.19. Use Table 4-3 to find the rate of return. Two passes through Table 4-3, which is reproduced as Table 6-3, shows a rate of return of 13 percent.

At an opportunity cost of 10 percent, Part C of Table 6-2 shows that the most you should pay for this stock is $63.60 per share. The maximum price is the sum of the $22.66 present value of the future dividends and the $40.94 present value when you sell the stock in 10 years.

This example shows that evaluating a stock is the same as evaluating a fixed-income security, such as a bond. The basic difference is that you have to allow for the gradual growth in dividends and stock prices when evaluating stocks.

Evaluating a stock is more complicated than this simple example suggests, however. The discounted cash flow solution is a minor part of the evaluation. The major part is

---

TABLE 6-2
Stock Evaluation—Example 6-1

A. The Firm

1. Stock Price, $/share	50
2. Dividends, $/share	2.50
3. Investment Period, years	10
4. Growth Rate, %/yr.	8
5. Gi Growth Factor at RT = Line 3 times Line 4	2.2255
6. Future Stock Price: Multiply Line 1 by Line 5	111.28

B. Discounting

7. Trial Discount Rate, %	10	15
8. Di Discount Factor at RT = Line 3 times Line 7	0.3679	0.2231
9. RT: Subtract Line 4 from Line 7. Multiply the result by Line 3	20	70
10. If Line 7 is greater than Line 4, enter a Dc Discount Factor at RT = Line 9. If Line 4 is greater, enter a Gc Growth Factor instead	0.9063	0.7192
11. Present Value of Stock Sale: Multiply Line 6 by Line 8	40.94	24.83
12. Present Value of Dividends: Multiply Line 2 by Lines 3 and 10	22.66	17.98
13. Present Value: Add Lines 11 and 12, then Subtract Line 1	13.60	−7.19

If Line 13 is positive, try a new discount rate 5 percentage points higher. If Line 13 is negative, try a new discount rate 5 percentage points lower. Use Table 4-3 to complete the solution for rate of return.

C. Maximum Allowable Price

Discount at your opportunity cost, and complete Lines 8 through 12. Continue below.

14. Maximum Allowable Price: Add Lines 11 and 2	63.60

---

analyzing the firm's performance. Based on that analysis and the outlook for the economy, you must project how fast the firm is likely to grow, and how fast future dividends and the price of the stock are likely to grow. Once you have projected future dividends and stock prices, the discounted cash flow solution is straightforward and simple.

The main objective of this chapter is to help you understand how corporations grow, and how that growth makes dividends and the price of the stock grow. This will serve as a framework for analyzing the firm's historical performance and projecting future dividends and stock prices. How, in the example above, did you project that the company would grow 8 percent per year? How did you decide that the firm would earn enough money to finance growth of 8 percent per year and still have enough left to pay half of its earnings out as dividends? How did you decide that the company could grow 8 percent per year, pay half of its earnings out as dividends, and not have to borrow more debt? What would happen to the analysis if the company grew faster or slower than projected, paid out more or less dividends, or took on more debt?

TABLE 6-3

Solve for Rate of Return—Example 6-1

	First Estimate	Second Estimate
1. Low Discount Rate, %	10	13.27
2. Present Value at Low Discount Rate	13.60	−1.05
3. High Discount Rate, %	15	15
4. Present Value at High Discount Rate	−7.19	−7.19
5. Subtract Line 1 from Line 3	5	1.73
A. Both Present Values Positive		
6. Subtract Line 4 from Line 2		
7. Divide Line 5 by Line 6, then Multiply by Line 4		
8. Estimated Return: Add Lines 3 and 7		
B. One Present Value Positive and One Negative		
9. Make Lines 2 and 4 positive, and Add them together	20.79	
10. Divide Line 5 by Line 9, then Multiply by Line 2	3.27	
11. Estimated Return: Add Lines 1 and 10	13.27	
C. Both Present Values Negative		
12. Make Lines 2 and 4 positive, and Subtract one from the other		6.14
13. Divide Line 5 by Line 12, then Multiply by Line 2		0.30
14. Estimated Return: Treat Line 13 as positive, and subtract it from Line 1		12.97

For a more accurate estimate, calculate present value at the estimated return. Then use this form again using the estimated return and Line 1 or Line 3, whichever is closer to the estimated return. Continue until successive estimates are essentially identical.

To answer these questions you must understand the basics of corporate growth. You need to understand how day-to-day operations generate cash, and how that cash pays for the firm's growth and pays for dividends. Finally, you need to understand how the cash the firm generates is reflected in the price of its stock.

The first step is to understand the corporation's financial structure, as reported on the corporation's balance sheet. That analysis identifies the financial core of the corporation, the financial engine that generates cash flow and earnings. Next, you will need to understand the corporation's profit and loss statement, which shows how much revenue the corporation received during the year, and how it used that revenue. The statement shows how much was left after paying operating costs, to pay interest and dividends, and to reinvest in the business.

A corporate cash flow diagram combines information from the balance sheet and the profit and loss statement. The cash flow diagram makes clear the relationship between the cash the corporation generates, the cash it needs to sustain growth, and the cash available for dividends. A straightforward model will capture the interrelationships among these factors. It will tell how the rate of return the firm earns, the fraction of earnings it reinvests and the fraction it pays out as dividends, and the fractions of debt and equity in its capital pool controls how fast it can grow.

CORPORATE FINANCIAL STRUCTURE

The balance sheet lays out the firm's financial structure. One side of the balance sheet lists the assets of the corporation—all of the items of value the corporation owns. The other side of the balance sheet lists the liabilities of the corporation—the claims of all interested parties on the assets of the corporation. Because there is a claim of ownership for every asset, total assets and total liabilities are always equal.

The two vertical bars in Fig. 5-2 show the balance sheet for the average U.S. manufacturing corporation in 1984. The bar on the left represents total assets; the bar on the right represents total liabilities. The two bars have the same height above the zero baseline because total assets and total liabilities are always equal. Stockholders own what's left of total assets after all other interested parties have satisfied their claims. Stockholder's equity adjusts to whatever value makes total assets equal total liabilities.

Assets

Assets are divided into current assets and long-term assets. Current assets are assets with an expected life of one year or less. Typical current assets are cash on hand, accounts receivable, and inventories. Current assets account for 41 percent of total assets of the average manufacturing corporation. Long-term assets are assets with an expected life greater than one year. The major long-term asset of most corporations is plant and physical equipment. Gross fixed assets are the firm's fixed plant and equipment valued at the price the firm originally paid for it. Net fixed assets are gross assets less accumulated depreciation. In 1984, gross fixed assets represented 67 percent of total assets and net fixed assets represented 38 percent of total assets.

Many investors do not understand depreciation. Depreciation is simply an accounting device to avoid distorting a firm's profits because of major capital expenditures. Suppose a normal, healthy firm earns 10 million dollars per year. One year the firm builds a new plant, and pays out 100 million dollars for it. If the firm charged that 100 million dollars as an expense the year it spent the money, the firm would show an apparent loss of 90 million dollars. There would be normal profits of 10 million dollars, less 100 million dollars spent for the new plant. Reporting a loss of 90 million dollars is obviously not a fair picture of that firm's condition.

To avoid this distortion, accountants recognize that the new plant will be productive for many years. They spread the cost of that plant over its estimated useful life. Suppose the firm expects the plant to have a productive life of 20 years. The accountants spread the 100 million dollar cost of the plant over the estimated 20-year life and charge $5 million as an expense in each of the 20 years. The $5 million yearly charge is depreciation. Profits in the year the firm builds the new plant will be more reasonable. There will be the normal $10 million, plus the profits the new plant earns, less $5 million in deprecia-

Fig. 6–2
TYPICAL BALANCE SHEET

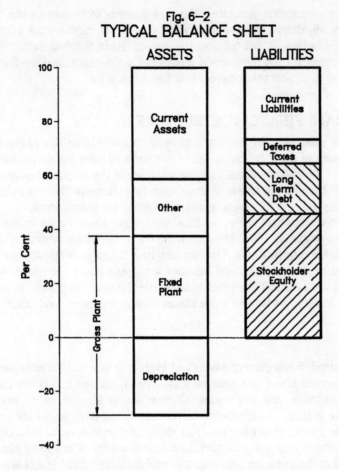

ASSETS   LIABILITIES

Per Cent

100

80 — Current Assets

60 —

Other

40 —

Fixed Plant   Gross Plant

20 —

0

Depreciation

-20 —

-40

Current Liabilities

Deferred Taxes

Long Term Debt

Stockholder Equity

tion. Depreciation is simply an accounting device to avoid distorting profits in those years when capital spending is unusually high.

Capital spending does not show on the books as an expense when the firm actually spends the money. Instead, capital spending shows up as an increase in fixed assets. As annual depreciation charges gradually recognize this spending as an expense, bookkeeping entries transfer credits from the net, fixed-asset account into an account called reserve for depreciation. When the plant finally reaches the end of its useful life, depreciation charges will have transferred all of the plant's cost from the net fixed-asset account to the depreciation reserve. In the process, all this money will have been charged as an expense.

Gross fixed assets is the total sum the corporation spent in past years on plant and equipment. The reserve for depreciation is the amount of this spending the firm has already charged as expense. Net fixed assets is the amount of this spending the firm has yet to charge to expense. Depreciation is an annual bookkeeping entry which is recorded as expense money the firm spent in earlier years.

Gross fixed assets are shown in Fig. 6-2 as a vertical bar extending both above and below the zero line. The part of the bar above the zero line is the firm's net fixed assets.

The part extending below the zero line is the firm's reserve for depreciation. Through 1984, the average U.S. manufacturing corporation had charged 43 percent of its prior capital spending as an expense. The firm has yet to charge the remaining 57 percent, though actually spent, as an expense. The firm shows this remaining amount as net fixed assets.

Each year, depreciation charges transfer some of the net fixed assets from above the zero line in Fig. 6-2 to the depreciation reserve below the zero line. The firm's total assets shrink by the amount of depreciation transferred. If these depreciation charges are not offset by new investment, the firm will become smaller. The firm must therefore reinvest all depreciation charges just to maintain zero growth.

Some investors erroneously believe that depreciation is an allowance for wear and tear on equipment. They believe the reserve for depreciation is a fund for replacing the plant when it wears out. Depreciation charges are simply an accounting device for spreading capital costs over a plant's useful life to avoid distorting profits. Firms spend the money represented by depreciation charges for operating purposes as they generate the money. No fund is built up to replace the plant. When the plant reaches the end of its life, the money to replace it will come from then current cash flow, or from new debt.

Liabilities

Liabilities are also divided into short-term liabilities with an expected life of one year or less, and long-term liabilities, with an expected life greater than one year. Short-term liabilities include accounts payable, wages payable, and loans payable. In 1984, 27 percent of the average manufacturing corporation's liabilities were short-term liabilities. Long-term liabilities include deferred taxes, long-term debt, minority interests, and stockholder's equity.

Deferred taxes are the government's claims for taxes the firm deferred by accelerating depreciation. You will see how these claims arise in the profit and loss statement. Deferred items represent roughly 8 percent of total liabilities. Minority stockholders are stockholders remaining from firms in which the corporation previously acquired a controlling, but not a complete interest.

Most firms finance growth partly by selling long-term bonds. They do not repay bonds in the usual sense, however. They roll the bonds over instead, then sell new bonds and use the proceeds to pay off older bonds as they mature. A firm does not have to repay long-term debt until the firm eventually goes out of business. In 1984, long-term debt represented 18 percent of the average manufacturing corporation's total liabilities.

Preferred stockholders receive a fixed dividend instead of a share of earnings. The fixed dividend obligation on preferred stock is similar to the fixed interest obligation on debt. Therefore, you can treat preferred stock like long-term debt.

Those assets remaining after claims by suppliers, the government, minority holders, or holders of the firm's debt belong to the stockholders. Those remaining assets make up stockholder's equity. In 1984, stockholders owned 46 percent of the assets of the average manufacturing corporation. The lower, right-hand block in Fig. 6-2 represents stockholder equity.

Stockholder's equity divided by the number of shares of stock outstanding is the book value per share. Analysts often compare stock prices to book value, although the stock might be valued higher or lower than the book value. Book value should concern you only insofar as it affects cash payments to you.

Capital Employed

The financial core of a corporation is the capital it employs on a permanent basis for earning a return for the suppliers of that capital. Capital employed is long-term debt supplied by the corporation's bondholders and preferred stockholders, and equity capital supplied by the corporation's common stockholders. The two shaded blocks in Fig. 6-2 represent capital employed. In 1984, 64 percent of the total capital used by the average manufacturing corporation was long-term capital. Of this amount, stockholders supplied 71 percent and bondholders supplied 29 percent.

The procedure for evaluating a stock centers on capital employed. An analysis shows how the firm uses this capital to generate a growing stream of earnings and dividends. This growing stream of earnings and dividends is what causes the price of the stock to grow.

Profit and Loss Statement

The balance sheet is a snapshot of the corporation's financial structure at a point in time. The profit and loss statement shows the cash flows that occur over a period of time. These cash flows determine the next period's balance sheet.

Corporations keep two sets of books. One set, called the financial books, shows the condition of the corporation as measured by generally accepted accounting principles. This is the financial record presented in the corporation's annual report. The second set, called the tax books, are the books the corporation uses to calculate its tax bill. The difference between the two sets of books is that the tax books take advantage of accelerated depreciation.

Figure 6-3 compares the two sets of books. Both show the same amount of sales and cash operating costs, but tax books usually show much more depreciation than financial books. Greater depreciation makes the corporation's taxable income smaller. Figure 6-3 also shows taxable income as the amount of sales leftover after deducting operating costs and depreciation. The bottom horizontal layer in Fig. 6-3 shows that the tax books result in lower taxes.

Tax book depreciation is higher because the government allows firms to accelerate depreciation. Firms shift some of the depreciation from the later years of productive equipment's life up to the earlier years. This shift of depreciation expense causes a corresponding shift of taxable income from the early years to the later years. The net result is to defer taxes. Deferring taxes is attractive because the corporation can use the money until the taxes eventually come due, and the present value of tax costs is lower.

If the firm calculated taxes from the financial books, the tax deduction for depreciation would be less, and taxable income and taxes would be higher. The extra taxes that would be due are shown by the layer labeled "deferred taxes" in the bottom left of Fig. 6-3. As Fig. 6-2 shows, each year's deferred taxes accumulate in the deferred tax account in long-term liabilities, which represent a tax claim by the government that must eventually be paid. As long as the corporation continues to grow, accelerated deprecia-

Fig. 6–3
CORPORATE PROFIT/LOSS STATEMENT

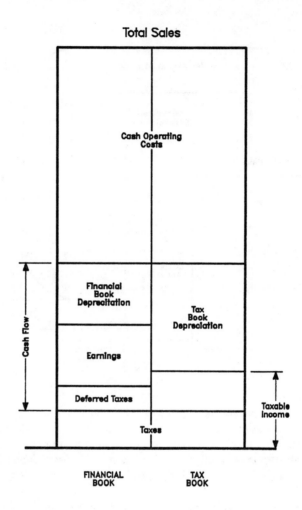

tion from investing in new plant and equipment will result in continued deferral of federal taxes. When growth slows, however, tax book depreciation will become smaller than financial book depreciation. Federal taxes will rise above those the firm would have calculated from its financial books, and the corporation will begin paying taxes they had previously deferred.

Cash Flow Diagram

The cash flow diagram in Fig. 6-4 shows how the cash flows described in the Profit and Loss Statement make the firm grow. The box in the lower left corner represents capital employed by the firm—long-term debt and stockholder's equity. The firm receives a

Fig. 6–4
CORPORATE CASH FLOW

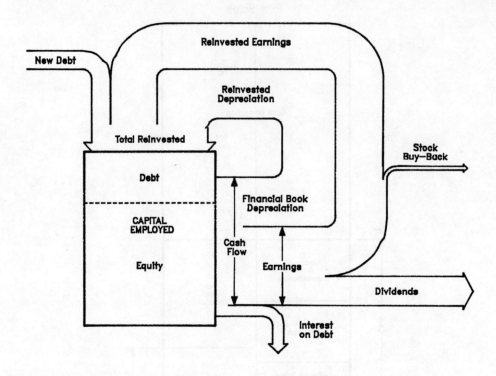

steady flow of revenue from selling its product. The amount left after paying cash operating costs is known as cash flow. Cash flow leaves the right side of the capital box.

Cash flow has two primary components. One is depreciation, a bookkeeping charge recognizing expense money spent in previous years. All depreciation is reinvested in the business. The second component is the earnings that are available to the suppliers of long-term capital.

The suppliers of long-term debt and preferred stockholders receive interest payments for the use of their money. Interest leaves the earnings stream at the bottom of the diagram. Management reinvests some of the earnings in the business. How much it reinvests depends on the investment opportunities it has and the cash required to finance those opportunities. The balance of the earnings is available to pay to stockholders as dividends. Dividends leave the earnings stream at the lower right corner of the diagram. Management might also use some of the earnings to buy back the firm's stock. A cash stream leaving the reinvested earnings stream in the middle right side of the diagram represents cash used to buy back stock.

The firm reinvests depreciation and that part of earnings not used to pay dividends, interest, or to buy back stock. It buys new plant and equipment. Reinvested earnings reenters the top of the capital box. Reinvested earnings is equity capital. Reinvested equity must be balanced by new debt to maintain the firm's target debt/equity ratio. Otherwise, the capital pool will gradually grow richer in equity capital and violate the steady-state assumption. New debt enters the capital box at the top left of the diagram.

The firm can pay out more in dividends than it earns. If it does, the flow of reinvested earnings at the top of the capital box will reverse. If dividends are greater than earnings, capital will be withdrawn to pay dividends. The firm will be liquidating itself, and will shrink in size.

Reinvested earnings and new debt adds to capital employed and makes the firm grow. The capital added by reinvesting depreciation just offsets the loss in capital when the firm first deducted that depreciation. All depreciation must be reinvested just to maintain zero growth. The investment that makes the firm grow is the capital invested above and beyond depreciation.

CORPORATE GROWTH MODEL

The review of this corporation's balance sheet focused on capital employed as the long-term core of capital the corporation employs to generate earnings. Capital employed is the sum of stockholder equity and long-term debt. The cash flow diagram in Fig. 6-4 showed how the firm divides the cash left after paying cash operating costs among earnings and depreciation, and how the firm either reinvests these cash flows to finance further growth, or pays the cash as dividends and interest to stockholders and bondholders.

The review of balance sheets, profit and loss statements, and cash flow diagrams provides only a qualitative understanding of how corporations grow. You must go beyond qualitative understanding and develop quantitative relationships to apply this understanding to evaluating stocks. Discounted cash flow analysis requires projections of the cash you will either spend or receive as a result of investing in a stock. You know the price of the stock, so all you need to do is estimate dividends and the cash you will receive when you finally sell the stock. Therefore, the model must define quantitatively how both dividends and stock prices grow with time.

Build a model of a corporation's growth by developing a simple relationship among the cash flows shown in Fig. 6-4. The goal is to develop a simple relationship for dividends and the price of the stock—the essential ingredients for evaluating a stock.

Three basic measures are important for modelling corporate growth. The first is a measure of the corporation's size. Use capital employed to measure size. The second is a measure of how efficiently the firm uses that capital to generate earnings. Use the firm's rate of return to measure efficiency. The third measure characterizes the firm's pool of capital. Characterize the pool by the fractions of debt and equity in the pool.

Earnings will depend on how large a pool of capital the firm employs and on how efficiently it uses that capital. Calculate earnings by multiplying the firm's capital employed by the rate of return the firm earns:

$$E = (R)(C)$$

E is earnings in millions of dollars, R is the firm's rate of return in decimal form, and C is capital employed, also in millions of dollars. A firm that earns a return of 12 percent on $100 million of capital employed would have earnings of (0.12)(100), or 12 million dollars.

Rate of return is a critical parameter. Analysts often base rate of return on stockholder equity instead of capital employed. The two are simply related:

$$R_C = (f_E)(R_E) \; ; \; R_E = R_C/f_E$$

Find the return on capital employed, R_C, by multiplying the return on stockholder's equity, R_E, by the fraction of equity capital in the firm's capital pool, f_E. Find the return on equity by dividing the return on capital employed by the equity fraction.

Example 6-2. A firm earns a return of 12 percent on capital employed. If the firm has 25 percent debt in its capital pool, what is the corresponding return on stockholder equity? Equity and debt make up the total capital pool. If debt is 25 percent of the pool, equity must be 75 percent, and the equity fraction is 0.75. The return on equity from the equation above is:

$$R_E = (12)/(0.75) = 16\%$$

Prudent use of debt leverages the return on equity above the return on capital employed. Calculate dividends by multiplying earnings by the firm's dividend payout fraction, where f_D is the dividend payout fraction:

$$\text{Dividends} = (f_D)(E)$$

Reinvested earnings are earnings not paid out as dividends, where $(1-f_D)$ is the reinvestment fraction:

$$\text{Reinvested Earnings} = (1-f_D)(E)$$

Suppose the firm earning \$2.40 per share has a dividend payout fraction of 0.4. Its reinvestment fraction is $(1-0.4)$, or 0.6. This firm would pay $(0.4)(\$2.40)$, or \$0.96 per share in dividends and reinvest $(0.6)(\$2.40)$, or \$1.44 per share. Find the firm's stock price by multiplying earnings per share by the price/earnings ratio:

$$P = (P/E)(E/N)$$

P is the stock price, P/E is the price/earnings ratio, N is the number of shares, and (E/N) is earnings per share. A firm with a price/earnings ratio of 10 and earnings of \$2.40 per share would have a stock price of $(10)(\$2.40)$, or \$24 per share.

How fast a firm grows depends on how fast it reinvests earnings and adds new debt to the top of the capital box shown in Fig. 6-4. The firm's growth rate is:

$$g = (1-f_D)(R_C)/(f_E)$$

The percentage growth rate in decimal form is g. This equation could be written more simply as the product of the reinvestment fraction, $(1-f_D)$, and the return on stockholder equity. Use the equation as written so you do not mask the effect of leverage. The more debt a firm carries, the lower its equity fraction is. Dividing by a lower equity fraction in the growth equation causes faster growth. The firm grows faster because it adds more new debt to balance reinvested earnings and maintain the equity fraction at the steady-state level.

The growth equation is critical for understanding how a firm grows and how that growth determines the growth of dividends and stock prices. The equation shows how growth depends on the firm's rate of return, on how much of its earnings it reinvests and how much it pays out as dividends, and on how much debt the firm carries. The rate of return is a prominent factor in the growth equation. The higher the rate of return, the more cash is available to finance growth, and the faster the firm can grow. The firm reinvests only part of its earnings. The balance is used to pay dividends. The reinvestment fraction, $(1-f_D)$, accounts for the fraction of earnings the firm reinvests. Reinvested earnings must be accompanied by new debt to maintain the firm's debt/equity ratio at the steady-state target level. Dividing by the equity fraction accounts for the new debt, and gives the total reinvestment above depreciation. This is the reinvestment that makes the firm grow. Under steady-state conditions, capital employed, earnings, dividends, and the stock price all grow at the same percentage rate given by the growth equation.

A firm does not grow just because it has the cash to pay for growth. It must also have profitable projects to invest in. Growing firms have more investment opportunities than they can finance. Mature firms often find it difficult to develop enough profitable projects to absorb all of the cash they generate. They should return the money they can't invest profitably to the shareholders, either as higher dividends, or as stock buybacks. It is usually easier to estimate a firm's growth rate than to estimate its dividend payout fraction. Rearrange the growth equation to find the dividend payout fraction the firm can pay and still finance that level of growth. The dividend payout fraction is:

$$f_D = 1 - (f_E) \, (g) \, /(R_C)$$

Table 6-4 provides a convenient form for calculating either the firm's growth rate, or the dividend payout fraction it can accommodate at any growth rate.

Example 6-3. A firm earns a 12 percent return on capital employed. It pays 40 percent of its earnings out as dividends and has an equity fraction of 0.75. How fast can it grow? Part A of Table 6-5 shows how to calculate growth. The firm will be able to finance growth of 9.6 percent per year.

Suppose this firm has an opportunity to grow faster. It can increase growth from 9.6 to 12 percent per year. How much would it have to lower its dividend payout fraction to finance the faster growth? Part B of Table 6-5 works out the new dividend payout frac-

---
TABLE 6-4
Growth and the Dividend Payout Fraction

1. Rate of Return, %   _____
2. Equity Fraction   _____

A. Growth Rate

3. Dividend Payout Fraction   _____
4. Reinvestment Fraction: Subtract Line 3 from 1.0   _____
5. Growth Rate, %/yr.: Multiply Line 1 by Line 4, then Divide by Line 2   _____

B. Dividend Payout Fraction

6. Growth Rate, %/yr.   _____
7. Multiply Line 2 by Line 6, then Divide by Line 1   _____
8. Dividend Payout Fraction: Subtract Line 7 from 1.0   _____

_____*TABLE 6-5*_____
Growth and the Dividend Payout Fraction—Example 6-3

1. Rate of Return, %	12
2. Equity Fraction	0.75
A. Growth Rate	
3. Dividend Payout Fraction	0.4
4. Reinvestment Fraction: Subtract Line 3 from 1.0	0.6
5. Growth Rate, %/yr.: Multiply Line 1 by Line 4, then Divide by Line 2	9.6
B. Dividend Payout Fraction	
6. Growth Rate, %/yr.	12
7. Multiply Line 2 by Line 6, then Divide by Line 1	0.75
8. Dividend Payout Fraction: Subtract Line 7 from 1.0	0.25

tion. To speed growth to 12 percent per year, this firm would have to lower its dividend payout fraction from 0.4 to 0.25.

Growth Model Implications

A growth model has much to say about a firm as it passes through the various stages of its life cycle. Consider a new firm at the beginning of its life cycle. It has developed a major new technology. Consumers want the product. There are no competitors. Orders are coming in faster than the firm can make the product. The strong demand and absence of competition allow the firm to charge a high price and earn a high return. The firm urgently needs money so it can add productive capacity to meet the strong demand.

How fast can such a firm grow? Their current high rate of return will help. The growth equation shows that the higher rate of return, the faster the growth. The firm will pay no dividends, so f_D will be zero, and the reinvestment fraction $(1 - f_D)$ will have the maximum value of value 1.0. The closer this fraction is to 1.0, the faster the firm will grow. The firm will also raise as much debt as it safely can. The equity fraction f_E will go down. The lower value of f_E in the growth equation's divisor makes the firm grow faster. Suppose this firm is able to earn a return of 25 percent, and raise enough debt to lower the equity fraction to 0.6. Substituting these values into the growth equation gives a growth rate of 42 percent per year:

$$g = (1-0)\ (0.25)/(0.6) = 0.42$$

Growth this fast might be more than the firm can manage effectively. Rapid growth might continue for several years, but then new competitors will enter the market. Competition will lower the price of the product, and the firm will earn a lower return. Market saturation will also slow growth. Suppose the firm's rate of return drops to 15 percent and growth slows to 20 percent per year. With less cash needed to finance the slower growth, the firm will have more cash available to pay dividends. Use the equation for the dividend payout fraction used earlier to calculate the dividends the firm will be able to pay:

$$f_D = 1 - (0.6)\,(0.2)/(0.15) = 0.20$$

The firm will now have enough cash left over after financing the slower growth to pay 20 percent of its earnings out as dividends. Prices will continue to fall as new competitors enter the market, and growth will continue to slow as the market matures. Suppose that, when the firm reaches maturity, its rate of return has dropped to 12 percent, and growth has slowed to 8 percent per year:

$$f_D = 1 - (0.6)\,(0.08)/(0.12) = 0.6$$

The firm can now pay 60 percent of its earnings out as dividends.

Eventually, new technology makes the firm's product obsolete. Growth slows further and might even disappear. The firm begins to die. Suppose in this terminal stage, growth slows to 4 percent per year and rate of return drops to 10 percent:

$$f_D = 1 - (0.6)\,(0.04)/(0.1) = 0.76$$

As opportunities for growth disappear, more cash becomes available to pay dividends. Alternatively, the firm might use this cash to reduce debt or to buy back stock.

The growth and dividend payout equations will be useful at each stage of a firm's life cycle. You can use them to project how fast capital, earnings, dividends, and stock prices are likely to grow, and the fraction of earnings the firm can pay as dividends.

Per Share Earnings, Dividends, and Stock Price

As a stockholder, you want to know how your share of capital, earnings, and dividends grows with time. To do this, divide the total capital, earnings, and dividends by the number of shares of stock outstanding. If a firm earning $12 million has five million shares of stock outstanding, earnings per share would be $12 million divided by five million shares, or $2.40 per share.

When dividing by the number of shares, you need to recognize that the number of outstanding shares changes gradually for most firms. You should be concerned about changes that dilute your claim to earnings and dividends. The number of outstanding shares could grow with time as firms issue stock to acquire other firms, or pay for employee benefit plans. Changes in the number of shares because of stock splits are irrelevant, because you have the same claim to earnings after the split as you did before. The number of outstanding shares could also decrease with time as a result of stock buyback programs. The number of shares of outstanding stock gradually grows for most firms, however. The equation for growth at a constant percentage growth rate is a reasonable way to describe this gradual growth:

$$N_T = N_o Gi_{n,T}$$

Find N_T, the number of shares outstanding at any time, by multiplying N_o, the number of current outstanding shares, by a $Gi_{n,T}$ growth factor from Appendix Table A1. Read the growth factor at the product of the share growth rate, n, and time. If the number of outstanding shares decreases with time, multiply by a Di discount factor instead. Work out the percentage growth or decay rate in the number of shares using this simple procedure:

1. Find how the number of outstanding shares has changed over the period covered by reading the firm's annual report. Divide the number of shares outstanding at the end of the period by the number of outstanding shares at the beginning. If the ratio of shares is greater than one, the result is a growth factor. If the ratio is less than one, the result is a discount factor.

2. If the ratio of shares is greater than one, look up the growth factor in Appendix Table A1 and read the corresponding RT product. If the ratio of shares is less than one, look up the discount factor in Appendix Table A3 and read the corresponding RT product.

3. Divide the RT product by the time period in years. The result is the share growth rate in percent per year. If the ratio of shares is greater than one, the share growth rate is positive. If the share ratio is less than one, the share growth rate is negative.

Calculating the growth rate this way averages the rate for the period. You might want to calculate growth over a more recent period, say, the last five years. This way, you can determine whether recent share growth differs significantly from the average for the longer period.

Example 6-4. Over a 10-year period, a firm's number of outstanding shares of stock increased gradually from 250 million to 263 million. What was the growth rate of the number of shares outstanding? The ratio of the final to the initial number of shares is 263/250, or 1.0520. Use the growth factors shown in Appendix Table A1 because the ratio is greater than 1.0. A growth factor of 1.0520 in Appendix Table A1 occurs at an RT product of 5.07. The growth rate is the RT product divided by the 10-year time period, or 5.07/10. Therefore, the shares have grown at an average rate of 0.507 percent per year.

Projecting Cash Flows

Future cash flows grow at the firm's steady-state growth rate. To project future cash flows, multiply the firm's initial capital, earnings, and dividends by the appropriate Gi growth factor, and divide by the number of outstanding shares. To project capital employed per share, multiply the initial capital per share, C_o/N_o, by a Gi growth factor:

$$\text{Capital/Share} = (C_o/N_o)\text{Gi}_{(g-n),T}$$

The net growth rate, $g - n$, is the difference between the firm's growth rate and the growth rate of the number of outstanding shares. Read the Gi growth factor at the product of this net growth rate and time. If the net growth rate is negative instead of positive, use a Di discount factor instead. The key factors that determine the value of a firm's stock all grow at the same net rate. Use the same Gi growth factor to project future values. Project earnings per share by multiplying capital per share by the firm's rate of return:

$$\text{Earnings/Share} = (R_C)\,(C_0/N_0)Gi_{(g-n),T}$$

Project dividends by multiplying earnings per share by the dividend payout fraction:

$$\text{Dividends/Share} = f_D\,(R_C)\,(C_0/N_0)\,Gi_{(g-n),T}$$

Project the price of the stock by multiplying earnings per share by the price/earnings ratio:

$$\text{Stock Price} = (P/E)\,(R_C)\,(C_0/N_0)\,Gi_{(g-n),T}$$

Rate of Return for Investing in Stock

All of the information you need to evaluate a mature stock under steady-state conditions is now available. You know the current price of the stock. The previous equations provided you with the dividends and the price of the stock at any future time. The discounted cash flow solution for the rate of return is a simple one. Your rate of return is the growth rate of the firm, plus the dividend yield, less the growth rate of the number of shares outstanding:

$$\text{Rate of Return} = g + D/P - n$$

The D/P term in this equation is the dividend yield—the dividend divided by the stock price. Therefore, the rate of return for investing in stock under steady-state conditions is dictated by the simple rule: The rate of return for investing in the stock of a mature firm under steady-state conditions is the firm's growth rate, plus the dividend yield, less the share growth rate.

Professional analysts call this equation the Dividend Growth Model, and use it with the dividend growth rate and the dividend yield. The Dividend Growth Model can sometimes be confusing, however. How do you measure the dividend growth rate and the dividend yield for a stock that pays no dividends? The growth rate does not apply just to dividends, as the previous equations make clear. Capital employed, earnings, dividends, and the price of the stock all grow at the same rate. The rate of return for a stock that pays no dividends is the growth rate of the firm less the growth rate of the number of outstanding shares.

Example 6-5. In Example 6-1 you evaluated a firm that grew 8 percent per year, paid dividends of $2.50 per share, and sold for $50 per share. The number of outstanding shares remained constant. You found that the rate of return for investing in that stock was 13 percent. Recalculate the rate of return using the Dividend Growth Model. To do this, substitute the appropriate values in the model:

$$\text{Rate of Return} = 0.08 + 2.50/50 - 0 = 0.13$$

The 13 percent rate of return agrees with the trial-and-error solution of Example 6-1.

The Dividend Growth Model shows that investors earn high returns from firms that grow rapidly and pay high dividends. Firms do not grow rapidly and pay high dividends at the same time. If a firm grows rapidly, most of the firm's earnings must be reinvested to finance this growth, and dividends will be small. If the firm pays high dividends, reinvested earnings will be small, and growth will be slow.

An alternative form of the Dividend Growth Model is more intuitively appealing:

$$\text{Rate of Return} = (1-f_D)\,(R_E) + f_D(E/P) - n$$

This equation shows that the investor's return is a weighted average of the firm's return on equity capital, R_E, and the earnings/price ratio, E/P, less the share growth rate. The weighting factors are $(1-f_D)$ on the return on equity, and f_D on the earnings/price ratio. Note that the two weighting factors add up to 1.0. The earnings/price ratio is the earnings yield; it is the reciprocal of the price/earnings ratio.

This equation appears different from the Dividend Growth Model because it emphasizes the firm's return on equity capital instead of its growth rate. In fact, both equations are exactly equivalent. They both give the same return to the investor. The equivalence can be shown for the firm in Example 6-5. That firm is growing 8 percent per year, has a dividend payout fraction of 0.5, and sells at a price/earnings ratio of 10. According to the growth equation, it must earn a 16 percent return on equity capital. The reciprocal of the 10 price/earnings ratio is 0.1. Your return is 13 percent, the same as the return given by the Dividend Growth Model:

$$\text{Rate of Return} = (1-0.5)\,(0.16) + (0.5)\,(0.1) - 0 = 0.13$$

If a firm pays no dividends, the weighting factor $(1-f_D)$ is 1.0 and the weighting factor f_D is zero. Your rate of return is then the same as the firm's return on equity, less the share growth rate. At the other extreme, the firm pays all of its earnings out as dividends. The weighting factor $(1-f_D)$ is zero, and the weighting factor f_D is 1.0. Your return is then the earnings yield (the earnings/price ratio), less the share growth rate.

Mathematically, your return is highest when both terms of the alternative model are high. You will not find both terms high at the same time, however. If the firm earns a high return, its price/earnings ratio will also be high. The first term of the alternative model will be high, but the second term will be low. If you find a stock selling for a low price/earnings ratio, the second term of the model will be high. The firm is likely to earn a low return, however, and the first term will be low.

The Critical Factors that Determine a Stock's Value

Still another form of the Dividend Growth Model is worth study because it shows clearly which factors are most important in determining a stock's value:

$$\text{Rate of Return} = [1 - (1 - Eq/P)\,(f_D)]\,(R_E) - n$$

The ratio Eq/P is stockholder equity per share divided by the stock price. This equation identifies the firm's return on equity as the most critical factor. Your return is a multiple of the firm's return on equity. The multiplier is the group of factors enclosed in brackets. The average stock has an equity/price ratio of about 0.68 and a dividend payout fraction of about 0.4. The multiplier for this average firm is $[1-(1-0.68)\,(0.4)]$, or 0.87.

Your return from investing in the typical stock is, therefore, about 87 percent of the firm's return on equity.

The most important way to raise your return is to choose a firm that earns a high return on equity. The next most important way is to increase the multiplier. The multiplier is 1.0 reduced by the group $(1 - Eq/P)f_D$. If you can make this group smaller, the multiplier will increase and come closer to 1.0. The easiest way to decrease this group is to reduce the dividend payout fraction. The dividend payout fraction is the second most critical factor. Choose a stock that pays little or no dividends. The dividend payout fraction is then zero, which makes the multiplier 1.0. Your return then rises to the firm's return on equity.

Lowering the dividend payout fraction is attractive if the firm has profitable investment opportunities. A lower dividend payout gives the firm more cash to reinvest in the business. Reinvesting earnings raises your return because the firm can earn a higher return reinvesting earnings than you can by withdrawing dividends, paying taxes on them, and then reinvesting the balance. If the firm earns a lower return, you shouldn't hold its stock.

A firm that pays all of its earnings out as dividends has a dividend payout fraction of 1.0. The multiplier then drops to the equity/price ratio. The product of this multiplier and the return on equity is E/P, the earnings/price ratio. The results at the extreme dividend payout fractions of zero and one are identical to the results shown in the previous models.

The final way to increase the multiplier is to choose stocks that sell at a high ratio of stockholder equity to price. The equity/price ratio is the final critical factor. A high equity/price ratio reduces the group $(1 - Eq/P)f_D$, and increases the multiplier. The group containing the equity/price ratio is multiplied by the dividend payout fraction. High equity/price ratios are therefore most effective when the dividend payout fraction is high. The effect of the equity/price ratio drops as the dividend payout fraction falls. At a dividend payout fraction of zero, the equity/price ratio does not affect your return.

Choosing a Stock

The alternative forms of the Dividend Growth Model show you how to choose stocks under steady-state conditions:

1. The most critical factor is the return the firm earns on its equity capital. The firm must be profitable. Choose a firm that earns a high rate of return.

2. The firm should carry a reasonable amount of debt. Debt leverages the firm's rate of return and makes the return on equity higher than the return on capital employed.

3. The firm should reinvest most of its earnings and pay only small or no dividends. In the extreme, the firm pays no dividends. Your return is the same as the firm's return on equity and independent of the price/earnings ratio. If the firm pays all of its earnings out as dividends, your return is equal to the earnings/price ratio. Your return will be lower because the earnings/price ratio is normally smaller than the firm's return on equity.

4. The firm's stock should sell at a high equity/price ratio, particularly if the firm pays a substantial fraction of earnings out as dividends. The equity/price ratio is less important if the firm pays only small dividends.

Your return does not depend on the price/earnings ratio for a firm that pays no dividends. This is a surprising result. Remember, at steady-state conditions, you will enjoy the same high price/earnings ratio when you sell a stock as you paid when you bought the stock.

The model suggests that growth stocks offer the highest return. Growth firms often earn high returns on equity. They pay no dividends. They reinvest all of their earnings to finance growth. For such firms, the model says your return is equal to the growth firm's return on equity. Unfortunately, this result is not reliable. The problem is that the steady-state model does not apply to growth stocks. A growth firm's rate of return, growth rate, and price/earnings ratio, are all likely to be lower when you sell the stock than they were when you bought the stock. Don't use the steady-state model for growth stocks; use the model developed in Chapter 7 instead.

WHY A STOCK HAS VALUE

The basic reason a stock has value is that stocks pay dividends. The stock price is the present value of this future stream of dividends, paid from the time you buy the stock until the firm eventually goes out of business. Future dividends are discounted at the investor's opportunity cost. Growth firms usually do not pay dividends because they need to reinvest all they earn to finance their rapid growth. If these firms never paid dividends, their stocks would be worthless. Growth stocks are valuable because growth eventually slows, and the cash these firms need to finance growth drops. More cash becomes available to pay dividends. By that time, a long period of rapid growth will have made the firm large. A large capital base will then be generating earnings. As a result, earnings and dividends will be high.

The market prices the stock at the present value of those future dividends. You might invest in a growth stock, hold it five years, receive no dividends, then sell the stock for a higher price than you paid for it. The price will be higher because the eventual dividends will be five years closer, and, therefore, discounted less heavily.

The time you hold a stock does not affect your rate of return in the steady-state model. The value of the stock at any time is equal to the present value of all future dividends flowing from that time out to infinity. When you eventually sell the stock, the selling price will be the present value of all the future dividends paid after you sell. The total present value—the present value of the dividends up to the time you sell, plus the present value of the dividends after you sell—will be the same, regardless of when, if ever, you sell the stock. Consequently, the time you hold the stock does not affect your rate of return. The investment period does not appear in the Dividend Growth Model or in the alternative form of that model.

Calculation Form for Stocks of Mature Firms

You can calculate your rate of return from investing in the stock of a mature firm by any of the three previous equations. You can also use the calculation form in Table 6-6. The

---
TABLE 6-6
Calculation Form—Stocks of Mature Firms

A. Characteristics of the Firm

1. Return on Capital Employed, % _____
2. Growth Rate, %/yr. _____
3. Share Growth Rate, %/yr. _____
4. Capital Employed, $millions _____
5. Shares Outstanding, millions _____
6. Equity Fraction _____
7. Stock Price, $/share _____
8. Return on Equity, %: Divide Line 1 by Line 6 _____
9. Dividend Payout Fraction: Divide Line 2 by Line 8. Subtract the result from 1.0 _____
10. Earnings, $/share: Multiply Line 1 by Line 4. Then Divide by Line 5 and by 100 _____
11. Dividends, $/share: Multiply Line 10 by Line 9 _____
12. Dividend Yield, %: Multiply Line 11 by 100. Then Divide by Line 7 _____
13. Rate of Return, %: Add Lines 2 and 12, then Subtract Line 3 _____

B. Maximum Allowable Price

14. Opportunity Cost, % _____
15. Investment Period, years _____
16. RT: Add Lines 3 and 14, then Subtract Line 2. Multiply the result by Line 15 _____
17. Di Discount Factor at RT = Line 16. If Line 2 is greater than the sum of Lines 3 and 14, use a Gi Growth Factor instead _____
18. Dc Discount Factor at RT = Line 16. If Line 2 is greater than the sum of Lines 3 and 14, use a Gc Growth Factor instead _____
19. Present Value of Stock Sale: Multiply Line 7 by Line 17 _____
20. Present Value of Dividends: Multiply Line 11 by Lines 15 and 18 _____
21. Maximum Allowable Price: Add Lines 19 and 20 _____

---

calculation form is better because it forces your projection of dividends to be consistent with your projections of the firm's rate of return and growth rate. The calculation form also shows you how to find the maximum price you should pay for the stock.

Enter the basic information about the firm and the stock in the first seven lines of Table 6-6. The key projections are the rate of return you expect the firm to earn and how fast you expect the firm to grow. Calculate the dividend yield consistent with this rate of return and the growth rate in line 12. Your rate of return in line 13 follows the Dividend Growth Model. Your return is the sum of the growth rate in line 2 and the dividend yield in line 12, less the share growth rate in line 3.

Calculate your maximum allowable price by entering your opportunity cost in line 14, and the time you expect to hold the stock in line 15. The RT product in line 16 is based on the sum of the opportunity cost and the share growth rate less the firm's growth rate. If the sum of your opportunity cost and the share growth rate is greater than the firm's growth rate, use the Di and Dc discount factors in lines 17 and 18. If the firm's growth rate is greater, use the Gi and Gc growth factors instead. Discount the final sale of the stock in line 19, then discount dividends in line 20. Add the present values of the final stock sale and dividends in line 21 to find the maximum price you should pay.

Example 6-6. You are interested in a mature firm that has $800 million in capital employed and 80 million shares of stock outstanding. The capital pool is 65 percent equity. You project the firm to earn a return of 12 percent on capital employed and to grow 8 percent per year. You expect the number of shares outstanding to grow slowly at 0.5 percent per year. The stock sells for $12 per share. What rate of return will you earn? If your opportunity cost is 12 percent and you expect to hold the stock five years, what is the most you should pay for it? Table 6-7 shows how to evaluate this stock.

Enter the basic information about the stock in lines 1 through 7. Calculate a dividend payout fraction of 0.567 in line 9. This payout fraction is consistent with your estimate of the firm's rate of return and growth rate. Use the payout fraction to calculate a dividend yield of 5.67 percent in line 12. The Dividend Growth Model gives your return as 13.17 percent in line 13. Your return is the sum of the firm's 8 percent per year growth rate and the 5.67 percent dividend yield, less the 0.5 percent per year share growth rate.

Use your 12 percent opportunity cost as the discount rate in line 14 to calculate the maximum allowable price. The net discount rate is the 12 percent opportunity cost plus the 0.5 percent share growth rate, less the 8 percent growth rate, or 4.5 percent. The most you should pay for this stock is the $9.58 present value of the future stock sale in line 19 plus the $3.04 present value of future dividends in line 20. Line 21 shows a maximum allowable price of $12.62.

Limitations of the Steady-State Model

The steady-state model does not apply to growth firms, whose growth and rate of return fall with time. In addition, the steady-state model also has limitations even when applied to mature firms. Ideally, growth rate, rate of return, the dividend payout fraction, and financial structure stay constant with time. The limitation is that dividends and stock prices cannot continue growing at a steady rate for an infinite time.

No company can grow at steady-state conditions forever. After a period of maturity, during which the steady-state model applies, companies become senile. Their product becomes obsolete. Growth slows, then turns negative. The firm cuts dividends and eventually omits them. The price/earnings ratio, which reflects the present value of future dividends, drops. The steady-state model no longer applies. Don't assume any company will continue paying dividends at a steady rate for an infinite time. You will calculate too high a rate of return and too high a maximum allowable price.

If you assumed the stock in Example 6-6 were held an infinite time and never sold, your maximum allowable price would be the present value of an infinite stream of future dividends. Current dividends are $0.68 per share. At a net discount rate of 4.5 percent, an infinite stream of dividends has a present value of ($0.68)/(0.045), or $15.11 per share. This maximum is 20 percent higher than the maximum price you calculated for a five-year investment period.

TABLE 6-7
Stocks of Mature Firms—Example 6-6

A. Characteristics of the Firm

1. Return on Capital Employed, %	12
2. Growth Rate, %/yr.	8
3. Share Growth Rate, %/yr.	0.5
4. Capital Employed, $millions	800
5. Shares Outstanding, millions	80
6. Equity Fraction	0.65
7. Stock Price, $/share	12
8. Return on Equity, %: Divide Line 1 by Line 6	18.46
9. Dividend Payout Fraction: Divide Line 2 by Line 8. Subtract the result from 1.0	0.567
10. Earnings, $/share: Multiply Line 1 by Line 4. Then Divide by Line 5 and by 100	1.20
11. Dividends, $/share: Multiply Line 10 by Line 9	0.68
12. Dividend Yield, %: Multiply Line 11 by 100. Then Divide by Line 7	5.67
13. Rate of Return, %: Add Lines 2 and 12, then Subtract Line 3	13.17

B. Maximum Allowable Price

14. Opportunity Cost, %	12
15. Investment Period, years	5
16. RT: Add Lines 3 and 14, then subtract Line 2. Multiply the result by Line 15	22.5
17. Di Discount Factor at RT = Line 16. If Line 2 is greater than the sum of Lines 3 and 14, use a Gi Growth Factor instead	0.7985
18. Dc Discount Factor at RT = Line 16. If Line 2 is greater than the sum of Lines 3 and 14, use a Gc Growth Factor instead.	0.8955
19. Present Value of Stock Sale: Multiply Line 7 by Line 17	9.58
20. Present Value of Dividends: Multiply Line 11 by Lines 15 and 18	3.04
21. Maximum Allowable Price: Add Lines 19 and 20	$12.62

Use the steady-state model for finite time periods only. Find your return and the maximum price you should pay based on buying the stock, collecting dividends for a finite time, and then selling the stock.

"CREATIVE" ACCOUNTING

Using the analysis developed in this chapter will, to a great extent, help you avoid any deceptions in a firm's annual report developed by "creative" accounting. The analytical methods in this chapter center on dividends and stock prices—factors that creative accounting cannot easily fix. The dividend check comes in the mail each quarter, and you have the money in your hands. If the firm overstates earnings, the dividend payout fraction will decrease just enough to compensate for the inflated earnings. In the same way, the market sets the price of the stock. If the firm overstates earnings, the price/earnings ratio will drop to compensate.

SHORT-TERM INVESTMENTS

The methods of evaluating stocks in this chapter work best with long-term investments, because they fit the steady-state assumption better. Earnings, dividends, and stock prices cluster around long-term trend lines. Deviations above and below the trend lines tend to balance each other. This method does not work as well for short-term investments, however. There is not enough time for deviations on one side of the trend line to balance deviations on the other side. Short-term investors hope for price appreciation. Time is too short to expect much contribution from dividends. Time is also too short to expect much price appreciation from the normal growth of the firm. Short-term investors count on extraordinary price increases beyond those the normal growth of the firm produces.

MAKING REALISTIC EVALUATIONS

The model in this chapter is a simple one. Simple models are a good place to start, because they make it easy to follow the development step-by-step. They also make it easier to understand discounted cash flow analysis of stocks. Simplification has a price, however. You cannot yet apply the evaluation method to real stocks because the model does not yet account for inflation and taxes.

You will learn how to account for inflation in Chapter 8 and taxes in Chapter 9. Chapter 11 contains calculation forms you can use for actual stocks. In Chapter 12, you'll learn how market interest rates, a firm's rate of return, growth, and dividends, investment periods, and commissions affect your rate of return and the maximum price you should pay for a typical stock.

The model developed in this chapter is for mature firms at steady-state conditions. The next chapter adapts a model to growth stocks, where the steady-state assumption is not appropriate. Do not begin analyzing real stocks until you read Chapter 11.

SUMMARY

☐ You need to discount three cash flows when you evaluate a stock: The cash you pay when you buy the stock, the stream of dividends you receive as long as you hold the stock, and the cash you recover when you finally sell the stock. Evaluating a stock is the same as evaluating a fixed-interest security, such as a bond, except that you must allow for stock prices and dividends to grow with time.

☐ The steady-state model tells how dividends and stock prices grow with time. The firm's growth rate and all of the factors that affect growth stay constant over time. The steady-state model leads to simple solutions for your rate of return and the maximum price you should pay.

☐ The financial core of a corporation is the long-term capital it employs—equity capital supplied by stockholders and debt capital supplied by bondholders. The model shows how this capital generates cash and how that cash finances the growth of the business and pays dividends and interest to stockholders and bondholders. The model also shows how the stock price grows as a result of the growth in earnings.

☐ At steady-state conditions, the capital a firm employs, its earnings, dividends, and the price of its stock, all grow at a constant percentage rate: $g = (1 - f_D) (R_C)/f_E$. It is often more useful to rearrange this equation to find the dividend payout fraction the firm can accommodate at any growth rate: $f_D = 1 - (f_E g/R_C)$. This equation shows how dividends increase as growth firms mature.

☐ Capital, earnings, and dividends per share and the price of the stock all grow at the difference between the firm's growth rate and the growth rate in shares outstanding. The future value is the current value multiplied by a Gi growth factor. Read the growth factor at the difference between the firm's growth rate and the share growth rate. The steady-state assumption leads to a simple solution for your rate of return: Rate of Return = $g + D/P - n$. Professional analysts call this equation the Dividend Growth Model. An alternative form of this model is more intuitively appealing: Rate of Return = $(1 - f_D) (R_E) + (f_D) (E/P) - n$. Still another form of this model clearly shows the critical factors that determine a stock's value: Rate of Return = $[1 - (1 - Eq/P)f_D] (R_E) - n$.

☐ A firm's return on equity is the most critical factor. A low dividend payout fraction is the second critical factor. If a firm reinvests all of its earnings and pays no dividends, your rate of return is the same as the firm's return on equity. If the firm pays all of its earnings out as dividends, your return is only the earnings yield, E/P. A high equity/price ratio is the final critical factor. High equity/price ratios are most important when the dividend payout fraction is also high. The equity/price ratio loses importance as the dividend payout fraction approaches zero. All three models give the same rates of return. These models suggest primary guidelines for choosing stocks:

1. A firm must be profitable. Choose a firm that earns a high rate of return.

2. A firm should carry a reasonable amount of debt. Debt leverages the return on equity above the return on capital employed.

3. A firm should reinvest most, if not all, of its earnings, and pay little or no dividends.

4. The stock should sell at a high ratio of stockholder equity to stock price.

☐ The maximum price you should pay for a stock is the present value of future dividends, plus the present value of the cash you receive when you finally sell the stock. Discount these cash receipts at your opportunity cost. The calculation form in Table 6-6 simplifies the calculation.

☐ The procedure for evaluating stocks in this chapter avoids deceptions from "creative" accounting. It depends on dividends and stock prices, both of which creative accounting cannot fix. If a firm overstates earnings, there will be compensating changes in the dividend payout fraction and the price/earnings ratio.

☐ The evaluation procedure developed in this chapter has been simplified by omitting inflation and taxes. A realistic evaluation must account for these factors, however.

Inflation is covered in Chapter 8 and taxes in Chapter 9. Chapter 11 contains calculation forms for realistic evaluations of stocks.

☐ The steady-state model is reasonable for mature firms, whose growth rates and financial parameters come reasonably close to the steady-state assumption. The steady-state model is not reasonable for growth firms, because rapid growth cannot continue forever. The next chapter will show you how to evaluate growth stocks.

7

Don't Pay Too Much
for Growth Stocks

THE PROCEDURE FOR EVALUATING STOCKS DEVELOPED IN THE LAST CHAPTER IS LIMITED to mature companies, where the steady-state assumption can reasonably be expected to apply. The factors that determine a stock's value—the firm's rate of return, how fast its capital, earnings, and dividends grow, it's capital structure, and the price/earnings ratio of its stock—all stay constant with time. The steady-state model is a good place to begin the analysis. It is simple, straightforward, and easy to understand. The model also provides a basic understanding of the factors that determine a stock's value, how the factors rank in importance, and how those factors operate. The analysis of stocks where the steady-state model does not apply builds on the steady-state model in Chapter 6 as a foundation. Therefore, if you didn't read Chapter 6, I recommend you do so before beginning this chapter.

The steady-state model is not always appropriate, even for mature firms. Investors could change their outlook on the future of the firm and bid the price/earnings ratio up or down as a result. Even if investors do not change their outlook for the firm, changes in market interest rates could change investor's opportunity costs. A change in opportunity costs changes the price/earnings ratio investors are willing to pay. In both cases, the price/earnings changes violate the steady-state assumption. The ratio is different when you sell the stock than it was when you bought it.

The steady-state model is not a good model for growth stocks. Growth firms might be growing rapidly and earning high returns. Rapid growth and high returns, however, cannot continue unchanged forever. Growth slows as a growth company matures, and the rate of return and the price/earnings ratio fall. This chapter adapts the analysis of the factors that determine a stock's value as the company gradually matures.

The steady-state model also does not apply to firms with temporarily depressed growth and earnings. If these firms recover, rate of return and growth will improve until they reach normal levels. Therefore, a model for unsteady-state conditions has to fit both growth firms, whose performance falls off with time, and temporarily depressed firms, whose performance gradually improves with time.

The basic analysis for the unsteady-state case is the same as the steady-state case. Gradually changing conditions, however, complicate the analysis. There are no simple equations for the rate of return and the maximum allowable price. You will have to solve for rate of return by trial and error.

CHANGES IN PRICE/EARNINGS RATIO

The simplest change from steady-state conditions is when the price/earnings ratio changes over the investment period. The firm might still follow the steady-state model. Growth, rate of return, dividend payout, and the capital structure, might stay constant throughout the investment period. Investors might even keep the same outlook for future dividends and growth, but market interest rates might change. When interest rates change, investors change the discount rate they use to value stocks. The result is a change in the price/earnings ratio and a departure from steady-state conditions.

The changing price/earnings case is evaluated the same way you evaluated the steady-state examples in Chapter 6 but with one difference. You must multiply the expected future earnings by an estimate of the future price/earnings ratio to determine the future price of the stock. Future price/earnings ratios depend strongly on future interest rates, which are difficult to predict. Evaluate the stock over a range of likely future price/earnings ratios. Then you can test how sensitive the rate of return and maximum allowable price are to future price/earnings ratios.

Suppose an investor buys a typical stock at an initial price/earnings ratio of 11. Figure 7-1 shows how changes in the price/earnings ratio affect his rate of return. The rate of return is sensitive to the final price/earnings ratio, particularly if the stock is held only a short time. The rate of return becomes less sensitive to the eventual price/earnings ratio the longer the stock is held.

In a short investment period, there is not enough time for dividend payments to amount to much, nor for the firm's normal growth in earnings to cause a large increase in the price of the stock. Changes in the price at which the stock is eventually sold caused by changes in the price/earnings ratio tend to be large compared to the other cash flows. If the stock is held for a longer period, the total of dividend payments and the appreciation in the stock price due to the firm's normal growth are larger. Changes in the final stock price caused by changes in the price/earnings ratio are then relatively less important.

Extreme changes in the price/earnings ratio are unpredictable. They do not come about because of the normal operation of the firm. They result from unexpected changes in factors such as market interest rates, acquisition by another firm, government regulation banning or restricting the firm's major product, technological breakthroughs, plant disasters, disasters to competitors, loss of key personnel, and the like. Unpredictable changes are part of the risk of investing in stocks.

Anyone who buys stocks in the hope of a quick "killing" are gambling, not investing. They are counting on unpredictable factors to make the stock price rise quickly. Investors are also happy to take advantage of unexpected gains in the price of the stock, but they base their expectations primarily on the more predictable growth of the firm, and the consequent rise in the price of the stock that growth causes.

EVALUATING GROWTH STOCKS

Growth stocks are often stocks of companies on the leading edge of technology. They are growing rapidly and earning high rates of return. They excite investor interest. A period of rapid growth stretches before them and they might possibly become the leaders of a new industry. These stocks are glamour stocks. The problem with growth

Fig. 7-1
Effect of Final Price/Earnings Ratio
S&P Average Stock

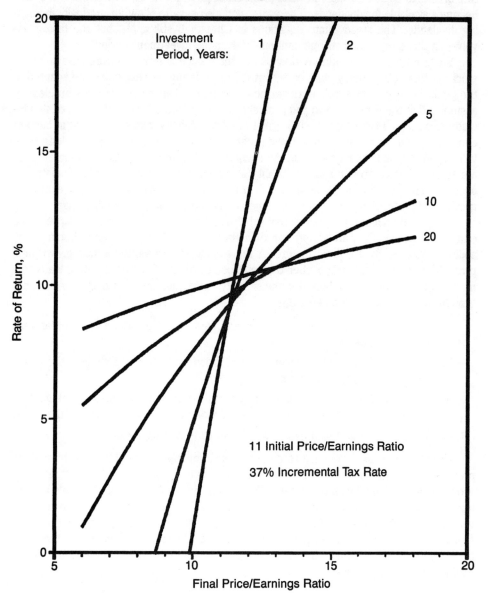

stocks is that investors have already recognized their high growth potential and bid the price of these stocks up to very high levels. High price/earnings ratios are to be expected, however. Investors are paying for future earnings, not current earnings. Price/ earnings ratios might be 50 or more. The price charged for this high growth could be so high, however, that you will not earn a reasonable return investing in it.

The basic analysis of growth stocks is similar to the analysis of mature stocks that fit the steady-state assumption except that you must allow for a gradual decline in the firm's rate of return, capital growth rate, and price/earnings ratio. As growth slows, more cash becomes available for dividends. Therefore, you also have to allow for gradually increasing dividends. The steady-state equations in Chapter 6 still apply, but the factors involved in those equations change continually over the investment period.

You have to discount future dividends and the proceeds from the eventual sale of the stock, just as in the steady-state case, but the discounting process has to be adapted to the gradual decay in the firm's performance. Professional analysts solve this problem by assuming that the firm's growth and profitability will go through several stages of steady-state growth. In a two-stage model, growth and profitability remain constant at current conditions in the first stage. Growth and profitability then suddenly collapse to long-term values and remain at those values in the second stage. Some analysts add an intermediate stage, in which growth and profitability stay constant for a time at intermediate values. The steady-state model is assumed to hold in each stage. The analyst estimates growth and profitability levels in each stage and how long each stage might last.

Analysts do not actually believe that growth and profitability suddenly collapse at the end of each stage. They are simply approximating in a crude way how growth and profitability decline as growth firms mature. A more realistic assumption is that growth and profitability decay continually rather than collapse suddenly. That assumption leads to a model with an infinite number of immeasurably short, steady-state stages. Analyze a growth stock by following these steps:

1. Project how fast the firm's rate of return, capital growth rate, and price/earnings ratio will decline as the firm matures.

2. Use the projection of the firm's capital growth rate to calculate how the firm's capital base will grow with time.

3. Use the estimates of capital employed, rate of return, and price/earnings ratio from the previous two steps to calculate dividends and the final price of the stock.

4. Find your rate of return by the usual trial-and-error solution.

Calculation forms make each step in the evaluation easy to do. The first three steps provide you with all of the information you need for a discounted cash flow analysis of growth stocks. The initial investment is the current price of the stock. A simple averaging procedure gives the present value of dividends. The averaging procedure requires values of dividends at times 11.3, 50, and 88.7 percent of the investment period. The first two steps provide the necessary values. The final cash flow depends on the stock price when you sell. Estimate the final stock price by multiplying the final earnings by the final price/earnings ratio.

Growth Stock Example

Suppose you are considering a growth stock. You are attracted by the firm's high growth of 30 percent per year. You are also attracted by the firm's high profitability. It is currently earning a 23 percent return. The firm has $5 of capital employed per share, and, at the current 23 percent return, earnings are $1.15 per share. The firm pays $0.18 per share in dividends. The stock sells for $46 per share. The price/earnings ratio is 40.

Investors are obviously valuing the stock at what they consider a fair multiple of future earnings, not today's earnings. You think this stock might be a good investment, and plan to hold it for 10 years.

Suppose your opportunity cost is 10 percent. How do you go about deciding whether this stock is attractive? How do you decide whether $46 is a fair price for this growing stream of future earnings and dividends, and a steadily increasing stock price?

Projecting Performance as a Growth Stock Matures

The first step to evaluating a growth stock is to project how fast you expect the firm's performance to fall as the firm matures. How fast will the firm's rate of return fall? How fast will growth slow? How fast will the price/earnings ratio fall? A simple model describes gradual decay. The model is based on any factor beginning at some starting value and gradually approaching (but never reaching) some long-run limiting value. The long-run value is the value that will exist many years from now when the firm has matured and is no longer a growth firm. Average values for a large group of stocks, such as the Standard and Poor's 500 stock average, are reasonable choices for long-run limits. You can adjust the rate at which each factor approaches its long-run limit to match your estimate of how fast that factor will fall as the firm matures. The model is:

$$V_T = V_\infty + (V_0 - V_\infty)\, Di_{k,T}$$

The value of the factor at any time, V_T is the long-run value V_∞ plus some fraction of the initial margin between the starting and long-run values, $(V_0 - V_\infty)$. That fraction is a Di discount factor. At zero time, the discount factor is 1.0, and the full initial margin is present. As time goes on, the Di discount factor gradually approaches zero. The falling discount factor makes the $(V_0 - V_\infty)$ part of the equation gradually approach zero, and the factor gradually approaches its long-run limiting value.

The decay rate, k, measures how fast the factor decays from its starting value towards the long-run limiting value. Choose a decay rate you think appropriate, then read the $Di_{k,T}$ discount factor from Appendix Table A3 at the product of the decay rate and time. You might find it easier to think in terms of a half-life rather than a decay rate. The half-life is the time required for a factor to move half-way from any starting value towards that factor's long-run limit. Estimate the half-life (in years), then find the decay rate from:

$$k = 69.3/(\text{Half-Life})$$

If you expect a firm's growth rate to approach long-run growth with a ten-year half-life, for example, the decay rate would be 69.3/10, or 6.93 percent per year.

Figure 7-2 shows how decay proceeds from a starting value towards a long-run limit over a range of half-lives. The starting value is taken as 100; the long-run limit as zero. With a long half-life, decay proceeds slowly. At shorter half-lives, decay is faster. The steady-state model corresponds to an infinite half life—the factor remains at the starting level forever. Figure 7-2 is a helpful guide in choosing a half-life that matches how rapidly you expect any factor in the unsteady-state model to decay from its current value towards an appropriate long-run limit.

Figure 7-2 was drawn using a factor that decays from some starting level towards

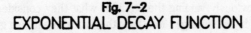

Fig. 7–2
EXPONENTIAL DECAY FUNCTION

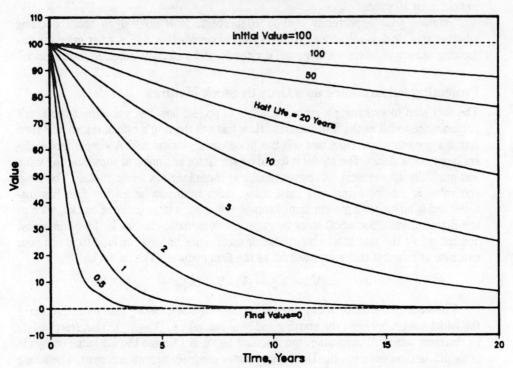

some lower, long-run limit. The model can also be used to describe the opposite case—a factor that grows from some starting level towards some higher, long-run limit. The corresponding chart would look like an inverted Fig. 7-2. The curves would all start from the bottom left corner and rise gradually towards the top right corner. You can use the inverted plot to describe how a factor, such as rate of return, recovers for a firm with temporarily depressed earnings.

Forecasting Rate of Return, Capital Employed, and P/E Ratio

Use this model to make the forecasts you need to evaluate this growth stock. You need to forecast how fast the firm's rate of return, capital growth rate, and price/earnings ratio will decay as the firm matures. The rate of return forecast is the most critical. The forecast of the capital growth rate is less critical. If the firm grows more slowly than you had forecast, the size of the firm, its earnings, and the price of its stock when you eventually sell will be lower than you had forecast. The slower growth, however, will have made more cash available for dividends, and you will receive more dividends than you had forecast. The gains from higher dividends tend to offset the shortfall from slower growth. If the firm grows faster than you had forecast, you will receive smaller dividends, but the stock price will be higher than you had forecast when you sell. The higher stock price offsets the lower dividends. The forecast of price/earnings ratio is critical if you plan to hold the stock only a short time, but becomes less critical the longer you plan to hold the stock.

The size of the firm, as measured by capital employed, is difficult to forecast directly. It is easier to forecast how fast you expect the capital growth rate to slow as the firm matures. The forecast of the capital growth rate determines how large capital employed will be at any time. You will be able to use the forecast of capital growth rate to calculate capital employed at any time.

Use the calculation form in Table 7-1 to project the firm's rate of return, capital growth rate, and the price/earnings ratio. These factors tend to follow the decay curves of Fig. 7-2. Enter the starting value and the long-run limit in lines 1 and 2 of the calculation form. Enter the difference between these two values in line 3. The difference is the component that will gradually decay as the factor you are projecting gradually approaches its long-run limit. Examine the decay curves in Fig. 7-2, and choose a half-life that best represents your judgment about how fast that factor will decay. Enter the half-life in line 4, and calculate the corresponding decay rate in line 5. Enter the time in line 6.

The bottom half of the calculation form contains four columns, one for each of the three intermediate times needed for calculating dividends, and a final column for the value at the end of the investment period. Line 7 contains the appropriate fraction of the investment period for each column. Calculate the RT products in line 9, read the corresponding Di discount factors from Appendix Table A3, and enter them in line 10. The amount of the initial margin ($V_o - V_\infty$) that remains at each time is the initial margin in line 3 multiplied by the discount factors in line 10. Line 11 shows these remaining values. Find the final value of the factor you are projecting by adding the long-run limit in line 12.

You will need forecasts for the firm's rate of return, capital growth rate, and price/

TABLE 7-1
Calculation Form
Projecting Rate of Return, Capital Growth Rate, and Price/Earnings Ratio

1. Starting Value				_____
2. Long-Run Limit				_____
3. Subtract Line 2 from Line 1				_____
4. Half-Life, years				_____
5. Decay Rate: Divide 69.3 by Line 4				_____
6. Investment Period, years				_____
7. Time Factors	0.113	0.5	0.887	1.0
8. Time: Multiply value in Line 7 by Line 6	_____	_____	_____	_____
9. Multiply each time in Line 8 by Line 5	_____	_____	_____	_____
10. Di Discount Factors from Appendix Table A-3 at the RT Products in Line 9	_____	_____	_____	_____
11. Multiply each value in Line 10 by Line 3	_____	_____	_____	_____
12. Factor Values: Add Lines 11 and 2	_____	_____	_____	_____

earnings ratio at the end of the investment period to estimate the final stock price. You will also need forecasts of the rate of return and the capital growth rate at three intermediate times to discount dividends.

Rate of Return

Use the calculation form to project how fast rate of return is likely to fall for this growth firm. The firm now earns a 23 percent rate of return. Suppose you expect return to line out at 9 percent when the firm eventually matures. After studying the decay patterns in Fig. 7-2, you decide that a five-year half-life describes how fast you expect rate of return to decay. Every five years the margin between the rate of return and the long-run limit will halve. The initial margin between the 23 percent starting return and the 9 percent long-run return is 14 percent. This initial margin will halve to 7 percent in five years. In turn, the 7 percent margin will halve to 3.5 percent in another five years:

Time, years	Half-Lives	Margin, %	Rate of Return
0	0	14	23
5	1	7	16
10	2	3.5	12.5
15	3	1.75	10.75
20	4	0.875	9.875
∞	∞	0.0	9.0

The rate of return comes closer and closer to the limiting value of 9 percent, but never reaches the limiting value. You can make the rate of return decay as slow or as fast as you think appropriate by choosing a suitable half-life. The longer the half-life, the slower the decay towards the long-run limit.

Example 7-1. Use the calculation form in Table 7-1 to project how this firm's rate of return decays from the 23 percent starting return towards the 9 percent long-run return at the end of the 10-year investment period and at the three intermediate times.

Table 7-2 shows the calculations. Enter the starting return of 23 percent and the long-run return of 9 percent in lines 1 and 2. Put the 14 percent difference between them in line 3. Enter the five-year half-life in line 4, and calculate a decay rate of 69.3/5, or 13.86 percent per year, in line 5. Enter the 10-year investment period in line 6.

Calculate the RT products needed for the Di discount factors in line 9. RT is the product of the time fraction in line 7, the investment period in line 6, and the decay rate in line 5. Enter the Di discount factors corresponding to these RT products in line 10. Multiply the starting margin in line 3 by the discount factors in line 11. The rate of return is the sum of the long-run return in line 2 and the decaying margin in line 12.

The calculation shows that this growth firm's rate of return will fall from 23 percent initially to 12.5 percent at the end of the 10-year investment period. You will need the returns calculated at the three intermediate times to discount dividends in Table 7-7.

Capital Growth Rate

Use the calculation form in Table 7-1 to forecast how rapidly capital growth is likely to slow as this growth firm matures.

TABLE 7-2
Projecting Rate of Return—Example 7-1

1. Starting Value				23
2. Long-Run Limit				9
3. Subtract Line 2 from Line 1				14
4. Half-Life, years				5
5. Decay Rate: Divide 69.3 by Line 4				13.86
6. Investment Period, years				10
7. Time Factors	0.113	0.5	0.887	1.0
8. Time: Multiply value in Line 7 by Line 6	1.13	5.0	8.87	10
9. Multiply each time in Line 8 by Line 5	15.7	69.3	122.9	138.6
10. Di Discount Factors from Appendix Table A-3 at the RT Products in Line 9	0.8547	0.5001	0.2925	0.2501
11. Multiply each value in Line 10 by Line 3	11.97	7.00	4.10	3.50
12. Factor Values: Add Lines 11 and 2	20.97	16.00	13.10	12.50

Example 7-2. The growth firm you are considering is currently growing 30 percent per year. You know that growth will gradually slow, and you project a long-run limit of 8 percent per year—approximately the GNP growth in undeflated dollars—when the firm eventually matures. You again expect growth to slow with a five-year half-life. What will the capital growth rate be at the end of the 10-year period and at the three intermediate times?

Table 7-3 shows how to project the capital growth rate. At a five-year half-life, the decay model shows that growth will slow from its starting value of 30 percent per year to 13.5 percent per year by the end of the 10-year investment period. The table also shows capital growth rates at the three intermediate times needed for discounting dividends.

Capital Employed

The projection of the capital growth rate determines what capital employed will be at any future time. You cannot forecast the two independently. The easiest way to project the size of the firm is to begin by projecting how fast you expect the capital growth rate to slow. Then use the growth projection to calculate capital employed at any time.

Your primary concern is with capital per share, which measures your share of capital employed. Capital per share grows at a slightly different rate than capital employed because of the gradual growth in the number of outstanding shares. For most firms, the number of outstanding shares grows slowly with time. Examine how fast the number of shares have been growing for the firm you are evaluating, and calculate the share growth rate as shown in Chapter 6.

The net growth rate of capital per share is the growth rate of capital employed, less the growth rate of the number of shares outstanding. Use the calculation form in Table 7-4 to convert your projection of capital growth rate to capital employed per share.

TABLE 7-3
Projecting Capital Growth Rate—Example 7-2

1. Starting Value				30
2. Long-Run Limit				8
3. Subtract Line 2 from Line 1				22
4. Half-Life, years				5
5. Decay Rate: Divide 69.3 by Line 4				13.86
6. Investment Period, years				10
7. Time Factors	0.113	0.5	0.887	1.0
8. Time: Multiply each value in Line 7 by Line 6	1.13	5.0	8.87	10
9. Multiply each time in Line 8 by Line 5	15.7	69.3	122.9	138.6
10. Di Discount Factors from Appendix Table A-3 at the RT Products in Line 9	0.8547	0.5001	0.2925	0.2501
11. Multiply each value in Line 10 by Line 3	18.81	11.00	6.44	5.50
12. Factor Values: Add Lines 11 and 2	26.81	19.00	14.44	13.50

Example 7-3. The growth firm you have been examining has $5 of capital employed per share. You expect the number of shares outstanding to grow slowly at a rate of 0.2 percent per year. Calculate capital per share at the end of the investment period and at the three intermediate times. Use the forecast of the capital growth rate from Example 7-2.

Use the calculation form in Table 7-4 to work out capital per share. Table 7-5 illustrates the calculation. Enter the basic information—starting capital employed, starting and long-run capital growth rates, half-life, growth in shares outstanding, and the investment period—in the first eight lines. List the time factors for the three intermediate times and the investment period in line 9. Lines 10 through 14 develop the average capital growth rate from the beginning of the investment to each time listed in line 10. Read Gi growth factors based on the average growth rates in line 14 and the times in line 10, and enter them in line 16. Find the capital per share in line 17 by multiplying the starting capital per share by the Gi growth factors in line 16. Capital per share is projected to grow from $5 initially to $35.85 at the end of the 10-year period.

This estimate of capital per share is much lower than you would have calculated if you had not allowed for the gradual slowing of growth. The Gi growth factor would have been 19.688 if capital per share grew steadily at 29.8 percent per year—the initial capital growth rate of 30 percent per year less the 0.2 percent per year growth in the number of shares outstanding. Capital per share at year 10 would have been estimated at $98.44, two and a half times the estimate allowing for gradually slowing growth rates.

Allowing for a gradual slowing of capital growth makes a big difference in the projected size of a growth firm during the investment period. The big difference in the size of the firm generates corresponding differences in projected dividends and stock prices, and in the attractiveness of growth stocks.

TABLE 7-4
Calculation Form—Capital Employed

1. Starting Capital Employed, $ per share				_____
2. Starting Capital Growth Rate, %/yr.				_____
3. Long-Run Capital Growth, %/yr.				_____
4. Growth in Shares Outstanding, %/yr.				_____
5. Subtract Line 3 from Line 2				_____
6. Half-Life for Capital Growth Rate, years				_____
7. Decay Rate: Divide 69.3 by Line 6				_____
8. Investment Period, years				_____
9. Time Factors	0.113	0.5	0.887	1.0
10. Time: Multiply each value in Line 9 by Line 8	_____	_____	_____	_____
11. RT: Multiply each value in Line 10 by Line 7	_____	_____	_____	_____
12. Dc Discount Factor from Appendix Table A4 at the RT Products in Line 11.	_____	_____	_____	_____
13. Multiply each value in Line 12 by Line 5	_____	_____	_____	_____
14. Average Growth Rate: Add Lines 3 and 13, then Subtract Line 4	_____	_____	_____	_____
15. Multiply each value in Line 14 by the corresponding values in Line 10	_____	_____	_____	_____
16. Gi Growth Factor from Appendix Table A1 at the RT Products in Line 15	_____	_____	_____	_____
17. Capital per Share: Multiply each value in Line 16 by Line 1	_____	_____	_____	_____

Price/Earnings Ratio

As a growth firm matures, growth slows and rate of return falls. The firm's price/earnings ratio reflect this erosion in growth and profitability and will fall as well. At maturity, the price/earnings ratio should approximate the price/earnings ratio for an average stock. The price/earnings ratio for the Standard and Poor's 500 stock average is a reasonable estimate for a growth stock's long-run price/earnings ratio.

The price/earnings ratio should decay about as fast as rate of return and capital growth decay. An average of the half-lives chosen for rate of return and capital growth decay is a reasonable estimate. Use the calculation form in Table 7-1 to estimate future price/earnings ratios. You need the price/earnings ratio only at the end of the investment period. Ignore the first three columns in Table 7-1.

Example 7-4. The growth stock you are considering has a current price/earnings ratio of 40. You expect this ratio to line out at 11 when the firm matures. Project a five-year half-life for the price/earnings ratio, the same as the half-life of the firm's rate of

TABLE 7-5
Capital Employed—Example 7-3

1. Starting Capital Employed, $ per share				5
2. Starting Capital Growth Rate, %/yr.				30
3. Long-Run Capital Growth, %/yr.				8
4. Growth in Shares Outstanding, %/yr.				0.2
5. Subtract Line 3 from Line 2				22
6. Half-Life for Capital Growth Rate, years				5
7. Decay Rate: Divide 69.3 by Line 6				13.86
8. Investment Period, years				10
9. Time Factors	0.113	0.5	0.887	1.0
10. Time: Multiply each value in Line 9 by Line 8	1.13	5.0	8.87	10
11. RT: Multiply each value in Line 10 by Line 7	15.7	69.3	122.9	138.6
12. Dc Discount Factor from Appendix Table A4 at the RT Products in Line 11.	0.9255	0.7214	0.5756	0.5411
13. Multiply each value in Line 12 by Line 5	20.36	15.87	12.66	11.90
14. Average Growth Rate: Add Lines 3 and 13, then Subtract Line 4	28.16	23.67	20.46	19.70
15. Multiply each value in Line 14 by the corresponding values in Line 10	31.8	118.4	181.5	197.0
16. Gi Growth Factor from Appendix Table A1 at the RT Products in Line 15	1.3744	3.2674	6.1411	7.1707
17. Capital per Share: Multiply each value in Line 16 by Line 1	6.87	16.34	30.71	35.85

return and capital growth rate. What will the price/earnings ratio be at the end of the 10-year investment period?

Use the calculation form in Table 7-1. Table 7-6 shows the results. The price/earnings ratio at the end of the 10-year investment period is estimated at 18.25.

Calculation Form for Evaluating Growth Stocks

Table 7-7 simplifies the evaluation of growth stocks. Use Table 7-1 first to project the firm's rate of return and capital growth rate at the three intermediate times and at the end of the investment period. Then use Table 7-4 to convert the projected growth rates to capital per share at the same four times. Also use Table 7-1 to project the price/earnings ratio at the end of the investment period.

The first six lines in Table 7-7 record basic information about the firm. You can fill them out quickly. Enter terminal values of capital employed and rate of return from

TABLE 7-6
Price/Earnings Ratio—Example 7-4

1. Starting Value				40
2. Long-Run Limit				11
3. Subtract Line 2 from Line 1				29
4. Half-Life, years				5
5. Decay Rate: Divide 69.3 by Line 4				13.86
6. Investment Period, years				10
7. Time Factors	0.113	0.5	0.887	1.0
8. Time: Multiply each value in Line 7 by Line 6				10
9. Multiply each time in Line 8 by Line 5				138.6
10. Di Discount Factors from Appendix Table A-3 at the RT Products in Line 9				0.2501
11. Multiply each value in Line 10 by Line 3				7.25
12. Factor Values: Add Lines 11 and 2				18.25

TABLE 7-7
Calculation Form—Growth Stocks

A. The Stock

1. Current Price, $/share _____

2. Final Capital, $/share, from Table 7-5 _____

3. Final Rate of Return, %, from Table 7-1 _____

4. Final Earnings: Multiply Line 2 by Line 3, then Divide by 100 _____

5. Equity Fraction _____

6. Final Price/Earnings Ratio from Table 7-1 _____

B. The Investor

7. Investment Period, years _____

C. Future Cash Flows

8. Future Price: Multiply Line 4 by Line 6 _____

9. Time Factors:	0.113	0.5	0.887
10. Time: Multiply each entry on Line 9 by Line 7			
11. Capital, $/share, from Table 7-4			
12. Growth Rate, %/yr., from Table 7-1			
13. Rate of Return, %, from Table 7-1			
14. Multiply Line 5 by Line 12, then Divide by Line 13			

Table 7-7. Continued.

15. Dividend Payout Fraction: Subtract Line 14
    from 1.0   _____ _____ _____

16. Dividends, $/share: Multiply Line 11 by
    Lines 13 and 15, then Divide by 100   _____ _____ _____

D. Discounting

17. Discount Rate, %   _____

18. Di Factor at RT = Line 7 times Line 17   _____

19. Present Value of Final Proceeds: Multiply
    Line 8 by Line 18   _____

20. Multiply each entry on Line 10 by Line 17   _____ _____ _____

21. Di Factor at RT = Line 20   _____ _____ _____

22. Multiply Line 16 by Line 21   _____ _____ _____

23. Add the first and last entries on Line 22;
    Multiply the result by 0.278   _____

24. Multiply the second entry on Line 22
    by 0.444   _____

25. Present Value of Dividends: Add Lines 23
    and 24; Multiply the result by Line 7   _____

26. Net Present Value: Add Lines 19 and 25,
    then Subtract Line 1   _____

If the present value on Line 26 is positive, try a new discount rate 5 percentage points higher. If Line 26 is negative, try a new discount rate 5 percentage points lower. Use Table 4-3 to complete the solution for rate of return.

E. Maximum Allowable Price

Enter your after-tax opportunity cost in Line and and complete Lines 18 through 25.

27. Maximum Allowable Price: Add Lines 19 and 25

_____

Tables 7-5 and 7-2 in lines 2 and 3. Multiply them together to give terminal earnings in line 4. Enter the stock's current price in line 1. Calculate the price at which you will eventually sell the stock in line 8 by multiplying terminal earnings in line 4 by the terminal price/earnings ratio from Table 7-6.

You will need dividends at the three intermediate times listed in line 10. Enter the rate of return, capital growth rate, and capital employed at those times in lines 11 through 13. The values are those you calculated in Tables 7-2, 7-3, and 7-5. The payout equation developed in Chapter 6 gives the dividend payout fraction consistent with any combination of the firm's rate of return, growth rate, and equity fraction. Calculate the dividend payout fraction in line 15. Multiply the capital employed by the rate of return at the three intermediate times, and the result is the earnings at those times. Multiply again by the dividend payout fraction to get the dividends in line 16.

Check the dividend payout fraction in line 15 to make sure it is reasonable. The payout fraction normally lies between zero and one. A payout fraction below zero is too low. You have assumed too fast a capital growth for the return the firm is earning. Either back off your growth projection, boost your rate of return projection, or both. A payout fraction above 1.0 is too high. It means the firm is liquidating itself.

All of the cash flows required for a discounted cash flow analysis are now available. Enter a trial discount rate in line 17. Enter a Di discount factor at that rate and the investment period in line 18, then discount the final stock sale in line 19. Calculate the present value of dividends at the three intermediate times in lines 20 through 25. Find the total present value in line 26 and the maximum allowable price in line 27.

The quickest way to use this table is to begin with your opportunity cost as the trial discount rate and work down to the maximum allowable price in line 27. If the market price is higher than your maximum allowable price, the stock is not attractive. There is no need to continue the analysis. The rate of return will be some value below your opportunity cost. If the market price is less than the maximum price you should pay, the stock might be attractive. Continue with a new trial discount rate 5 percentage points higher, and proceed to calculate your rate of return. Use Table 4-3 to complete the calculation for the rate of return. You will then be able to compare this stock with other investment opportunities.

Example 7-5. Complete the evaluation of the growth stock begun in the previous examples. Find your rate of return and the maximum price you should pay. Assume your opportunity cost is 8 percent. Table 7-8 completes the calculation. Rates of return, capital growth rates, capital employed, and the price/earnings ratio were developed in Tables 7-2, 7-3, 7-5, and 7-6. Enter these values in the appropriate places in Table 7-8.

Most firms maintain a stable mix of debt and equity in their capital pool. Assume this growth firm keeps its capital pool constant at 35 percent debt and 65 percent equity, typical values of the average firm. Enter 0.65 as the equity fraction in line 5.

The price of the stock when you sell in year 10 is the product of the price/earnings ratio and earnings per share at that time. Table 7-5 shows that capital employed reaches $35.85 per share in year 10. Table 7-2 shows that the firm's rate of return reaches 12.5 percent. Multiply both figures together and find earnings of $4.48 per share in line 4. Multiply again by the price/earnings ratio of 18.25 projected in Table 7-6 for year 10. The stock price should be $81.76 per share, as shown in line 8.

Begin discounting at your 8 percent opportunity cost. Line 19 shows that the present value from the sale of the stock is $36.73 per share. Line 25 shows the present value of dividends total $3.95 per share. Total present value, including the initial investment, is -5.32 per share. The negative present value shows that this growth stock is not attractive. The present value is negative, and the rate of return is less than your opportunity cost.

Continue working on Table 7-8, and calculate a maximum allowable price of $40.68 per share in line 27. The current market price of $46 per share is above the $40.68 maximum price you should pay. This growth stock is not attractive, and the analysis could end at this point. If you continued with additional trial discount rates, you would find a rate of return of 6.7 percent for investing in this stock.

The assumption that this growth firm's performance will fall off with a five-year half-life leads to a rate of return below your 8 percent opportunity cost. Although the stock

TABLE 7-8
Growth Stocks—Example 7-5

A. The Stock

1. Current Price, $/share			46
2. Final Capital, $/share, from Table 7-5			35.85
3. Final Rate of Return, %, from Table 7-1			12.5
4. Final Earnings: Multiply Line 2 by Line 3, then Divide by 100			4.48
5. Equity Fraction			0.65
6. Final Price/Earnings Ratio from Table 7-1			18.25

B. The Investor

7. Investment Period, years			10

C. Future Cash Flows

8. Future Price: Multiply Line 4 by Line 6			81.76
9. Time Factors:	0.113	0.5	0.887
10. Time: Multiply each entry on Line 9 by Line 7	1.13	5.0	8.87
11. Capital, $/share, from Table 7-5	6.87	16.34	30.71
12. Growth Rate, %/yr., from Table 7-1	26.81	19.00	14.44
13. Rate of Return, %, from Table 7-1	20.97	16.00	13.10
14. Multiply Line 5 by Line 12, then Divide by Line 13	0.831	0.772	0.716
15. Dividend Payout Fraction: Subtract Line 14 from 1.0	0.169	0.228	0.284
16. Dividends, $/share: Multiply Line 11 by Lines 13 and 15, then Divide by 100	0.24	0.60	1.14

D. Discounting

17. Discount Rate, %			12.7
18. Di Factor at RT = Line 7 times Line 17			0.4493
19. Present Value of Final Proceeds: Multiply Line 8 by Line 18			36.73
20. Multiply each entry on Line 10 by 17	9.0	40.0	71.0
21. Di Factor at RT = Line 20	0.9139	0.6703	0.4916
22. Multiply Line 16 by Line 21	0.2193	0.4022	0.5604
23. Add the first and last entries on Line; 22; Mulitply the result by 0.278			0.2168
24. Multiply the second entry on Line 22 by 0.444			0.1786

Table 7-8. Continued.

25. Present Value of Dividends: Add Lines
    23 and 24; Multiply the result by Line 7   3.95
26. Net Present Value: Add Lines 19 and
    25, then Subtract Line 1   −$5.32

If the present value on Line 26 is positive, try a new discount rate 5 percentage points higher. If Line 26 is negative, try a new discount rate 5 percentage points lower. Use Table 4-3 to complete the solution for rate of return.

E. Maximum Allowable Price
Enter your after-tax opportunity cost in Line 17 and complete Lines 18 through 25.

27. Maximum Allowable Price: Add Lines 19 and 25 $40.68

appears to be attractive because of the firm's rapid growth and the high return it earns, the stock costs too much, given your assumptions about how fast the firm will mature and your opportunity cost.

Effect of Half-Life
The critical assumption in this analysis is that the firm's rate of return, capital growth rate, and price/earnings ratio will all decay with a five-year half-life. Extend the analysis and test how sensitive the results are to half-lives. Figure 7-3 shows the rate of return and the maximum allowable price/earnings ratio for this growth stock over a range of half-lives. The results are plotted in Fig. 7-3 and listed below:

Half-Life, yrs.	Rate of Return, %	Maximum Allowable Price $/Share	Maximum P/E Ratio
4	3.3	20.23	17.6
5	6.7	27.77	24.1
6	9.5	35.99	31.3
8	13.5	52.95	46
10	16.2	69.25	60
20	22.6	130	113
50	27.0	201	175
Steady-State	30.2	408	355

The top plot in Fig. 7-3 shows how the rate of return varies with the half-life. The rate of return for investing in this growth stock does not reach your 8 percent opportunity cost until a half-life of 7.2 years. Therefore, deciding on whether or not to invest in this growth stock does not require a precise estimate of half-lives. Instead, the decision requires an estimate of whether growth and profitability will decay slowly enough so that the half-life will be longer than 7.2 years. If you judge that decay will be slow and the half-life will be longer than 7.2 years, then this growth stock is attractive. If you judge that decay will be faster, and that the half-life will be shorter than 7.2 years, this growth stock is not attractive.

The bottom plot of Fig. 7-3 shows how the maximum allowable price/earnings ratio varies with half-life. This plot is consistent with the top plot. The maximum allowable price/earnings ratio does not reach the current market ratio of 40 until the half-life reaches 7.2 years.

If you had used the steady-state model to evaluate this growth stock, you would have calculated a 30.2 percent rate of return and a maximum allowable price/earnings ratio of 408—far too optimistic an evaluation. Using the unsteady-state model and allowing for gradual decay in the firm's growth, rate of return, and price/earnings ratio gives much more realistic evaluations of growth stocks.

SUMMARY

☐ A growth stock does not follow the steady-state assumption. Its growth rate, rate of return, dividend payout, capital structure, and price/earnings ratio do not stay constant during the investment period. Evaluating a growth stock is basically the same as evaluating the stock of a mature firm at steady-state conditions, except that you must allow for gradual change in the factors that affect the stock's value.

☐ The simplest unsteady-state case is one in which the price/earnings ratio, when you eventually sell the stock, differs from the ratio when you first purchased it. This case is evaluated simply by using estimates of the future price/earnings ratio in the discounted cash flow solution. The rate of return for investing in a stock is sensitive to changes in the price/earnings ratio if the stock is held only a short time, but becomes less sensitive the longer you hold the stock.

☐ Growth stocks require an allowance for a gradual slowing of growth, a gradual fall in profitability and price/earnings ratio, and a gradual increase in dividends as growth firms mature. Stocks of temporarily depressed firms require an allowance for gradually increasing growth, profitability, price/earnings ratio, and dividends as these firms recover.

☐ A decay model describes how any factor in the analysis gradually decays from some initial value towards a long-run limit. A half-life controls how fast any factor decays

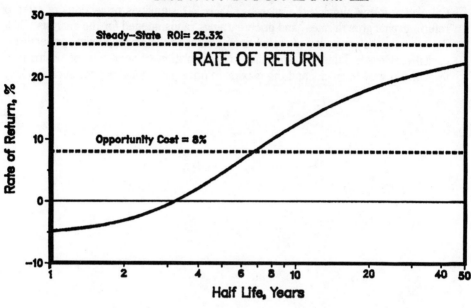

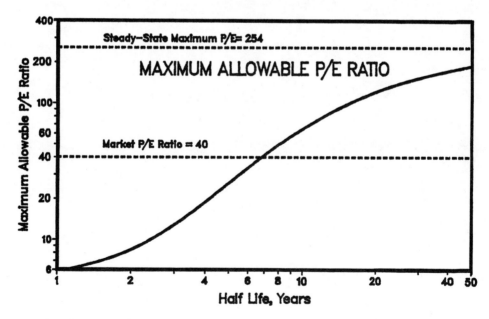

from its initial value towards its long-run limit. Figure 7-2 is a helpful guide for estimating half-lives.

☐ Calculation forms simplify the analysis. Table 7-1 simplifies projections of rates of return, capital growth rates, and price/earnings ratios needed for the analysis. Table 7-4 converts the projection of capital growth rates to the corresponding projection of capital employed. Table 7-7 simplifies the calculation of your rate of return from investing in growth stocks and the maximum price you should pay for such stocks.

8

Will Anything Be Left After Inflation?

INFLATION, THE GRADUAL INCREASE IN THE PRICES OF GOODS AND SERVICES OVER time, has been a problem throughout history. Inflation is undesirable because prices and interest rates rise. Deflation, the gradual decay in prices over time, is even more undesirable. In periods of severe deflation, businesses fail, factories close, and people are thrown out of work. Zero inflation is the paper-thin dividing line between inflation and deflation. Zero inflation is ideal, but governments cannot manage their economies precisely enough to land exactly on that thin dividing line. The practical choice is somewhere between inflation and deflation. Bitter experience with severe deflation during the Great Depression of the 1930s showed that inflation is better than deflation. The goal is to control inflation at some small but acceptable level.

Because of inflation, part or all of your gain from investing in securities is illusory. You might have invested $1,000 in a stock and later sold the stock for $1,500, for an apparent gain of 50 percent. If prices inflated 50 percent while you held the stock, however, your $1,500 will buy no more goods and services than the $1,000 you started with. Your real gain will have been zero. Therefore, don't be misled by looking only at the apparent gains from investments. Know your real gain in purchasing power, and adjust for inflation when you evaluate securities.

MEASURING INFLATION

The Bureau of Labor Statistics regularly publishes price indices for a large number of goods and services sold in our economy. Several series are combined to provide price indices for particular sectors and groups in the economy. The Consumer Price Index measures the price of a market basket of goods and services the average consumer buys. Another economy yardstick is the GNP, or Gross National Product, Deflator, which is a composite price index of all the goods and services bought throughout the economy. The GNP Deflator is the broadest measure of inflation in the economy. Figure 8-1 shows how the GNP Deflator has grown since 1972. It has increased steadily throughout the period. A market basket of goods and services that cost $46 in 1972 had risen to $110 in 1989.

The rate of inflation measures how fast the GNP Deflator increases, and is shown by how steeply the curve in Fig. 8-1 is rising. The inflation rate is the slope of the GNP Deflator curve. Figure 8-2 shows these slopes calculated for moving, one-year periods. The inflation rate is uneven. During this period, the inflation rate was, at times, high. At other times, it was low. Inflation ranged from a high of 12 percent per year in 1975 to a

Fig. 8–1
GNP DEFLATOR

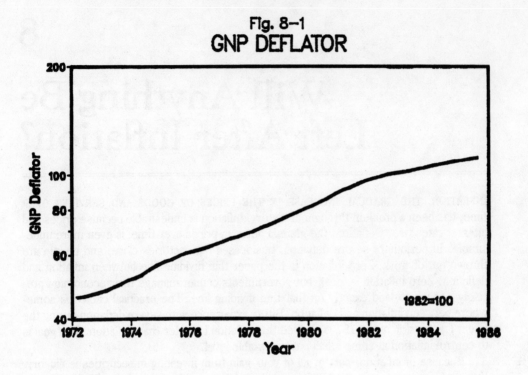

1982=100

Fig. 8–2
INFLATION RATE

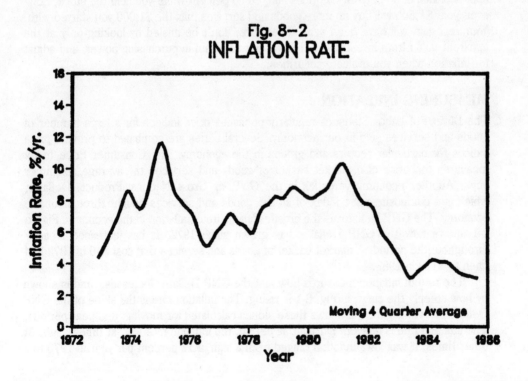

Moving 4 Quarter Average

low of 3 percent per year in 1985. Many forecasters during 1989 projected long-run inflation of about 5 percent per year.

ALLOWING FOR INFLATION IN SECURITY ANALYSIS

The simplest assumption for inflation is that the inflation rate stays constant with time.
Under steady-state conditions, prices inflate at a constant percentage rate. The Gi
growth factor in Appendix Table A1 describes growth at a constant percentage rate.
Therefore, you can find future prices by multiplying the current price by a Gi growth
factor:

$$P_T = P_o Gi_{i,T}$$

The future price, P_T, is the current price, P_o, multiplied by the growth factor $Gi_{i,T}$.
Read this growth factor from Appendix Table A1 at the product of the inflation rate and
time.

Deflating future prices means adjusting future prices to prices àt today's purchasing
power. Deflating is equivalent to discounting future cash flows to find their present value.
The deflated price is simply the future price multiplied by a Di discount factor from
Appendix Table A3. Read the discount factor $Di_{i,T}$ at the product of the inflation rate and
time:

$$P_o = P_T Di_{i,T}$$

RATE-OF-RETURN CALCULATIONS

The essence of finding your rate of return by discounted cash flow is to multiply each
increment of cash you spend or receive by a discount factor. You then add all of the discounted cash flows, and adjust the discount rate so that the sum of the discounted cash
flows equals zero. To allow for inflation, you must also deflate all future cash flows.
Deflate future cash flows by multiplying them by a second discount factor, $Di_{i,T}$ read
from Appendix Table A3 at the product of the inflation rate and time. The second discount factor is a deflator, which converts future cash flows to dollars at today's purchasing power.

Multiplying future cash flows by both the $Di_{R,T}$ discount factor and the $Di_{i,T}$ deflator
is the same as multiplying by the single discount factor $Di_{(R+i),T}$. Read this discount factor at the sum of the discount rate and the inflation rate. You can see that the discount
rate that makes present value zero is the sum of a discount rate and an inflation rate. The
sum of the two rates is the nominal rate of return. The component R is the real rate of
return, and the component i is the inflation rate

The rates of return you found in previous chapters were nominal rates of return.
Inflation was ignored. In effect, you set the inflation rate equal to zero. The discount rate
that made present values equal to zero was the nominal rate of return. If inflation is not
zero, the inflation rate that makes present values equal to zero is the sum of the real rate
of return and the inflation rate. To find your real rate of return, you must subtract the
inflation rate from the nominal discount rate. Follow these two simple steps to allow for
inflation when you evaluate investments:

1. Calculate the return on investment in the normal way. By trial and error, find the
   discount rate that makes all the discounted cash flows add up to zero. That dis-

count rate is the nominal rate of return—the sum of the real rate of return and an inflation rate. The nominal rate of return is a return not adjusted for inflation.

2. Subtract the projected inflation rate from the rate of return you found in Step 1. The result is the real rate of return—the return in dollars of constant purchasing power. Some examples will make the allowance for inflation clear.

Example 8-1. Frank does not trust banks. Neither does he trust the stock market. He hides $1,000 in his mattress, and recovers the money five years later. Inflation proceeded at the rate of 6 percent per year during those five years. What is the rate of return on his "investment?"

There are two cash flows: −$1,000 when he hides the money, and $1,000 when he recovers it. Discount these cash flows exactly as in the previous examples, but discount at the sum of the discount rate and the inflation rate. Set the total present value equal to zero:

$$-1,000 + 1,000 \text{ Di}_{(R+6),5} = 0$$

Note that you must evaluate the Di discount factor at the sum of the discount rate and the 6 percent per year inflation rate. The solution for the discount factor is:

$$\text{Di}_{(R+6),5} = 1,000/1,000 = 1.0$$

Appendix Table A3 shows that the discount factor is 1.0 at an $(R+i)T$ product of zero:

$$(R+6)*5 = 0$$

The only way for this product to equal zero is for $(R+6)$ to be zero, that is, for R to be −6 percent. While Frank's money was hidden in the mattress, his real rate of return was minus 6 percent, that is, minus the inflation rate.

Example 8-2. Harry is smarter than Frank. Harry put his $1,000 in a bank savings account and earned 5.5 percent interest. He left his interest to compound in the account, so that when he withdrew his money five years later, it had grown to ($1,000) $(\text{Gi}_{5.5,5})$, or $1,316.50. What was Harry's real rate of return?

Set up the discounted cash flow solution just as in the preceding example. The solution for the discount factor is:

$$-1,000 + 1,316.53*\text{Di}_{(R+6),5} = 0$$
$$\text{Di}_{(R+6),5} = 1,000/1,316.53 = 0.7596$$

Read from Appendix Table A3 that a discount factor of 0.7596 occurs at an $(R+i)T$ product of 27.5:

$$(R+6)*5 = 27.5$$
$$R+6 = 27.5/5 = 5.5$$
$$R = 5.5-6 = -0.5$$

Harry's real rate of return was minus 0.5 percent. The interest Harry earned on his savings account was not high enough to compensate for inflation, although he was better off than he would have been if he had hidden his $1,000 in his mattress. Even so, he lost purchasing power at the rate of 0.5 percent per year.

Review the examples of investing in bonds and stocks in Chapters 5, 6, and 7. The real rate of return for these examples is the rate of return calculated in those examples, less the expected inflation rate.

EARNING A REAL RETURN ON INVESTMENT

These examples teach a critical lesson. If you expect to earn a real return on an investment (if you expect to increase your purchasing power), that investment must earn a nominal return higher than the anticipated inflation rate. Suppose you need a real rate of return of 3 percent, and you expect inflation to be 6 percent per year. You must insist on a nominal rate of return of 3 percent plus 6 percent, or 9 percent from any investment. The additional 6 percent is an inflation premium.

You can now see why interest rates increase when lenders expect inflation to rise. Lenders recognize that an increase in inflation will reduce their real rate of return. They compensate by adding an inflation premium to the interest rate they charge, which protects their real rate of return. If lenders expect inflation to increase by 1 percentage point per year, they will raise the nominal interest rates they charge by 1 percentage point. The two increases offset each other, and leave the lender's real interest rate unchanged. Interest rates rise during periods of inflation because of the inflation premium lenders add to protect their real interest rates.

There are frequent references to the "real interest rate" in the financial press. The real interest rate is simply the nominal interest rate less the expected or the historic inflation rate. Figure 2-1 in Chapter 2 shows nominal and real interest rates over the past 15 years. The nominal interest rate is the interest rate reported by the government. The curve for real interest rates is the nominal interest rate curve less the inflation rate.

ALLOWING FOR INFLATION WHEN CALCULATING MAXIMUM ALLOWABLE PRICE

The maximum allowable price you should pay for any security is the sum of all future cash flows you expect to receive from that security—a stream of interest or dividend payments, and the cash you receive when you redeem a security or sell a stock—all discounted at your opportunity cost. Inflation will erode the purchasing power of those future cash flows. To remove the effects of inflation you must deflate all future cash flows by multiplying them by the deflator $Di_{i,T}$.

You must deflate all costs, including your opportunity cost. An opportunity cost is the rate of return you could earn from the next best use of your money. The next best use of your money will normally be investing in some alternative security, or prepaying a debt and saving interest costs. Adjust the opportunity cost for inflation just like you adjust any other rate of return. Subtract the expected inflation rate from your nominal opportunity cost.

The two inflation adjustments, deflating future cash flows and subtracting the inflation rate from your nominal opportunity cost, cancel each other. There is no net adjustment. Continue to find the maximum allowable price by discounting the sum of all future cash flows you expect from that security at your nominal opportunity cost. There is no need to deflate future cash flows, nor to deflate your opportunity cost.

Example 8-3. In Example 6-6, you analyzed a stock and found a maximum allowable price of $12.62 per share at a 12 percent opportunity cost. What is the maximum allowable price if you expect 5 percent per year inflation?

Deflate your 12 percent opportunity cost by subtracting the expected inflation rate of 5 percent. Your real opportunity cost is $(12-5)$, or 7 percent. Now, discount all future cash flows at the sum of the real 7 percent opportunity cost and the 5 percent inflation rate. The total discount rate is $(7+5)$, or 12 percent.

The two inflation adjustments, deflating the opportunity cost and discounting at the sum of the opportunity cost and the inflation rate, offset each other. The net discount rate is 12 percent—the same discount rate you used in Example 6-6. Therefore, the maximum allowable price is $12.62 per share, the same price you calculated in Example 6-6.

SUMMARY

☐ Inflation makes part, or all, of the gains from investing in securities illusory. Because of inflating prices, your gain in real purchasing power is less than the nominal gain from the investment.

☐ Adjust the future cash flows expected from investing in any security to cash flows at today's purchasing power. Multiply each future cash flow by the deflation factor, $Di_{i,T}: P_o = P_T Di_{i,T}$. Where i is the expected inflation rate. The deflation factor is a discount factor; read it from Appendix Table A3.

☐ The real interest rate or rate of return from any investment is the nominal interest rate or rate of return, less the expected inflation rate. Use this simple two-step rule to adjust rate of return for inflation:

1. Calculate the rate of return without regard for inflation.
2. Subtract the expected inflation rate from the rate of return calculated in Step 1.

☐ To earn a real return from an investment, you must earn a greater return than the expected inflation rate. The nominal rate of return is the sum of the real return and the inflation rate.

☐ When calculating the maximum price you should pay for any security, the two adjustments for inflation—deflating future cash flows and deflating your opportunity cost—offset each other. Regardless of the expected inflation rate, the most you should pay for any security is the sum of all future nominal cash flows you expect from that security, discounted at your nominal opportunity cost.

9

Will Anything Be Left After Taxes?

ANY INCOME YOU EARN FROM YOUR INVESTMENT PROGRAM IS SUBJECT TO TAXES. YOU will have to allow for the bite federal and state taxes take out of investment income to find your net gain from investing in securities. Consequently, you must analyze all of your investment opportunities on an after-tax basis.

INCREMENTAL TAX RATES

The critical distinction to make in allowing for taxes is to distinguish between incremental and average tax rates. Figure 9-1 illustrates the idea of an incremental tax rate. The diagram shows how the federal government taxes the income of married taxpayers who file joint returns. The first several thousand dollars of each family's income is free of taxes. Individuals will receive a personal exemption of $2,000 in 1989. Beginning in 1990, these exemptions will be adjusted for inflation. For a family of four, exemptions shield the first $8,000 of 1989 income from federal taxes. Each taxpayer is also entitled to a standard deduction, which depends on the taxpayer's marital status. A married couple filing a joint return could take a standard deduction of $5,200 in 1989. The standard deduction is also adjusted for inflation. The standard deduction, together with four exemptions, will then shield the first $13,200 of this family's income from taxes. Taxpayers with deductions higher than the standard can itemize and claim the higher deductions.

Income greater than the total of exemptions and deductions is taxable, and is taxed at the rates shown in Fig. 9-1. There are two basic tax rates. The first increment of taxable income is taxed at a low rate of 15 percent. The second increment is taxed at a higher rate of 28 percent. The income level at which the tax rate jumps from 15 to 28 percent depends on marital status. For married taxpayers filing jointly, the tax rate jumps at a taxable income of $29,750. For single taxpayers, the tax rate jumps at a taxable income of $17,850. These break points are also adjusted for inflation.

The dashed rectangles in Fig. 9-1 represent the 5 percent surcharge that more affluent taxpayers must pay. This surcharge brings their tax rate to 33 percent. For married taxpayers filing jointly, the 5 percent surcharge begins at a taxable income of $71,900 and continues until a taxable income of $149,250. The surcharge for single taxpayers begins at a taxable income of $43,150 and continues until a taxable income of $89,560. The 5 percent surcharge gradually eliminates the benefits of the lower, 15 percent tax rate. By the end of the surcharge bracket, all taxable income is taxed at an equivalent single rate of 28 percent.

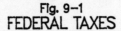

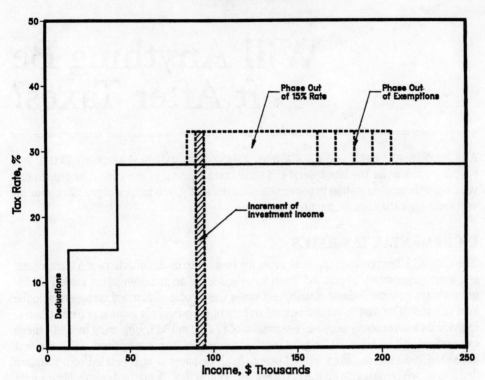

The 5 percent surcharge continues across additional income brackets of $10,920. There is one such bracket for each personal exemption, as shown by the smaller dashed rectangles at the right of the diagram. Each $10,920 bracket removes the benefit of one personal exemption. The 5 percent surcharge results in wealthy taxpayers paying at a 28 percent effective rate on all taxable income, and receiving no personal exemptions. The income levels at which tax rates change are also adjusted for inflation.

Consider an investor who has a total income of $90,000, four exemptions, and who takes the standard deduction. Figure 9-1 shows that this investor will be taxed at a rate of 33 percent on his last dollar of income. The tax rate on the last dollar of taxable income is the incremental or marginal tax rate. Suppose that investor receives an additional $5,000 per year in investment income. The investment income will add to his base income, which is shown as a shaded vertical strip in Fig. 9-1. Figure 9-1 clearly shows that the additional income will be taxed at the investor's 33 percent incremental tax rate.

Investment income adds to your base income and is taxed at your incremental tax rate. Therefore, the basic rule for allowing for taxes in security analysis is: All your investment income will be taxed at your incremental tax rate. If your incremental tax rate is 33 percent, the government will take 0.33 dollars out of every investment dollar you earn, and you will keep only $(1-0.33)$, or 0.67 dollars. The quantity $(1-0.33)$ is the after-tax factor. Find your after-tax income by multiplying your before-tax income by your after-tax factor. In the example shown in Fig. 9-1, the investor's incremental tax rate is 33 percent, and his after-tax factor is $(1-0.33)$, or 0.67. His after tax income is:

$$\text{Net After-Tax Income} = (0.67)\ (\$5,000) = \$3,350$$

Examine your federal and state tax returns and determine the tax rate you will pay on the last dollar of taxable income. That rate is your incremental tax rate, and is the tax rate you should use to allow for taxes when you evaluate securities. The average tax rate is the total taxes divided by total income. The average tax rate is less than the incremental tax rate because the average includes previous blocks of income taxed at either 0, 15, or 28 percent. The government taxes investment income at the incremental tax rate, not the average tax rate. Therefore, use the incremental tax rate when you evaluate securities.

STATE TAXES

Besides federal taxes, the state also taxes your investment income. State taxes vary from state to state, but the average tax rate is about 6 percent. Check your state tax return and determine the tax rate you paid on your last dollar of income. If you itemize deductions on your federal tax return, you can deduct state taxes from taxable income. The deduction saves federal taxes, and partially offsets the state tax. Also, if you itemize deductions on your federal tax return, find your net incremental state tax rate by multiplying the gross state tax rate by your federal after-tax factor.

Suppose an investor pays an incremental federal tax rate of 33 percent, and an incremental state tax rate of 6 percent. If he itemizes deductions, his net incremental state tax rate will be the gross state tax rate of 6 percent multiplied by the after-tax factor $(1-0.33)$, or 4 percent. His total incremental tax rate is the sum of the 33 percent federal rate and the 4 percent state rate, or 37 percent.

If this investor does not itemize deductions, there will be no federal offset against state taxes. His total incremental tax rate will be the sum of the 33 percent federal tax rate and the 6 percent state tax rate, or 39 percent. A total incremental tax rate of 37 percent is used for the examples worked out in this book. Review your federal and state tax returns and determine the appropriate incremental tax rate for your own situation.

ORDINARY INCOME AND CAPITAL GAINS

The Tax Reform Act of 1986 removed the distinction between ordinary income and capital gains. Both kinds of income are now taxed at the same rate. Tax laws change often, however, and a future law could restore favorable treatment for capital gains. Therefore, this book keeps the flexibility for taxing ordinary income and capital gains differently.

Before the new tax law, the rate at which earnings were taxed depended on the kind of earnings you received. Dividends and interest were taxed as ordinary income. Capital gains—the difference between the price at which you sell a security and the price you originally paid for that security—was taxed at lower rates. Sixty percent of capital gains was tax-free and the remaining 40 percent was taxed as ordinary income.

If you invested in a rapidly growing company that reinvested all of its earnings and paid no dividends, all your gain came from an increase in the price of the stock. Taxes were low because all your gain was taxed at favorable capital gains tax rates. If you invested in a mature company that grew slowly and paid a large fraction of its earnings out as dividends, more of your gain came as dividends and less as a capital gain. Taxes were higher because dividends are taxed as normal income. Taxes were highest if you invested in a security such as a certificate of deposit, because all of your gain came as interest, and was taxed as ordinary income.

An investor in the then maximum 50 percent tax bracket, paid a 50 percent tax on only 40 percent of the capital gain. That is equivalent to a tax of only 20 percent on the total capital gain. The higher the investor's incremental tax rate, the greater the advantage from low capital gains tax rates.

ALLOWING FOR TAXES IN SECURITY ANALYSIS

To allow for taxes when evaluating a security, simply convert all future cash flows you expect from the security to an after-tax basis. This book treats ordinary income and capital gains separately in case the government restores favorable treatment for capital gains in a future tax law. Cash flows such as dividends and interest are taxed as ordinary income. Find your after-tax income by multiplying dividends and interest by your after-tax factor. An investor with a 37 percent incremental tax rate would multiply dividend and interest income by $(1-0.37)$, or 0.63.

A capital gain is the difference between the price at which you sell a security and the price you originally paid for that security. Find your tax on capital gains by multiplying the gain by the appropriate tax rate. Since the Tax Reform Act of 1986, all capital gains is taxed as ordinary income. The appropriate tax rate is now the same incremental tax rate you pay on interest and dividends. If a future tax law reduces capital gains taxes, use the lower rate. The calculation forms in Chapter 11 recognize that tax laws can change and you can use different tax rates for ordinary and capital gains taxes.

Your opportunity cost must also be on an after-tax basis. Suppose the next best thing you can do with your money is to prepay a mortgage on which you are paying 10 percent interest. Your before-tax opportunity cost is 10 percent. If you itemize deductions, your after-tax opportunity cost will be less. When you prepay a mortgage, you lose the tax deduction from the interest costs you save. Federal taxes rise as a result. The net saving in interest cost is the gross saving less the increased federal taxes. Find your after-tax opportunity cost by multiplying your before-tax opportunity cost by your after-tax factor. Suppose your incremental tax rate is 37 percent. Prepaying the 10 percent mortgage will yield a before-tax opportunity cost of 10 percent and an after-tax opportunity cost of $(1-0.37)$ (10), or 6.3 percent.

Calculate your after-tax opportunity cost this way only if you itemize deductions on your federal tax return. If you don't itemize but take only the standard deduction instead, the savings in interest cost will not increase your taxable income. Your after-tax opportunity cost will then be the same as your before-tax cost.

If the next best use of your money is some alternative investment, your after-tax opportunity cost is the after-tax rate of return you could earn from that investment. Evaluating an investment in any security on the basis of the net return after taxes involves the following steps.

RATE OF RETURN

To calculate the rate of return for an investment, convert all cash flows you expect from the investment to an after-tax basis. Multiply cash flows that are taxed at ordinary rates, such as interest and dividends, by your after-tax factor. Multiply capital gains by the tax rate that applies to capital gains, and include the tax as a negative cash flow in the discounted cash flow analysis. After you convert all cash flows to an after-tax basis, calculate the rate of return from the investment by the usual discounted cash flow method.

MAXIMUM ALLOWABLE PURCHASE PRICE

To determine the maximum allowable purchase price of an investment, convert all future cash flows you expect from the investment—interest, dividends, the cash from the eventual sale of the security, and commissions—to cash flows after taxes. Convert your opportunity cost to an after-tax cost. The maximum price you should pay is the sum of all future after-tax cash flows discounted at your after-tax opportunity cost.

DISCOUNTED CASH FLOW ANALYSIS INCLUDING TAX EFFECTS

You will normally have to find your after-tax rate of return from any investment by using trial-and-error methods. Simple, fixed-interest securities such as bank savings accounts are an exception, because all the gain is in the form of interest payments. You recover the initial investment at the end of the investment period. There is no capital gain and no capital gains tax. Find your after-tax return from a bank savings account by multiplying the bank's interest rate by your after-tax factor. If the bank pays 5.5 percent interest and your incremental tax rate is 37 percent, your after-tax return is $(1-0.37)(5.5)$, or 3.47 percent.

Example 9-1. In Example 8-2, you saw how Harry put $1,000 in a bank savings account that paid 5.5 percent interest. His real rate of return was only −0.5 percent, because prices inflated 6 percent per year while his money was invested. Harry's incremental federal and state tax rate totals 37 percent. What is his real rate of return after taxes?

Harry's after-tax return is the before-tax interest rate multiplied by his after-tax factor: $R = (1-0.37)(5.5) = 3.47\%$. With inflation at 6 percent per year, Harry's real rate of return is: $R = 3.47 - 6 = -2.53\%$. Because the government takes 37 percent of Harry's interest income in taxes, Harry's real rate of return drops from −0.5 to −2.53 percent.

This example should make you wary of ''conservative'' investments like bank savings accounts and certificates of deposit. After you allow for inflation and taxes, these investments often result in a loss in purchasing power.

TAX-DEFERRED SAVINGS PLANS

You can defer taxes by investing in your company's pension plan and deferred compensation (401k) plan, and in Individual Retirement Accounts (IRAs) or Keogh Plans. These plans are attractive because your money grows without being taxed during the period you contribute to the plan. Only when you retire and begin withdrawing from the plan does the government tax your earnings. Deferring taxes is advantageous. Savings grow faster when they are not taxed, and the present value of taxes is less the longer you can defer taxes. The after-tax rate of return from an IRA plan depends on the before-tax rate of return the security you invest in earns, your incremental tax rate at the time you make the investment and at the time you recover your investment, and on the number of years you invest your money. Your rate of return also depends on how much of the investment you can deduct from taxable income when you make the investment, and on how much of the withdrawals are taxable.

The Economic Recovery Tax Act of 1981 allowed you to deduct your IRA contributions from your taxable income in the year you contributed to the IRA. The entire amount is taxed when you withdraw it from the plan after age 59 and a half.

The Tax Reform Act of 1986 eliminated the deduction of the initial IRA investment from taxable income for many taxpayers. Single taxpayers with adjusted gross incomes over $35,000, married taxpayers filing jointly with adjusted gross incomes over $50,000, and married taxpayers filing separately with any adjusted gross income can no longer deduct their investment. Eliminating this initial tax savings makes IRA plans less attractive.

The calculation form in Table 9-1 simplifies the analysis of IRA plans. The form will adapt to any likely changes in the tax laws governing IRA plans. Part A of the form records the before-tax rate of return from the investment in the IRA plan in line 1 and the number of years before you withdraw the proceeds in line 2. Part B records tax information. Enter your incremental tax rate when you invest in the IRA in line 3, and the incremental tax rate when you withdraw in line 4. Enter the fraction of the initial investment

---
TABLE 9-1
Calculation Form—IRA Plans

A. The IRA Investment

 1. Rate of return before Taxes, %   _____

 2. Time until Investment Recovered, years   _____

B. Taxes

 3. Divide Incremental Tax Rate (%) at Time of Investment by 100   _____

 4. Divide Incremental Tax Rate (%) at Time of Withdrawal by 100   _____

 5. Fraction of Investment Deductible at Time of Investment   _____

 6. Fraction of Withdrawal Taxable at Withdrawal   _____

C. Rate of Return

 7. Multiply Line 5 by Line 3; Subtract the result from 1.0   _____

 8. Multiply Line 6 by Line 4; Subtract the result from 1.0   _____

 9. Divide Line 7 by Line 8   _____

10. Enter Line 9 in your calculator and tap the ln(x) key   _____

11. Multiply Line 10 by 100 and Divide by Line 2   _____

12. Rate of Return, %: If Line 11 is positive, subtract it from Line 1. If
    Line 11 is negative, add it to Line 1._____

TABLE 9-2
Taxes on IRA Plans

Fraction of Investment Deductible from Taxable Income

Marital Status	Adjusted Gross Income (AGI)	Fraction Deductible
Married	Less than $40,000	1.0
	$40,000 to $50,000	(50,000 - AGI)/10,000
	More than $50,000	0
Single	Less than $25,000	1.0
	$25,000 to $35,000	(35,000 - AGI)/10,000
	More than $35,000	0

Fraction of Withdrawal that is Taxable

A. Current (1989) Law

	Fraction of Investment Deductible	Fraction of Withdrawal Taxable
All Deductible	Fraction = 1.0	1.0
None Deductible	Fraction = 0	$1 - Di_{R,T}$*

B. Possible Tax Law Change: Adjust Gains for Inflation

	Fraction of Investment Deductible	Fraction of Withdrawal Taxable
All Deductible	Fraction = 1.0	$Di_{i,T}$*
None Deductible	Fraction = 0	$D_{i,T} - Di_{R,T}$*

*Discount factors read at product of return on IRA investment, or inflation rate times the IRA investment period in years.

you can deduct from your taxable income in line 5, and the fraction of your withdrawal that is taxable in line 6. Table 9-2 will help you choose the appropriate fractions for lines 5 and 6. If you can deduct your initial investment, all of your withdrawal will be taxable. If you cannot deduct the investment, only part of your withdrawals are taxable. Suppose you cannot deduct the initial investment, your IRA investment earns a before-tax return of 10 percent, and you withdraw the proceeds 20 years later. Table 9-2 shows that the fraction of your withdrawal that will be taxed is 1.0 minus a Di discount factor. The Di discount factor for a 10 percent return and a 20-year investment period is 0.1353. The fraction taxable is (1 − 0.1353), or 0.8647.

Changes in the tax treatment of IRA's will most likely affect the fraction deductible in line 5 and the fraction taxable in line 6. Adjust these fractions to conform to any changes in IRA regulations. One change being considered is to adjust the gain from the IRA for inflation before taxing the gain. If you can deduct the initial investment, the fraction taxable will be a Di discount factor read at the inflation rate. Suppose this proposal is adopted, and you expect 5 percent per year inflation in the previous example. Table 9-2 shows that the fraction of your withdrawal that is taxable is a Di discount factor at a 5 percent discount rate and a 20-year investment period. The taxable fraction is 0.3679. If you cannot deduct the initial investment, Table 9-2 shows that the fraction taxable is the difference between discount factors read at the expected inflation rate and the before-tax return from the IRA investment. In this example, the fraction taxable is (0.3679 – 0.1353), or 0.2326. Follow the directions in the form and find your after-tax rate of return in line 12.

Most investors wait until retirement before withdrawing money from their IRA plans. Their incremental tax rates are likely to be lower in retirement than the tax rates when they first invested the money. Not only do these investors benefit from deferring taxes, they might also benefit from a lower tax rate when they do pay the tax.

Example 9-2. An investor with an incremental tax rate of 37 percent invests in a security paying 10 percent interest. Compare his after-tax returns if he:

A. Invests without the benefit of deferred taxes.

B. Invests in an IRA and qualifies for the initial tax savings. He withdraws the proceeds from the IRA after he retires 20 years later. Calculate his rate of return if his incremental tax rate drops to 30 percent after he retires, stays at 37 percent, or increases to 44 percent.

C. Invests in an IRA but has too much income to qualify for the initial tax savings. His incremental tax rate after he retires drops to 30 percent. Explore how the rate of return varies over a range of investment periods.

D. The same as Case C, except that the tax law is changed and taxable gains from the IRA are adjusted for inflation. Calculate the after-tax return if the investor expects 5 percent per year inflation.

Case A: Find the after-tax rate of return by multiplying the before-tax return by the investor's after-tax factor:

$$R = (1-0.37)\,(10) = 6.3\%$$

The after-tax return is 6.3%.

Case B: Calculate the rate of return using Table 9-1. Table 9-3 shows the calculation for a final tax rate of 30 percent. The initial investment is deductible, which makes the fraction in line 5 1.0. Because the initial investment was deductible, withdrawals are fully taxable, and the taxable fraction in line 6 is also 1.0. The after-tax rates of return are:

Final Incremental Tax Rate, %	After-Tax Rate of Return, %
30	10.53
37	10.00
44	9.41

If the incremental tax rate is the same when you withdraw the money as when you first invested the money, the after-tax rate of return is equal to the before-tax return on the IRA investment, even though the proceeds

_____TABLE 9-3_____
IRA Plans—Example 9-2A
Initial Investment Deductible

A. The IRA Investment

1. Rate of Return before Taxes, %   10
2. Time until Investment Recovered, years   20

B. Taxes

3. Divide Incremental Tax Rate (%) at Time of Investment by 100   0.37
4. Divide Incremental Tax Rate (%) at Time of Withdrawal by 100   0.30
5. Fraction of Investment Deductible at Time of Investment   1
6. Fraction of Withdrawal Taxable at Withdrawal   1

C. Rate of Return

7. Multiply Line 5 by Line 3; Subtract the result from 1.0   0.63
8. Multiply Line 6 by Line 4; Subtract the result from 1.0   0.7
9. Divide Line 7 by Line 8   0.9000
10. Enter Line 9 in your calculator and tap the ln(x) key   −0.1054
11. Multiply Line 10 by 100 and Divide by Line 2   −0.527
12. Rate of Return, %: If Line 11 is positive, subtract it from Line 1. If
    Line 11 is negative, add it to Line 1.   10.53

are eventually taxed. If this investor's incremental tax rate drops to 30 percent after he retires, his after-tax return increases by 0.53 percentage points.

Case C: Table 9-4 shows how to calculate the rate of return when you cannot deduct the initial investment from taxable income. The fraction deductible in line 5 is then zero. Table 9-2 shows that the fraction taxable in line 6 is 1.0 minus a Di discount factor. At a 10 percent return and a 20-year time period, the Di discount factor is 0.1353. The fraction taxable is (1.0 − 0.1353), or 0.8647.

The evaluation is for an investment period of 20 years and a final increment tax rate of 30 percent. The after-tax return is 8.50 percent. After-tax returns for investment periods ranging from 1 to 40 years for this example are:

Investment Period, yrs.	Rate of Return, %
1	7.10
5	7.49
10	7.90
20	8.50
30	8.88
40	9.13

TABLE 9-4
IRA Plans—Example 9-2C
Initial Investment Not Deductible

A. The IRA Investment

1. Rate of Return before Taxes, % — 10
2. Time until Investment Recovered, years — 20

B. Taxes

3. Divide Incremental Tax Rate (%) at Time of Investment by 100 — 0.37
4. Divide Incremental Tax Rate (%) at Time of Withdrawal by 100 — 0.30
5. Fraction of Investment Deductible at Time of Investment — 0
6. Fraction of Withdrawal Taxable at Withdrawal — 0.8647

C. Rate of Return

7. Multiply Line 5 by Line 3; Subtract the result from 1.0 — 1
8. Multiply Line 6 by Line 4; Subtract the result from 1.0 — 0.7406
9. Divide Line 7 by Line 8 — 1.3503
10. Enter Line 9 in your calculator and tap the ln(x) key — 0.3003
11. Multiply Line 10 by 100 and Divide by Line 2 — 1.502
12. Rate of Return, %: If Line 11 is positive, subtract it from Line 1. If Line 11 is negative, add it to Line 1. — 8.50

For short investment periods, the rate of return is modestly higher than the 6.3 percent return this investor could earn from the same security and paying normal income taxes. The 8.50 percent return for a 20-year investment is well below the 10.53 percent return this investor could earn if he could deduct the initial investment from his taxable income. As the investment grows in the IRA, the rate of return increases slowly, but never reaches the 10.53 percent return available to lower-income taxpayers who qualify for the initial tax savings. The Tax Reform Act of 1986 makes IRA plans much less attractive for investors who cannot deduct the initial IRA investment from their taxable income.

Case D: This case is worked out in Table 9-5. It is similar to Case C, except that the taxable fraction in line 6 is the difference between Di discount factors read at the inflation rate and at the before-tax return on the IRA investment. At a 5 percent per year inflation rate and a 20-year time period, the Di discount factor is 0.3679. The Di discount factor at the IRA investment's 10 percent return is 0.1353. The fraction taxable in line 6 is the difference between the two, (0.3679−0.1353), or 0.2326.

This change in the tax laws, if enacted, would raise this investor's return from 8.50 percent in Case C to 9.64 percent.

TABLE 9-5
IRA Plans—Example 9-2D
Only Inflation-Adjusted Gain Taxable

A. The IRA Investment

1. Rate of Return before Taxes, %	10
2. Time until Investment Recovered, years	20

B. Taxes

3. Divide Incremental Tax Rate (%) at Time of Investment by 100	0.37
4. Divide Incremental Tax Rate (%) at Time of Withdrawal by 100	0.30
5. Fraction of Investment Deductible at Time of Investment	0
6. Fraction of Withdrawal Taxable at Withdrawal	0.2326

C. Rate of Return

7. Multiply Line 5 by Line 3; Subtract the result from 1.0	1
8. Multiply Line 6 by Line 4; Subtract the result from 1.0	0.9302
9. Divide Line 7 by Line 8	1.0750
10. Enter Line 9 in your calculator and tap the ln(x) key	0.0723
11. Multiply Line 10 by 100 and Divide by Line 2	0.362
12. Rate of Return, %: If Line 11 is positive, subtract it from Line 1. If Line 11 is negative, add it to Line 1.	9.64

TAX-FREE SECURITIES

The interest (but not the capital gain) from some securities is free of taxes. The interest from municipal bonds is free of federal taxes. Use just the state tax rate to find your after-tax income from municipal bonds. If you itemize deductions, multiply the state tax rate by the federal after-tax factor. Interest from federal government bonds is free of state and local taxes. Use just the federal incremental tax rate to find after-tax returns from federal securities.

Suppose an investor with a 33 percent incremental federal tax rate and a 6 percent incremental state tax rate buys a 7 percent municipal bond. If he itemizes deductions, his net state tax rate will be $(1 - 0.33)$ (6), or 4 percent. His state after-tax factor will be $(1 - 0.04)$, or 0.96, and his after-tax return will be (0.96) (7), or 6.72 percent. If he buys an 8 percent federal bond, his after-tax factor will be $(1 - 0.33)$, or 0.67, and his after-tax return will be (0.67) (8), or 5.36 percent.

Tax-free bonds are not as attractive as you might first think. Investors bid the prices of tax-free bonds up to the point where after-tax returns are approximately the same for tax-free and taxable bonds. Tax-free bonds are more attractive to taxpayers with high incremental tax rates.

SUMMARY

☐ Taxes reduce your return from investing in securities and you must take them into account when you evaluate securities. The government taxes investment income at your incremental tax rate—the tax rate on your last dollar of taxable income. Current (1989) federal tax rates are either 15 or 28 percent. More affluent taxpayers pay a 5 percent surcharge, which brings their incremental tax rate to 33 percent.

☐ Income from interest and dividends is taxed as ordinary income. Capital gains used to be taxed at a lower capital gains rate, but the Tax Reform Act of 1986 now taxes capital gains as ordinary income. Future tax laws might again tax capital gains at lower rates.

☐ Incremental state tax rates average 6 percent. If you itemize and deduct state taxes on your federal return, the deduction offsets part of your state tax. Find your net incremental state tax rate by multiplying the gross tax rate by your after-tax factor. An investor with a 33 percent incremental federal tax rate has a federal after-tax factor of $(1-0.33)$, or 0.67. If he itemizes deductions and pays a 6 percent incremental state tax, his net incremental state tax rate drops to $(0.67)(6)$, or 4 percent. His total incremental tax rate is the sum of the 33 percent federal rate and the net 4 percent state rate, or 37 percent.

☐ Find after-tax income by multiplying your before-tax income by your after-tax factor.

☐ Find the rate of return from investing in any security by normal discounted cash flow methods. Convert all cash flows to after-tax cash flows and include capital gains taxes as a negative cash flow. After calculating the after-tax rate of return from investing in the security, subtract the anticipated inflation rate to find the real after-tax rate of return.

☐ Find the maximum price you should pay for any security by converting all of the cash flows from that security to an after-tax basis. Then discount those cash flows at your after-tax opportunity cost.

☐ Tax-deferred savings plans such as company pension plans, (401k) deferred compensation plans, and IRA and Keogh plans are attractive because your money grows faster when taxes are deferred, and the present value of taxes is less. The Tax Reform Act of 1987 makes IRA plans less attractive for investors who cannot deduct the initial investment from taxable income. A calculation form makes IRA plans easy to analyze.

10

Analyzing Financial Data

By NOW, YOU SHOULD UNDERSTAND THE ARITHMETIC OF SECURITY ANALYSIS. THE arithmetic is straightforward. Estimate future cash flows, look up growth or discount factors from a table, substitute those factors in a calculation form, and carry out a prescribed sequence of simple arithmetic.

The arithmetic of security analysis is rigorous. The procedure gives the correct rate of return and maximum allowable price you should pay for any security, given the estimates of growth and profitability you supply. Any errors in the analysis arise from errors in projecting the future growth and profitability of the firm. If you make optimistic forecasts of the firm's growth and profitability, you will calculate optimistic returns for investing in that security. If you make pessimistic projections, you will calculate pessimistic returns. The errors arise from the projections, not from the arithmetic.

Developing reasonable projections for a firm's growth and profitability is a critical part of security analysis. Your evaluation of any security will not be reliable unless the underlying growth and profitability projections are also reliable. Therefore, let's examine how you should analyze a firm and project its future growth and profitability.

The steady-state model in Chapter 6 demonstrated how corporations grow and how that growth causes dividends and stock prices to grow. That model identified the rate of return the firm earns and how fast it grows as the critical factors that determine how attractive any firm and its stock are. The firm will adjust the percentage of earnings it pays out as dividends to be consistent with the return it earns and how fast it grows. The proportions of debt and equity in the firm's capital pool are less critical. The equity and debt fractions are stable and are easy to predict. You must also know the price/earnings ratio the market will pay for that firm's stock. These factors—rate of return, growth rate, and price/earnings ratio—are the critical factors you must forecast from the data available on each firm.

Begin by analyzing the firm's historical performance. What rate of return has the firm earned? Has the return been stable or erratic? Is the rate of return affected by the nation's economy? How fast has the firm grown? Is growth stable? What dividends can you expect? What are the debt and equity fractions in the firm's capital pool? What price/earnings ratio will the market pay for the stock? How does the firm compare to others in the same industry?

Analyzing a firm's historical record establishes the basic financial parameters of the firm, and the stability of those parameters. It also provides a starting point for projecting future performance. Consequently, you need to know how to forecast how these parameters might change in the future.

SOURCES OF COMPANY DATA

The primary source of data for any company is that company's annual report. Many companies also publish a statistical supplement, which provides more detail on the firm's physical and financial operations. Write to the companies you are considering and request copies of both reports. Additional data is also available from the 10K report the company files with the Securities and Exchange Commission.

Several publications provide historical records of financial performance for many firms and a brief analysis of the current outlook for those firms. Valuable reference books for financial data include *Valueline*, the *Standard and Poor's Stock Market Encyclopedia*, and *Moody's Handbook of Common Stocks*. More detailed information about a company is available from *Moody's Industrial Manual*. Your local library should have some or all of these sources.

The historical record tells how the company has performed in the past and shows whether performance was stable or erratic. The historical record is the best measure of the quality of the firm's management. Firms tend to follow historical trends; they do not normally collapse or become highly profitable overnight. Trends do change, however, so before projecting the historical performance into the future, look for any recent developments that might cause the historical trends to change. Several publications discuss recent developments for individual companies, and suggest how those developments might affect future performance. Publications you might find useful include *The Wall Street Transcript*, *Barrons*, and *Forbes*. The *Wall Street Transcript* contains presentations company managements make to security analysts, and a feature called the *Roundtable*. The *Roundtable* focuses on a major industry, and invites analysts who follow that industry to discuss the industry's problems, and the outlook for individual firms in that industry. Your broker might also be able to supply an analysis of the firm you are evaluating.

THE BASIC DATA

The sources previously cited contain much information on individual stocks. This information includes the data you need to evaluate a stock, but not always in the form you need to use the analysis developed in Chapter 6. You will have to make some simple adjustments to the published data.

The most important published data to adjust is reinvested earnings. Reinvested earnings is the only factor that makes equity capital grow in the steady-state model you developed in Chapter 6. This assumption is true for the idealized firm, but is only roughly true for an actual firm. Reinvested earnings are the primary reason equity capital grows, but a variety of other factors also contribute to equity growth. You must allow for these factors, or the growth equation of Chapter 6 will be only roughly, not rigorously, true. The simplest way to allow for these factors is to adjust reinvested earnings to include all of the factors that make stockholder equity grow. Adjust reinvested earnings by redefining reinvested earnings as the year-to-year change in stockholder equity. Reinvested earnings adjusted this way are primarily the reinvested earnings the firm reports, but it also includes all of the other factors that make equity grow.

Your description of the firm must be consistent. When you adjust reinvested earnings, you must also make corresponding adjustments in all the factors that involve reinvested earnings. These factors are reported earnings, rate of return, and the dividend payout fraction, and price/earning ratio. Reported earnings are the sum of dividends and reinvested earnings. You must define adjusted earnings as the sum of dividends and the year-to-year change in stockholder equity. Adjust the rate of return by dividing adjusted earnings by capital employed. Adjust the dividend payout fraction and price/earning ratio by dividing dividends and the stock price by adjusted earnings. Smaller adjustments include calculating average capital employed and the average equity fraction in the capital pool.

Suppose you are interested in growth stocks, and you choose the Hewlett-Packard Company as a possible investment. Your first step will be to read Hewlett-Packard's annual report. Learn about the company's products and the markets it operates in. Collect the basic financial data on the company from the annual report, and from the other sources listed in the *Sources of Company Data* section. Develop a historical record of Hewlett-Packard's performance for at least five years, preferably 10 years.

Most annual reports include a five- or 10-year historical summary of financial results. The calculation form in Table 10-1 will help you extract the key data from this historical summary and make all of the necessary adjustments. Table 10-2 shows how to use this form to analyze Hewlett-Packard. Let's proceed through the table line-by-line and learn how to use it.

Capital Employed

Hewlett-Packard's annual report lists stockholder's equity and long-term debt. You will calculate capital employed, the capital growth rate, the equity fraction in the capital pool, and adjusted reinvested earnings from these data. Line 1 in Table 10-2 lists stockholder's equity. Line 4 lists long-term debt. Both lines come directly from the annual report. Most of a firm's long-term debt is shown under long-term liabilities in the firm's balance sheet. Part of the long-term debt might come due during the year and will be shown separately as a short-term liability. Use the total of both parts of long-term debt. If the firm has preferred stock, add the stock to the debt. Treat preferred stock like debt because the firm pays a fixed dividend on the preferred stock, the same as it pays a fixed interest on its debt. Subtract the prior year's stockholder equity from the current year's stockholder equity to find the year-to-year change in equity in line 3. This change is the adjusted reinvested earnings.

The capital employed is the total of debt and equity (the total of lines 1 and 4) and is shown as line 5. These values of equity, debt and capital employed are year-end values. Earnings are generated over the course of the year. Be consistent when you calculate rate of return, and divide earnings by the average capital employed during the year. Add the current and the previous year's stockholder equity and divide by 2 to find the average stockholder equity in line 2. Calculate average capital employed in line 6 the same way.

The equity fraction measures the average value of equity during the year. The average equity fraction in line 7 is the average equity divided by the average capital employed.

TABLE 10-1
Calculation Form—Analyzing a Firm

A. Capital Structure

Year:

	19	19	19	19	19	19
1. Stockholder Equity, $millions						
2. Average Stockholder Equity						
3. Annual Gain in Stockholder Equity						
4. Long-Term Debt, $millions						
5. Capital Employed: Add Lines 1 and 4						
6. Average Capital Employed, $millions						
7. Equity Fraction: Divide Line 2 by Line 6						

B. Profitability

8. Reported Earnings, $millions						
9. Dividends, $millions						
10. Adjusted Earnings: Add Lines 3 and Line 9						
11. Adjusted/Reported Earnings: Divide Line 10 by Line 8						
12. Rate of Return, %: Divide Line 10 by Line 6; Multiply the result by 100						
13. Dividend Payout Fraction: Divide Line 9 by Line 10						

C. Growth

14. Growth in Capital Employed: Use Table 10-3						

D. Outstanding Stock

15. Number of Shares, millions						
16. Price/Earnings Ratio						
17. Price/Earnings Ratio, S&P 500						
18. Relative Price Earnings Ratio: Divide Line 16 by Line 17						

TABLE 10-2
Analyzing a Firm—Hewlett-Packard

Year:	1976	1977	1978	1979	1980	1981	1982	1983	1984	1985
A. Capital Structure										
1. Stockholder Equity, $millions	677	824	1002	1235	1547	1920	2349	2887	3545	3982
2. Average Stockholder Equity		751	913	1119	1391	1734	2135	2618	3216	3764
3. Annual Gain in Stockholder Equity		147	178	233	312	373	429	538	658	437
4. Long-Term Debt, $millions	8	12	10	15	29	26	39	71	81	102
5. Capital Employed: Add Lines 1 and 4	685	836	1012	1250	1576	1946	2388	2958	3626	4084
6. Average Capital Employed, $millions		761	924	1131	1413	1761	2167	2673	3292	3855
7. Equity Fraction: Divide Line 2 by Line 6		0.99	0.99	0.99	0.98	0.98	0.99	0.98	0.98	0.98
B. Profitability										
8. Reported Earnings, $millions		122	153	203	269	312	383	432	547	489
9. Dividends, $millions		11.4	13.9	21.3	24.1	27.0	30.1	40.8	51.3	56.5
10. Adjusted Earnings: Add Lines 3 and 9		158	192	254	336	400	459	579	709	494
11. Adjusted/Reported Earnings: Divide Line 10 by Line 8		1.30	1.25	1.25	1.25	1.28	1.20	1.34	1.30	1.01
12. Rate of Return, %: Divide Line 10 by Line 6; Multiply the result by 100		20.8	20.8	22.5	23.8	22.7	21.2	21.7	21.5	12.8
13. Dividend Payout Fraction: Divide Line 9 by Line 10		0.072	0.072	0.084	0.072	0.068	0.066	0.070	0.072	0.114
C. Growth										
14. Growth in Capital Employed: Use Table 10-2		19.9	19.1	21.1	23.2	21.1	20.5	21.4	20.4	11.9
D. Outstanding Stock										
15. Number of Shares, $millions		227.8	232.1	236.6	240.9	245.3	250.7	254.9	256.5	256.9
16. Price/Earnings Ratio		18.3	14.5	14.0	14.6	17.8	14.6	24.0	17.7	18.0
17. Price/Earnings Ratio, S&P 500		8.8	8.0	7.4	9.2	7.9	11.4	12.4	9.9	14.8
18. Relative Price/Earnings Ratio: Divide Line 16 by Line 17		2.08	1.81	1.89	1.59	2.25	1.28	1.94	1.79	1.22

Earnings

Earnings in line 8 come directly from the annual report. You are analyzing the firm, not the shareholders. Use total earnings, not earnings per share. Dividends are also taken directly from the annual report and listed in line 9. Adjusted earnings are the sum of dividends and the year-to-year change in stockholder equity. Calculate adjusted earnings in line 10 by adding lines 3 and 9. Adjusted earnings should be reasonably close to reported earnings. The ratio of adjusted to reported earnings in line 11 will be reasonably close to 1.0 if the adjustment is small.

Rate of Return

The adjusted rate of return is adjusted earnings divided by the average capital employed and multiplied by 100 to express the result as a percentage. Line 12 lists Hewlett-Packard's annual rates of return.

Dividend Payout Fraction

The adjusted dividend payout fraction is reported dividends divided by adjusted earnings, and is listed on line 13.

Growth and Shares Outstanding

You will calculate growth rates frequently. The calculation form in Table 10-3 simplifies the calculation, and gives continuous growth rates consistent with the growth factors in Appendix Table A1 and A2. Use this table to calculate the year-to-year capital growth rates in line 14. An example of this calculation is shown in Table 10-4. The number of shares outstanding in line 15 comes directly from the annual report.

Price/Earnings Ratios

A firm's annual report often lists average values of price/earnings ratios. Valueline, Standard and Poor's, and Moody's also report price/earnings ratios. Annual price/earnings ratios for Hewlett-Packard are shown in line 16 of Table 10-1. Price/earnings ratios are more meaningful if you divide them by the price/earnings ratio for the Standard and Poor's 500 stock average. Dividing by the Standard and Poor's average removes the influence of market interest rate. The relative price/earnings ratio measures how investors value the firm relative to all other firms. Relative price/earnings ratios are shown in line 18.

TABLE 10-3
Calculating Growth Rates

1. Most Recent Value _____

2. Earlier Value _____

3. Years between Values in Lines 1 and 2 _____

4. Divide Line 1 by Line 2 _____

5. Enter Line 4 in your calculator and tap the ln(x) key _____

6. Growth Rate, %/yr.: Multiply Line 5 by 100, then divide by Line 3 _____

The simple adjustments outlined in Table 10-1 convert the data that is normally available to you in the form you need to analyze an investment using the model developed in Chapter 6.

ANALYTICAL TOOLS

You need to analyze all of the historical data to develop an understanding of Hewlett-Packard's financial performance and how Hewlett-Packard compares to other companies in the same business. A few simple analytical tools can help you develop this understanding. There are three basic tools. The first tool is for calculating the growth rates of factors like capital employed, earnings, dividends, stock prices, and sales. Growth rates must be continuous so that the calculated rates will be consistent with the growth rates, discount rates, and inflation rates in the growth model. The second tool is for measuring how stable the factors that control the attractiveness of the proposed investment are. It is not enough to know that a firm has some average growth rate and rate of return. You also want to know if those growth rates and rates of return are stable or whether they fluctuate widely from one year to the next. The third tool is for comparing a firm with other firms in the same industry.

Plotting

Financial data is often presented in tables such as Table 10-2. Tables are an excellent way to store data, but a poor way to analyze data. The key data is buried in a mass of less important data. Seeing trends in tables of data is extremely difficult. The process involves plotting the data mentally. Plots show trends and relationships much more clearly than tables do. Therefore, you'll want to move immediately from tables to plots, and analyze the data on graph paper.

There are several types of graph paper that are extremely helpful in analyzing data. Arithmetic paper, in which both the horizontal and vertical scales are simple arithmetic scales, is the most common. Because percentage changes are usually more meaningful than absolute changes, however, graph paper with at least one axis scaled logarithmically is much more useful. Semilog paper has one axis scaled in logarithmic coordinates. Plots on semilog paper are an excellent way to measure growth rates. Log-log paper has both axes scaled in logarithmic coordinates. Probability paper is useful for analyzing stability and for comparing one firm with other firms in the industry. If you are not familiar with these types of graph paper, read Appendix B for directions on how to use them.

Logarithmic scales are particularly useful because equal distances on a logarithmic scale represent equal percentage changes. Percentage changes are usually the most meaningful way to measure change. A one dollar increase in stock price from $1 to $2 per share, for example, is a large change; it represents a doubling in value. On the other hand, the same one dollar increase from 100 to 101 dollars per share is trivial; it represents only a one percent change. Logarithmic scales put such changes in proper perspective. The first change appears large on a logarithmic scale, and the second change appears trivial.

Growth Rates

Figure 10-1 shows two ways to plot financial data. The top plot is an arithmetic plot of Hewlett-Packard's earnings from 1968 through 1985. The earnings scale is a simple

Fig. 10–1
HEWLETT–PACKARD EARNINGS

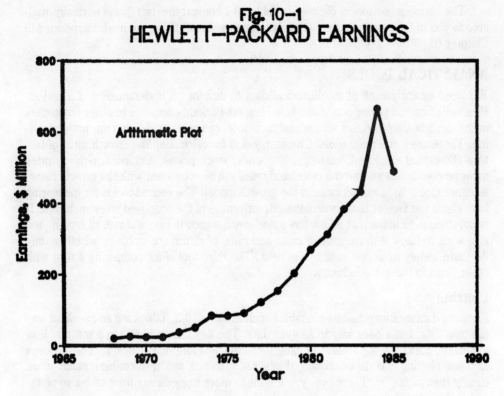

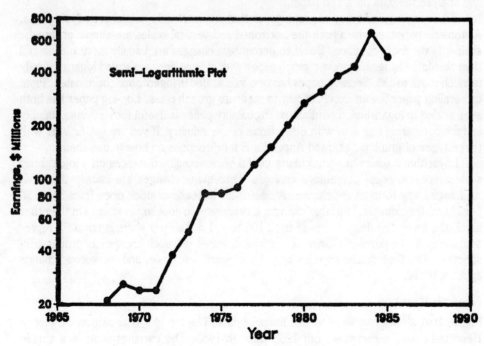

arithmetic scale. Arithmetic plots are usually a poor way to plot data, because they often have a "gee whiz" appearance. In this case, earnings appear to grow slowly in the early 1970s, and then suddenly speed up in later years. The apparent speed-up in growth is deceptive. Despite the steeply rising curve, percentage growth rates might be holding steady, or even declining. Percentage growth rates are more important. You cannot tell from an arithmetic plot whether the percentage growth rate is increasing, holding steady, or falling off.

Semilogarithmic plots avoid this deception. They are much more informative. Take a look at the bottom plot shown in Fig. 10-1. The lower half of Fig. 10-1 contains the same data as the upper half. But the appearance of slow growth during the early years followed by faster growth in the later years in the upper part of Fig. 10-1 does not show up in the lower part. The reverse is true—earnings were growing faster (the curve is steeper) in the earlier years than in the later years.

The great advantage of semilog plots is that any quantity that is growing or decaying at a constant percentage rate plots as a straight line on semilog paper. The slope of the line measures the growth or decay rate. If the quantity is growing, the line slopes upwards to the right. The faster the growth, the steeper the line. If the quantity is decaying, the line will slope downwards to the right. A horizontal line means no growth. If the growth rate is changing, the data plots as a curve instead of a straight line. The slope of the curve at any point measures the growth rate at that point.

Semilog paper shows you immediately whether the variable is growing at a constant percentage growth rate and whether that growth rate is changing with time. You can also judge whether the growth rate is stable or erratic by how badly the data scatters around a curve drawn through the data.

The semilog plot of Hewlett-Packard's earnings is repeated in Fig. 10-2 to illustrate the use of semilog plots for measuring growth rates. The plot shows several straight line segments. Each segment represents a period when Hewlett-Packard's earnings grew at a constant percentage rate. The straight line segment in the early 1970s is steeper than the straight line segment of the later 1970s, but both are steeper than the straight line segment of the 1980s. These changing slopes show that earnings growth was slowing over the period. Growth was fastest during the early 1970s, slower during the later 1970s, and even slower during the 1980s. Growth measured by the calculation form in Table 10-2 for these straight line segments is:

Period	Earnings Growth, %/yr.
1971 – 1974	41
1976 – 1980	26.7
1980 – 1983	16.2

The slope of the straight line drawn through Hewlett-Packard's earnings measures the average growth rate during that time period. Note that the annual earnings do not fall exactly on these straight lines. A straight line drawn between two adjacent data points will, therefore, have a different slope than a straight line drawn through several points. Consequently, year-to-year growth rates are different than the average growth rate over a longer time period. Growth rates over periods longer than one year are more meaningful. They represent more experience and are more stable.

Fig. 10–2
HEWLETT PACKARD EARNINGS

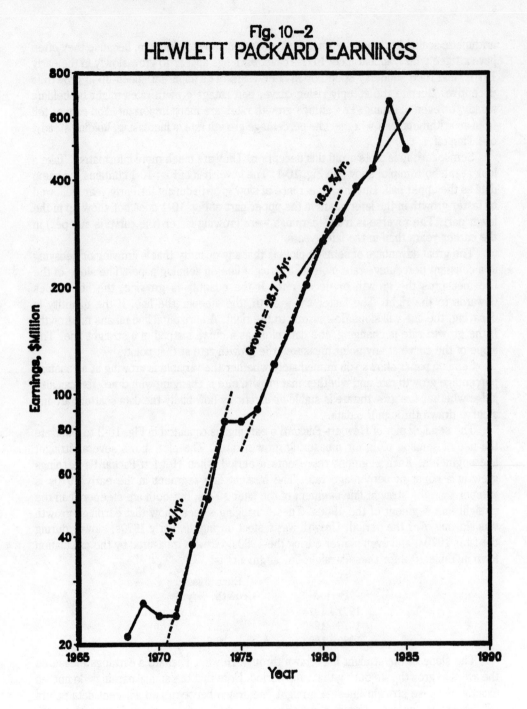

You can easily calculate growth rates using the form in Table 10-2. Draw the best straight line you can through the data on a semilog plot. Read a point at each end of the line, enter the values in Table 11-2, and calculate the growth rate. The best straight line that can be drawn through a set of data is known as a "least-squares" line. Many hand calculators include linear regression, which is the method for calculating the least-squares line. The least-squares growth rate is the slope of that line. Keep in mind that you are working in semilogarithmic coordinates. Use the ln(x) key on your calculator to convert earnings to ln(earnings) before entering the data into your calculator's linear regression program. The least-squares growth rate for Hewlett-Packard's earnings from 1976 through 1980 is 26.77 percent per year, a value that agrees well with the slope of the line drawn by eye.

While least-squares growth rates can be calculated directly on a hand calculator, it is best to plot the data on semilog paper first. Least-squares growth rates are meaningful only for straight-line relationships. The plot identifies the time periods where the data plot is a reasonably straight line. All the data might fall on a straight line or, as in the Hewlett-Packard example, it might fall on several lines of different slope. The plot might also show that a curve fits the data better than a straight line. You might want to measure growth rates at several times. In this case, draw straight lines tangent to the curve at those times, and measure the slopes of the tangent lines.

Plot data like capital employed, earnings, dividends, stock prices, cash flow, book value, and sales, where percentage changes are more important than absolute changes, on semilog paper. Semilog paper is the best way to show whether these factors are growing at constant percentage growth rates or if growth rates are gradually changing with time. Negative numbers and zero cannot be plotted on logarithmic coordinates. If the firm whose earnings you are plotting has occasional losses, you will have to skip those points when plotting earnings. If the firm has many losses, history will not be helpful for projecting how the firm might recover in the future. You might do better to look for another stock.

Growth Multiples

One shortcoming of semilog graph paper is that the data points march to the right the same distance each year, regardless of whether that year was one of economic boom or one of economic bust. A horizontal scale that reflects the health of the economy in each year rather than just the passage of time is more informative. The data points then march to the right each year a distance proportional to the strength of the economy in that year. In severe recessions, the data might retrogress for a year or two, and move back to the left.

The logarithm of some measure of economic activity, such as Gross National Product (GNP), is a good choice for the horizontal scale. The GNP series is available both in current dollars and in constant dollars, that is, dollars deflated to dollars of constant purchasing power. Use the current dollar series because data from annual reports are in current dollars. A plot of log (earnings) against log (GNP) is a log-log plot, because both the vertical and horizontal scales are logarithmic.

The GNP is a gross measure of economic activity. You might be able to focus on a more appropriate measure of economic activity for the particular stock you are considering. If you are considering the stock of a defense contractor, for example, you might substitute federal spending on defense in place of GNP. For a company making household furnishings, you might substitute consumer spending on durable goods. As long as you stay with major components of the GNP, you should be able to find published forecasts for those components.

The horizontal scale is usually too compressed on normal log-log graph paper because the economy does not grow enough in a five- to 10-year period. An easy way to expand the horizontal scale is to switch to semilog paper. Use the ln(x) key on your calculator to convert the GNP to ln(GNP), and plot ln(GNP) on the horizontal arithmetic

Fig. 10-3
HEWLETT–PACKARD
EARNINGS GROWTH MULTIPLE

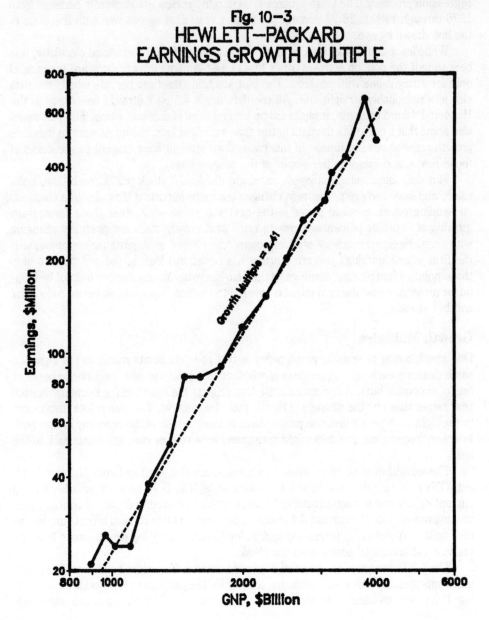

scale. The result is still a log-log plot, but you can now expand the ln(GNP) scale to any convenient width.

Figure 10-3 shows Hewlett-Packard's earnings plotted against current-dollar GNP on log-log graph paper. The data plots more smoothly because the ln(GNP) scale compensates for annual fluctuations in economic activity. The slope of a log-log plot is a critical measure of growth called the growth multiple. Growth multiples give growth in earnings, dividends, capital, etc., as a multiple of growth in the GNP. You might expect current dollar GNP to grow 8 percent per year. You would then expect a firm with a growth multiple of 1.5 to grow (1.5) (8), or 12 percent per year.

The growth multiple is calculated just like the growth rate—by measuring the slope of the best straight line you can draw through the data. Table 10-4 simplifies the calculation of growth multiples. Draw the best straight line through the data, read a point at each end of the line, enter the data in Table 10-5, and calculate the growth multiple.

Table 10-6 works out the growth multiple for Hewlett-Packard. Draw the best straight line through Hewlett-Packard's earnings in Fig. 10-3, and read earnings of $750 million at one end at a GNP of $4,331 billion, and earnings of $16.3 million at a GNP of $884 billion at the other. Hewlett-Packard's growth multiple is 2.41, as worked out in Table 10-5. During the 1972 – 1983 period, Hewlett-Packard's earnings grew 2.41 times as fast as the GNP.

Growth multiples are extremely useful because they not only measure growth, they also tie growth into the growth of the national economy. Forecasts of economic growth are widely available. *The Blue Chip Indicators*, a widely-quoted newsletter pub-

---

TABLE 10-4
Hewlett-Packard Capital Growth from 1977 to 1978

1. Most Recent Value	924
2. Earlier Value	761
3. Years between Values in Lines 1 and 2	1
4. Divide Line 1 by Line 2	1.214
5. Enter Line 4 in your calculator and tap the ln(x) key	0.1941
6. Growth Rate, %/yr.: Multiply Line 5 by 100, then divide by Line 3	19.41

TABLE 10-5
Calculating Growth Multiples

1. Most Recent Value	_____
2. GNP at that Time	_____
3. Earlier Value	_____
4. GNP at the time of Line 3	_____
5. Divide Line 1 by Line 3. Enter in your calculator and tap the ln(x) key	_____
6. Divide Line 2 by Line 4. Enter in your calculator and tap the ln(x) key	_____
7. Growth Multiple: Divide Line 5 by Line 6	_____

_____*TABLE 10-6*_____
Growth Multiple for Hewlett-Packard Earnings

1. Most Recent Value	750
2. GNP at that Time	4,331
3. Earlier Value	16.3
4. GNP at the time of Line 3	884
5. Divide Line 1 by Line 3. Enter in your calculator and tap the ln(x) key	3.8289
6. Divide Line 2 by Line 4. Enter in your calculator and tap the ln(x) key	1.5891
7. Growth Multiple: Divide Line 5 by Line 6	2.41

lished in Sedona, Arizona, regularly collects and publishes forecasts of a group of economists. Each November, *Business Week* magazine collects the GNP forecasts from a large group of analysts, and report both the individual forecasts and the average forecast of the group.

Growth companies grow faster than the GNP, and, therefore, have growth multiples higher than 1.0. As these firms mature, the growth multiple gradually falls and eventually reaches 1.0 at maturity. If the growth multiple is decaying, a log-log plot will show curvature instead of a straight line. Proceed just as you did with curvature in semilog plots. Draw tangents to the curve at several points. The slopes of these tangent lines are the growth multiples at those times.

A reasonable projection for a growth company is that growth will begin at the current growth multiple. The growth multiple will gradually decay as the company matures and approach a long-run limit of 1.0. At maturity, growth will slow to the growth rate of the national economy. The decay model in Fig. 7-2 can be used to project future values of the growth multiple. Economists predict long-run growth in real GNP of about 3 percent per year, and long-run inflation at about 5 percent per year. Current dollar GNP grows at the sum of real GNP growth and the inflation rate, in this case 5 percent plus 3 percent, or 8 percent per year. At a growth multiple of 2.41, you might project Hewlett-Packard's current earnings to grow (2.41) (8), or 19.3 percent per year. Growth should gradually slow to 8 percent per year as the growth multiple approaches 1.0 at maturity.

After a period of maturity, firms normally enter a period of decline. Growth might slow from the GNP growth rate to the population growth rate, or even lower. Population growth is about one percent per year. If you expect growth to approach population growth as a long-run limit, use a real, long-run limiting growth rate of 1 percent per year. Nominal growth is the sum of the real growth and the inflation rate, approximately 1 percent plus 5 percent, or 6 percent per year.

Stability

In addition to measuring the absolute levels of variables such as growth, rate of return, dividend payout fraction, and the like, you also want to know how stable those variables are. A firm might have earned an average return of 15 percent over the past 10 years. You will feel much more confident about that stock if that 15 percent came from averaging 10 annual returns that varied narrowly between 14 and 16 percent than if it came from 10 annual returns that ranged from −5 to +23 percent.

A series of annual measurements of variables like rate of return, growth rate, etc., do not scatter in a haphazard way around the average value. These variables tend to distribute themselves around the average value in a systematic way. Statisticians call the way measurements distribute themselves around the average value the normal distribution.

The normal distribution is an excellent way to measure both the average value of a variable, such as rate of return, and the range over which the return is likely to fluctuate. The normal distribution of rates of return for two firms, both of which earn a 15 percent average return, are shown in Fig. 10-4. The height of the distribution shows the relative likelihood of reaching any rate of return. The distribution is highest at the average return. Therefore, the average return is the most likely return. The distribution falls off on either side of the average. Therefore, returns that differ from the average return are less likely. The farther the return is from the average, the lower the distribution curve is, and the less likely is that return. Most returns are reasonably close to the average return. Only a few lie far from the average.

Firm A in Fig. 10-4 is stable. Its rates of return fluctuate in a narrow band. Firm B is much less stable. Its rates of return fluctuate in a much broader band. It takes only two

Fig. 10−4
RATE OF RETURN STABILITY

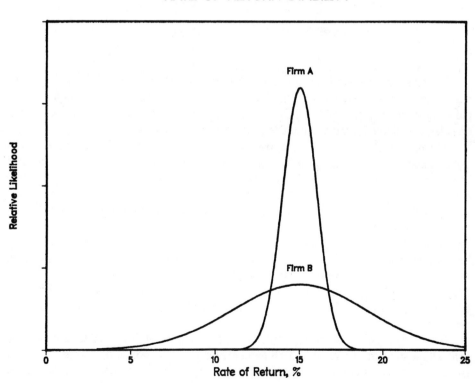

measures to completely define normal distributions such as those shown in Fig. 10-4. One measure is the average result, which locates the peak of the curve. The second measure is the standard deviation, which measures how broadly the distribution spreads.

The standard deviation is an excellent way to measure the stability of factors such as rate of return and growth rate, and to compare the stability of different firms. The standard deviation is extremely informative because it is linked to probability. If you know the standard deviation, you can find the probability that the factor you are estimating will lie in any given range.

Many hand calculators automatically calculate both the average and the standard deviation of a set of observations. Check the instructions for your calculator for obtaining the average and standard deviation for a set of observations. Try calculating Hewlett-Packard's average rate of return and standard deviation from the data in Table 10-2. You should find an average return of 16.72 percent and a standard deviation of 1.79 percentage points.

The standard deviation is useful because it tells you how confident you can be that a variable lies in any given range. If you insist on 100 percent confidence, the range must be infinite because the variable could have any value. If you are willing to settle for something less, say, 95 percent confidence, the range narrows to a useful one. The confidence range is a multiple of the standard deviation. The confidence level multiples are:

Confidence Level	Multiple of Standard Deviation
50	0.67
80	1.28
90	1.65
95	1.96
99	2.58

For example, the confidence multiple for 95 percent confidence extends approximately two standard deviations on either side of the average value. The confidence multiple is somewhat higher with small samples of data. Appendix Table A5 lists values of the confidence multiple for various confidence levels and sample sizes.

Try applying Appendix Table A5 to estimating the likely range of rates of return you should expect for Hewlett-Packard. The average of the nine Hewlett-Packard rates of return shown in Table 10-2 is 16.72 percent. The standard deviation is 1.79 percent. The confidence multiple for 50 percent confidence with nine observations is 0.703. Therefore, you can be 50 percent confident, barring a basic change in Hewlett-Packard's performance, that a future return will fall within 16.72 plus or minus (0.703) (1.79), or within 16.72 plus or minus 2.24 percent. The confidence range broadens if you want to be more confident about the rate of return. At 90 percent confidence, the confidence multiple is 1.833. The rate of return is likely to fall in the wider band of 16.72 plus or minus (1.833) (3.18), or 20.87 plus or minus 5.83 percent. At the 90 percent confidence level, one return out of 10 should lie outside this band. One does—the 12.8 percent return in 1985.

Standard deviations provide a direct way to compare the stability of different firms. A firm with a standard deviation of 6.36 percent, for example, would have rates of return twice as unstable as Hewlett-Packard's. If you compare standard deviations for several firms, be sure to measure them over the same time period so that all firms in the sample experience the same pattern of economic growth and recession.

Firm A in Fig. 10-4 has a tight distribution; the standard deviation is only 1 percent. Rate of return is stable. If this stability continues, 90 percent of future rates of return can be expected to lie within plus or minus (1.833) (1), or within 1.833 percentage points of the average return. Firm B's standard deviation is 4 percent. Firm B is four times more unstable than Firm A. Ninety percent of its future rates of return are likely to lie within (1.833) (4), or 7.33 percentage points of the average return.

The normal distribution also permits you to judge whether an observation differs enough from all of the others that it can be considered an outlier. Something is different about that observation. A group of observations that all belong to the same family scatter around the average result according to the normal distribution. Ninety-five percent of the observations for large samples should lie within two standard deviations of the average result. Any observation that differs from the average result by more than about three standard deviations can be considered an outlier. It does not have the same characteristics as the other observations. In some way, that observation is different from the others.

Probability Graph Paper

A useful application of the normal distribution is testing whether there are any unusually good or unusually poor firms in an industry. If you would like to know, for example, whether any firm has an unusually high or an unusually low rate of return, growth rate, or price/earnings ratio. Suppose none of the firms in an industry is unusual. You would then find just the normal scatter of rates of return, growth rates, and price/earnings ratios around the average values for that industry. These values should fit a normal distribution. If any firm is unusual, it should lie off the normal distribution.

A special type of graph paper called probability paper is used for such tests. Probability paper has a horizontal probability scale specially constructed so that any set of results that fit a normal distribution will plot as a straight line. If none of the firms in an industry has an unusual rate of return, then the rates of return for the firms in that industry should plot as a reasonably straight line on probability paper. A firm with an unusually high rate of return will plot above the line established by the other firms. A firm with an unusually poor rate of return will plot below the line.

ANALYSIS OF HEWLETT-PACKARD DATA

How can you use these basic tools to analyze Hewlett-Packard's performance? The most critical factors are the rate of return Hewlett-Packard earns and how fast it grows. You should examine these factors more carefully and compare Hewlett-Packard to other firms in the computer industry. To aid in this comparison, Table 10-7 lists data for 28 firms in the computer industry from 1981 to 1985.

Rate of Return

The best way to compare Hewlett-Packard's returns with the other computer companies is to plot the returns on probability paper as shown in Fig. 10-5. If you are not familiar with probability paper, you can read about how to use it in Appendix C.

TABLE 10-7
Performance of Computer Firms, 1981 – 1985

Firm	Rate of Return, %		Capital Growth, %/yr.		P/E Ratio
	Average	Standard Deviation	Average	Standard Deviation	
Ahmdal	7.6	3.6	17.1	11.2	26.2
Apollo Computer	−1.4	31.4	90	56.7	33.3
Apple Computer	23.3	10.8	14.7	11.9	12.4
Burroughs	7.9	2.0	4.0	8.9	12.2
Centronics	−11.1	12.5	−8.3	34.5	—
Commodore	24.6	33.0	35.1	42.5	—
Computervision	12.1	14.0	21.3	24.4	—
Control Data	7.6	7.7	−0.7	21.6	—
Convergent Technology	10.3	9.3	87.5	80.8	61
Cray Research	19.0	5.3	26.2	15.1	21.8
Data General	7.4	3.0	13.3	8.5	50
Datapoint	4.2	10.5	12.1	42.3	26.9
Dataproducts	7.8	4.4	6.8	9.1	18.4
Digital Equipment	10.9	3.0	17.5	5.4	15.7
Gerber Scientific	13.1	4.8	24.5	17.0	11.8
Hewlett-Packard	16.3	2.0	19.6	4.0	19.3
Honeywell	10.2	1.1	5.5	4.3	11.5
Integraph	24.0	4.0	58.2	36.6	18.5
IBM	21.4	2.6	12.9	3.6	13.2
NCR Corp.	12.6	1.4	4.0	4.8	13.3
Paradyne	6.0	10.8	27.3	26.5	27.2
Prime Computer	17.8	4.0	18.0	3.4	17.3
SCI Systems	12.8	1.0	43.8	24.3	12.8
Seagate Technology	31.8	30.1	114	91	9.7
Sperry Corp.	7.5	1.4	6.0	4.2	15.9
Tandem Computer	12.2	4.3	31.7	39.5	20.9
Telex	20.6	4.6	25.3	20.5	11.4
Wang Labs B	13.4	5.8	30.2	15.6	56

Note that the data points lie reasonably close to a straight line. The average unadjusted return for the 28-company group is 12.5 percent, as read at the midpoint (the 50 percent point) of the distribution. The standard deviation is 8.0 percent. All of the points lie close to the straight line, which indicates that no firm had an unusually high or an unusually low rate of return. The top firm, Seagate Technology, and the bottom firm, Centronics, had the returns one should expect for the highest and the lowest firm in a sample of 28 firms with a standard deviation of 8.0 percent.

Hewlett-Packard's 16.7 percent rate of return was higher than the returns for 70 percent of the firms in this industry. Only eight firms—Seagate Technology, Commodore, Intergraph, Apple, IBM, Telex, Cray Research, and Prime Computer—had higher returns. You might want to expand your search and examine these stocks as potential investments.

Fig. 10–5
RATE OF RETURN

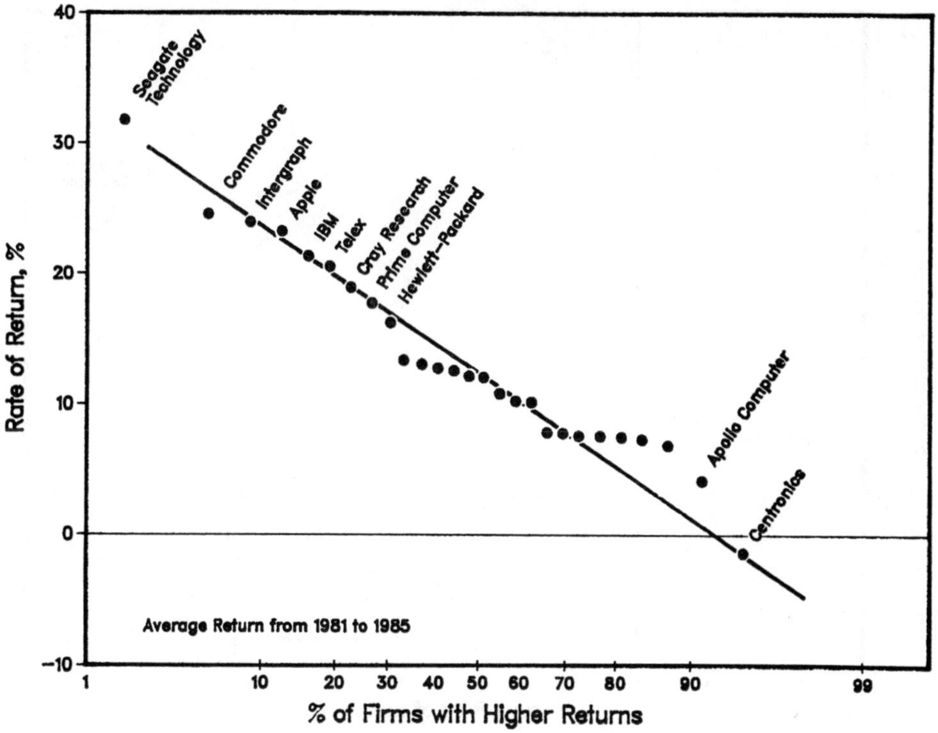

Average Return from 1981 to 1985

(Y-axis: Rate of Return, %)
(X-axis: % of Firms with Higher Returns)

Data points labeled: Seagate Technology, Commodore, Intergraph, Apple, IBM, Telex, Cray Research, Prime Computer, Hewlett-Packard, Apollo Computer, Centronics

Stability of Rate of Return

The rate of return should be stable as well as high. Returns should scatter in a narrow band rather than a wide band. Figure 10-6 shows the standard deviation of the rate of return plotted against the average return for the same companies. The desirable combination of high returns and low standard deviations are to the right of the plot near the horizontal axis.

Hewlett-Packard shows up well in this comparison. Seventeen firms had standard deviations below about 5 percent. Six firms, including Hewlett-Packard, also have average returns higher than 15 percent. Five firms—Intergraph, IBM, Telex, Cray Research, and Prime Computer—had higher average returns than Hewlett-Packard and standard deviations below about 5 percent.

Seagate Technology and Commodore, the firms with the highest average returns in Fig. 10-5, do not look so attractive in Fig. 10-6. Their returns were unstable, with standard deviations of 30 and 33 percent, respectively. If you were to make your selection on the basis of high and stable rates of return, Figs 10-5 and 10-6 show that six firms—Intergraph, IBM, Telex, Cray Research, Prime Computer, and Hewlett-Packard—are the best candidates.

Fig. 10-6
STABILITY OF RATE OF RETURN

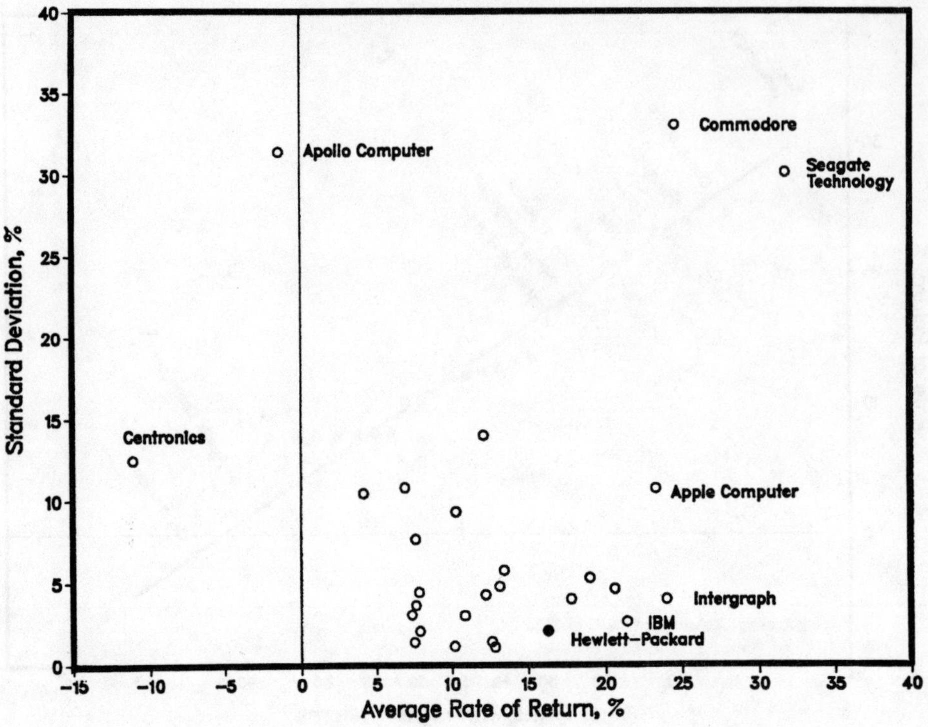

Capital Growth

Least-squares capital growth rates measured for year-end data from 1980 through 1985, are plotted on probability paper in Fig. 10-7. Most firms lie on a straight line passing through an average capital growth rate of 20 percent per year at the midpoint of the distribution. Five firms—Seagate Technology, Apollo Computer, Convergent Technology, Intergraph, and SCI System—had unusually high capital growth. Data points for these firms lie above the line drawn through the other companies. Hewlett-Packard lies at the midpoint of the distribution, which indicates that capital growth rate was average for this industry.

Stability of Capital Growth

Figure 10-8 contrasts the stability of capital growth, as measured by the standard deviation of the five annual capital growth rates from 1980 to 1985, with the growth rate for the period. Firms with high, stable capital growth lie to the right of the plot near the horizontal axis. Beyond a capital growth of about 20 percent per year, however, none of the firms lie near the horizontal axis. Very high growth is associated with instability— with high standard deviations.

Fig. 10–7
CAPITAL GROWTH RATE

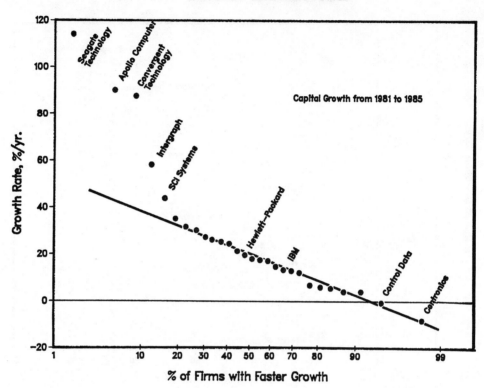

There appears to be a boundary, suggested by the slanting dashed line, that shows the most stability you can expect at any given growth rate. According to this line, capital growth becomes unstable above about 20 percent per year. Hewlett-Packard lies at that point, with a capital growth of 19.6 percent per year and a standard deviation of 4 percent. The firms with exceptional capital growth—Seagate Technology, Apollo Computer, and Convergent Technology—have very unstable growth, with standard deviations ranging from 56 to 91 percent.

Price/Earnings Ratios

The price you have to pay to participate in this industry is a critical element in the analysis. The price/earnings ratios for this group of computer stocks in mid-1986 are plotted on probability paper in Fig. 10-9. Price/earnings ratios are plotted on a logarithmic scale because percentage changes in price/earnings ratios are more meaningful than absolute changes.

Hewlett-Packard's price/earnings ratio of 19 is about average for the group. Forty percent of the companies in the group are more expensive than Hewlett-Packard, while 60 percent are less expensive. Convergent Technology, Wang, and Data General have unusually high price/earnings ratios, as shown by their location above the curve estab-

Fig. 10-8
STABILITY OF CAPITAL GROWTH

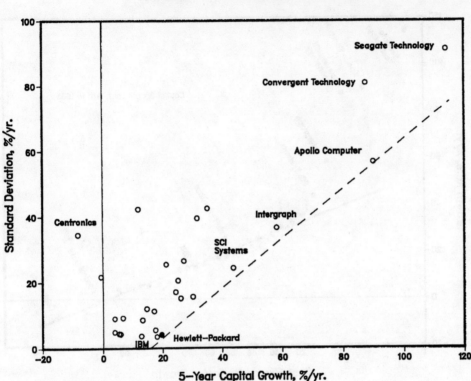

lished by the other companies. Seagate Technology, Telex, Honeywell, and Gerber Scientific are the least expensive companies.

Three companies—IBM, Prime Computer, and Hewlett-Packard—stood out in Figs. 10-6 and 10-8 as having both high and stable rates of return and high and stable capital growth. IBM is the least expensive of this group, with a price/earnings ratio of 13. Prime is slightly less costly than Hewlett-Packard with a price/earnings ratio of 17. You might want to look more carefully at IBM and Prime Computer.

Basis for Hewlett-Packard Evaluation

This analysis of Hewlett-Packard applies to Hewlett-Packard's historical performance. There is no assurance that Hewlett-Packard will perform as well in the future as it has in the past. You must decide how much of this historical performance will continue in the future. You will have to judge which elements of performance to modify when you project Hewlett-Packard's future.

The computer industry entered a slump in 1985. This slump affected Hewlett-Packard, as shown by the drop in its rate of return from 21.5 percent in 1984 to 12.8 percent in 1985. Capital growth also slowed from 20.4 to 11.9 percent per year. While the industry is likely to recover from the slump, it is by no means assured that the rate of return

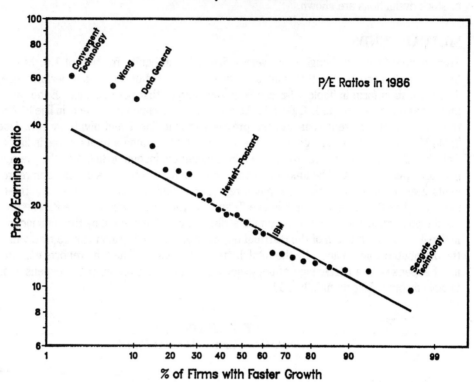

Fig. 10-9
PRICE/EARNINGS RATIO

and capital growth will recover to pre-slump levels. The computer industry is maturing, and you should expect some drop in return and slowing of growth.

You will need to use your own judgment in estimating the rate of return and capital growth rate Hewlett-Packard might recover to. Because Hewlett-Packard is a growth stock, you also need to project how fast the rate of return, capital growth rate, and the price/earnings ratio will decay towards their long-run limits. Hewlett-Packard's debt and equity fractions are stable and can be projected at their current values. The following table shows one reasonable set of assumptions about Hewlett-Packard's future performance:

	Initial Value	Half-Life, yrs.	Long-Run Value
Rate of Return	16	7	12
Capital Growth Rate	18	7	9
Price/Earnings Ratio	19	7	13
Equity Fraction	0.975	–	0.975
Share Growth Rate, %/yr.	1.8	–	–

Be wary about accepting someone else's estimates of how any company will perform in the future. Analyze the historical record along the lines suggested in this chapter, then make your own assessment of how that firm is likely to perform in the future. This analysis of Hewlett-Packard continues in Chapter 15, where several practical examples of stock evaluations are shown.

MUTUAL FUNDS

Treat mutual funds as though they were a firm with an equity fraction of 1.0. Mutual funds publish a prospectus that contains a historical record of the fund's performance. The calculation form in Table 10-8 can help you analyze that performance. Enter year-end net asset values in line 1. Calculate the average asset value for the year in line 2. Add the entry for the current year and the previous year in line 1 and divide by two. Use Table 10-3 to find the annual growth rates in line 3. List the fund's total income in line 4. Calculate the fund's rate of return in line 5 by dividing the income in line 4 by the average net asset value in line 2. The fund will report how much of each year's distribution represents investment income and how much represents capital gains. List the investment income in line 6, the capital gains in line 7, and the total distribution in line 8. The dividend payout fraction in line 9 is the total distribution in line 8 divided by the total income in line 4. Find the fraction of the distribution taxed as a capital gain in line 10 by dividing the distributed gains in line 7 by the total distribution in line 8. The fund reports management expenses as a percentage of net asset value. You must report those expenses as taxable income. List them in line 11.

TABLE 10-8
Calculation Form—Mutual Funds

	19___	19___	19___	19___	19___
1. Net Asset Value, $/share year end					
2. Average NAV, $/share					
3. NAV Growth, %/yr.					
4. Total Fund Income, $/share					
5. Rate of Return, % (Line 4/Line 2) × 100					
Distributions					
6. Interest					
7. Capital Gains					
8. Total					
9. Dividend Payout Fraction (Line 8/Line 4)					
10. Capital Gains, % (Line 7/Line 8) × 100					
11. Fund Expense, % of NAV					
Average Results					
12. Rate of Return, Average					
13. Rate of Return, Standard Deviation					
14. Total Income					
15. Total Distributions					
16. Payout Fraction: Divide Line 15 by Line 14					
17. Least-Squares NAV Growth, %/yr.					
18. Consistent Rate of Return: Subtract Line 16 from 1.0. Divide the result into Line 17					

The bottom section of the calculation form completes the analysis. Find the fund's average rate of return and the standard deviation of those returns in lines 12 and 13. Your hand calculator should develop these results automatically. The standard deviation measures how stable the fund's rate of return is. Calculate these results for the whole period and for the most recent five years. Compare the two results to determine whether the fund's return is steady or falling.

Simple averages for factors like rate of return, dividend payout fraction, and growth rate are apt to be distorted by wild values in any given year. It is better to work with averages that are not as sensitive to occasional wild values. Calculate an average dividend payout fraction in line 16 by adding dividends in line 15 for a period of years and dividing by total income in line 14 for the same period. Calculate a least-squares growth rate for net asset value for the same period in line 17. Use your calculator's regression program to calculate the growth rate. Remember to convert net assets to the natural logarithm of net assets before you enter that value in your calculator's regression program. Calculate an average rate of return that is consistent with the dividend payout and net asset growth rate in line 18. Find the average return by subtracting the dividend payout fraction in line 18 from 1.0 and dividing the result into the growth rate in line 17.

Table 10-9 shows how you would use this calculation form to analyze the Magellan Fund, which is a popular stock mutual fund. The entries in lines 1, 4, 6, 7, 8, and 11 come directly from the fund's prospectus. Develop the rest of the entries as previously outlined.

The Magellan Fund has averaged a 25.2 percent return over the 1981–1989 period, and an 18 percent average return over the most recent five years. Returns are unstable, however, the standard deviation is slightly larger than the average return. This instability makes it difficult to forecast the fund's future returns. Least-squares asset growth in line 17 is 10.5 percent per year for the whole period, and 7.4 percent per year for the most recent five years. The average dividend payout fraction in line 16 is 0.51 for the whole period, and 0.58 for the most recent five years. The rate of return in line 18 that is consistent with this average dividend payout and growth rate is 21.4 percent for the whole period, and 17.6 percent for the most recent five years.

This evaluation of the Magellan Fund continues in the next chapter, which includes a calculation form for evaluating mutual funds. The Magellan Fund will be evaluated based on the analysis in Table 10-9.

AFTER THE INVESTMENT

After you have invested in a stock, track the stock. See whether the firm is living up to your projections of growth and profitability. Check whether the price of the stock is growing as you anticipated.

Tracking Stock Prices

Stock prices can be tracked simply by plotting the stock price against time. There are several additional steps you can take to make the plot more informative. The first step is to plot stock prices on semilog paper. Follow percentage changes in price rather than absolute changes. Remember that a one dollar gain from $1 to $2 per share doubles your money, while that same one dollar gain from $100 to $101 per share is only a 1 percent

TABLE 10-9
Magellan Fund
Dollar Amounts in Dollars per Share

	1989	1988	1987	1986	1985	1984	1983	1982	1981
1. Net Asset Value, $/share year end	52.92	44.10	59.85	55.34	37.69	35.21	34.25	19.68	29.82
2. Average NAV, $/share	48.51	51.98	57.60	46.52	36.45	34.73	26.97	24.75	22.60
3. NAV Growth, %/yr.	18.2	−30.5	7.8	38.4	6.8	2.8	55.4	−41.6	66.2
4. Total Fund Income, $/share	9.72	−6.01	11.81	20.08	6.54	3.10	16.13	0.36	14.96
5. Rate of Return, % (Line 4/Line 2) × 100	20.0	−11.6	20.5	43.2	17.9	8.9	59.8	1.5	66.2

Distributions

	1989	1988	1987	1986	1985	1984	1983	1982	1981
6. Interest	0.90	0.72	0.46	0.65	0.37	0.26	0.33	0.58	0.39
7. Capital Gains	—	9.02	6.84	1.78	3.69	1.88	1.23	9.92	0.13
8. Total	0.90	9.74	7.30	2.43	4.06	2.14	1.56	10.50	0.52
9. Dividend Payout Fraction (Line 8/Line 4)	0.093	−1.621	0.618	0.121	0.621	0.690	0.097	−29.2	0.035
10. Capital Gains, % (Line 7/Line 8) × 100	0	92.6	93.7	73.3	90.9	87.9	78.9	94.5	25.0
11. Fund Expense, % of NAV	1.08	1.14	1.08	1.08	1.12	1.04	0.85	1.34	1.23

Average Results

	Total Period	Last 5 Years
12. Rate of Return, Average	25.2	18.0
13. Rate of Return, Standard Deviation	26.2	19.5
14. Total Income	76.69	42.14
15. Total Distributions	39.15	24.43
16. Payout Fraction: Divide Line 15 by Line 14	0.51	0.58
17. Least-Squares NAV Growth, %/yr.	10.5	7.39
18. Consistent Rate of Return: Subtract Line 16 from 1.0. Divide the result into Line 17	21.4	17.6

gain. Semilog plots are more informative because they show these changes in proper perspective.

Add perspective to the plot by adding, say, the last five years of historical stock prices to the plot. Also, plot your projected prices as determined by your projection of earnings and the price/earnings ratio. You can then tell whether the stock is following your price forecast and whether current price behavior is a continuation or a break from past performance.

Track the growth rate of the stock price by recalling that any quantity that grows at a constant percentage rate plots as a straight line on semilog graph paper. Measure the growth rate of the stock's price by drawing a straight line through the data and measuring its slope. Price data tend to be "noisy"; prices tend to scatter around the line rather than lie exactly on the line. Draw the best straight line you can through the cloud of data points. Don't be alarmed by an occasional point lying off the line. But a series of points departing from the line may signal the beginning of a new price trend.

If stock prices fall on a curved line instead of a straight line, you know that the growth rate is changing. You can measure changing growth rates by drawing straight lines, tangent to the curve, at several points along the curve, and measuring the slopes of these lines.

Relative Stock Price

The price of the stock might change because of a change in the outlook for the firm or because of a change in market interest rates. You can separate changes caused by the firm from changes caused by the market by tracking changes in the price of the stock relative to the average price of all stocks. First, develop an initial reference point by dividing the price at which you buy the stock by the price of the Standard and Poor's stock average at that time. Then track the ratio of the stock price to the price of the Standard and Poor's average stock. Convert this ratio to a price index by dividing the ratio by the initial reference point at the time you bought the stock. Multiply by 100 to make the index start at 100.

Plot this price index on semilog paper. The slope of the best straight line through the data measures the growth of the stock relative to the growth of the market. If the price of the stock increases faster than the market, the price index will grow above 100, and the data points will lie on a line sloping upwards to the right. If the stock grows only as fast as the market, the data points will lie on a horizontal line. If the stock grows more slowly than the market, the price index will fall below 100 and the data points will lie on a line sloping downward to the right.

Effect of the Economy

Changes in the price of the stock could also reflect ups and downs in the national economy. You can allow for changes in the economy by substituting some measure of the economy, such as the GNP, for time. Plot stock prices and relative prices against the GNP on log-log graph paper. Stock prices should then move a horizontal distance that depends on the health of the economy during that time period. The slope of such log-log plots measures the growth in the price of the stock as a multiple of the growth of the economy. Use the GNP in current dollars because stock prices are in current dollars.

Periods of one quarter are the shortest periods you can plot in this way, because the GNP data is only available quarterly. These plots will also be too cramped in the horizontal direction if you use normal log-log paper. You can avoid this difficulty by converting the GNP to ln(GNP) on your calculator, and plotting stock price against ln (GNP) on semilog graph paper. The horizontal scale is still a log scale because you have converted the GNP to ln(GNP). Adjust the horizontal ln(GNP) scale to spread the data points a convenient distance apart. Other measures of the economy, such as consumer spending on durable goods, or federal spending on defense, might be more appropriate than the GNP, depending on the business of the firm.

Growth and Earnings

Update the analysis that led you to invest in the stock as soon as the firm's next financial report becomes available. Plot sales and earnings on semilog paper, and add several years of historical data so you can judge whether current data represents a departure from historical trends. These plots are more useful if you plot sales and earnings against ln(GNP) instead of against time. You can then make an allowance for the strength of the economy in each quarter.

SUMMARY

☐ Make a few simple adjustments to published data on a firm. Adjust earnings, rate of return on capital employed, average capital employed, and the average equity fraction to put the financial data normally available into the form needed for the evaluation models developed in this book.

☐ The best way to understand the story financial data has to tell is to plot the data. Percentage changes are usually more meaningful than absolute changes. Plot the data on logarithmic scales, because distances on a logarithmic scale measure percentage changes. Semilog plots, in which one scale is logarithmic, are useful for interpreting growth rates. A quantity that grows at a constant percentage rate plots as a straight line on semilog paper. If the growth rate is changing, the data plots as a curved line. Plotting data, such as earnings, capital, and dividends, against the logarithm of some measure of economic activity, such as the GNP, is more informative. The slope of these log-log plots is the growth multiple, which gives the growth of the firm as a multiple of the growth in the economy.

☐ The standard deviation is the best way to measure the stability of a firm's rate of return and capital growth rate. Plot rate of return against the standard deviation of rate of return for all of the firms in an industry to locate firms with high and stable rates of return. Locate firms with rapid and stable capital growth in the same way.

☐ Identify firms with unusually high or unusually low rates of return, capital growth, and price/earnings ratios by plotting those factors on probability paper for all of the firms in an industry. If those firms have just the normal scatter of results, the data plots as a straight line. Firms with unusually high results plot above the line; and firms with unusually poor results, plot below the line.

☐ Treat mutual funds as a firm that has an equity fraction of 1.0. A calculation form shows how to analyze information from the fund's prospectus to extract the data you need to evaluate the fund.

☐ After investing in a stock, plot stock price on semilog graph paper to track the growth in the stock's price. Distinguish changes in price caused by changes in the outlook for the firm from changes caused by changes in market interest rates by plotting the ratio of the stock price to the Standard and Poor's 500 stock average. Track progress of the firm by plotting stock prices and sales and earnings from the firm's quarterly reports against some index of economic activity, such as the GNP. Plot on log-log graph paper, and update your analysis of the firm each time the firm issues its annual report.

11

Calculation Forms for Practical Use

THE CALCULATION FORM IN THE PRECEDING CHAPTERS WERE SIMPLIFIED TO ILLUSTRATE the basic features of analysis. Now it is time to go beyond simplified forms and work with calculation forms you can use to evaluate real securities. The forms in this chapter cover all of the factors that determine the profitability of an investment, which can help you choose the best securities for your investment program.

Evaluating securities is much easier if you keep the evaluation problem in perspective. You do not need to calculate rates of return to three decimal places. Any security you evaluate is going to require some type of a forecast. You might have to forecast a firm's growth and profitability or future price/earnings ratios or interest rates. Forecasting is difficult and is prone to error. Errors in your forecasts can generate errors much larger than errors in the second or third decimal place of a calculated rate of return. Calculating returns to too many decimal places is wasted effort. The calculation forms in this chapter give returns accurate to the first decimal place. One decimal place is all the accuracy you need to manage your investment program effectively.

On the other hand, taxes are not so simplified. The U.S. tax code is complex, and a calculation form that includes every jiggle in the code would be more complicated than you would be willing to use. Jiggles affect the second or third decimal place in a calculated return. Worry about the jiggles when you make out your tax return, not when you evaluate securities. It's wasted effort.

Spend your time understanding the cash flows you expect a security to generate. If you are evaluating a stock, spend most of your time analyzing the firm as outlined in Chapter 10. Carefully consider the rate of return you expect the firm to earn and how fast you expect the firm to grow. If the firm is a growth firm, think about how fast you expect the firm to mature. If you are evaluating a bond, spend most of your time checking the bond's safety and call features. Working the calculation forms should take the least amount of your time.

TUNING THE ANALYSIS TO YOUR SITUATION

The analysis examples in preceding chapters show how some nameless investor would evaluate securities. That's fine for illustrating the method, but when you analyze your own investments, you want to recognize that you are different from other investors. Depending on your taxable income and the state where you happen to live, your incremental tax rate is likely to be different. You are also likely to have a different set of alternative investments, which will make your opportunity cost different.

The first step in gaining control over your investment program is to determine your incremental tax rate and your opportunity cost. Once you understand these factors, you can tune the analysis to your particular situation and judge whether any security is a good choice for you.

Determining Your Incremental Tax Rate

Use Table 11-1 to determine your incremental tax rate. Examine your latest federal and state tax returns, and find the tax rate you paid on your last dollar of taxable income. Enter your incremental federal tax rate on line 1 and your incremental state tax rate on line 3. If you itemize deductions on your federal tax return, complete the first section of Part B. If you use the standard deduction instead, complete the second section of Part

---
TABLE 11-1
Incremental Tax Rates

A. Federal Taxes

  1. Tax Rate on Last Dollar of Taxable Income, % _____

  2. Federal After-Tax Factor: Divide Line 1 by 100, then Subtract the result from 1.0 _____

B. State Taxes

  3. Tax Rate on Last Dollar of Taxable Income, % _____

You Itemize Federal Deductions

  4. Tax Rate after Federal Offset: Multiply Line 3 by Line 2 _____

  5. Total Incremental Tax Rate, %: Add Lines 1 and 4 _____

  6. Net After-Tax Factor: Divide Line 5 by 100, then subtract the result from 1.0 _____

You Do Not Itemize

  7. Total Incremental Tax Rate, %: Add Lines 1 and 3 _____

  8. Net After-Tax Factor: Divide Line 7 by 100, then subtract the result from 1.0 _____

C. Capital Gains Tax

  9. Capital Gains Tax, % _____

You Itemize Federal Deductions

10. Multiply Line 2 by Line 3, then divide by Line 1. Add the result to 1.0 _____

11. Total Capital Gains Tax, %: Multiply Line 9 by Line 10 _____

You Do Not Itemize

12. Divide Line 3 by Line 1. Add the result to 1.0 _____

13. Total Capital Gains Tax: Multiply Line 9 by Line 12 _____

B. Part C allows you to treat capital gains separately from ordinary income in case future tax laws restore more favorable capital gains treatment.

Table 11-2 shows how an investor with a 33 percent incremental federal tax rate and a 6 percent incremental state tax rate would use this form. If he itemized deductions on his federal return, his total incremental tax rate in line 5 would be 37 percent, and his after-tax factor would be 0.63. If he used the standard deduction instead, his total incremental tax rate in line 7 would be 39 percent, and his after-tax factor would be 0.61. Tax rates on capital gains are the same as tax rates on ordinary income in 1989. Part C shows that his total capital gains tax rate would also be 37 or 39 percent, depending on whether or not he itemizes deductions.

Use the incremental tax rates from Table 11-1 for taxable investment income. Some securities are tax-free. The interest on U.S. government bonds is free of state and local taxes. Use just the federal tax rate in line 1 to convert interest to an after-tax basis. The

---
TABLE 11-2
Incremental Tax Rates—Example 11-1

A. Federal Taxes

1. Tax Rate on Last Dollar of Taxable Income, %	33
2. Federal After-Tax Factor: Divide Line 1 by 100, then subtract the result from 1.0	0.67

B. State Taxes

3. Tax Rate on Last Dollar of Taxable Income, %	6

You Itemize Federal Deductions

4. Tax Rate after Federal Offset: Multiply Line 3 by Line 2	4
5. Total Incremental Tax Rate, %: Add Lines 1 and 4	37
6. Net After-Tax Factor: Divide Line 5 by 100, then Subtract the result from 1.0	0.63

You Do Not Itemize

7. Total Incremental Tax Rate, %: Add Lines 1 and 3	39
8. Net After-Tax Factor: Divide Line 7 by 100, then Subtract the result from 1.0	0.61

C. Capital Gains Tax

9. Capital Gains Tax, %	33

You Itemize Federal Deductions

10. Multiply Line 2 by Line 3, then Divide by Line 1. Add the result to 1.0	1.1218
11. Total Capital Gains Tax, %: Multiply Line 9 by Line 10	37.0

You Do Not Itemize

12. Divide Line 3 by Line 1. Add the result to 1.0	1.1818
13. Total Capital Gains Tax: Multiply Line 9 by Line 12	39.0

interest from state and local bonds is free of federal taxes. Use the state and local tax rate in line 3 or 4 to convert interest from state and local bonds to an after-tax basis. Only the interest from tax-free bonds is free of taxes. Capital gains are fully taxable.

Determining Your Opportunity Cost

The next step in gaining control over your investment program is to determine your opportunity cost. Examine the returns available from investments with clearly stated returns. Convert them to an after-tax basis. See what your return would be if you made each investment in an IRA plan. Make sure you will earn a real return. Subtract the inflation rate you expect from after-tax returns to estimate your real after-tax returns.

Table 11-3 can help you estimate your opportunity cost. Table 11-4 shows how you might use this form in 1989. The table is based on a 37 percent incremental tax rate. Adjust the results to your own tax rate. The top part of the form shows typical investments you might make. These investments include bank savings accounts, money market funds, certificates of deposit, T-Bills and treasury bonds, Ginnie Maes, tax-free bonds, and a 401(k) plan. Enter the before-tax return you expect from these investments in the first column of the form. Convert these returns to an after-tax basis in the second column.

TABLE 11-3
Calculation Form—Opportunity Cost

Rate of Return, %

A. Investment Opportunities	Before Tax	Nominal	After Tax IRA Plans Deductible? Yes	No
_____	_____	_____	_____	_____
_____	_____	_____	_____	_____
_____	_____	_____	_____	_____
_____	_____	_____	_____	_____
_____	_____	_____	_____	_____
_____	_____	_____	_____	_____

B. Debt Repayment

_____	_____	_____	
_____	_____	_____	
_____	_____	_____	
_____	_____	_____	

Use Table 9-1 to find what your after-tax returns would be if you made these investments in an IRA plan. Enter the IRA results in either the third or fourth column, depending on whether or not you can deduct the IRA investment from taxable income. I have assumed an incremental tax rate of 37 percent both when you invest the money in the IRA, and when you withdraw it 30 years later.

Also, examine the opportunities you have to repay debt and save interest costs. The Tax Reform Act of 1987 continues the deductibility of mortgage interest, but phases out the deductibility of credit card interest. Enter your mortgage and credit card interest rates on the bottom part of the form.

At 5 percent per year inflation, the first and third investments in this list earn negative or zero real after-tax returns. You will lose purchasing power if you invest in them. They provide the incentive to search for better returns.

Now, examine the form and look for the highest after-tax return. That is, the investment that determines your opportunity cost. The most attractive opportunity in this list is the 401(k) savings plan. Your employer might offer such a plan, and contribute 50 cents or more for every dollar you invest. The money is typically invested in your employer's stock, in treasury bonds, or in a money market fund. Your money grows tax-free until you retire. The 401(k) plan earns a much higher return than any other investment listed above. If a 401(k) plan is available, invest the maximum amount your employer permits.

The most attractive opportunity after the 401(k) plan is paying credit-card debt. If you owe money on credit cards, your opportunity cost in this example will be 18 percent. Don't consider any other investment unless that investment promises a return greater than 18 percent. Earning such a high return is difficult in a competitive market. Avoiding 18 percent credit-card interest is likely to be your next, most attractive investment. Pay your credit-card debt promptly to avoid these high interest costs.

If you use the standard deduction on your federal tax return, your next most attractive opportunity is to repay your mortgage and avoid 10 percent after-tax interest charges. Your opportunity cost will then be 10 percent. If you itemize deductions, paying off your mortgage saves only 6.3 percent interest and is less attractive. Your next best investment is then a Ginnie Mae in an IRA plan. Your opportunity cost drops to either 9.8 or 8.4 percent, depending on whether you can deduct the investment from taxable income. If you cannot find any alternative investments with a higher return, invest up to the IRA limit.

After you have reached the IRA limits, you are restricted to the returns in the second column of the table. The next best investment in this example is tax-free bonds. Your opportunity cost will then be 6.7 percent. You are now ready to examine stocks and bonds, but you must insist on an after-tax return greater than 6.7 percent. If you cannot find any stocks or bonds that promise a higher return, invest in the tax-free bonds. Tax-free bonds might not be the next best investment, however, if your incremental tax rate is less than the 37 percent rate in this example. One of the other investments in Table 11-4 will then determine your opportunity cost.

There are many stocks and bonds available in the market that might pay better returns. Examine stocks in companies you believe have a promising future, or that might be undervalued. Examine bonds that appear to offer favorable interest rates. The investor in Table 11-4 would use a 6.7 percent opportunity cost when evaluating these alterna-

TABLE 11-4
Opportunity Cost

Rate of Return, %

| | Before Tax | Nominal | After Tax — IRA Plans Deductible? | |
			Yes	No
A. Investment Opportunities				
Super NOW Account	5.1	3.2	5.1	4.0
Money Market Fund	8.7	5.5	8.7	7.3
Certificates of Deposit				
One Year—Average	8.0	5.0	8.0	6.6
One Year—High Return	9.2	5.8	9.2	7.8
U.S. T-Bills (One Year)	8.1	5.4	8.1	6.7
Treasury Bonds (10 Years)	8.4	5.6	8.4	7.0
Ginnie Mae	9.8	6.2	9.8	8.4
Tax-Free Bonds	6.7	6.7	6.7	6.7
401(k) Savings Plan	50+	50+	–	–
B. Debt Repayment				
Mortgage				
Itemize Deductions	10	6.3		
Don't Itemize	10	10		
Credit Card Debt	18	18		

tive investments to ensure against investing in a security less attractive than tax-free municipal bonds.

Interest rates fluctuate continually. Fluctuating interest rates change the returns on investment opportunities. Consequently, your opportunity cost will fluctuate as a result. Therefore, you should track interest rates, which are reported in publications such as *Barrons, The Wall Street Journal*, and in the financial pages of your daily newspaper. Adjust your opportunity cost whenever interest rates change significantly.

PRACTICAL CALCULATION FORMS

Use the forms in this chapter to evaluate actual securities. The forms will make the evaluation easy, and follow a consistent pattern. An initial section records basic information about the security. A second section records information about you. A third section develops estimates of the cash flows that security should generate. A fourth section discounts these cash flows. A final section calculates the maximum price you should pay for that security.

The forms are much easier to use than they might first appear. You will not be ready to use these forms until you have first studied the security. If you are evaluating a stock, you will have analyzed the firm as suggested in Chapter 10. You will have estimated the rate of return the firm will earn and how fast the firm will grow. You will have estimated future price/earnings ratios. If you are evaluating a bond, you know the bond's cost, interest rate, years to maturity, and call features. You know your incremental tax rate and how long you plan to hold the security. The first two sections of the calculation forms simply record that information, so you will be able to fill them out quickly. The balance of the form consists of a sequence of simple arithmetic steps.

After a little experience, you'll find that these forms take just a few minutes to complete. Learn how to calculate growth and discount factors on your hand calculator instead of looking them up in the tables. This will speed the process substantially. You should spend most of your time analyzing the investment along the lines suggested in Chapter 10, and only a small amount of time on the calculation form.

The quickest way to use the form is to begin with your opportunity cost as the first trial discount rate. Work down to the present value at the bottom of the discounting section or the maximum allowable price at the bottom of the form. If the present value is negative, or if the security costs more than the maximum allowable price, it is not attractive. There is no need for further calculation. If the present value is positive, or if the security costs less than the maximum allowable price, it might be attractive. Continue with the form and calculate the rate of return you should expect. The rate of return allows you to compare this investment with alternative investments.

Don't worry too much about minor factors like commissions. Assume a 2.5 percent commission if you use a full-service broker and a 1 percent commission if you use a discount broker. If the stock appears to be attractive, ask your broker for the actual commission and adjust the evaluation. Each form is illustrated by an example. Work through the example carefully to make sure you know how to use the form.

Certificates of Deposit

The government taxes the interest from certificates of deposit with maturities longer than one year as though the interest were paid each month. You must pay taxes during the life of the certificate, even though you cannot withdraw your money without penalty until the certificate matures.

Find your after-tax return from a certificate of deposit by multiplying the certificate's equivalent continuous interest rate by your after-tax factor. The calculation form in Table 11-5 simplifies the evaluation. Enter the certificate's interest rate in line 1, and the number of times per year the certificate compounds interest in line 2. List your after-tax factor in line 3. Lines 4 through 6 develop the certificate's equivalent continuous interest rate. If the certificate compounds continuously, skip lines 4 and 5, and enter the certificate's interest rate directly in line 6. Multiply by your after-tax factor to find your after-tax return in line 7.

Example 11-1. A certificate of deposit pays 9 percent interest compounded quarterly. What is the after-tax return to an investor with a 37 percent incremental tax rate? Table 11-6 shows the solution. The certificate's equivalent interest rate in line 6 is 8.90 percent. At an after-tax factor of 0.63, the after-tax return is 5.61 percent. If prices inflate 5 percent per year, the real return is only 0.61 percent.

_____TABLE 11-5_____
Calculation Form—Certificates of Deposit

A. The Certificate
1. Certificate's Interest Rate, %   _____
2. Compounding Frequency, times per year*   _____
3. Divide Incremental Tax Rate (%) by 100, Subtract the result from 1.0   _____
4. Divide Line 1 by Line 2 and by 100. Add 1.0 to the result   _____
5. Enter Line 4 in your calculator and tap the ln(x) key   _____
6. Equivalent Continuous Interest Rate: Multiply Line 5 by Line 2 and by 100   _____

B. Rate of Return
7. Multiply Line 6 by Line 3   _____

*If the certificate pays interest continuously, skip Lines 4 and 5, and enter the certificate's interest rate in Line 6.

_____TABLE 11-6_____
Certificates of Deposit—Example 11-3

A. The Certificate
1. Certificate's Interest Rate, %   9
2. Compounding Frequency, times per year*   4
3. Divide Incremental Tax Rate (%) by 100, Subtract the result from 1.0   0.63
4. Divide Line 1 by Line 2 and by 100. Add 1.0 to the result   1.0225
5. Enter Line 4 in your calculator and tap the ln(x) key   0.0223
6. Equivalent Continuous Interest Rate: Multiply Line 5 by Line 2 and by 100   8.90

B. Rate of Return
7. Multiply Line 6 by Line 3   5.61

*If the certificate pays interest continuously, skip Lines 4 and 5, and enter the certificate's interest rate in Line 6.

Bonds

Use the calculation form in Table 11-7 to evaluate bonds. Record the bond's price, interest rate, and years to maturity in Part A of the form. Bond prices in the financial pages of your newspaper are based on a face value of $100. Follow this convention when you enter the bond's price in line 1.

    Enter your incremental tax rate for ordinary income and for capital gains, along with the time you expect to hold the bond, in Part B. If you expect the bond to be called, enter the call price in lines 18 and 22. Adjust your investment period to the call time. If

TABLE 11-7
Calculation Form—Bonds

A. The Bond

1. Bond Price _____
2. Divide Commission (%) by 100; Add the result to 1.0 _____
3. Bond Cost: Multiply Line 1 by Line 2 _____
4. Bond Interest Rate, % _____
5. Years to Maturity _____

B. The Investor

6. Divide Incremental Tax Rate (%) by 100 _____
7. After-Tax Factor: Subtract Line 6 from 1.0 _____
8. Divide Capital Gains Tax Rate (%) by 100 _____
9. Investment Period, years _____

C. Future Cash Flows

If the bond is redeemed at maturity, enter 100 in Lines 18 and 22, then skip to Line 23. If you expect the bond to be called, enter the call price in Lines 18 and 22 and skip to Line 23.

10. Subtract Line 9 from Line 5 _____
11. Future Market Interest Rate, % _____
12. Di Factor at RT = Line 10 times Line 11 _____
13. Dc Factor at RT = Line 10 times Line 11 _____
14. Multiply Line 4 by Lines 10 and 13 _____
15. Multiply Line 12 by 100 _____
16. Future Price: Add Lines 14 and 15 _____
17. Enter 1.0 if the bond is redeemed at maturity. Otherwise, Divide commission (%) by 100, then Subtract the result from 1.0 _____
18. Future Price Less Commission: Multiply Line 16 by Line 17 _____
19. Divide 100 by Line 3. Enter in your calculator, and tap the ln(x) key _____
20. Divide Line 19 by Line 5, then Multiply by 100 _____
21. Gi Factor at RT = Line 9 times Line 20 _____
22. Tax Basis: Multiply Line 3 by Line 21 _____
23. Capital Loss Credit: If Line 3 is less than Line 18, enter zero and continue on Line 24. Otherwise, Subtract Line 18 from Line 3, and Multiply the result by Line 8. Skip to Line 26. _____
24. Capital Gains Tax: Multiply the difference between Lines 18 and 22 by Line 8. _____
25. Tax on Market Discount: If Line 3 is greater than 100, enter zero. Otherwise, Subtract Line 3 from Line 22, and Multiply the result by Line 6. _____
26. Final Proceeds: Add Lines 18 and 23, then Subtract Line 25. If Line 18 is greater than Line 22, Subtract Line 24. If Line 22 is greater, Add Line 24. _____

D. Discounting

27. Trial Discount Rate, % _____

28. Di Factor at RT = Line 27 times Line 9 _____

29. Dc Factor at RT = Line 27 times Line 9 _____

30. Gc Factor at RT = Line 27 times 0.5 _____

31. Present Value of Interest: Multiply Line 4 by Lines 7, 9, and 29, then Divide by Line 30 _____

32. Present Value at Redemption: Multiply Line 26 by Line 28 _____

33. Present Value: Add Lines 31 and 32, then Subtract Line 3 _____

If the present value in Line 33 is positive, try a new discount rate 5 percentage points higher. If Line 33 is negative, try a new discount rate 5 percentage points lower. Use Table 4-3 to speed the solution for rate of return.

E. Maximum Allowable Price (Approximate)

Enter your opportunity cost as the discount rate in Line 27, and complete Lines 28 through 31.

34. Divide Line 9 by Line 5 _____

35. Subtract Line 8 from 1.0 then Multiply by Lines 18 and 28 _____

36. Subtract Line 6 from Line 8. Multiply the result by Lines 28 and 34, and by 100 _____

37. Add Lines 31 and 35, then Subtract Line 36 _____

38. Multiply Line 6 by Line 34 _____

39. Subtract Line 34 from 1.0. Multiply the result by Line 8, then Add Line 38 _____

40. Multiply Line 28 by Line 39; Subtract the result from 1.0 _____

41. Maximum Allowable Price: Divide Line 37 by Lines 2 and 40 _____

you redeem the bond at maturity, the redemption value will be $100. Enter $100 in lines 18 and 22, and continue the evaluation in line 23. If you expect to sell the bond before it matures, you will have to estimate the future selling price. Lines 10 through 18 develop this estimate, based on your estimate of the future market interest rate on comparable bonds in line 11.

Capital gains are fully taxable, even those from tax-free bonds. The government considers the gain a combination of two gains. It taxes one as ordinary income and the other as a capital gain. You might buy a bond at a discount from its $1,000 face value. That discount is called the market discount. The government considers market discount a form of interest, and taxes it as ordinary income. The balance of the gain is a capital gain and is taxed as a capital gain.

You can use either of two methods to figure the market discount. The calculation form uses the constant interest rate method, because that method gives slightly more favorable results. The market discount is the gain from your original cost to your tax basis. The form develops the tax basis in line 22. Line 25 gives the tax on the market discount. The capital gain or loss is the difference between the net selling price and the tax basis. The form develops the capital gain tax or credit on line 24. Line 26 shows the final proceeds—the selling price less taxes and commissions—when you sell the bond.

Discount the cash flows in Part D. If the present value in line 33 is negative, the bond is not attractive. The calculation can end at this point. If the present value is positive, repeat Part D with a second discount rate 5 percentage points higher. Then use Table 4-3 to complete the solution for rate of return.

Part E develops the maximum price you should pay for the bond. The calculation uses the rateable interest method in place of the constant interest method to avoid a trial-and-error solution. Both methods give the same maximum price when capital gains and ordinary income are taxed at the same rate. There will be a small error if the government lowers the capital gains tax.

You can calculate a more accurate maximum price if the capital gains tax changes. If the present value in line 33 is positive, repeat Table 11-7 with a new bond price, 5 percent higher than the original price. If the present value is negative, use a new price, 5 percent lower. Discount again at your opportunity cost. You will then have a present value at the original bond price and a second present value at the new price.

You previously used Table 4-3 to estimate rate of return. You can also use Table 4-3 to estimate maximum price. Use bond prices in place of rates of return, and enter both sets of values in Table 4-3. Follow the directions, and calculate a more accurate maximum allowable price.

Example 11-2. The bond tables in your daily newspaper quote a price of $81 for a bond that pays 6 percent interest and matures in 11 years. You expect to hold the bond for five years. Your incremental tax rate is 37 percent. What rate of return should you expect from this bond? If your opportunity cost is 7 percent, what is the most you should pay for the bond?

Table 11-8 shows how to evaluate this bond. Enter the basic data on the bond in Part A and your tax rates and expected investment period in Part B. Because you will not hold the bond until it matures, you will have to estimate the bond's price when you sell five years from now. The future price depends on market interest rates at that time. Suppose you estimate that similar bonds will then pay 7 percent interest. Enter that estimate on line 11, and calculate a future bond price of $95.10 in line 16.

The tax on the market discount is developed in lines 19 through 25. Calculate in line 20 that a constant interest rate of 1.83 percent will make your original cost grow to the $100 face value at maturity 11 years from now. At that interest rate, your original cost will grow to $89.65 in line 22 when you sell in five years. That value is your tax basis. The gain from your original cost to the $89.65 tax basis is the market discount. Line 25 shows you will pay a tax of $2.90 on this discount. The difference between the actual net selling price and the $89.65 tax basis is a capital gain. You will pay a tax of $1.67 on this gain, as line 24 shows.

Part D shows that present value at your 7 percent opportunity cost is −$3.01. The negative present value means this bond is not attractive. The rate of return will be below your opportunity cost. If you continue the evaluation, you will find a rate of return of 6.2 percent. Part E shows that you should not pay more than $76.98 for this bond.

TABLE 11-8
Evaluating Bonds—Example 11-4

A. The Bond

1. Bond Price	81
2. Divide Commission (%) by 100; Add the result to 1.0	1.01
3. Bond Cost: Multiply Line 1 by Line 2	81.81
4. Bond Interest Rate, %	6
5. Years to Maturity	11

B. The Investor

6. Divide Incremental Tax Rate (%) by 100	0.37
7. After-Tax Factor: Subtract Line 6 from 1.0	0.63
8. Divide Capital Gains Tax Rate (%) by 100	0.37
9. Investment Period, years	5

C. Future Cash Flows

If the bond is redeemed at maturity, enter 100 in Lines 18 and 22, then skip to Line 23. If you expect the bond to be called, enter the call price in Lines 18 and 22 and skip to Line 23.

10. Subtract Line 9 from Line 5	6
11. Future Market Interest Rate, %	7
12. Di Factor at RT = Line 10 times Line 11	0.6570
13. Dc Factor at RT = Line 10 times Line 11	0.8166
14. Multiply Line 4 by Lines 10 and 13	29.40
15. Multiply Line 12 by 100	65.70
16. Future Price: Add Lines 14 and 15	95.10
17. Enter 1.0 if the bond is redeemed at maturity. Otherwise, Divide commission (%) by 100, then Subtract the result from 1.0	0.99
18. Future Price Less Commission: Multiply Line 16 by Line 17	94.15
19. Divide 100 by Line 3. Enter in your calculator, and tap the ln(x) key	0.2008
20. Divide Line 19 by Line 5, then Multiply by 100	1.83
21. Gi Factor at RT = Line 9 times Line 20	1.0958
22. Tax Basis: Multiply Line 3 by Line 21	89.65
23. Capital Loss Credit: If Line 3 is less than Line 18, enter zero and continue on Line 24. Otherwise, Subtract Line 18 from Line 3, and Multiply the result by Line 8. Skip to Line 26.	0
24. Capital Gains Tax: Multiply the difference between Lines 18 and 22 by Line 8	1.67
25. Tax on Market Discount: If Line 3 is greater than 100, enter zero. Otherwise, Subtract Line 3 from Line 22, and Multiply the result by Line 6.	2.90
26. Final Proceeds: Add Lines 18 and 23, then Subtract Line 25. If Line 18 is greater than Line 22, Subtract Line 24. If Line 22 is greater, Add Line 24.	89.58

Table 11-8. Continued.

D. Discounting

27. Trial Discount Rate, %   7

28. Di Factor at RT = Line 27 times Line 9   0.7047

29. Dc Factor at RT = Line 27 times Line 9   0.8437

30. Gc Factor at RT = Line 27 times 0.5   1.0177

31. Present Value of Interest: Multiply Line 4 by Lines 7, 9, and 29, then
    Divide by Line 30   15.67

32. Present Value at Redemption: Multiply Line 26 by Line 28   63.13

33. Present Value: Add Lines 31 and 32, then Subtract Line 3   – $3.01

If the present value in Line 33 is positive, try a new discount rate 5 percentage points higher. If Line 33 is negative, try a new discount rate 5 percentage points lower. Use Table 4-3 to speed the solution for rate of return.

E. Maximum Allowable Price (Approximate)

Enter your opportunity cost as the discount rate in Line 27, and complete Lines 28 through 31.

34. Divide Line 9 by Line 5   0.455

35. Subtract Line 8 from 1.0 then Multiply by Lines 18 and 28   41.80

36. Subtract Line 6 from Line 8. Multiply the result by Lines 28 and 34,
    and by 100   0

37. Add Lines 31 and 35, then Subtract Line 36   57.47

38. Multiply Line 6 by Line 34   0.1684

39. Subtract Line 34 from 1.0. Multiply the result by Line 8, then Add
    Line 38   0.3701

40. Multiply Line 28 by Line 39; Subtract the result from 1.0   0.7392

41. Maximum Allowable Price: Divide Line 37 by Lines 2 and 40 $76.98

Zero Coupon Bonds

Table 11-9 is the calculation form for evaluating zero coupon bonds. The form parallels the form for normal bonds, except that there is no entry for interest payments. Zero coupon bonds do not pay interest, they sell at a deep discount from face value instead, which is called original issue discount. The government considers this discount a form of interest, and taxes it as ordinary income. You pay a tax each year on this phantom interest, even though you do not receive the interest until you sell the bond.

Use Table 11-9 just like you used Table 11-7 for normal bonds. The form taxes phantom interest by the constant interest rate method because this method gives a slightly higher return. Part E of the form uses the rateable interest method instead to avoid a trial-and-error solution for the maximum allowable price. If you need a more accurate maximum price, use the same procedure recommended in the section on normal bonds.

Example 11-3. A zero coupon bond 10 years from maturity is priced at $41. You plan to hold the bond for six years. Your incremental tax rate is 37 percent. What rate of

TABLE 11-9
Calculation Form—Zero Coupon Bonds

A. The Bond
1. Bond Price
2. Divide Commission (%) by 100; Add the result to 1.0
3. Bond Cost: Multiply Line 1 by Line 2
4. Years to Maturity

B. The Investor
5. Divide Incremental Tax Rate (%) by 100
6. Divide Capital Gains Tax Rate (%) by 100
7. Investment Period, years

C. Future Cash Flows
If the bond is redeemed at maturity, enter 100 in Lines 13 and 17, then skip to Line 18.
8. Subtract Line 7 from Line 4
9. Future Market Interest Rate, %
10. Di Factor at RT = Line 8 times Line 9
11. Future Price: Multiply Line 10 by 100
12. Divide Commission (%) by 100, Subtract the result from 1.0
13. Future Price Less Commission: Multiply Line 11 by Line 12
14. Divide 100 by Line 3. Enter in your calculator, and tap the ln(x) key
15. Divide Line 14 by Line 4, then Multiply by 100
16. Gi Factor at RT = Line 7 times Line 15
17. Tax Basis: Multiply Line 3 by Line 16
18. Capital Gains Tax: Multiply the difference between Lines 13 and 17 by Line 6
19. Final Proceeds: If Line 13 is greater than Line 17, Subtract Line 18 from Line 13. If Line 17 is greater, Add Lines 13 and 18.

D. Discounting
20. Trial Discount Rate, %
21. Di Factor at RT = Line 20 times Line 7
22. Present Value of Final Proceeds: Multiply Line 19 by Line 21
23. RT: Multiply the difference between Lines 15 and 20 by Line 7
24. Dc Factor at RT = Line 23. If Line 15 is greater than Line 20, use a Gc Factor instead
25. Present Value of Tax on Imputed Interest: Multiply Line 3 by Lines 5, 7, 15, and 24, then divide by 100
26. Present Value: Subtract Lines 3 and 25 from Line 22

If the present value on Line 26 is positive, try a new discount rate 5 percentage points higher. If Line 26 is negative, try a discount rate 5 percentage points lower. Use Table 4-3 to complete the solution for rate of return.

Table 11-9. Continued.

E. Maximum Allowable Price (Approximate)

Enter your opportunity cost as the discount rate in Line 20, and complete Line 21.

27. Dc Factor at RT = Line 20 times Line 7 _____

28. Divide Line 7 by Line 4 _____

29. Subtract Line 6 from 1.0; Multiply the result by Lines 13 and 21 _____

30. Multiply Line 5 by Line 27 _____

31. Multiply Line 6 by Line 21; Subtract the result from Line 30 _____

32. Multiply Line 28 by Line 31 and by 100 _____

33. Subtract Line 32 from Line 29 _____

34. Multiply Line 5 by Lines 27 and 28 _____

35. Subtract Line 28 from 1.0; Multiply the result by Lines 6 and 21 _____

36. Subtract Lines 34 and 35 from 1.0 _____

37. Maximum Allowable Price: Divide Line 33 by Lines 2 and 36 _____

return should you expect? What is the most you should pay for this bond if your opportunity cost is 7 percent?

Table 11-10 shows how to evaluate this bond. Enter the basic data on the bond in Part A and your tax rate and expected investment period in Part B. You will have to estimate the price of the bond when you sell it in six years. Suppose you estimate that market interest rates then will be 7 percent. Enter this estimate on line 9, and calculate a future price, less commissions, of $74.82 in line 13.

Line 15 shows a constant interest rate of 8.82 percent for figuring your tax basis. At that rate, line 17 shows that your tax basis when you sell in six years will be $70.30. The difference between your original $41.41 cost and the $70.30 tax basis is the phantom interest. This interest is taxed as ordinary income during the period you hold the bond. The difference between the $74.82 net selling price and the $70.30 tax basis is taxed as a capital gain. The capital gains tax in line 18 is $1.67.

Discounting at your 7 percent opportunity cost results in a present value of −$1.92 in line 26. The negative present value means this bond is not attractive. If you continue the calculation, you will find a rate of return of 6.3 percent. The maximum allowable price from Part E is $37.64, about 10 percent below the current market price. If you use Table 4-3, you will estimate a more accurate maximum price of $38.22—1.5 percent higher than the maximum calculated from Table 11-10.

Ginnie Maes (GNMA)

Use the calculation form in Table 11-11 to evaluate Ginnie Maes (GNMA), mortgage-backed securities. The form uses a face value of $100 to conform to the way financial pages quote GNMA prices. Enter the basic data on the GNMA in Part A. The firms who service the underlying mortgages collect a service fee of 0.5 percent. Line 5 adds this fee back to the GNMA interest rate to find the interest rate on the underlying pool of

_____*TABLE 11-10*_____
Zero Coupon Bonds—Example 11-3

A. The Bond

1. Bond Price	41
2. Divide Commission (%) by 100; Add the result to 1.0	1.01
3. Bond Cost: Multiply Line 1 by Line 2	41.41
4. Years to Maturity	10

B. The Investor

5. Divide Incremental Tax Rate (%) by 100	0.37
6. Divide Capital Gains Tax Rate (%) by 100	0.37
7. Investment Period, years	6

C. Future Cash Flows

If the bond is redeemed at maturity, enter 100 in Lines 13 and 17, then skip to Line 18.

8. Subtract Line 7 from Line 4	4
9. Future Market Interest Rate, %	7
10. Di Factor at RT = Line 8 times Line 9	0.7558
11. Future Price: Multiply Line 10 by 100	75.58
12. Divide Commission (%) by 100, Subtract the result from 1.0	0.99
13. Future Price Less Commission: Multiply Line 11 by Line 12	74.82
14. Divide 100 by Line 3. Enter in your calculator, and tap the ln(x) key	0.8816
15. Divide Line 14 by Line 4, then Multiply by 100	8.82
16. Gi Factor at RT = Line 7 times Line 15	1.6976
17. Tax Basis: Multiply Line 3 by Line 16	70.30
18. Capital Gains Tax: Multiply the difference between Lines 13 and 17 by Line 6	1.67
19. Final Proceeds: If Line 13 is greater than Line 17, Subtract Line 18 from Line 13. If Line 17 is greater, Add Lines 13 and 18.	73.15

D. Discounting

20. Trial Discount Rate, %	7
21. Di Factor at RT = Line 20 times Line 7	0.6570
22. Present Value of Final Proceeds: Multiply Line 19 by Line 21	48.06
23. RT: Multiply the difference between Lines 15 and 20 by Line 7	10.9
24. Dc Factor at RT = Line 23. If Line 15 is greater than Line 20, use a Gc Factor instead	1.0565
25. Present Value of Tax on Imputed Interest: Multiply Line 3 by Lines 5, 7, 15, and 24, then divide by 100	8.57
26. Present Value: Subtract Lines 3 and 25 from Line 22	−$1.92

If the present value on Line 26 is positive, try a new discount rate 5 percentage points higher. If Line 26 is negative, try a discount rate 5 percentage points lower. Use Table 4-3 to speed the solution for rate of return.

Table 11-10. Continued.

E. Maximum Allowable Price (Approximate)

Enter your opportunity cost as the discount rate in Line 20, and complete Line 21.

27. Dc Factor at RT = Line 20 times Line 7	0.8166
28. Divide Line 7 by Line 4	0.6
29. Subtract Line 6 from 1.0; Multiply the result by Lines 13 and 21	30.97
30. Multiply Line 5 by Line 27	0.3021
31. Multiply Line 6 by Line 21; Subtract the result from Line 30	0.0590
32. Multiply Line 28 by Line 31 and by 100	3.54
33. Subtract Line 32 from Line 29	27.43
34. Multiply Line 5 by Lines 27 and 28	0.1813
35. Subtract Line 28 from 1.0; Multiply the result by Lines 6 and 21	0.0972
36. Subtract Lines 34 and 35 from 1.0	0.7215
37. Maximum Allowable Price: Divide Line 33 by Lines 2 and 36	$37.64

mortgages. Enter the nominal mortgage term in line 6, and the actual life in line 7. Actual mortgage lives average about 12 years.

Part C develops future cash flows. Line 13 shows the mortgagee's annual payments per $100 of mortgage. You recover your investment gradually as mortgagees pay off their mortgages. Line 15 shows the balance of the investment you will recover at the end of the mortgage's actual life.

Discount the cash flows in Part D. Lines 23 and 24 give the present value of the mortgage payments during the life of the mortgage and the investment you recover at the end of the actual life. Line 27 shows the present value of the service fees and the taxes on the mortgage interest. Line 29 gives the net present value for the investment. Find the maximum price you should pay in Part E of the calculation form.

Example 11-4. An 8 percent GNMA, 30-year mortgage certificate was quoted at $93 in 1989. Assume the underlying mortgages will be paid in 12 years. Your incremental tax rate is 37 percent. What rate of return should you expect from this investment? What is the most you should pay if your opportunity cost is 7 percent?

Table 11-12 shows how to evaluate this investment. The GNMA interest rate in line 4 is 8 percent. Add the 0.5 percent service fee in line 5 to find the 8.5 percent interest rate on the underlying mortgages. At this mortgage interest rate, line 13 shows that mortgagees will make annual mortgage payments of $9.22 per $100 of mortgage. Mortgagees will pay off $15 of the mortgage during the 12-year life. When the mortgage is prepaid in year 12, line 15 shows that you will recover a balance of $85.

Line 23 shows a $74.85 present value of the annual mortgage payments. Line 27 shows that you will lose $26.61 of this amount in taxes and service fees. Line 24 shows that the balance of the investment you recover in year 12 has a present value of $36.69.

The net present value in line 29 is −$9.97. The negative present value shows that this investment is not attractive. The maximum allowable price in line 33 is $81.25—13 percent below the quoted price of $93. If you continue the analysis, you will find a 5.7 percent rate of return.

_____*TABLE 11-11*_____
Calculation Form—Ginnie Maes

A. The Ginnie Mae
1. Price   _____
2. Divide Commission (%) by 100 and Add the result to 1.0   _____
3. Cost: Multiply Line 1 by Line 2   _____
4. GNMA Interest Rate, %   _____
5. Add 0.5 to Line 4   _____
6. Mortgage Term, years   _____
7. Expected Life, years   _____

B. The Investor
8. Divide the Incremental Tax Rate (%) by 100   _____
9. Divide the Capital Gains Tax Rate (%) by 100   _____

C. Future Cash Flows
10. Gc Factor at RT = Line 5 times Line 6   _____
11. Dc Factor at RT = Line 5 times Line 6   _____
12. Dc Factor at RT = Line 5 times the difference between Lines 6 and 7   _____
13. Mortgage Payments, $/yr.: Divide 100 by Lines 6 and 11   _____
14. Divide Line 7 by Line 6; Subtract the result from 1.0   _____
15. Investment Recovered When Mortgage Repaid: Multiply Line 14 by
    100 and by Line 12. Divide the result by Line 11.   _____
16. Capital Gains Tax: Subtrate Line 3 from 100, Multiply the result by
    Line 9   _____
17. Multiply Line 4 by Line 8, then add 0.5. Divide the result by Line 5   _____

D. Discounting
18. Trial Discount Rate, %   _____
19. Di Factor at RT = Line 18 times Line 7   _____
20. Dc Factor at RT = Line 18 times Line 7   _____
21. RT: Subtract Line 18 from Line 5; Multiply the result by Line 7   _____
22. Gc Factor at RT = Line 21. If Line 18 is greater than Line 5, use a
    Dc Factor instead.   _____
23. Present Value of Mortgage Payments: Multiply Line 13 by Lines 7
    and 20   _____
24. Present Value of Recovered Investment: Multiply Line 15 by Line 19   _____
25. Divide Line 22 by Line 10   _____
26. Divide Line 20 by Line 11, then Subtract Line 25   _____
27. Present Value of Service Fee and Tax on Interest: Multiply 100 by
    Lines 7, 17, and 26. Then Divide by Line 6   _____
28. Present Value of Capital Gains Tax: Multiply Line 16 by Line 19   _____

Table 11-11. Continued.

29. Present Value: Add Lines 23 and 24, then Subtract Lines 3 and 27. If Line 3 is less than 100, Subtract Line 28. If Line 3 is greater than 100, Add Line 28 _____

If Line 29 is positive, choose a discount rate 3 percentage points higher. If Line 29 is negative, choose a discount rate 3 percentage points lower. Use Table 4-3 to complete the calculation for rate of return.

E. Maximum Allowable Price
Use your opportunity cost as the trial discount rate in Line 18, and complete Lines 19 through 27.

30. Multiply Line 9 by Line 19 and by 100 _____
31. Add Lines 23 and 24, then Subtract Lines 27 and 30 _____
32. Multiply Line 9 by Line 19; Subtract the result from 1.0 _____
33. Maximum Allowable Price: Divide Line 31 by Lines 2 and 32 _____

TABLE 11-12
Ginnie Maes—Example 11-4

A. The Ginnie Mae
1. Price — 93
2. Divide Commission (%) by 100 and Add the result to 1.0 — 1.01
3. Cost: Multiply Line 1 by Line 2 — 93.93
4. GNMA Interest Rate, % — 8
5. Add 0.5 to Line 4 — 8.5
6. Mortgage Term, years — 30
7. Expected Life, years — 12

B. The Investor
8. Divide the Incremental Tax Rate (%) by 100 — 0.37
9. Divide the Capital Gains Tax Rate (%) by 100 — 0.37

C. Future Cash Flows
10. Gc Factor at RT = Line 5 times Line 6 — 4.6302
11. Dc Factor at RT = Line 5 times Line 6 — 0.3615
12. Dc Factor at RT = Line 5 times the difference between Lines 6 and 7 — 0.5121
13. Mortgage Payments, $/yr.: Divide 100 by Lines 6 and 11 — 9.22
14. Divide Line 7 by Line 6; Subtract the result from 1.0 — 0.6
15. Investment Recovered When Mortgage Repaid: Multiply Line 14 by 100 and by Line 12. Divide the result by Line 11. — 85.00

Table 11-12. Continued.

16. Capital Gains Tax: Subtrate Line 3 from 100, Multiply the result by
    Line 9 .... 2.25
17. Multiply Line 4 by Line 8, then add 0.5. Divide the result by Line 5 .... 0.407

D. Discounting

18. Trial Discount Rate, % 7
19. Di Factor at RT = Line 18 times Line 7 .... 0.4317
20. Dc Factor at RT = Line 18 times Line 7 .... 0.6765
21. RT: Subtract Line 18 from Line 5; Multiply the result by Line 7 18
22. Gc Factor at RT = Line 21. If Line 18 is greater than Line 5, use a
    Dc Factor instead. 1.0957
23. Present Value of Mortgage Payments: Multiply Line 13 by Lines 7
    and 20 .... 74.85
24. Present Value of Recovered Investment: Multiply Line 15 by Line 19 .... 36.69
25. Divide Line 22 by Line 10 .... 0.2366
26. Divide Line 20 by Line 11, then Subtract Line 25 .... 1.6348
27. Present Value of Service Fee and Tax on Interest: Multiply 100 by
    Lines 7, 17, and 26. Then Divide by Line 6 .... 26.61
28. Present Value of Capital Gains Tax: Multiply Line 16 by Line 19 .... 0.97
29. Present Value: Add Lines 23 and 24, then Subtract Lines 3 and 27. If
    Line 3 is less than 100, Subtract Line 28. If Line 3 is greater than
    100, Add Line 28 .... −9.97

If Line 29 is positive, choose a discount rate 3 percentage points higher. If Line 29 is negative, choose a discount rate 3 percentage points lower. Use Table 4-3 to complete the calculation for rate of return.

E. Maximum Allowable Price

Use your opportunity cost as the trial discount rate in Line 18, and complete Lines 19 through 27.

30. Multiply Line 9 by Line 19 and by 100 .... 15.97
31. Add Lines 23 and 24, then Subtract Lines 27 and 30 .... 68.96
32. Multiply Line 9 by Line 19; Subtract the result from 1.0 .... 0.8403
33. Maximum Allowable Price: Divide Line 31 by Lines 2 and 32 .... 81.25

Stocks of Mature Firms

To evaluate stocks of mature firms, begin the evaluation by analyzing the firm's historical record as suggested in Chapter 10. Estimate the rate of return you expect the firm to earn and how fast you expect it to grow. Read the firm's capital employed, the equity fraction in the capital pool, and the number of outstanding shares from Table 10-1. If you believe that the firm's rate of return and growth rate will hold steady during the period

TABLE 11-13
Calculation Form—Stocks of Mature Firms

A. The Firm

1. Stock Price, $/share   _____

2. Divide Commission (%) by 100, and Add the result to 1.0   _____

3. Net Cost: Multiply Line 1 by Line 2   _____

4. Rate of Return, %   _____

5. Growth Rate, %/yr.   _____

6. Equity Fraction   _____

7. Dividend Payout Fraction: Multiply Line 5 by Line 6, then Divide by
   Line 4. Subtract the result from 1.0   _____

8. Capital Employed, $millions   _____

9. Shares Outstanding, millions   _____

10. Share Growth Rate, %/yr.   _____

11. Dividend: Multiply Line 4 by Lines 7 and 8. Then Divide by Line 9
    and by 100   _____

B. The Investor

12. Divide Incremental Tax Rate (%) by 100; Subtract the result from 1.0 _____

13. Divide Capital Gains Tax Rate (%) by 100   _____

14. Investment Period, years   _____

C. Cash Flows

15. RT: Subtract Line 10 from Line 5, then Multiply by Line 14   _____

16. Gi Factor at RT = Line 15   _____

17. Future Stock Price, $/share: Multiply Line 1 by Line 16   _____

18. Divide Commission (%) by 100, Subtract the result from 1.0   _____

19. Net Sale: Multiply Line 17 by Line 18   _____

20. Capital Gains Tax: Subtract Line 3 from Line 19. Multiply the result
    by Line 13   _____

21. Final Cash Flow: Subtract Line 20 from Line 19   _____

D. Discounting

22. Trial Discount Rate, %   _____

23. Di Factor at RT = Line 14 times Line 22   _____

24. RT: Add Lines 10 and 22, then Subtract Line 5. Multiply the result
    by Line 14   _____

25. Dc Factor at RT = Line 24. If Line 5 is greater than the sum of
    Lines 10 and 22, use a Gc Factor instead.   _____

26. Present Value of Dividends: Multiply Line 11 by Lines 12, 14, and 25 _____

27. Present Value of Final Cash Flow: Multiply Line 21 by Line 23   _____

28. Net Present Value: Add Lines 26 and 27, then Subtract Line 3   _____

Table 11-13. Continued.

If the present value on Line 28 is positive, try a discount rate 5 percentage points higher. If Line 28 is negative, try a discount rate 5 percentage points lower. Use Table 4-3 to speed the solution for rate of return.

E. Maximum Allowable Price

Enter your opportunity cost as the discount rate in Line 22, and complete Lines 23 through 27.

29. Subtract Line 13 from 1.0. Multiply the result by Lines 19 and 23 _____

30. Add Lines 26 and 29 _____

31. Multiply Line 13 by Line 23. Subtract the result from 1.0 _____

32. Maximum Allowable Price: Divide Line 30 by Lines 2 and 31 _____

---

you plan to hold the stock, the firm is mature. Use the calculation form in Table 11-13 to evaluate the stock.

Enter the basic data on the stock and the firm in Part A. Enter the rate of return you expect the firm to earn in line 4, how fast you expect it to grow in line 5, and the equity fraction in the firm's capital pool in line 6. Line 7 shows the dividend payout fraction that is consistent with this rate of return, growth rate, and equity fraction. Line 11 shows the corresponding dividend per share. Enter your after-tax factor, capital gains tax rate, and the period you expect to hold the stock in Part B.

Part C develops the cash flows you should expect from this stock. At steady-state conditions, per-share capital, earnings, dividends, and the stock price all grow at the firm's growth rate, less the growth rate of shares outstanding. The growth factor in line 16 shows how these factors will grow during the time you hold the stock. To find the price when you sell the stock, multiply the current stock price by the growth factor in line 16. The final cash flow in line 21 is the proceeds from the sale of the stock, less capital gains taxes and commissions.

Discount these cash flows in Part D. Begin discounting at your opportunity cost. The Dc discount factor in line 25 is used to discount dividends. This discount factor depends on the discount rate, the firm's growth rate, and the growth rate of outstanding shares. If the firm's growth rate is greater than the sum of the discount rate and the share growth rate, the net rate is a growth rate. In this case, use a Gc growth factor in place of the Dc discount factor. Line 28 shows the net present value at the discount rate in line 22. Part E of the calculation form develops the maximum price you should pay.

Example 11-5. You are interested in a mature firm that earns a 12 percent return and is growing steadily at 8 percent per year. The firm has $1,250 million of capital employed, 60 percent of which is equity capital. Forty million shares of stock are outstanding. You expect the number of shares to grow gradually at 0.5 percent per year. The current price is $45 per share. At a 12 percent return and $31.25 of capital per share, earnings are (0.12)(31.25), or $3.75 per share. The price/earnings ratio is (45)/(3.75), or 12. You plan to hold the stock for five years. What rate of return should you expect? If your after-tax opportunity cost is 7 percent and you pay a 37 percent incremental tax rate, what is the most you should pay for this stock?

Table 11-14 illustrates the evaluation. Enter the basic data about the stock in Part A. Line 7 shows that a dividend payout fraction of 0.6 is consistent with a 12 percent return, 8 percent per year growth rate, and an equity fraction of 0.6. The initial dividends in line 11 are $2.25 per share.

At steady-state conditions, the stock price will grow 7.5 percent per year—the firm's 8 percent per year growth rate, less the 0.5 percent per year growth in outstanding shares. At this net growth over a five-year period, the Gi growth factor in line 16 is 1.4550. Line 17 shows a stock price of $65.47 when you sell in five years. After a 1 percent commission and a $7.17 capital gains tax, line 21 gives your net proceeds from the sale as $57.65.

Begin discounting at your 7 percent opportunity cost. The firm's 8 percent per year growth rate is greater than the sum of the 7 percent discount rate and the 0.5 percent per year share growth rate. The net rate is a growth rate of 0.5 percent. Therefore, a Gc growth factor is used in line 25 to discount dividends. Discounting is straightforward. The net present value in line 28 is $2.36 per share. The maximum allowable price from line 32 is $48.16 per share.

This stock might be an attractive investment. The present value at your opportunity cost is positive, and the current price is 6.5 percent below the maximum price you should pay. If you discount again at a higher discount rate and use Table 4-3 to complete the calculation, you will find a rate of return of 8.1 percent. Whether you invest in this stock or not depends on how this 8.1 percent return compares with the returns you expect from alternative investment opportunities.

TABLE 11-14
Stocks of Mature Firms—Example 11-5

A. The Firm

1. Stock Price, $/share	45
2. Divide Commission (%) by 100, and Add the result to 1.0	1.01
3. Net Cost: Multiply Line 1 by Line 2	45.45
4. Rate of Return, %	12
5. Growth Rate, %	8
6. Equity Fraction	0.6
7. Dividend Payout Fraction: Multiply Line 5 by Line 6, then Divide by Line 4. Subtract the result from 1.0	0.6
8. Capital Employed, $millions	1,250
9. Shares Outstanding, millions	40
10. Share Growth Rate, %/yr.	0.5
11. Dividend: Multiply Line 4 by Lines 7 and 8. Then Divide by Line 9 and by 100	2.25

B. The Investor

12. Divide Incremental Tax Rate (%) by 100; Subtract the result from 1.0	0.63

Table 11-14. Continued.

13. Divide Capital Gains Tax Rate (%) by 100	0.37
14. Investment Period, years	5

C. Cash Flows

15. RT: Subtract Line 10 from Line 5, then Multiply by Line 14	37.5
16. Gi Factor at RT = Line 15	1.4550
17. Future Stock Price, $/share: Multiply Line 1 by Line 16	65.47
18. Divide Commission (%) by 100, Subtract the result from 1.0	0.99
19. Net Sale: Multiply Line 17 by Line 18	64.82
20. Capital Gains Tax: Subtract Line 3 from Line 19. Multiply the result by Line 13	7.17
21. Final Cash Flow: Subtract Line 20 from Line 19	57.65

D. Discounting

22. Trial Discount Rate, %	7
23. Di Factor at RT = Line 14 times Line 22	0.7047
24. RT: Add Lines 10 and 22, then Subtract Line 5. Multiply the result by Line 14	2.5
25. Dc Factor at RT = Line 24. If Line 5 is greater than the sum of Lines 10 and 22, use a Gc Factor instead.	1.0126
26. Present Value of Dividends: Multiply Line 11 by Lines 12, 14, and 25	7.18
27. Present Value of Final Cash Flow: Multiply Line 21 by Line 23	40.63
28. Net Present Value: Add Lines 26 and 27, then Subtract Line 3	2.36

If the present value on Line 28 is positive, try a discount rate 5 percentage points higher. If Line 28 is negative, try a discount rate 5 percentage points lower. Use Table 4-3 to speed the solution for rate of return.

E. Maximum Allowable Price

Enter your opportunity cost as the discount rate in Line 22, and complete Lines 23 through 27.

29. Subtract Line 13 from 1.0. Multiply the result by Lines 19 and 23	28.78
30. Add Lines 26 and 29	35.96
31. Multiply Line 13 by Line 23. Subtract the result from 1.0	0.7393
32. Maximum Allowable Price: Divide Line 30 by Lines 2 and 31	$48.16

Growth Stock

To evaluate a growth stock, begin the evaluation by analyzing the firm as suggested in Chapter 10. If you expect the firm's rate of return to change during the period you plan to hold the stock, estimate the long-run return and the half-life that measures how fast rate of return will decay. Then use Table 7-1 to estimate rates of return at the three intermediate times needed for discounting dividends and at the end of the investment

TABLE 11-15
Calculation Form—Growth Stocks

A. The Stock

1. Current Price, $/share _____
2. Divide Commission (%) by 100; Add the result to 1.0 _____
3. Net Cost: Multiply Line 1 by Line 2 _____
4. Final Capital, $/share, from Table 7-5 _____
5. Final Rate of Return, %, from Table 7-1 _____
6. Final Earnings: Multiply Line 4 by Line 5, then Divide by 100 _____
7. Equity Fraction _____
8. Final Price/Earnings Ratio from Table 7-1 _____

B. The Investor

9. Divide Incremental Tax Rate (%) by 100; Subtract the result from 1.0 _____
10. Divide Capital Gains Tax Rate (%) by 100 _____
11. Investment Period, years _____

C. Future Cash Flows

12. Future Price: Multiply Line 6 by Line 8 _____
13. Divide Commission (%) by 100; Subtract the result from 1.0 _____
14. Net Sale: Multiply Line 12 by Line 13 _____
15. Capital Gains Tax: Subtract Line 3 from Line 14. Multiply the result by Line 10 _____
16. Net Proceeds: Subtract Line 15 from Line 14 _____
17. Time Factors: ___0.113___   ___0.5___   ___0.887___
18. Time: Multiply each entry on Line 17 by Line 11 _____ _____ _____
19. Capital, $/share, from Table 7-5 _____ _____ _____
20. Growth Rate, %/yr., from Table 7-1 _____ _____ _____
21. Rate of Return, %, from Table 7-1 _____ _____ _____
22. Multiply Line 7 by Line 20, then divide by Line 21 _____ _____ _____
23. Dividend Payout Fraction: Subtract Line 22 from 1.0 _____ _____ _____
24. Dividends, $/share: Multiply Line 19 by Lines 21 and 23, then Divide by 100 _____ _____ _____

D. Discounting

25. Discount Rate, % _____
26. Di Factor at RT = Line 25 times Line 11 _____
27. Present Value of Final Proceeds: Multiply Line 16 by Line 26 _____

Table 11-15. Continued.

28. Multiply each entry on Line 18 by
Line 25   _____ _____ _____

29. Di Factor at RT = Line 28   _____ _____ _____

30. Multiply Line 9 by Lines 24 and 29   _____ _____ _____

31. Add the first and last entries on Line 30; Multiply the result by
0.278   _____

32. Multiply the second entry on Line 30 by 0.444   _____

33. Present Value of Dividends: Add Lines 31 and 32; Multiply the
result by Line 11   _____

34. Net Present Value: Add Lines 27 and 33, then Subtract Line 3   _____

If the present value on Line 34 is positive, try a discount rate 5 percentage points higher. If Line 34 is negative, try a discount rate 5 percentage points lower. Use Table 4-3 to complete the solution for rate of return.

E. Maximum Allowable Price

Enter your after-tax opportunity cost in Line 25 and complete Lines 26 through 33. Continue with Line 35.

35. Subtract Line 10 from 1.0. Multiply the result by Lines 14 and 26   _____

36. Add Lines 33 and 35   _____

37. Multiply Line 10 by Line 26. Subtract the result from 1.0   _____

38. Maximum Allowable Price: Divide Line 36 by Lines 2 and 37   _____

period. In the same way, use Table 7-1 to estimate how fast you expect the firm's growth rate to slow. Then use Table 7-5 to convert the projection of growth rates into the cor-

Example 11-6. In Chapter 7, you evaluated a growth firm that earned a return of 23 percent and was growing 30 percent per year. The firm employed $5 of capital per share, of which 65 percent was equity capital. The stock sold for $46 per share. You projected that the firm's rate of return would gradually approach a long-run limit of 9 percent, that capital growth would approach a long-run limit of 8 percent per year, and that the price/earnings ratio would gradually approach a long-run value of 11. These factors approached their long-run limits with five-year half-lives. You planned to hold the stock for 10 years. In Chapter 7, you ignored taxes and commissions and concluded that you could earn a return of 6.7 percent. Now you want to recognize the effect of taxes and commissions. What return should you expect if your incremental tax rate is 37 percent and you pay a discount broker a 1 percent commission? What is the most you should pay if your after-tax opportunity cost is 8 percent?

Table 11-16 shows how to evaluate this growth stock. Before using the calculation form, you will have analyzed the firm and used Table 7-1 to project the firm's rate of return, growth rate, and price/earnings ratio. You will also have used Table 7-5 to convert the growth projection to the corresponding projection of capital employed per share. These projections were developed in Chapter 7. Enter the projections in the appropriate blanks in Parts A and C of Table 11-16.

TABLE 11-16
Growth Stocks—Example 11-6

A. The Stock

1. Current Price, $/share	46
2. Divide Commission (%) by 100; Add the result to 1.0	1.01
3. Net Cost: Multiply Line 1 by Line 2	46.46
4. Final Capital, $/share, from Table 7-5	35.85
5. Final Rate of Return, %, from Table 7-1	12.5
6. Final Earnings: Multiply Line 4 by Line 5, then Divide by 100	4.48
7. Equity Fraction	0.65
8. Final Price/Earnings Ratio from Table 7-1	18.25

B. The Investor

9. Divide Incremental Tax Rate (%) by 100; Subtract the result from 1.0	0.63
10. Divide Capital Gains Tax Rate (%) by 100	0.37
11. Investment Period, years	10

C. Future Cash Flows

12. Future Price: Multiply Line 6 by Line 8			81.76
13. Divide Commission (%) by 100; Subtract the result from 1.0			0.99
14. Net Sale: Multiply Line 12 by Line 13			80.94
15. Capital Gains Tax: Subtract Line 3 from Line 14. Multiply the result by Line 10			12.76
16. Net Proceeds: Subtract Line 15 from Line 14			68.18
17. Time Factors:	0.113	0.5	0.887
18. Time: Multiply each entry on Line 17 by Line 11	1.13	5.0	8.87
19. Capital, $/share, from Table 7-5	6.87	16.34	30.71
20. Growth Rate, %/yr., from Table 7-1	26.80	19.00	14.44
21. Rate of Return, %, from Table 7-1	20.97	16.00	13.10
22. Multiply Line 7 by Line 20, then Divide by Line 21	0.831	0.772	0.716
23. Dividend Payout Fraction: Subtract Line 22 from 1.0	0.169	0.228	0.284
24. Dividends, $/share: Multiply Line 19 by Lines 21 and 23, then Divide by 100	0.24	0.60	1.14

D. Discounting

25. Discount Rate, %	8
26. Di Factor at RT = Line 25 times Line 11	0.4493
27. Present Value of Final Proceeds: Multiply Line 16 by Line 26	30.63

Table 11-16. Continued.

28. Multiply each entry on Line 18 by Line 25	9.0	40.0	71.0
29. Di Factor at RT = Line 28	0.9136	0.6703	0.4918
30. Multiply Line 9 by Lines 24 and 29	0.1381	0.2534	0.3532
31. Add the first and last entries on Line 30; Multiply the result by 0.278			0.1366
32. Multiply the second entry on Line 30 by 0.444			0.1125
33. Present Value of Dividends: Add Lines 31 and 32; Multiply the result by Line 11			2.49
34. Net Present Value: Add Lines 27 and 33, then Subtract Line 3			−$13.34

If the present value on Line 34 is positive, try a discount rate 5 percentage points higher. If Line 34 is negative, try a discount rate 5 percentage points lower. Use Table 4-3 to complete the solution for rate of return.

E. Maximum Allowable Price

Enter your after-tax opportunity cost in Line 25 and complete Lines 26 through 33. Continue with Line 35.

35. Subtract Line 10 from 1.0. Multiply the result by Lines 14 and 26	22.91
36. Add Lines 33 and 35	25.40
37. Multiply Line 10 by Line 26. Subtract the result from 1.0	0.8338
38. Maximum Allowable Price: Divide Line 36 by Lines 2 and 37	$30.16

Project future cash flows in Part C. The final earnings and price/earnings ratio recorded in Part A give a stock price of $81.76 when you sell in 10 years. After capital gains taxes and commissions, line 16 shows you will net $68.18 from the sale.

The entries for times 11.3, 50, and 88.7 percent of the investment period are used to calculate dividends consistent with your projections of the firm's rate of return, capital and share growth rate, and equity fraction. Line 24 shows how dividends grow as slowing growth frees more funds to pay dividends.

Discount these cash flows in Part D. Begin with your after-tax opportunity cost as the first trial discount rate. Line 27 shows that the net proceeds when you sell the stock in 10 years have a present value of $30.63. Dividends are discounted and converted to an after-tax basis in lines 28 through 33. Line 33 shows that dividends have a present value of $2.49 per share. Net present value in line 34 is − $13.34 per share. The maximum allowable price in line 38 is $30.16 per share.

Taxes and commissions make this stock even less attractive than calculated in Chapter 7. The maximum allowable price is 34 percent below the current market price. If you continue the evaluation, you will find a rate of return of only 4.6 percent—significantly less than the 6.7 percent return found before taxes and commissions were included.

Mutual Funds

Use Table 11-17 to evaluate mutual funds. Begin the evaluation by analyzing the fund's historical performance, as outlined in Chapter 10. That analysis provides the information

TABLE 11-17
Calculation Form—Mutual Funds

A. The Fund

1. Price _____

2. Divide Fee (%) by 100, Add the result to 1.0 _____

3. Cost: Multiply Line 1 by Line 2 _____

4. Rate of Return, % _____

5. Dividend Payout Fraction _____

6. Growth, %/yr.: Subtract Line 5 from 1.0, Multiply the result by Line 4 _____

7. Capital Gain Fraction _____

8. Expense, % or NAV _____

9. Initial Distribution: Multiply Line 1 by Lines 4 and 5. Divide the result by 100 _____

B. The Investor

10. Divide Incremental Tax Rate (%) by 100 _____

11. Divide Capital Gains Tax Rate (%) by 100 _____

12. Investment Period, years _____

C. Future Cash Flows

13. Gi Growth Factor at RT = Line 6 times Line 12 _____

14. Future NAV: Multiply Line 1 by Line 13 _____

15. Divide Fee (%) on Sale by 100; Subtract the result from 1.0 _____

16. Net Sales: Multiply Line 14 by Line 15 _____

17. Subtract Line 7 from 1.0. Multiply the result by Line 10 _____

18. Average Tax Rate on Fund Distributions: Multiply Line 7 by Line 11. Add the result to Line 17 _____

19. Capital Gains Tax: Subtract Line 3 from Line 16. Multiply the result by Line 11 _____

20. Net Proceeds: Subtract Line 19 from Line 16 _____

D. Discounting

21. Trial Discount Rate, % _____

22. Di Discount Factor at RT = Line 12 times Line 21 _____

23. RT: Subtract Line 6 from Line 21. Multiply the result by Line 12 _____

24. Dc Discount Factor at RT = Line 23. If Line 6 is greater than Line 21, use a Gc Factor instead. _____

25. Present Value of Net Sale: Multiply Line 20 by Line 22 _____

26. Present Value of Distributions: Subtract Line 18 from 1.0. Multiply the result by Lines 9, 12, and 24 _____

27. Multiply Line 1 by Lines 8 and 12. Divide the result by 100 _____

Table 11-17. Continued.

28. Present Value of Tax on Fund Expenses: Multiply Line 10 by Lines
    24 and 27   _____

29. Present Value: Add Lines 25 and 26, then Subtract Lines 3 and 28   _____

If Line 29 is positive, choose a discount rate 5 percentage points higher, and repeat Lines 22
through 29. If Line 29 is negative, choose a discount rate 5 percentage points lower. Use Table
4-3 to complete the calculation for rate of return.

E. Maximum Allowable Price

Use your opportunity cost as the discount rate in Line 21, and complete Lines 22 through 28.
Then continue below:

30. Subtract Line 11 from 1.0. Multiply the result by Lines 16 and 22   _____

31. Add Lines 26 and 30, then Subtract Line 28   _____

32. Multiply Line 11 by Line 22. Subtract the result from 1.0   _____

33. Maximum Allowable Price: Divide Line 31 by Lines 2 and 32   _____

you need to complete Part A of Table 11-17. Record your tax rate and your investment
period in Part B of the form.

Part C of the calculation form develops the future cash flows you expect the fund to
generate. Line 14 shows the net asset value when you sell. Line 16 gives the net proceeds after sales fees. Line 18 gives the average tax rate you will pay on distributions
from the fund. Line 19 gives capital gains taxes. Line 20 develops the net proceeds after
capital gains taxes.

Begin discounting at your opportunity cost in line 21. If the discount rate in line 21 is
greater than the growth rate of net asset value in line 6, use a Dc discount factor in line
24. If the growth rate is greater, use a Gc growth factor instead. If you meet the 2 percent test and can deduct the fund's expenses on your federal tax return, enter a zero in
line 28. If you cannot deduct these expenses, you will have to include them as taxable
income. Line 28 shows the present value of your tax obligation. Line 29 gives the total
present value. The fund might be attractive if the present value on line 19 is positive.
Continue discounting at a higher discount rate, and use Table 4-3 to calculate the rate of
return you should expect.

Example 11-7. You analyzed the Magellan Fund's historical performance in Chapter
10, and recorded your results in Table 10-9. Over the past five years, you found that net
asset value grew 7.39 percent per year. The fund paid 58 percent of its earnings out as
dividends. You found a rate of return of 17.6 percent consistent with this growth rate and
dividend payout. You expect this performance will continue for the next five years. The
fund sells at a net asset value of $52.92 per share, plus a 3 percent sales fee. There is no
fee when you sell your shares. What rate of return can you expect if you invest in this
fund and hold your shares for five years? What is the maximum price you should pay?
Your incremental tax rate is 37 percent and your opportunity cost is 7 percent.

Use Table 11-17 to evaluate the fund. Table 11-18 shows the evaluation. Enter the
$52.92 net asset value in line 1. Line 3 shows your cost will be $54.51, including the 3
percent sales fee. Enter the fund's 17.6 percent rate of return in line 4, the 0.58 divi-

TABLE 11-18
Mutual Funds—Example 11-7

A. The Fund

1. Price — 52.92

2. Divide Fee (%) by 100, add the result to 1.0 — 1.03

3. Cost: Multiply Line 1 by Line 2 — 54.51

4. Rate of Return, % — 17.6

5. Dividend Payout Fraction — 0.58

6. Growth, %/yr.: Subtract Line 5 from 1.0, Multiply the result by Line 4 — 7.39

7. Capital Gain Fraction — 0.9

8. Expense, % or NAV — 1.1

9. Initial Distribution: Multiply Line 1 by Lines 4 and 5. Divide the result by 100 — 5.40

B. The Investor

10. Divide Incremental Tax Rate (%) by 100 — 0.37

11. Divide Capital Gains Tax Rate (%) by 100 — 0.37

12. Investment Period, years — 5

C. Future Cash Flows

13. Gi Growth Factor at RT = Line 6 times Line 12 — 1.4470

14. Future NAV: Multiply Line 1 by Line 13 — 76.58

15. Divide Fee (%) on Sale by 100; Subtract the result from 1.0 — 1.0

16. Net Sales: Multiply Line 14 by Line 15 — 76.58

17. Subtract Line 7 from 1.0. Multiply the result by Line 10 — 0.037

18. Average Tax Rate on Fund Distributions: Multiply Line 7 by Line 11. Add the result to Line 17 — 0.37

19. Capital Gains Tax: Subtract Line 3 from Line 16. Multiply the result by Line 11 — 8.17

20. Net Proceeds: Subtract Line 19 from Line 16 — 68.41

D. Discounting

21. Trial Discount Rate, % — 7

22. Di Discount Factor at RT = Line 12 times Line 21 — 0.7047

23. RT: Subtract Line 6 from Line 21. Multiply the result by Line 12 — 1.95

24. Dc Discount Factor at RT = Line 23. If Line 6 is greater than Line 21, use a Gc Factor instead. — 1.0098

25. Present Value of Net Sale: Multiply Line 20 by Line 22 — 48.21

26. Present Value of Distributions: Subtract Line 18 from 1.0. Multiply the result by Lines 9, 12, and 24 — 17.18

Table 11-18. Continued.

27. Multiply Line 1 by Lines 8 and 12. Divide the result by 100	2.91
28. Present Value of Tax on Fund Expenses: Multiply Line 10 by Lines 24 and 27	1.09
29. Present Value: Add Lines 25 and 26, then Subtract Lines 3 and 28	9.79

If Line 29 is positive, choose a discount rate 5 percentage points higher, and repeat Lines 22 through 29. If Line 29 is negative, choose a discount rate 5 percentage points lower. Use Table 4-3 to complete the calculation for rate of return.

E. Maximum Allowable Price

Use your opportunity cost as the discount rate in Line 21, and complete Lines 22 through 28. Then continue below:

30. Subtract Line 11 from 1.0. Multiply the result by Lines 16 and 22	34.00
31. Add Lines 26 and 30, then Subtract Line 28	50.09
32. Multiply Line 11 by Line 22. Subtract the result from 1.0	0.7393
33. Maximum Allowable Price: Divide Line 31 by Lines 2 and 32	65.78

dend payout fraction in line 5, and the 7.39 percent per year net asset value growth rate in line 6. The capital gain fraction and the fund's expenses in lines 7 and 8 come directly from the analysis of the fund in Table 10-9. At the conditions you projected in Part A, line 9 shows your initial dividend should be $5.40 per share.

Enter your tax rates and the five-year investment period in Part B. The Gi growth factor for a 7.39 percent per year growth rate and a five-year investment period in line 13 is 1.4470. At that growth factor, line 14 shows you should be able to sell your shares for $76.58 in five years. Because ordinary income and capital gains are taxed at the same rate (1989), line 18 shows you will pay a 37 percent tax on distributions from the fund. The net proceeds after a capital gains tax of $8.17 is $68.41, as line 20 shows.

Begin discounting at your 7 percent opportunity cost in line 21. Use a Gc growth factor in line 24 because the 7.39 percent per year net asset growth rate is greater than the 7 percent discount rate. The present value of distributions from the fund is $17.18 in line 26. Present value of the net proceeds when you sell is $48.21 in line 25. Assume you do not meet the 2 percent test on your federal tax return, and have to report the fund's expenses as taxable income. Line 29 shows a net present value of $9.79 for this investment.

The positive present value shows that the Magellan Fund might be an attractive investment. If you continue the analysis and use Table 4-3 to complete the solution, you will find a rate of return of 10.8 percent. The Magellan Fund is attractive, provided you have no alternative investments that offer higher returns.

Part E of the calculation form shows that you should not pay more than $65.78. The fund's price in this example is 17 percent below the maximum you should pay.

SUMMARY

☐ The first step in gaining control over your investment program is to know your incremental tax rate and your opportunity cost. Calculation forms simplify both tasks. Once you know these basic factors, you can tune security analysis to your particular situation.

☐ Calculation forms simplify security evaluation. The forms in this chapter cover certificates of deposit, bonds, zero coupon bonds, mortgage-backed securities, stocks of mature firms, mutual funds, and growth stocks. With a little practice, you should be able to work through these forms in just a few minutes.

☐ When you evaluate a security, spend most of your time developing an understanding of the cash flows you expect that security to generate. If you are evaluating a stock, analyze the firm as the last chapter suggests. Make careful projections of the return you expect the company to earn and how fast you expect it to grow. If the firm is a growth firm, estimate how fast it is likely to mature. If you are evaluating a bond, spend your time checking the bond's safety and call features. Calculating the rate of return and the maximum price you should pay should take only a small part of the total evaluation time.

12

Investment Results with Typical Stocks

CHAPTER 6 DEVELOPED THE THEORETICAL BASIS FOR VALUING A STOCK. NOW IT'S time to learn what that theory can tell us about real stocks. How important are market interest rates? How important are commissions? Can long-term investors achieve better results than short-term traders who move in and out of the market frequently? How critical is the rate of return the firm earns? The dividends it pays? The debt it carries? Let's examine a typical stock, and see how these factors affect the stock's value.

THE TYPICAL STOCK

What is a typical stock? Perhaps the best definition is the statistics Standard and Poor's maintains on a broad group of 500 major stocks. The statistics include earnings, dividends, capital structure, stock prices, and the number of outstanding shares. This chapter uses Standard and Poor's 500 stock average to describe the typical stock.

Chapter 6 showed you that a firm's rate of return, growth rate, price/earnings ratio, and debt level are the primary factors that determine a stock's value. Dividends are also important, but the dividends a firm is able to pay depends on the rate of return the firm earns, how fast it is growing, and the equity fraction in its capital pool. Once you project these three factors, the growth equation of Chapter 6 fixes the dividends a firm is able to pay.

Figure 12-1 shows the characteristics of the typical stock, as measured by the Standard and Poor's 500 stock average from 1970 through 1988. The rate of return shown in the upper-left plot fluctuates with the state of the economy. Return on capital employed varied from 6.5 percent to 11.7 percent, and the typical firm averaged a 9 percent return. Return on equity varied from 11.2 percent to 17.8 percent, and the average return was 14.1 percent. Growth of capital employed, shown in the upper-right plot, ranged from 6.4 percent to 14.1 percent, and growth averaged 9.4 percent per year over the whole period. Growth has been slowing. Over the most recent 10 years, growth slipped to 8.5 percent per year.

The lower-left plot shows the dividend payout fraction. The typical firm paid 35 percent of its earnings out as dividends in the 1970s. Dividends have been rising as growth slowed. The dividend payout fraction over the most recent five years averaged 0.55. Most firms try to maintain stable growth of dividends. They keep dividends stable even though earnings fluctuate. During a year when earnings are unusually low, firms frequently maintain dividend payments and allow the dividend payout fraction to rise. Firms might even pay a dividend when the firm loses money just to maintain a record of steady

Fig. 12-1

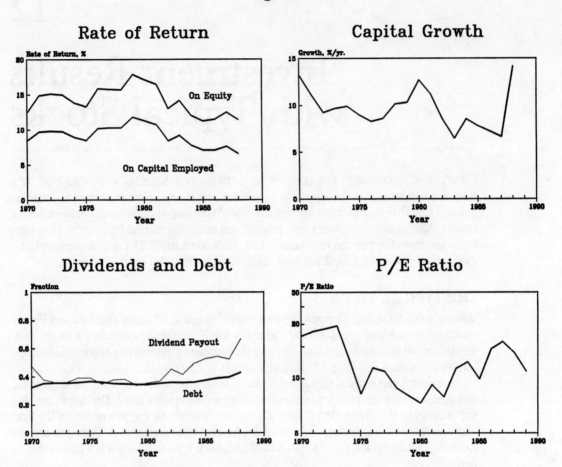

dividends. The firms then compensate by allowing the dividend payout fraction to fall in a subsequent year when earnings are unusually high. Over time, the dividend payout fraction averages out as the target level management sets.

The typical firm has a stable equity fraction, as the lower-left plot shows. The typical firm carried 65 percent equity and 35 percent debt in its capital pool. The amount of debt firms have taken on to finance the recent wave of acquisitions lowered the equity fraction to 0.57.

Price/earnings ratios are more volatile as can be seen in the lower-right plot. Price/earnings ratios varied from a high of 19.5 in 1972 to a low of 7.3 in 1979. The typical stock sold at a price/earnings ratio of 12 in 1989. Price/earnings ratios change as market interest rates change. Changing interest rates change investor's opportunity costs and the discount rate they use to value securities. The price/earnings ratio also changes as investors change their expectations of the firm's future earnings. Firms that have not borrowed heavily to finance acquisitions should resemble the typical firm during the 1970 to 1984 period. Based on the data in Fig. 9-1, current values for the typical firm are:

Rate of Return, %	
on Capital Employed	9
on Stockholder Equity	13.8
Dividend Payout Fraction	0.4
Debt Fraction	0.35
Equity Fraction	0.65
Price/Earnings Ratio	11

Capital growth is also a critical parameter, but it cannot be estimated independently of the firm's rate of return, dividend payout, and equity fraction. The growth equation in Chapter 6 shows how the firm's growth rate depends on the dividend payout fraction, f_D, the return on capital employed, R, and equity fraction f_E:

$$g = (1-f_D) \; (R)/(f_E)$$

The capital growth rate for the typical firm with the characteristics listed above is:

$$g = (1-0.4) \; (0.09)/(0.65) = 0.083$$

Therefore, capital employed in the typical firm grows about 8.3 percent per year under steady-state conditions.

EVALUATING THE AVERAGE STOCK

The Dividend Growth Model in Chapter 6 showed the rate of return you should expect under steady-state conditions. That model ignores taxes, inflation, and broker's commissions, however. The Dividend Growth Model gives a return of 11.9 percent for this typical stock:

$$\text{Rate of Return} = g-n+(f_D)/(P/E) = 0.083-0+(0.4)/(11) = 0.119$$

If you expect 5 percent per year inflation, the real rate of return is 11.9 minus 5, or 6.9 percent.

Taxes, inflation, and broker's commissions reduce this return significantly. The calculation forms in Chapter 11 account for these factors, and provide realistic estimates of the after-tax rate of return you should expect from investing in a typical stock.

Example 12-1. Suppose you consider investing in this typical stock. Assume the firm employs one billion dollars of capital and has 20 million shares outstanding. At a 9 percent return, earnings are $4.50 per share. At a price/earnings ratio of 11, the stock costs $49.50 per share. What rate of return should you expect if your incremental tax rate is 37 percent? What is the most you should pay if your after-tax opportunity cost is 7 percent? Assume you use a full-service broker, and pay a 2.5 percent commission, and hold the stock for 10 years.

Table 12-1 shows the evaluation. Enter the characteristics of the stock in Part A and your tax rate and the investment period in Part B. Line 17 shows a price of $113.52 when you sell in 10 years. Line 21 shows net proceeds of $88.50 after capital gains taxes and commissions.

Discounting at your 7 percent opportunity cost gives a present worth of $5.32 per share. Line 32 shows a maximum allowable price of $55.86, 13 percent higher than the

TABLE 12-1
Calculation Form—Example 12-1

A. The Firm

1. Stock Price, $/share	49.50
2. Divide Commission (%) by 100, and Add the result to 1.0	1.025
3. Net Cost: Multiply Line 1 by Line 2	50.74
4. Rate of Return, %	9
5. Growth Rate, %	8.3
6. Equity Fraction	0.65
7. Dividend Payout Fraction: Multiply Line 5 by Line 6, then divide by Line 4. Subtract the result from 1.0	0.4
8. Capital Employed, $millions	1,000
9. Shares Outstanding, millions	20
10. Share Growth Rate, %/yr.	0
11. Dividend: Multiply Line 4 by Lines 7 and 8. Then Divide by Line 9 and by 100	1.80

B. The Investor

12. After-Tax Factor	0.63
13. Divide Capital Gains Tax Rate (%) by 100	0.37
14. Investment Period, years	10

C. Cash Flows

15. RT: Subtract Line 10 from Line 5, then Multiply by Line 14	83
16. Gi Factor at RT = Line 15	2.2933
17. Future Stock Price, $/share: Multiply Line 1 by Line 16	113.52
18. Divide Commission (%) by 100, Subtract the result from 1.0	0.975
19. Net Sale: Multiply Line 17 by Line 18	110.68
20. Capital Gains Tax: Subtract Line 3 from Line 19. Multiply the result by Line 13	22.18
21. Final Cash Flow: Subtract Line 20 from Line 19	88.50

D. Discounting

22. Trial Discount Rate, %	7
23. Di Factor at RT = Line 14 times Line 22	0.4966
24. RT: Add Lines 10 and 22, then Subtract Line 5. Multiply the result by Line 14	13
25. Dc Factor at RT = Line 24. If Line 2 is greater than the sum of Lines 21 and 6, use a Gc Factor instead.	1.0679
26. Present Value of Dividends: Multiply Line 11 by Lines 12, 14, and 25	12.11
27. Present Value of Final Cash Flow: Multiply Line 21 by Line 23	43.95
28. Net Present Value: Add Lines 26 and 27, then Subtract Line 3	5.32

Table 12-1. Continued.

If the present value on Line 28 is positive, try a discount rate 5 percentage points higher. If
Line 28 is negative, try a discount rate 5 percentage points lower. Use Table 4-3 to speed the
solution for rate of return.

E. Maximum Allowable Price

Enter your opportunity cost as the discount rate in Line 22, and complete Lines 23 through 27.

29. Subtract Line 13 from 1.0. Multiply the result by Lines 19 and 23	34.63
30. Add Lines 26 and 29	46.74
31. Multiply Line 13 by Line 23. Subtract the result from 1.0	0.8163
32. Maximum Allowable Price: Divide Line 30 by Lines 2 and 31	55.86

$49.50 market price. If you continue the calculation, you will find a rate of return of 8.1
percent. The real return after 5 percent per year inflation is 3.1 percent.

Consequently, allowing for taxes and commissions reduces the rate of return for
investing in the average stock about one-third—from 11.9 percent calculated from the
Dividend Growth Model to 8.1 percent. At the expected inflation rate of 5 percent, taxes
and commissions cut the real rate of return by more than half—from 6.9 percent to 3.1
percent.

Broker's Commissions and the Investment Period

Your broker will charge a commission when you buy a stock, and a second commission
when you later sell the stock. Commissions from full-service brokers average about 2.5
percent of the value of the stock. Discount brokers charge a lower commission of about
1 percent of the value of the stock. A commission is part of the cost of investing in stocks
and is included in the calculation forms in the last chapter.

How commissions affect your return depends on how long you hold the stock. If you
are a long-term investor, commissions will be small relative to the dividends you collect
and the gain in stock price over a long investment period. But if you are a short-term
investor, dividends and stock prices will not have much time to grow in the short
time you hold the stock. Commissions will then be much larger relative to the other cash
flows.

Figure 12-2 shows how broker's commissions and the investment period affect the
rate of return for investing in the average stock. The plot shows returns with no commissions, with commissions of 1 percent typical of discount brokers, and 2.5 percent commissions typical of full-service brokers. Investment periods range from 0.5 to 20 years.
The investor's federal and state incremental tax rate totals 37 percent. Figure 12-2
shows that commissions can eat up most of the return available to short-term investors.

Fig. 12-2
EFFECT OF COMMISSIONS
AND INVESTMENT PERIOD

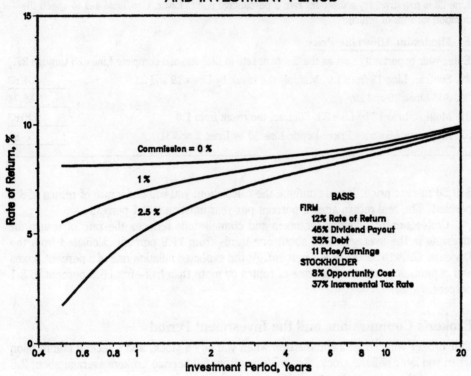

The results are:

Investment	Rate of Return, %		
	Commission		
Period, years	% of Stock Price:		
	0	**1**	**2.5**
0.5	7.58	5.02	1.22
1	7.64	6.34	4.40
2	7.75	7.08	6.08
5	8.07	7.77	7.34
10	8.53	8.37	8.13
20	9.23	9.14	9.00

Brokers capture most of the gains from investors who hold their stock for only short periods. An investor who holds an average stock only half a year and who pays a 2.5 percent commission loses 84 percent of the potential return available at no commission. His rate of return drops from 7.58 percent without a commission to only 1.22 percent with a 2.5 percent commission. Even investors who use discount brokers lose 34 percent of the potential rate of return. An investor who holds his stock 10 years instead of only one-half year loses only 4.7 percent of the potential rate of return at 2.5 percent commission, and only 1.9 percent of the potential return at a 1 percent commission.

The lesson of Fig. 12-2 is clear. Avoid short-term investments in stocks and frequent switches from one stock to another. Brokers capture most of the return from such investments. Analyze companies carefully, and invest only in those companies you think you will be comfortable holding for several years. Use a discount broker, and your returns will be even higher, particularly if you invest for short periods.

Long-term investors have an added advantage. Commissions are a smaller part of the total cash flows the longer you hold a stock. Therefore, your rate of return increases steadily the longer you hold the stock. These results show that you can raise your rate of return from typical stocks about 44 percent by holding your stock 10 years instead of one year, and by dealing with a discount broker. The examples in the rest of this chapter are for 10-year investments so that commissions do not distort the effects of the other factors under study.

EFFECT OF MARKET FACTORS ON PRICE/EARNINGS RATIO

You are now ready to make realistic evaluations of how market interest rates, the rate of return a mature firm earns, how fast it grows, the dividends it pays, and the amount of debt it carries in its capital pool affect the maximum price/earnings ratio you should pay for a typical stock.

Assume that you hold the stock 10 years, and then sell it at an average price/earnings ratio of 11. You use a discount broker, and pay a commission of 1 percent when you buy the stock and again when you later sell the stock. Your after-tax opportunity cost is 7 percent.

Effect of Market Interest Rate

Market interest rates fluctuate continually in order to match the supply of funds to the demands for loans. As market interest rates fluctuate, your opportunity cost fluctuates in step. The result is a continual fluctuation in the maximum price/earnings ratio you should pay for any security. Figure 12-3 shows that market interest rate strongly affects the maximum allowable price/earnings ratio you should pay for a typical stock. The lower the interest rate, the higher the maximum allowable price/earnings ratio:

Market Interest Rate, %	Maximum Allowable Price/Earnings Ratio	
Incremental Tax Rate, %:	0	37
4	21.9	18.4
6	18.4	14.5
8	15.4	11.6
10	13.0	9.5
12	11.0	7.8
14	9.3	6.4

The price of stocks, like the price of bonds, is sensitive to market interest rates. Stocks and bonds fluctuate in value for the same basic reason: changing interest

Fig. 12-3
EFFECT OF INTEREST RATE

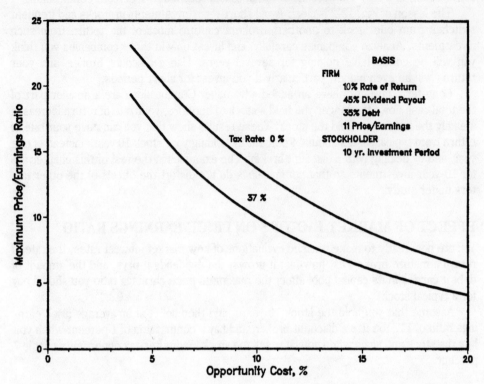

rates mean changing opportunity costs, and a corresponding change in the present value of future dividends, interest payments, and redemption values.

Because market interest rates affect stock prices so strongly, you cannot evaluate a stock solely on the basis of the firm's prospects for future growth and earnings. If market interest rates change during the period you hold the stock, the stock's price/earnings ratio will change as a result. Falling interest rates raise the price/earnings ratio and the rate of return you will earn from the stock. Rising interest rates lower the price/earnings ratio and your rate of return. In this example, each 1 percentage point change in interest rate changes the price/earnings ratio for the average stock 10 percent at an incremental tax rate of 37 percent.

Investors with high opportunity costs (i.e., investors with attractive alternate investments) cannot justify high price/earnings ratios for typical stocks. An investor with a 14 percent opportunity cost and a 37 percent incremental tax rate, for example, cannot afford to pay a price/earnings ratio higher than 6.4 for a typical stock. An investor whose alternate investment is a tax-free bond paying 8 percent interest has an 8 percent opportunity cost. If his incremental tax rate were also 37 percent, he could afford to pay a price/earnings ratio of 11.6 for the same stock.

Tax rates also affect the maximum price/earnings ratio you should pay for a stock. Taxes have a stronger effect at higher opportunity costs. At an opportunity cost of 6 percent, reducing the tax rate from 37 percent to 0 percent raises the maximum allowable price/earnings ratio 27 percent. At a 12 percent opportunity cost, the same reduction in tax rate raises the maximum allowable price/earnings ratio 41 percent.

Effect of the Firm's Rate of Return

The higher the return a firm earns, the more cash it has available to pay dividends and to finance growth. Higher dividends and faster growth makes the stock more attractive, and you can afford to pay more for it. Figure 12-4 shows how the firm's rate of return affects the maximum allowable price/earnings ratio. The firm's capital growth rate is held constant at the 8.3 percent per year average for the typical stock. With growth held constant, changes in the firm's rate of return cause corresponding changes in the firm's dividend payout. The higher the return the firm earns, the more you can afford to pay for it:

Firm		Investor	
Rate of Return, %	Dividend Payout, %	Maximum Allowable Price/Earnings Ratio	
Incremental Tax Rate, %:		0	37
8	32.5	15.7	12.1
10	46.0	17.2	13.2
12	55.0	18.1	14.0
14	61.4	18.8	14.5
16	66.3	19.3	14.9

In the neighborhood of the 9 percent return a typical firm earns, each 1 percentage point increase in a firm's rate of return raises the maximum allowable price/earnings ratio about 4.3 percent. These results are most accurate at a typical firm's 9 percent rate of return, where the assumption that the stock can be sold 10 years later at a price/earnings ratio of 11 is most reasonable. Firms that earn higher returns are above average. They are worth more than indicated above because they can be sold 10 years later at a price/earnings ratio higher than 11. Similarly, firms earning less than a 9 percent return are below average. They are worth less than indicated above because they probably cannot be sold at a price/earnings ratio of 11 in 10 years.

The high maximum allowable price/earnings ratio for firms that earn high rates of return also depends on the assumption that the high rate of return will continue unchanged over the 10-year investment period. The higher the rate of return, the less tenable is this assumption. The steady-state model is not a good choice for these firms. Use the unsteady-state model for such firms, and allow for the rate of return to decay gradually over time.

Effect of Dividend Payout

A firm might pay more or less dividends than Standard and Poor's average firm, depending on whether it is growing faster or slower than the average firm. A firm growing faster than the average firm needs cash to finance the faster growth. Faster-growing firms commonly raise the needed cash by paying smaller dividends and reinvesting more of their earnings. Similarly, a firm that grows more slowly than the average firm has more of its earnings available for dividends, and can afford a higher dividend payout.

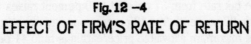

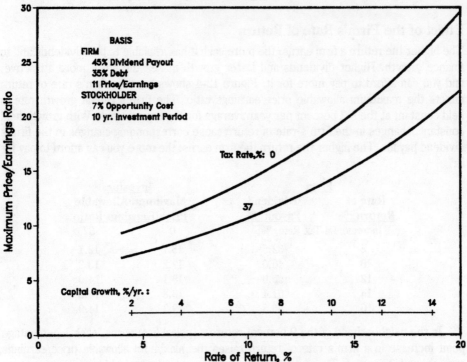

Figure 12-5 shows how the trade-off between growth and dividend payout affects the maximum allowable price/earnings ratio you should pay for the typical stock. Firms that reinvest more of their earnings and pay less dividends are worth more than firms that pay more dividends:

Dividend Payout, %:	Capital Growth, %/yr.	Incremental Tax Rate, %:	Maximum Allowable Price/Earnings Ratio
		0	37
0	13.9	21.4	16.5
20	11.1	18.7	14.4
40	8.3	16.5	12.8
60	5.5	14.8	11.5
80	2.8	13.5	10.4
100	0	12.5	9.6

The lower the dividend payout, the faster the firm can grow, and the more investors can afford to pay for the stock. Changes in dividend payout and growth rate do not affect the stock's value as much as changes in the firm's rate of return does.

The typical firm with a 40 percent dividend payout grows 8.3 percent per year. An investor with a 7 percent opportunity cost and a 37 percent incremental tax rate could afford to pay a price/earnings ratio of 12.8 for this stock. If that firm did not grow at all, it

Fig. 12–5
EFFECT OF DIVIDEND PAYOUT

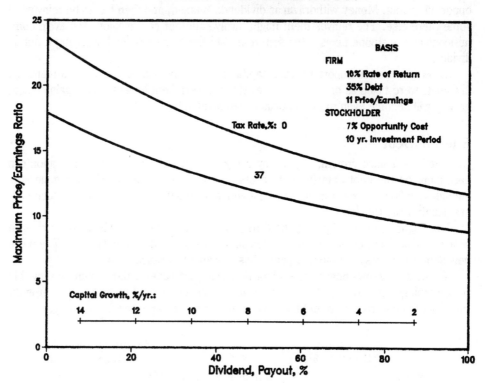

could raise its dividend payout to 100 percent, but the maximum allowable price/earnings ratio would drop to 9.6. If that firm uncovered enough new investment opportunities to grow 13.9 percent per year and eliminated dividends to finance those opportunities, the maximum allowable price/earnings ratio would rise to 16.5.

These calculations show that, other things being equal, firms with lower dividend payouts (and faster growth) are worth more than firms with higher dividend payouts (and slower growth), provided the firm reinvests the money not paid out as dividends in profitable projects. These calculations are based on steady-state growth, and selling the stock at a price/earnings ratio of 11 in 10 years. If the firm growing 13.9 percent per year could maintain that growth for 10 years, it would likely sell at a price/earnings ratio higher than 11 and be worth more than shown above. If it could not maintain that growth, use the unsteady-state model and allow for slowing growth.

Other things being equal, the amount of earnings the firm pays out in dividends and how much it reinvests should not affect the value of the stock. The stock's value depends primarily on the return the firm earns on the capital it employs. How this return is divided between dividends and reinvestment is immaterial. But the firm normally earns a higher return than the investor can from his next best investment opportunity. Otherwise, the investor shouldn't hold that stock. If the firm can earn a higher return, investors benefit more from leaving their money in the firm than from withdrawing it as dividends. In this example, growth is worth more than dividends because the firm earns 9 percent on the capital it reinvests, whereas the investor can earn only his 7 percent opportunity cost. Money withdrawn as dividends is taxed, and then has to be reinvested somewhere else. The reinvestment might involve another commission. You avoid commissions and postpone taxes if the firm reinvests the money instead of paying it out as dividends.

Growth was more important when capital gains received favorable tax treatment and dividends were taxed as ordinary income. If the government lowers capital gains taxes, growth will become even more important than dividends.

Effect of Debt

Corporations finance growth, in part, by carrying debt. As long as the corporation can earn more on the debt than the debt costs, and as long as the corporation generates enough cash flow to cover the interest cost with a reasonable margin of safety, stockholders benefit from the debt.

The higher the debt fraction the firm carries, the more new debt it borrows each year to balance reinvested earnings and maintain the target debt/equity ratio. The more new debt it borrows, the more capital it has available to finance growth.

Figure 12-6 shows how debt level for the typical firm affects the maximum allowable price/earnings ratio you should pay for its stock. The added debt finances faster growth. Investors benefit from more debt as long as the firm can carry that debt safely:

Debt, %:	Capital Growth, %/yr.	Maximum Allowable Price/Earnings Ratio	
		Incremental Tax Rate, %: 0	37
0	5.0	12.8	9.9
10	5.5	13.4	10.4
20	6.2	14.2	11.0
30	7.1	15.3	11.8
40	8.3	17.0	13.1
50	9.9	19.6	15.1

The curves for debt shown in Fig. 12-6 are flatter than the curves for rate of return and dividend payout in Figs. 12-4 and 12-5. Therefore, debt is not as powerful as the firm's rate of return and dividend payout for making capital employed grow faster and raising the value of the stock.

The typical firm carries 35 percent debt and grows 8.3 percent per year. An investor with a 7 percent opportunity cost and a 37 percent incremental tax rate could afford to pay a maximum price/earnings ratio of 12.8 for this stock. If the firm paid off its debt and maintained a 40 percent dividend payout, growth would slow to 5.4 percent per year, and the maximum allowable price/earnings ratio would drop to 9.9. If the firm developed new investment opportunities, it could finance growth up to 9.9 percent per year by raising its debt level to 50 percent. At the faster growth, the maximum allowable price/earnings ratio would increase to 15.1. More debt means faster growth and higher stock values, provided that the added debt is used for profitable projects.

Fig. 12–6
EFFECT OF DEBT

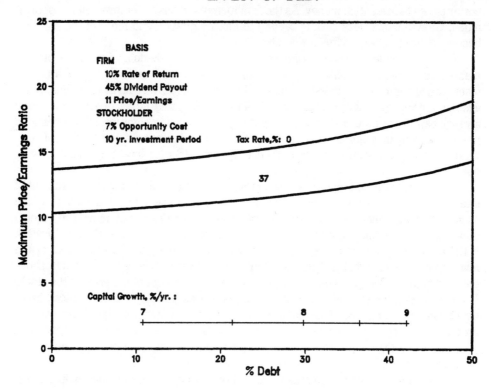

Importance of Attractive Investment Opportunities

The calculations of how the firm's rate of return, growth rate, dividend payout, and debt affect the maximum price/earnings ratio you should pay for a typical stock all depend on one critical assumption: that the firm has attractive opportunities for reinvesting the money that it does not pay out to stockholders as dividends. That assumption might not always be true.

The money a firm earns belongs to its stockholders. Ideally, managements continually assess how much of these earnings they should reinvest in the business and how much they should pay to the stockholders as dividends. The firm's managers continually look for investment opportunities in their particular area of the business. The firm needs some investments just to maintain the existing plant. Investments are also needed to make existing plants more efficient, to meet the growth in demand for the firm's existing products. Some investments move the firm into new areas.

Managements continually assess these investment proposals. They accept those that meet profitability standards, and reject those that do not. Managements then adjust dividend and debt policy to finance the needed investments. As long as management can earn a higher return by reinvesting earnings in the business than stockholders can by taking the dividends, paying taxes, and reinvesting the money elsewhere, the stockholder benefits when management reinvests earnings. Growth companies in the early stages of their life cycle need all the money they can get to finance rapid growth, and they frequently pay no dividends. Stockholders benefit because they do not normally have any better places to invest that money. As the firm matures, it has fewer investment opportunities. Growth slows, less cash is needed to finance growth, and more of the earnings become available to pay out as dividends.

As a stockholder, you do not know in any detail the schedule of proposed investments management is considering. You do not know how attractive they are, nor whether management is reinvesting money that would better be paid as dividends. Managements normally maintain stable growth in dividends, and target dividends at some average payout fraction. If stockholders get used to receiving some traditional dividend payout fraction, management might also get used to reinvesting some traditional reinvestment fraction, whether it has attractive opportunities for investing that money or not.

A major acquisition program is a danger sign. It indicates that the firm has run out of internally-developed opportunities. Instead of returning the unneeded money to the shareholders as higher dividends, management might use the money to finance acquisitions. Acquisitions have a poor record. They frequently turn out poorer than anticipated. If the acquired firm is an attractive investment, stockholders can buy the stock at the market price. A firm that acquires another firm, however, must pay a premium above the market price. The premium typically amounts to 60 percent of the price of the stock. Because market forces continually adjust the price of each stock so that the stock earns only a competitive return, a firm that pays a 60 percent premium is likely to earn a below-average return on that acquisition. The acquiring firm needs a great deal of synergism —usually more than is possible—to offset this premium and make the acquisition economically attractive.

Harold Geneen made a remarkable record of building ITT through acquisitions during his tenure as chief executive officer. He acquired over 300 firms in 18 years—nearly one and one-half acquisitions per month. Mr. Geneen was recognized not only for his ability to acquire other companies, but also for his ability to manage them once acquired. Growth in ITT's sales and profits averaged 18 percent per year over that period. But stockholders received little benefit from this remarkable achievement, as Professor Lorie of the University of Chicago pointed out in a *Wall Street Journal* review of the book *Geneen*, by R.J. Schoenberg.[1] A stockholder who bought ITT stock at the beginning of Mr. Geneen's acquisition program and sold it at the end earned a nominal return of only 3.2 percent on his investment. After deducting inflation, which averaged 4.0 percent per year during this period, that stockholder's real rate of return was −0.8 percent. The stockholder did not even keep up with inflation. He would have done better investing in the Standard and Poor's average stock. If stockholders did not benefit from an acquisition program managed by an executive of Mr. Geneen's caliber, they are not likely to benefit from acquisition programs managed by ordinary executives.

Stockholders of firms that begin a major acquisition program can reasonably expect that the acquisitions will lower the firm's future rate of return, and thereby lower the value of that firm's stock. A major acquisition program is a signal to move your money to some other firm, preferably one that is still growing by internally-developed projects.

---

[1] *Wall Street Journal*, March 19, 1985.

MUTUAL FUNDS

Mutual funds have become a popular way for the average person to invest in the stock market. Mutual funds are pools of money managed by professional investors and invested in stocks they believe to be promising. The fund is continually supervised, and money is shifted from one stock to another as changing conditions warrant. Fund are available with a variety of investment objectives, such as growth funds, aggressive growth funds, income funds, balanced income/growth funds, foreign stock funds, bond funds, money market funds, and funds that specialize in particular industries.

An investment firm might operate a variety of funds and allow you to switch from one fund to another as your investment goals change. Some funds do not charge any load, some funds charge loads of 2 to 3 percent, and others, loads up to an 8.5 percent maximum. There is a movement among no-load funds to begin charging a load. There might also be a redemption fee if you sell your shares before some minimum investment period, typically five years.

You must pay taxes on your income from mutual funds. The fund sends periodic statements detailing the source of its earnings, and stating which earnings are taxable as ordinary income and which are taxable as capital gains.

The expenses of operating a mutual fund are paid out of the fund's income. Operating expenses typically run 1.5 percent of the fund's assets. Stating expenses as a percentage of assets make the expenses look small, but 1.5 percent of assets might amount to 15 percent of earnings, an amount not so small. Expenses are listed in a statistical table in the fund's prospectus. Funds are also allowed to dip into the fund's assets under the SEC's 12b-1 rule to help pay marketing expenses. The SEC is forcing more complete disclosure of operating expenses in the fund's advertising.

Mutual funds claim advantages of professional management, diversification among a wide variety of stocks, and lower commissions. A number of studies, however, show that a majority of these professionally-managed funds earn less than an investment in Standard and Poor's average stock—less than an investor who picks stocks by throwing darts at the financial page. A study reported in the July, 1985 issue of Consumer Reports rated 289 mutual funds based on the return to an investor who made $2,000 IRA investments each year over the five-year period 1980 to 1984. Nearly 80 percent of these funds earned less than an investment in the Standard and Poor's average stock, which earned a 13.5 percent return during the same period. The distribution of rate of return these funds earned was:

5 % of funds earned	19.0 %	or more;	95%	earned less	
10 %	"	16.2 %	"	90%	"
20 %	"	13.6 %	"	80%	"
50 %	"	9.4 %	"	50%	"
70 %	"	5.1 %	"	30%	"
90 %	"	3.5 %	"	10%	"
95 %	"	0.1 %	"	5%	"

The average mutual fund earned a return of 9.4 percent—30 percent less than the 13.5 percent return earned by the Standard and Poor's average stock in the same time period. The best of the 289 funds earned a return of 28.2 percent. The worst earned a return of −26.1 percent. Four percent of the funds either earned no return or lost money. Consequently, the poor track record of mutual funds should encourage you to choose your own stocks, and to analyze them by the methods described in this book.

BUYING STOCKS ON MARGIN

When you buy stocks on margin you borrow part of the money from your broker. Buying stocks on margin extends your ability to invest in stocks. The Federal Reserve Board limits the amount brokers can loan on stocks. The current limit is 50 percent. If you were to buy $5,000 worth of stock on margin, for example, $2,500 is the most your broker could loan. Check with your broker first, however, because he will not loan money on all stocks.

Borrowing is a way to leverage your investment. If you can borrow money at 10 percent interest and invest in a stock that earns a 13 percent return, you have gained by borrowing. If the stock earns only an 8 percent return, you have lost.

Interest on broker's loans is tax-deductible, so figure your interest cost on an after-tax basis. Project the after-tax rate of return you expect to earn on the stock by the methods in this book. If you are confident the stock you are considering will earn a higher return than the after-tax interest rate your broker charges, you might want to consider buying on margin so you can acquire more of the stock.

Interest rates on margin accounts fluctuate frequently. Therefore, you should frequently reassess stocks bought on margin to reassure yourself that the stock still earns a return higher than the broker's interest rate. If the margin between the return you expect from the stock and the interest rate on your margin account drops below the level you are comfortable with, consider either paying off the margin debt, or selling the stock.

The danger of buying stocks on margin is that the price of the stock might go down rather than up. Your broker has rules on the minimum equity you must maintain in a margin account. If your stock drops enough to bring your equity below this minimum, your broker will issue a margin call, and ask you to deposit more money in your account. If you are unable to do so, your broker has the right to sell your stock and use the proceeds to reduce your margin loan. Consequently, he might sell when you would prefer to hold on.

SUMMARY

☐ The typical firm, as represented by Standard and Poor's 500 stock average, earns a 9 percent rate of return on capital employed, which grows 8.3 percent per year. The firm pays 40 percent of its earnings out as dividends, and carries 35 percent debt and 65 percent equity in its capital structure. In 1989, stock of this average firm sold at a price/earnings ratio of 11.

☐ Brokers capture most of the gain from short-term stock investments. Hold your stock for several years to minimize the percentage of the gain your broker captures. Also use discount brokers as well.

☐ Taxes, inflation, and commissions are important factors affecting the rate of return from investing in stocks. When these factors are ignored, the average stock appears to offer an 11.9 percent rate of return. At 5 percent per year inflation, the real rate of return appears to be 6.9 percent, but a 37 percent incremental tax rate and a 2.5

percent broker's commission reduces the nominal return one-third—from 11.9 percent to 8.1 percent. The real return halves—from 6.9 percent to 3.1 percent.

☐ Changes in market interest rates change investor's opportunity costs, and therefore, the rate at which investors discount future cash flows. For an investor with a 7 percent opportunity cost and a 37 percent incremental tax rate, a 1 percentage point drop in interest rates raises the maximum price/earnings ratio he should pay about 10 percent.

☐ The rate of return a firm earns is the most critical factor in determining your rate of return and the maximum price you should pay for that firm's stock. The dividend payout fraction and the amount of debt the firm carries are less important. For an investor with a 7 percent opportunity cost, each 1 percentage point rise in the firm's rate of return raises the maximum allowable price and price/earnings ratio about 4.3 percent.

☐ Companies that pay low dividends (and grow faster) are worth more than companies that pay high dividends (and grow slower), provided the money not paid in dividends is invested in profitable projects. Carrying more debt raises a firm's value by allowing that firm to grow faster, provided the firm uses the debt to finance profitable growth opportunities and has enough cash flow to cover interest payments by a comfortable margin. Faster growth justifies higher price/earnings ratios for firms that carry more debt.

☐ The higher price/earnings ratio justified for firms that earn high returns, have low dividend payouts and high debt depends critically on the firm having attractive investment opportunities for the money it doesn't pay out as dividends. The firm might not always have such opportunities. If the firm has a stable dividend policy, it also has a stable reinvestment policy. Management might be tempted to invest at a steady rate whether it has attractive investment opportunities or not. A major acquisition program is a danger sign. It signals that the firm has run out of internally-developed projects. Future returns are likely to suffer because acquisitions have a poor record. In this case, it might be wise to sell out and invest your money elsewhere.

☐ Mutual funds are a popular way to invest in stocks. Mutual funds provide the advantage of professional management, diversification, and lower commissions. A number of studies, however, show that mutual funds, on average, earn less than the Standard and Poor's 500 stock average. A recent study of 289 mutual funds over the 1980–1984 period found that nearly 80 percent of these funds earned less than the Standard and Poor's average stock during the same period.

☐ Buying stocks on margin is a way to extend your ability to invest in stocks. You might want to consider buying on margin if you are confident the after-tax return on the stock exceeds, by a comfortable margin, the after-tax interest rate your broker charges on margin loans.

13

Deciding When to Sell

YOU DO NOT ACTUALLY MAKE A PROFIT FROM A SECURITY UNTIL YOU FINALLY SELL THAT security. Previous chapters guided you through the investment problem. Use that material to analyze firms you think have a bright future. The analysis will steer you away from stocks that cost too much and toward stocks that promise a reasonable return. Suppose you invest in those stocks. Now what? Do you sell as soon as the stock price rises a small amount? Do you hold on in hopes of even greater future gains? Do you put the stock away as a long-term investment? What if the stock price drops instead of going up?

Locating promising securities is only part of the investment problem. Once you invest in a security, a new question arises: "When should I sell the security?" The economics of selling a security is similar to the economics of investing in the security, and this chapter can help you find the right time to sell. Your decision to invest in the security was based on the best estimates you could make of the cash flows you expected that security to generate at the time you made the investment. As time passes, however, the circumstances that formed the basis of your analysis will change. New information becomes available. Market interest rates might change, thereby changing price/earnings ratios and your opportunity cost. The firm will not grow exactly as you had forecast, nor will profits be exactly as you had forecast. As the firm's actual performance unfolds, track the stock and update your analysis. If the firm performs better than expected, you might want to acquire more of its stock. If the firm performs worse than you expected, you will wonder whether you should sell the stock and invest the money in some other security.

You might also discover a new investment opportunity that was not available when you made the original investment. The new opportunity might raise your opportunity cost. You may wonder whether to sell the original investment to make money available for the new investment. All of these changes will affect the attractiveness of continuing to hold the original security.

BASIS OF THE ANALYSIS

You are free to call your broker at any time and order him to sell your security. If you do so, you will collect the market price of the security, less the broker's commission. You might also have to pay a capital gains tax. Each day you do not call your broker and sell the security, you forego the use of that money. In return for foregoing the money, you continue to collect interest or dividends, and enjoy any appreciation in the price of the security. You postpone recovering that money until a later time.

Foregoing money you could otherwise collect is the cost you pay for continuing your investment in that security. You are, in effect, investing the money you could otherwise collect in order to continue receiving dividends or interest and price appreciation. You can analyze that "investment," and calculate the rate of return for leaving that money invested. If the rate of return is higher than your current opportunity cost, keep your money invested in that security. If not, consider selling the security and investing the money in the alternative investment.

Theoretically, you could make the analysis each day, and calculate whether you should sell the security or keep it one more day. Such a procedure would locate, to the day, the best time to sell the security. This procedure is not practical, however, because you cannot forecast the gain from keeping a security for as short a time as one more day. More likely, a quarterly or an annual reappraisal is the most you can justify based on new information, unless a major development makes a basic change in your estimate of the firm's future.

Firms issue quarterly reports on sales and earnings, and a more detailed annual report. Track the firm's quarterly reports and see whether progress is reasonably close to your projections. Track stock prices; check whether they are reasonably close to the prices you had forecast. If the firm deviates in a significant way from your forecast, update your analysis of the firm. Make a new analysis of whether to sell the security. Make a more detailed analysis when the firm issues its annual report. Update your analysis to reflect the new information available on the security. Make any changes the new information warrants in your forecast of the firm's rate of return, growth rate, earnings, and dividends. If market interest rates change, make the corresponding changes in your opportunity cost and your forecast of price/earnings ratios. Proceed in this way on an annual basis, or more frequently if new information warrants, and judge whether to hold the security one more year or sell it.

Suppose you buy a stock and hold it for a year. You might find, after the year has passed, that the price of the stock is higher than you had forecast. Only an improved outlook for the firm, or a drop in market interest rates and investor's opportunity costs, justifies a higher stock price. Read what analysts are now saying about the firm. Ask your broker if he knows of any reason for a brighter outlook. Repeat your analysis, with appropriate allowance for any change in the firm's outlook and in price/earnings ratios. If you still cannot justify the stock's high price, you might conclude that the stock is over-priced. Price will eventually return to a more rational level. If you use the more rational stock price as your estimate of the price one year later, your analysis will show a low rate of return for keeping the stock. You might consider selling the stock now before its price drops to a more rational level.

You might also find, after the year has passed, that the price of the stock is lower than you had forecast. Only a poorer outlook for the firm, and/or an increase in market interest rates and investor's opportunity costs, justifies a lower stock price. Read what analysts are saying about the firm. Repeat your analysis, with an allowance for a poorer outlook for the firm, if appropriate, and lower price/earnings ratios. If you still cannot justify the stock's low price, you might conclude that the stock is underpriced. Price will eventually rise to a more rational level. If you use the rational stock price as your estimate of the price one year later, your analysis will show a high rate of return for keeping the stock. You might consider keeping the stock on the basis of a reasonable chance of a recovery in price.

The analysis of when to sell is basically identical to the analysis for investing in a security. The primary difference is that you use the money foregone by not selling today in place of the original investment cost. The price you originally paid for the security is a sunk cost. It does not enter the calculation, except as it affects capital gains and capital gains taxes.

CALCULATION FORM FOR SELLING SECURITIES

The calculation form in Table 13-1 simplifies the analysis of when to sell a stock. Completing the form can tell you whether to sell the stock now or keep it one more year. The form parallels the calculation forms in Chapter 11 for analyzing stocks. The first section covers the stock and your estimates of how the firm will perform in the coming year. The second section records your tax rates. The third section develops cash flows. Line 13 shows the money you forego by not selling now. Line 14 shows the cash you should expect if you sell the stock a year from now.

Part D of the calculation form discounts the cash flows. Choose your after-tax opportunity cost as the first trial discount rate. If discounting at your opportunity cost gives a negative present value in line 29, keeping the stock another year is not attractive. You could earn a higher return by selling the stock and putting that money in whatever investment determines your opportunity cost. If discounting at your opportunity cost gives a positive present value, the stock might be worth keeping. Choose a new trial discount rate 5 percentage points higher and repeat lines 25 through 28. Enter the present values at these two discount rates in Table 4-3, and complete the solution for rate of return. Once you know the rate of return, you can compare keeping this stock another year against all of your other investment opportunities.

The rate of return you should expect from holding on to the stock depends on the current price of the stock. The higher the price, the more money you forego by not selling the stock now. The maximum amount of money you should forego occurs at a critical price, which just reduces your return to your opportunity cost. If the current market price is higher than this critical price, your return for keeping the stock will be below your opportunity cost, and you should consider selling the stock. If the current market price is below this critical price, your return will be higher than your opportunity cost, and you should consider keeping the stock. Section E of the calculation form develops the critical price from cash flows discounted at your after-tax opportunity cost.

The original cost of the stock does not enter the analysis, except in calculating the capital gains tax. Economic analysis deals with decisions about cash when you still have a choice of whether to invest or not. Once you invest the cash, it becomes a "sunk" cost and is irrelevant when making decisions involving future investments. Therefore, the analysis of whether to sell a stock does not depend on what you originally paid for the stock. Instead, the analysis depends on the amount of money you forego by keeping the stock instead of selling it now.

Example 13-1. Three years ago, you bought a stock for $28 per share, plus a 1 percent commission. You expected the firm to earn a 12 percent return and to grow 12 percent per year. Based on that growth, you expected a stock price of $39.50 today. Today's price, however, is only $34 per share. Should you sell the stock or keep it one more year? Your after-tax opportunity cost is 7 percent.

TABLE 13-1

Calculation Form—When to Sell a Stock

Basis: Sell Now or Keep the Stock One More Year

A. The Stock

1. Original Cost, including Commissions, $/share _____

2. Current Price, $/share _____

3. Divide Commission (%) by 100, Subtract the result from 1.0 _____

4. Current Proceeds: Multiply Line 2 by Line 3 _____

5. Projected Earnings Next Year, $/share _____

6. Projected Dividends Next Year, $/share _____

7. Projected Price/Earnings Ratio _____

8. Proceeds from Sale in One Year; Multiply Line 5 by Lines 3 and 7 _____

B. The Investor

9. Divide Incremental Tax Rate (%) by 100, and Subtract the result from 1.0 _____

10. Divide Capital Gains Tax Rate (%) by 100 _____

C. Future Cash Flows

11. Capital Gains Tax Now: Subtract Line 1 from Line 4. Multiply the result by Line 10. _____

12. Capital Gains Tax in One Year: Subtract Line 1 from Line 8. Multiply the result by Line 10. _____

13. Money Foregone: Subtract Line 11 from Line 4. (Add Line 11 if Line 1 is greater than Line 4) _____

14. Net Cash in One Year: Subtract Line 12 from Line 8. (Add Line 12 if Line 1 is greater than Line 8) _____

D. Discounting

15. Trial Discount Rate, % _____

16. Di Factor at RT = Line 15 _____

17. Dc Factor at RT = Line 15 _____

18. Present Value of Sale in One Year: Multiply Line 14 by Line 16 _____

19. Present Value of Dividends: Multiply Line 6 by Lines 9 and 17 _____

20. Present Value: Add Lines 18 and 19, then Subtract Line 13. _____

If the present value on Line 20 is positive, try a discount rate 5 percentage points higher. If Line 20 is negative, try a discount rate 5 percentage points lower. Use Table 4-3 to complete the calculation for rate of return.

E. Critical Stock Price

Enter your opportunity cost as the discount rate in Line 15, and complete Lines 21 through 25.

21. Subtract Line 10 from 1.0. Multiply the result by Lines 8 and 16 _____

22. Subtract Line 16 from 1.0. Multiply the result by Lines 1 and 10. _____

23. Add Lines 19 and 21, then Subtract Line 22 _____

24. Subtract Line 10 from 1.0. Multiply the result by Line 3 _____

25. Critical Price: Divide Line 23 by Line 24 _____

After reviewing the latest information available on the firm, you conclude you were optimistic about how fast the firm could grow. Therefore, you reduce your growth estimate from 12 percent to 10 percent per year. You conclude that a return of 12 percent is still a reasonable estimate. The stock has sold at a price/earnings ratio of 11, and you expect this ratio to hold for the coming year. With earnings of $3.50 per share and a price/earnings ratio of 11, the stock price less commissions one year from now should be $38.12 per share.

Table 13-2 shows how you would decide whether to sell this stock. Enter your original cost, including commissions, in line 1 and the current price in line 2. Enter your estimates of the firm's future performance in lines 5 through 7. Record your incremental tax rate in Part B of the form.

Part C develops cash flows in the coming year consistent with your projections in Part A. Line 11 shows a capital gains tax of $1.99 per share if you sell now. Line 12 shows a capital gains tax of $3.64 per share if you sell a year from now. The money you forego by not selling now is the current price of $34 per share, less commissions and the capital gains tax. Line 13 shows you will forego $31.67 per share. This is the amount you are "investing" to share in the coming year's growth. If you sell one year from now, line 14 shows your net proceeds should be $34.48 per share.

Enter your 7 percent after-tax opportunity cost in line 15, and calculate a present value of $1.45 per share in line 20. The positive present value shows it might pay to keep the stock another year. Part E of the form develops the critical price. The critical price is what this stock is worth to you today. At your 7 percent opportunity cost, line 25 shows a value of $36.32 per share. If you continue the evaluation, you'll find that you should earn a return of 11.6 percent by keeping the stock for another year.

SUMMARY

☐ The economics for selling a security are similar to the economics for investing in a security. The difference is that the "investment" is the cash you forego by not selling the security now. You forego the market price of the security, less broker's commissions, and a capital gains tax. The price you originally paid for the security is irrelevant, except as an element in calculating the capital gain.

☐ The calculation form in Table 13-1 simplifies evaluating whether you should sell a stock now or keep it one more year. The form also develops a critical stock price. If the current market price is above the critical price, consider selling the stock now. If the current market price is below the critical price, consider keeping the stock one more year.

☐ Your original investment decision was based on the best information you had at the time. A firm does not grow exactly as you forecast, however. Market interest rates might have changed and caused a change in price/earnings ratio. When new information becomes available, or when a firm issues its next annual report, update your analysis of the firm. Use Table 13-1 to calculate the return you should expect for holding the security one more year. If the rate of return is higher than your opportunity cost, keep your money invested in the security. If

TABLE 13-2

When to Sell a Stock—Example 13-1

Basis: Sell Now or Keep the Stock One More Year

A. The Stock

1. Original Cost, including Commissions, $/share	28.28
2. Current Price, $/share	34
3. Divide Commission (%) by 100, Subtract the result from 1.0	0.99
4. Current Proceeds: Multiply Line 2 by Line 3	33.66
5. Projected Earnings Next Year, $/share	3.50
6. Projected Dividends Next Year, $/share	1.60
7. Projected Price/Earnings Ratio	11
8. Proceeds from Sale in One Year; Multiply Line 5 by Lines 3 and 7	38.12

B. The Investor

9. Divide Incremental Tax Rate (%) by 100, and Subtract the result from 1.0	0.63
10. Divide Capital Gains Tax Rate (%) by 100	0.37

C. Future Cash Flows

11. Capital Gains Tax Now: Subtract Line 1 from Line 4. Multiply the result by Line 10.	1.99
12. Capital Gains Tax in One Year: Subtract Line 1 from Line 8. Multiply the result by Line 10.	3.64
13. Money Foregone: Subtract Line 11 from Line 4. (Add Line 11 if Line 1 is greater than Line 4)	31.67
14. Net Cash in One Year: Subtract Line 12 from Line 8. (Add Line 12 if Line 1 is greater than Line 8)	34.48

D. Discounting

15. Trial Discount Rate, %	7
16. Di Factor at RT = Line 15	0.9324
17. Dc Factor at RT = Line 15	0.9658
18. Present Value of Sale in One Year: Multiply Line 14 by Line 16	32.15
19. Present Value of Dividends: Multiply Line 6 by Lines 9 and 17	0.97
20. Present Value: Add Lines 18 and 19, then Subtract Line 13	1.45

If the present value on Line 20 is positive, try a discount rate 5 percentage points higher. If Line 20 is negative, try a discount rate 5 percentage points lower. Use Table 4-3 to complete the calculation for rate of return.

E. Critical Stock Price

Enter your opportunity cost as the discount rate in Line 15, and complete Lines 21 through 25.

21. Subtract Line 10 from 1.0. Multiply the result by Lines 8 and 16	22.39
22. Subtract Line 16 from 1.0. Multiply the result by Lines 1 and 10.	0.71
23. Add Lines 19 and 21, then Subtract Line 22	22.65
24. Subtract Line 10 from 1.0. Multiply the result by Line 3	0.6327
25. Critical Price: Divide Line 23 by Line 24	36.32

not, consider selling the security and investing in the investment that determines your opportunity cost.

☐ Update your analysis of a firm more frequently if its quarterly reports indicate that your forecast of the firm's progress is in serious error.

☐ If the stock price grows faster than a more favorable outlook for the firm, or on lower market interest rates, justifies, your analysis will show that the stock is overpriced. You might want to sell before any price correction occurs. Similarly, the stock price might grow more slowly than a poorer outlook for the firm or higher market interest rates justify. Your analysis might then show that the stock is underpriced, and you might decide to keep the stock in anticipation it will recover to a more rational stock price.

14

What are the Chances
I Will Lose Money?

DISCOUNTED CASH FLOW ANALYSIS IS A RIGOROUS WAY TO EVALUATE SECURITIES. IT gives the correct rate of return you should earn and the most you should pay for any security. Yet, even though discounted cash flow analysis is mathematically correct, the analysis is subject to considerable uncertainty. The uncertainty arises from the projections you must make when you evaluate a security. You must project the rate of return the firm will earn and how fast it will grow. You must project the dividends the firm will pay. You must project the price/earnings ratio when you finally sell the stock, or a future interest rate if you sell a bond before it matures. Projections have errors. Projection errors generate corresponding errors in the rates of return and the maximum allowable price you calculate.

The returns available from securities are inversely related to the risk of the security. Institutions that offer safe securities do not have to offer as high a real interest rate to sell their securities as sellers of riskier securities do. The nominal interest rate safe securities pay is likely to be close to the expected inflation rate. The riskier the security, the higher the real interest rate the issuer must offer to get investors to buy those securities. Interest rates offered in 1989 and the net return after 37 percent taxes and 5 percent inflation were:

	Interest Before Taxes	Rate, % After Taxes	Real Interest Rate at 5%/yr. Inflation
Junk Bonds	14.0	8.8	3.8
10-Year Treasury Bonds	8.4	5.6	0.6
Certificates of Deposit	8.0	5.0	0.0
U.S. Savings Bonds	7.8	5.2	0.2
High-Grade Corporate Bonds			
1 – 10 Years	9.1	5.7	0.7
10 Years Plus	9.3	5.9	0.9
Tax Exempt 10-Year Bonds	7.4	7.4	2.4
Money Market Funds	8.6	5.4	0.4
Super-NOW Bank Savings Accounts	5.1	3.2	−1.8

Real after-tax interest rates cover a wide range. Super-NOW bank savings accounts paid a low of minus 1.8 percent. Junk bonds paid a high of 3.8 percent. The wide variation in risk from one security to another complicates the problem of evaluating securities. You cannot simply calculate a rate of return for each security and invest your money in those securities that offer the highest returns. If you do, you will build a portfolio of risky securities. You need a way to measure how risky each investment is. You can then choose a level of risk you are comfortable with, and invest in securities that offer the highest returns at that risk level.

Each investor has his own aversion to risk. Some investors are willing to gamble everything to make a killing. Most investors cannot accept the loss if an all-or-nothing gamble fails. They will accept lower returns in exchange for greater safety. Some investors value safety so highly they will invest only in the safest securities. Your risk profile changes with time. When you are young, you might accept more risk for the chance of earning higher returns and making your fortune grow faster. If your investments fail, you still have time to recover. As you become older, you become more averse to risk, and are more concerned with preserving your principal, which you depend on to finance retirement. Your investing strategy will change. You will avoid risky securities and switch your investments to safer securities.

This chapter illustrates a straightforward way to allow for risk. The method is the Monte Carlo technique. The method develops the range of possible rates of return you might earn from investing in a security, and gives the probability of each return. Risk analysis allows you to fine-tune security analysis to match your own tolerance for risk. You will be able to set an assurance level. The Monte Carlo method also tells you the rate of return you can expect at that assurance level. The method is not complicated, and you will be able to do the calculations on a hand calculator.

MONTE CARLO METHOD

Evaluating a security requires projecting the future cash flows you expect that security to generate. Projecting the future is uncertain. Cash flows do not usually turn out exactly as you project them to. Actual cash flows fall in a band extending both above and below the cash flows you project. Therefore, you must think of your cash flow projections as a range of possible values, not as a specific outcome. Values near the center of the range are more likely than values near either extreme. Such a range of values, together with the associated probability of achieving any given value, is known as a probability distribution.

The Monte Carlo method works with probability distributions for each of the factors involved in evaluating a security. The method translates these probability distributions to the corresponding probability distributions for the rate of return and the maximum allowable price for that security. The basic idea is straightforward:

1. Establish a probability distribution for each factor you think contributes significantly to the uncertainty of the evaluation. The probability distribution summarizes your best estimate of the range in which that factor might lie. It also defines the probability of each possible outcome. A calculation form can help you set up these distributions. The critical factors you should consider for probability distributions are the firm's rate of return, growth rate, and the future price/earnings ratio. If the stock is a growth stock, you should also set up probability distributions for the half-lives of these factors. The future interest rate is the critical factor when evaluating bonds you plan to sell before they mature.

2. Choose a random value for each factor from its probability distribution. These choices represent one possible set of values those factors could have.

3. Evaluate the investment using the random values chosen in Step 2. Calculate the rate of return and the maximum allowable price. The calculated rate of return and the maximum allowable price are one possible outcome from that investment. Save the results.

4. Go back to Step 2. Choose a new set of random values, and repeat the process. Each repetition yields one more possible rate of return and maximum allowable price. Repeat the process enough times so that you can establish a probability distribution for rate of return and maximum allowable prices. Ideally, you should do Monte Carlo analysis on a computer. You can then examine the results of, say, 1,000 random outcomes. But you can get surprisingly good results with a hand calculator and just a few random outcomes. A calculation form can simplify the procedure.

5. Plot the calculated random rates of return and maximum allowable prices on probability paper. The key points on this plot are the expected outcome and the chance of losing money, that is, earning a return less than your opportunity cost. Read the expected outcome at the midpoint of the distribution. Read the probability of losing money at the point where the rate of return is equal to your opportunity cost. You can also set an assurance level to define your tolerance for risk, and read the rate of return you should expect at that assurance level.

Probability Distributions

The key step in applying the Monte Carlo method is establishing probability distributions. You must set up a schedule of the values each uncertain factor might have, and the probability of reaching any of those values. The normal distribution discussed in Chapter 10 is a poor choice for this schedule, because it forces errors to be distributed symmetrically on either side of the most likely value. For example, you might project that a firm is most likely to earn a 10 percent return and that there is only a 10 percent chance that rate of return could be as much as 2 percentage points higher. The symmetry of the normal distribution forces you to assume that there is also only a 10 percent chance that the rate of return could be as much as 2 percentage points lower. But you might think an unsymmetrical distribution matches your feelings about likely rates of return better than a symmetrical distribution does. You might feel, for example, that low returns are more likely than high returns and allow a 10 percent chance that the return might be 3 instead of 2 percentage points lower.

The beta distribution avoids the limitations of symmetrical distributions. The beta distribution can be symmetrical, or it can have any degree of asymmetry. The symmetrical distribution is almost identical to the normal distribution. Figure 14-1 shows examples of a symmetrical and an unsymmetrical distribution. The horizontal scale shows the range of values the uncertain factor might have; the vertical scale shows the relative likelihood of finding those values. Values where the distribution curve is high are more likely than values where the curve is low. The most likely estimate lies at the peak of each distribution. The height of the distribution curve approaches zero at either extreme. Therefore, extreme high values and extreme low values are unlikely.

The area under the distribution curve measures the probability that the factor will lie

Fig. 14-1
BETA DISTRIBUTIONS

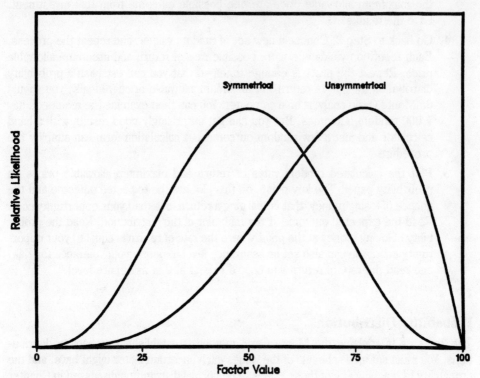

in any given range. The factor must lie somewhere between the extreme low value and the extreme high value of the distribution. Therefore, the total area under the distribution corresponds to 100 percent probability. The probability that the actual value will lie in any range is the percentage of the total area that lies in that range. For example, half of the area under the symmetrical distribution in Fig. 14-1 lies below the most likely value. Therefore, the probability that the actual value will be less than the most likely value is 50 percent. More than half of the area under the unsymmetrical distribution in Fig. 14-1 lies below the most likely value. Therefore, the probability of an actual value lower than the most likely value is more than 50 percent for that distribution.

Plotting probability distributions as shown in Fig. 14-1 is the best way to illustrate the basic idea that values near the most likely value (where the curve is high) are more likely than values near either extreme, where the curve is low. A related distribution called the cumulative distribution is more useful in practice, because it deals directly with probability. A cumulative distribution shows the cumulative area under bell-shaped distributions like those in Fig. 14-1. Probability begins at zero at the extreme low value of the factor, and gradually increases towards 100 percent at the extreme high value.

Figure 14-2 shows a group of cumulative beta distributions. The left vertical scale measures probability. It shows the cumulative area under probability distributions like those in Fig. 14-1. The bottom horizontal scale shows corresponding values of the

Fig. 14–2

PROBABILITY DISTRIBUTIONS

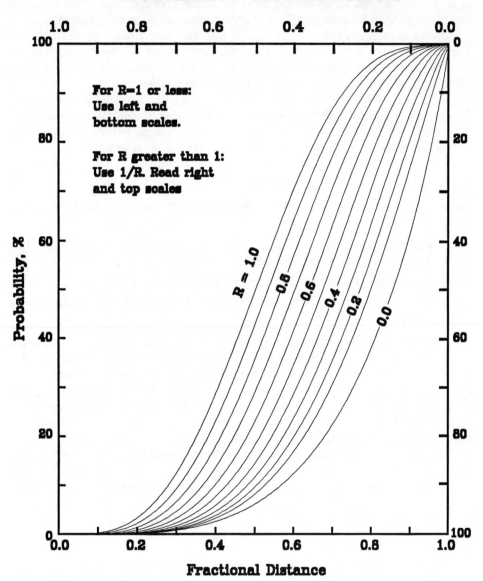

uncertain factor. The scale for factor values is normalized to begin at zero at the extreme low value of the factor and end at 1.0 at the extreme high value. The R parameter on each curve measures the asymmetry of the distribution. The asymmetry ratio, R, is the ratio of the distance above the most likely value to the distance below:

$$R = (H - ML)/(ML - L)$$

where H, ML, and L are the high, most likely, and low values in the range of possible values. The symmetrical distribution has the same distance above the most likely value as below, and so has an asymmetry ratio, or R value, of 1.0. Distributions skewed towards high values have smaller R ratios and intermediate degrees of asymmetry.

Distributions skewed towards low values have asymmetry ratios greater than 1.0. They are not shown in Fig. 14-2 to avoid complicating the plot. These curves are identical to the ones shown, except that they are reversed both from top to bottom and from left to right, and are located to the left of the distributions plotted.

You can read values for distributions with R ratios greater than 1.0 from the distributions plotted in Fig. 14-2. Use the reciprocal of the R value. If R is 2, for example, read the curve drawn for R = 1/2, or 0.5. Read the probability scale at the right side of the plot, and read the normalized factor value scale at the top of the plot.

Using the Probability Distribution

Use a simple three-step process to pick random values for each uncertain variable from Fig. 14-2:

1. Enter the vertical scale of Fig. 14-2 at a random probability between 0 and 100. Read the random probability from Appendix Table A6.
2. Read across horizontally to the appropriate distribution curve.
3. Read down vertically to a normalized value of the uncertain factor on the horizontal scale.

Appendix Table A6 contains a thousand random numbers from 0 to 100. Estimate the number of random numbers you will need. If you decide to set up probability distributions for five uncertain factors, for example, and you plan to calculate five random outcomes, you will need a total of 25 random numbers. Enter Table A6 at a random location, and consecutively read 25 random numbers. Enter each random number into the vertical scale in Fig. 14-2. Read across to the appropriate asymmetry curve, then read down to a random value for that factor.

Imagine for a moment that the appropriate distribution in Fig. 14-2 is a vertical line. When you read across to this vertical line at any random number and then read down, you will always read the same value on the horizontal scale. Therefore, a vertical distribution represents a factor whose value is known with certainty. Now, imagine that the line is no longer vertical, but has a slight tilt instead. Now when you read across to the tilted line and then read down, you will read a range of values that lies in a narrow band centered on the most likely value.

The middle 70 percent of the curves plotted in Fig. 14-2 are, roughly, lines at a small tilt. About 70 percent of the time, the random number will fall in this range. You will then read values for the uncertain factor that clusters near the most likely value. About 15 percent of the time, the random number will lie where the curve bends at the top of the plot. You will then read high values farther removed from the most likely value. About 15 percent of the time, the random number will lie where the curve bends at the bottom of the plot. You will then read low values farther removed from the most likely value. Selecting values this way generates a set of random values that match your feeling about the values each uncertain factor is likely to have.

Establishing a Probability Distribution

You need only three estimates to establish a probability distribution for each uncertain factor. One estimate is the most likely value. In any case, you need this estimate. The other two are estimates of how high or low you expect the value of that factor might be. Estimating the extreme high and low values is difficult. Move in from the extremes of the distribution, and estimate the upper and lower values at the 10 percent probability level instead. Think over the range of values each factor might have, then choose a high estimate such that any actual value has only a 10 percent chance of exceeding high that estimate. In the same way, choose a low estimate such that any actual value has only a 10 percent chance of being lower than that low estimate.

The firm's historical record provides some guidance on making these low and high 10 percent probability estimates. These estimates lie roughly 1.28 standard deviations on either side of the most likely value in a symmetrical distribution. The analysis of Hewlett-Packard in Chapter 10, found that Hewlett-Packard averaged a 20.9 percent rate of return with a standard deviation of 3.18 percentage points. The 10 percent and 90 percent probability estimates lie roughly 1.28 times 3.18, or 4.1 percentage points on either side of the 20.9 percent average return. Suppose you choose 20.9 percent as the most likely estimate for Hewlett-Packard's return. A reasonable low estimate would then be 2.09 − 4.1, or 16.8 percent. A reasonable high estimate would be 20.9 + 4.1, or a 25.0 percent return. These estimates can be adjusted further if you think the distribution should be asymmetrical.

You can estimate the uncertainty in the capital growth rate by plotting historical data on capital employed for the past five to 10 years against time on semilog graph paper. The data will scatter, and will not plot exactly as a straight line. You might take as your high growth rate estimate the slope of the steepest line you can reasonably draw through these data. Take as your low growth rate estimate the slope of the flattest line you can reasonably draw.

Calculation Form for
Generating Random Values

The calculation form in Table 14-1 simplifies setting up probability distributions and generating random values from them. The first part of the form sets up the probability distribution. Enter the most likely and the high and low 10 percent probability estimates on lines 1, 2, and 3. Calculate the distance below the most likely value in line 4, and the distance above the most likely value in line 5. Calculate the asymmetry ratio by dividing line 5 by line 4, or line 4 by line 5, whichever gives a result of 1.0 or less. Enter the result in line 6. If line 5 is less than line 4, the asymmetry ratio is less than 1.0. Use the left and bottom scales when you read values from Fig. 14-2. If line 5 is greater than line 4, the asymmetry ratio is greater than 1.0. Use the right and top scales when you read values from Fig. 14-2. Use the ratio in line 6 to locate the appropriate asymmetry curve in Fig. 14-2.

Lines 7 through 11 develop the information you need to convert values read from the normalized top and bottom scales in Fig. 14-2 to actual values for the factor. Lines 7 and 8 require reading horizontal distances at the 10 and 90 percent probability levels from Fig. 14-2. The easiest way to read distances in Fig. 14-2 is to use a centimeter scale.

TABLE 14-1
Calculation Form—Generating Random Values

A. Setting Up the Probability Distribution

1. Most Likely Value   _____

2. High Estimate   _____

3. Low Estimate   _____

4. Subtract Line 3 from Line 1   _____

5. Subtract Line 1 from Line 2   _____

6. R Ratio: If Line 5 is greater than Line 4, Divide Line 4 by Line 5. If
   not, Divide Line 5 by Line 4. Round to the nearest tenth.   _____

7. Read the Horizontal Distance in Fig. 14-2 at 90 percent probability*   _____

8. Read the Horizontal Distance in Fig. 14-2 at 10 percent probability*   _____

9. Subtract Line 8 from Line 7   _____

10. Subtract Line 3 from Line 2, then Divide by Line 9   _____

11. Multiply Line 10 by Line 7; Subtract the result from Line 2   _____

B. Generating Random Values

12. Enter a random number from Appendix Table A6   _____

13. Read a Horizontal Distance* from Fig. 14-2 at the probability in
    Line 12   _____

14. Random Value: Multiply Line 10 by Line 13. Add Line 11 to the
    result   _____

---

*If Line 5 is less than Line 4, use the left vertical scale, and read the horizontal distance from the left edge of Fig. 14-2 to the appropriate distribution curve. If Line 5 is greater than Line 4, use the right vertical scale, and read the horizontal distance from the appropriate distribution curve to the right edge of Fig. 14-2.

The centimeter scale is easier to use because it is a decimal scale. It avoids the bother of converting fractions to decimals you would have with a scale graduated in inches. Each centimeter is divided into ten millimeters. The scale markings of 1, 2, 3, etc., represent 10, 20, 30, etc., millimeters.

Line the centimeter scale parallel to the top and bottom edges of Fig. 14-2. If line 5 is less than line 4, the asymmetry ratio is less than 1.0. Set the zero mark on the centimeter scale at the 10 percent probability mark on the left vertical scale of Fig. 14-2. Then measure the distance between the left side of Fig. 14-2 and the appropriate curve. Repeat the measurement at the 90 percent probability mark on the left vertical scale. Measure all distances in millimeters. If line 5 is greater than line 4, the asymmetry ratio is greater than 1.0. Use the reciprocal (1.0 divided by R) of the asymmetry ratio, which will be less than 1.0. Use the right-hand probability scale. Set the ruler's zero mark on the appropriate curve at the 10 and the 90 percent probability levels. Then measure the distance from the appropriate curve to the right side of Fig. 14-2.

Lines 1 through 11 set up the probability distribution for each uncertain factor. You only have to fill these lines out once for each uncertain factor. The actual random values are generated in lines 12 through 14. These are the only lines you need to repeat to generate another random value.

Generate a random value by reading a random number from Appendix Table A6. Enter this number in line 12. Follow the footnote in Table 14-1, and locate this random number on either the left or the right vertical scale in Fig. 14-2. Then measure the horizontal distance to the curve whose R value is listed in line 6. Follow the steps in the calculation form, and generate the random value on line 14.

Don't make setting up probability distributions and generating random numbers any more difficult than it really is. You do not need to read precise values from Fig. 14-2. Keep the process simple. The asymmetry ratio is only an estimate because the values you use to derive it are estimates. Round the asymmetry ratio in line 6 to the nearest tenth. Rounding avoids having to interpolate between curves when you read values from Fig. 14-2.

Set up probability distributions only for the critical factors in the evaluation. The critical factors are the rate of return you expect the firm to earn, the firm's growth rate, and the price/earnings ratio when you sell. Half-lives are also critical if you use the unsteady-state evaluation. Set up the distribution in lines 1 through 11 of the calculation form for each factor. Then decide on the number of random outcomes you will evaluate, and read the random numbers consecutively from Appendix Table A6 for each factor. Line up your centimeter scale horizontally on Fig. 14-2, and read the distance from the curve to the left or right edge of the plot for each random probability. Then calculate the corresponding factor values in line 14 of the calculation form. Repeat the process for each uncertain factor.

Example 14-1. Suppose you estimate that a particular firm is most likely to earn a rate of return of 12 percent. You believe there is only a 10 percent chance that rate of return will be higher than 14 percent. But you believe lower returns are more likely, and estimate that there is a 10 percent chance that rate of return could be as low as 8 percent. Use the calculation form in Table 14-1 to choose 10 random values for rate of return based on these probability estimates.

Table 14-2 shows the solution. The first 11 lines set up the probability distribution and translate normalized readings from the top and bottom scales into random values of rate of return. Line 6 shows that you will be reading values from the R = 0.5 distribution curve in Fig. 14-2. Enter random numbers into the left scale of Fig. 14-2 because line 5 is less than line 4. Measure distances from the left edge of the plot to the R = 0.5 distribution curve. Read distances in lines 7, 8, and 13 of the calculation form in millimeters.

Enter Appendix Table A6 at a random location and read 10 random numbers. In this example, the first random number is 76.5. Lay your centimeter scale at the 76.5 percent probability level on the left vertical scale, and measure the horizontal distance from the left edge of Fig. 14-2 to the R = 0.5 distribution curve. This distance measures 85 millimeters on the author's copy of Fig. 14-2. Enter 85 millimeters in line 13. Line 14 translates this distance to a rate of return of 12.88 percent. Generate the other random rates of return from the remaining random numbers by repeating lines 12 through 14. The 10 random rates of return generated this way are:

Random Number	Rate of Return, %
76.5	12.88
14.1	8.59

Random Number	Rate of Return, %
21.5	9.35
71.2	12.68
7.5	7.55
62.7	12.01
56.7	11.73
53.1	11.54
6.2	7.26
72.1	12.68

Distributions with R Greater than 1.0

If you believe a high result is more likely than a low result, more of the probability distribution will lie above the most likely value. The R ratio will then be greater than 1.0. You will then need to use the top and right-hand scales when reading random values from Fig. 14-2. The calculation form in Table 14-1 includes the proper adjustments for R

TABLE 14-2
Generating Random Values—Example 14-1

A. Setting Up the Probability Distribution

1. Most Likely Value	12
2. High Estimate	14
3. Low Estimate	8
4. Subtract Line 3 from Line 1	4
5. Subtract Line 1 from Line 2	2
6. R Ratio: If Line 5 is greater than Line 4, Divide Line 4 by Line 5. If not, Divide Line 5 by Line 4. Round to the nearest tenth.	0.5
7. Read the Horizontal Distance in Fig. 14-2 at 90 percent probability*	94
8. Read the Horizontal Distance in Fig. 14-2 at 10 percent probability*	46
9. Subtract Line 8 from Line 7	48
10. Subtract Line 3 from Line 2, then Divide by Line 9	0.125
11. Multiply Line 10 by Line 7; Subtract the result from Line 2	2.25

B. Generating Random Values

12. Enter a random number from Appendix Table A6	76.5
13. Read a Horizontal Distance* from Fig. 14-2 at the probability in Line 12	85
14. Random Value: Multiply Line 10 by Line 13. Add Line 11 to the result	12.88

---

*If Line 5 is less than Line 4, use the left vertical scale, and read the horizontal distance from the left edge of Fig. 14-2 to the appropriate distribution curve. If Line 5 is greater than Line 4, use the right vertical scale, and read the horizontal distance from the appropriate distribution curve to the right edge of Fig. 14-2.

TABLE 14-3
Generating Random Values—Example 14-2

A. Setting Up the Probability Distribution

1. Most Likely Value	12
2. High Estimate	15
3. Low Estimate	10
4. Subtract Line 3 from Line 1	2
5. Subtract Line 1 from Line 2	3
6. R Ratio: If Line 5 is greater than Line 4, Divide Line 4 by Line 5. If not, Divide Line 5 by Line 4. Round to the nearest tenth.	0.7
7. Read the Horizontal Distance in Fig. 14-2 at 90 percent probability*	68
8. Read the Horizontal Distance in Fig. 14-2 at 10 percent probability*	20
9. Subtract Line 8 from Line 7	48
10. Subtract Line 3 from Line 2, then Divide by Line 9	0.104
11. Multiply Line 10 by Line 7; Subtract the result from Line 2	7.93

B. Generating Random Values

12. Enter a random number from Appendix Table A6	35.7
13. Read a Horizontal Distance* from Fig. 14-2 at the probability in Line 12	36
14. Random Value: Multiply Line 10 by Line 13. Add Line 11 to the result	11.67

*If Line 5 is less than Line 4, use the left vertical scale, and read the horizontal distance from the left edge of Fig. 14-2 to the appropriate distribution curve. If Line 5 is greater than Line 4, use the right vertical scale, and read the horizontal distance from the appropriate distribution curve to the right edge of Fig. 14-2.

ratios greater than 1.0. The adjustments are:

1. Invert the asymmetry ratio by dividing line 4 by line 5 so that the inverted ratio in line 6 is less than 1.0.

2. Enter random numbers from Appendix Table A6 into the right instead of the left vertical scale of Fig. 14-2.

3. Read horizontal distances from the appropriate distribution curve to the right instead of the left edge of the plot.

Example 14-2. Repeat Example 14-1 with a most likely return of 12 percent, only this time assume that the high rate of return estimate is 15 percent and the low estimate is 10 percent. This example is worked out in Table 14-3.

This distribution is skewed towards high values, and the R ratio is 1.5, which is greater than 1.0. Adjust to an R ratio below 1.0 in line 6 by dividing line 4 by line 5. The inverted R ratio is 0.667. Round this ratio to 0.7 in line 6. Use the right probability scale in Fig. 14-2 because line 5 is greater than line 4. Read horizontal distances from the appropriate probability curve to the right edge of the plot.

Enter the 10 random numbers in line 12, as in Example 14-1, and calculate random values of rate of return in lines 13 through 14. The corresponding random rates of return are:

Random Number	Rate of Return, %
35.7	11.67
47.2	12.24
88.5	15.00
94.4	15.63
73.7	13.66
54.3	12.30
44.8	12.16
51.0	12.39
13.9	10.34
93.7	15.47

Linking

Not all variables involved in security analysis fluctuate independently of one another. Some variables are linked—they move up and down together. Other variables might be inversely linked—when one moves up, the other moves down. Allow for this linking when you choose random values. You might believe a variable will fluctuate independently of the other variables. Pick random values for that variable independently of the random values you choose for any other variable. Variables such as the long-run rate of return, the long-run price/earnings ratio, and the long-run capital growth rate are linked and are all likely to move up and down together. If the long-run rate of return is high, the long-run price/earnings is also likely to be high. If the long-run rate of return is low, the long-run price/earnings ratio is also likely to be low. Long-run capital growth is not likely to be high unless the long-run rate of return is also high. The half-lives that describe how fast a growth company is likely to mature are also likely to be linked. If the rate of return decays rapidly, capital growth and the price/earnings ratio are also likely to decay rapidly.

Allow for this linking by using the same random number to generate random values of the linked variables. Using the same random number forces random values to be chosen at the same relative position in each probability distribution. Suppose you decide that the long-run rate of return, capital growth, and price/earnings ratio will all fluctuate up and down together. Define a probability distribution for each variable to match the likely range of values you think each variable might assume. Use a single random number to choose random values for all three variables, however. If you choose a random number of 91.2, for example, enter all three probability distributions at a random number of 91.2. Random values for all three factors will then be chosen at the same relative position at the high end of each distribution. If you believe these factors will all decay together, their half-lives will also be linked. Pick a new random number, and use that number to choose all three half-lives from the probability distributions for the three half-lives.

Some variables might be inversely linked—if one has a high value, the other is likely to have a low value. Choose inversely linked values by using one random number to select a value for one variable, and the complement of that random number to select the value of the other variable. If you use a random number of 91.2 to select the random value for one variable, for example, use the complement, 100−91.2, or 8.8, to select the random value of the other variable.

GROWTH STOCK EXAMPLE

A growth stock is an excellent candidate for risk analysis. There is considerable uncertainty about how fast rate of return, capital growth rate, and the price/earnings ratio are likely to decay as the firm matures. The long-run limits these critical variables are decaying towards are also uncertain. The Monte Carlo method can be illustrated by using it to analyze the risk for investing in the growth stock evaluated in Chapter 11. In the case of the growth stock evaluated in Chapter 11, all of the variables that affect profitability were at their most likely values, which are shown in Table 14-4. At these values, the growth stock offered a rate of return of 4.6 percent. Maximum allowable price was $30.16 per share.

The firm's rate of return, growth rate, and the future price/earnings ratio at which the market will value this growth stock are the critical variables. The uncertainty in these variables, together with the uncertainty in how fast these variables decay towards their long-run values, generates most of the uncertainty in the calculated profitability of the investment. These are the variables that justify probability distributions. The other variables in the table are relatively certain. Use the most likely values of these variables in the analysis.

TABLE 14-4
Most Likely Values—Growth Stock Example

Firm:		Most Likely Value
Rate of Return, %		
	Initial	23.
	Long-Run	10.
	Half-Life, years	5.
Capital Growth Rate, %/yr.		
	Initial	30.
	Long-Run	8.
	Half-Life, years	5.
Price/Earnings Ratio		
	Long-Run	13.
	Half-Life, years	5.
Initial Stock Price, $/share		46.50
Initial Capital Employed, $million		50.
Growth in Outstanding Shares, %/yr.		0.5
Debt Fraction		0.35
Equity Fraction		0.65
Investor:		
Opportunity Cost, %		8.
Incremental Tax Rate, %		37.
Investment Period, years		10.

You have now singled out the variables that contribute most to the risk in investing in this growth stock. The next step is to review the firm's financial history, particularly the ranges over which these critical factors have fluctuated. Examine stability both for this firm and for others in the same industry, as you did in Chapter 10. Draw upon your general knowledge of how firms perform, and estimate likely ranges for these critical factors at the 10 and 90 percent probability levels.

Use Table 14-1 to develop probability distributions and random values for these variables. Developing probability distributions requires judgment. The half-lives are likely to be the most critical variable. You might develop a basis for estimating reasonable half-lives by examining former growth stocks that have since matured. Look up the history of those stocks, and see how fast rate of return, capital growth, and the price/earnings ratio decayed. Measure the half-life that characterizes that decay.

The analysis of this growth stock is developed in Table 14-5. Consider the likely range of values each of the uncertain variables might have. Suppose you examine past experience, and develop the estimates listed in Table 14-5 of how high and how low each variable might be. Enter these values in lines 1 through 3 in Table 14-5. You believe the estimates of the initial rate of return and capital growth rate are independent, so pick independent random values for these variables. You also believe that the long-run values of rate of return, capital growth rate, and price/earnings ratio are linked and all of them move up and down together. Use a single random number to make the random values for these factors move up and down together. Identical half-lives have been chosen for the decay in rate of return, capital growth rate, and price/earnings ratio. Therefore, a single probability distribution will define the likelihood of any half-life.

There are only six probability distributions to deal with. There is one each for the initial and long-run rate of return and capital growth rate. There is one for the long-run price/earnings ratio, and one for the three half-lives. The R ratios for these distributions are developed in line 6.

Because of the linking among these variables, you only need four random numbers in line 12. Note that line 5 is less than line 4, except for the half-lives. Therefore, the R ratios will be less than 1.0 for all factors except the half-lives. Enter random numbers for all factors except half-lives in the left probability scale of Fig. 14-2. Measure horizontal distances from the left edge of the plot to the appropriate probability curve. Enter random numbers for the half-lives in the right probability scale. Read horizontal distances from the appropriate probability curves to the right edge of the plot. Line 13 contains the measured distances, and line 14 contains the random values calculated for these variables.

Values are now available for all the variables required for a discounted cash flow analysis. Calculate the rate of return and the maximum allowable price using the calculation form in Table 11-15. This particular set of random values yields a rate of return of 4.60 percent and a maximum allowable price of $30.57 per share. These results represent one possible outcome for investing in this growth stock. Save these results.

Now choose a new set of four random numbers and repeat the analysis beginning at line 14 of Table 14-5. Each repetition generates one more possible outcome. Continue generating random outcomes until the distribution of the outcomes stabilizes. You can follow how the distribution of the outcome stabilizes by tracking the results. Plot the average and the standard deviation of the estimated rate of return against the trial num-

TABLE 14-5

Risk Analysis—Growth Stock Example

A. Develop Probability Distributions

	Initial Values		Long-Run Values			Half-Lives
	Rate of Return, %	Growth Rate %/yr.	Rate of Return, %	Growth Rate %/yr.	P/E Ratio	All Variables
1. Most Likely Value	25	30	10	8	13	5
2. High Estimate	27	32	12	10	15	7
3. Low Estimate	22	27	6	5	8	4
4. Line 1 – Line 3	3	3	4	3	5	1
5. Line 2 – Line 1	2	2	2	2	2	2
6. R: (Line 5)/(Line 4) or (Line 4)/(Line 5)[1]	0.7	0.7	0.5	0.7	0.4	—
7. Distance, 90% Prob., mm.	87	87	93	87	96	62
8. Distance, 10% Prob., mm.	39	39	46	39	49	14
9. Line 7 – Line 8	48	48	47	48	49	48
10. (Line 2 – Line 3) Divided by Line 9	0.104	0.104	0.128	0.104	0.149	0.063
11. Multiply Line 10 by Line 7; Subtract the result from Line 2.	17.95	22.95	0.10	0.95	0.70	3.09
B. Random Value Selection						
12. Random Number[2]	98.1	33.7	53.5	53.5	53.5	49.2
13. Distance at Probability in Line 12	97	56	74	66	77	34
14. Random Value: Line 10 times Line 13, then Add Line 11	28.0	28.8	9.6	7.8	12.1	5.2

[1] Use right-hand probability scale in Figure 13-2.

[2] Long-run fluctuations are linked together; half-life fluctuations are also linked together.

ber. The average deviation and the standard deviation will fluctuate at first, but will settle down after a surprisingly few random outcomes. Continue calculating new random outcomes until the average and the standard deviation of the outcomes stabilize.

Figure 14-3 shows how the average value of the rates of return and the standard deviation stabilizes in this example. The plot compares the results with only a few random outcomes with the results obtained after 500 random outcomes. The average return and the standard deviation are unstable at first because they are based on only a few outcomes. By the fifth outcome, the average rate of return is 4.83 percent, reasonably close to the average return of 4.11 percent for 500 random outcomes. The standard deviation is 2.76, essentially identical to the standard deviation of 2.77 obtained with 500 random outcomes.

Plot the random outcomes on probability paper so you can read the probability of earning any given return. Figure 14-4 compares the estimates you will be able to make for rate of return after calculating five, 10, and 20 random outcomes to the corresponding estimates after calculating 500 random outcomes. The results after only five random outcomes are reasonably close to the results after 500 random outcomes, as shown in the top plot. The average return, read at the midpoint of the distribution, is 4.83 percent, compared to 4.11 percent after 500 random outcomes. Five random outcomes shows that there is an 87 percent chance of losing money, that is, of earning less than this investor's 8 percent opportunity cost. This probability is quite close to the 92 percent chance indicated by 500 random outcomes.

As shown in the middle plot of Fig. 14-4, doubling the calculation load to 10 random outcomes gives only marginal improvement. The average return is 4.58 percent, slightly closer to the 4.11 percent average for 500 random outcomes. The chance of losing money is still 87 percent. Doubling the calculation load again to 20 random outcomes gives a further marginal improvement in results, as shown in the bottom plot. The average return is now 4.32 percent, and the chance of losing money is 90 percent.

The best estimate of the expected rate of return is the average of the 500 random outcomes, or 4.11 percent. This return is somewhat less than the return of 4.6 percent obtained in Chapter 11 when all of the variables were at their most likely values. The distribution curve for 500 random outcomes shows only a 44 percent chance of reaching or exceeding this 4.6 percent return.

The best estimate of the maximum allowable price is the average of the 500 random outcomes, or $29.85 per share. This price is also somewhat lower than the maximum price of $30.16 calculated in Chapter 11 with all of the variables at their most likely values.

The probability distributions plotted in Fig. 14-4 show the probability of reaching any rate of return from this investment. They help you match this investment to your risk profile. A critical estimate is the probability of earning a return higher than your opportunity cost. Ninety percent of the random outcomes show a return less than 8 percent. Therefore, this growth stock offers only a 10 percent chance of exceeding the 8 percent opportunity cost. A conservative investor might insist on at least a 90 percent assurance of reaching the calculated outcome. Five random outcomes shows this investor he can only count on a rate of return of 1.1 percent at the 90 percent assurance level. Ten percent of the random outcomes are below a 1.1 percent return, the other 90 percent are above.

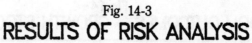

Fig. 14-3
RESULTS OF RISK ANALYSIS

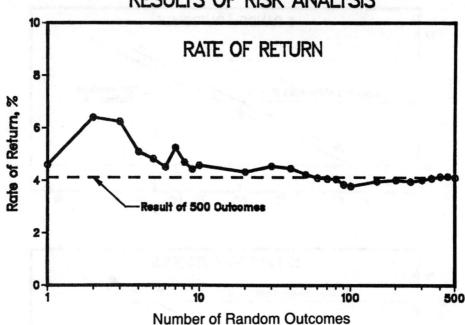

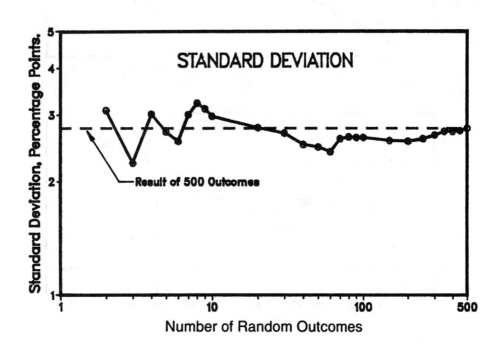

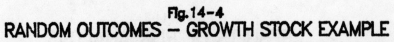

Fig. 14-4
RANDOM OUTCOMES – GROWTH STOCK EXAMPLE

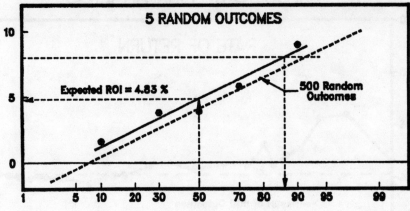

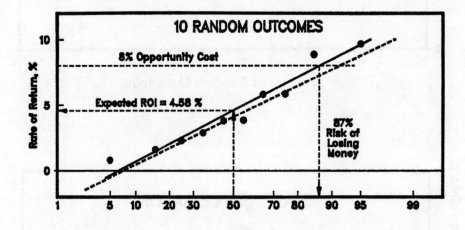

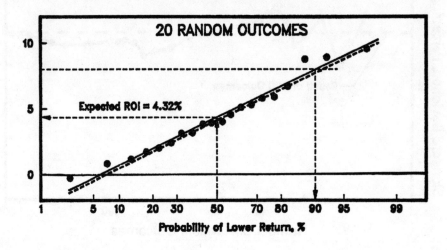

If you have access to a computer, you might feel more confident about your results by calculating several hundred random outcomes. This example shows you can get surprisingly good results by calculating as few as five random outcomes. The difference between a 4.8 percent return from five random outcomes and a 4.1 percent return from 500 random outcomes is not significant. Either result tells you this stock is not an attractive investment. The expected return is well below the 8 percent opportunity cost. Adding more random outcomes refines the result slightly, but does not change the investment from unattractive to attractive.

Calculating five random outcomes by hand is a reasonable task. In this example, assumptions made about linking reduced the number of probability distributions to only six. Use the Monte Carlo method. Even a small number of random outcomes will give you a much better feel for the likely range of outcomes than a single evaluation with all factors at their most likely values.

SOME PRACTICAL SUGGESTIONS

All of the uncertain factors in security analysis contribute to the resulting uncertainty in evaluating any security. Normally, only a few critical factors contribute most of the uncertainty. There is no need to develop a probability distribution for each uncertain factor in the analysis. Concentrate instead on those few critical factors that are difficult to forecast, and therefore, the most uncertain. The remaining factors normally make only a minor contribution to the final uncertainty. Don't bother with probability distributions for these factors.

You can get useful results with fewer probability distributions. Six probability distributions were developed for the growth stock in this chapter to illustrate risk analysis. But three of those factors—the firm's long-run rate of return, capital growth rate, and price/earnings ratio—are reasonably well known. They are values typical of mature firms. The critical uncertain factors are the half-lives—how fast you expect the firm's current return, growth rate, and price/earnings ratio to decay towards these long-run values. You can simplify the analysis by developing a single probability distribution for the three half-lives and the firm's initial rate of return and growth rate. The analysis would then involve only three probability distributions. The result would still be a useful indication of the risk for investing in that growth stock.

SUMMARY

☐ The Monte Carlo method is the best way to analyze the risk involved in investing in securities. It duplicates the way errors made projecting the critical factors generate corresponding errors in the rate of return and maximum allowable price.

☐ The essence of the Monte Carlo method is to develop probability distributions for the critical factors involved in evaluating a stock. The critical factors are the firm's rate of return, capital growth rate, and future price/earnings ratio, as well as the half-lives of these factors. Choose a random set of values for these factors from these probability distributions. The rate of return and maximum allowable price you obtain using a set of random values represent one possible outcome for investing in that security. Repeat the process until you accumulate enough random outcomes to develop probability distributions for the rate of return and the maximum allowable price.

☐ The expected outcome is the average of the random outcomes. Read the probability of losing money from a plot of the returns on probability paper. Losing money means earning a return below your opportunity cost. Read the probability of any other outcome from the probability plot. Decide on the degree of assurance you need to invest in stocks. Read the return you can expect at that assurance level from the probability plot.

☐ The Monte Carlo method is normally done on a computer, where the results of several hundred random outcomes can be examined. You can obtain useful results by calculating just a few random outcomes, however. As few as five random outcomes gave useful results for the growth stock example evaluated in this chapter.

Applying Security Analysis

THE PRINCIPAL OBJECTIVE OF THIS BOOK IS TO SHOW YOU HOW TO ANALYZE INVESTMENTS using the same state-of-the-art methods modern corporations use. The calculation forms in Chapter 11 simplify the analysis. This chapter shows you how you can apply these methods to real securities by following an investor as he analyzes six securities—a growth stock, a blue-chip stock, a stock in a hot industry, a stock with a low price/earnings ratio, a stock recommended by an "expert," and a bond.

The analyses were first made in March of 1987. March of 1987 is a significant time for testing methods for analyzing stocks. The Standard and Poor's 500 price/earnings ratio was 20, a very high level. With stocks that expensive, finding a stock priced low enough to yield an attractive return will be difficult. On October 19, 1987, approximately seven months later, the stock market crashed. The Dow-Jones Industrial average fell 508 points in a single day. A reliable method for analyzing securities would have told investors not to buy stock in the spring of 1987 because stocks were overpriced. You will see that the method for analyzing securities taught in this book gave the investor the correct advice.

The analysis was updated in November 1989. The market had recovered from the 1987 crash, but had suffered a 190-point mini-crash on October 13, 1989. Stocks were priced more realistically in the fall of 1989. The price/earnings ratio for the Standard and Poor's 500 stock average was 14. At that ratio, finding attractive stocks ought to be easier.

Let's follow an investor as he applies the evaluation methods of this book. His first step is to define his situation. What is his incremental tax rate? What is his after-tax opportunity cost? What inflation rate does he expect? How long does he intend to hold these securities? When he has answered these questions, he can begin to evaluate investment opportunities.

Suppose this investor completes Table 11-1, and finds an incremental tax rate of 37 percent. He also completes Table 11-3 and finds that high after-tax opportunity cost is set by a tax-free bond with a 7 percent return. He intends to hold any securities he buys for 10 years. He is concerned about risk, and will use the Monte Carlo method to explore the risk in each stock. Prices are those in effect in March of 1987 and November of 1989.

A word of caution! Do not invest in the securities used as examples in this chapter on the basis of the evaluations in this chapter. By the time you read them, they will be out of date. You are investing your money. Invest it on the basis of how you expect that security to grow, not on how someone else expects the security to grow. By all means, evaluate the security by the methods in this book, but make your own analysis of how you expect a company to perform, and use your own estimates of the future cash flows you expect that security to generate.

GROWTH STOCKS

Our investor's first interest is growth stocks. Growth stocks are glamour stocks. There is a certain intuitive appeal in investing in a company that is growing rapidly. The problem is that other investors have already recognized the rapid growth and might have bid the price of the stock so high that it now costs too much to participate in the rapid growth. Consequently, the primary question our investor must ask is whether the growth stock is overpriced.

You used Hewlett-Packard as an example of a growth stock in Chapter 10, and used the data through 1986 to analyze Hewlett-Packard's financial performance. Hewlett-Packard's historical performance is detailed in Table 15-1. In March 1987, this investor would only have had data through 1986 to work with. Hewlett-Packard appeared to be attractive compared to other computer stocks. Suppose the investor carries out the analysis in Chapter 10 and chooses Hewlett-Packard as a way to participate in the growing computer industry. The primary risk in a growth stock is that it might cost too much. The current high profitability and rapid growth might also decay too fast. Hewlett-Packard could be an excellent investment if its high return and rapid growth persists for an extended period. It would be a poor investment if the rate of return and growth decayed rapidly. Suppose the investor analyzes risk by the Monte Carlo method, and makes the

TABLE 15-1
Hewlett-Packard

Dollar Amounts in Millions

	1982	1983	1984	1985	1986	1987	1988	E1989
Stockholder Equity	2349	2887	3545	3982	4374	5022	4533	5285
Long-Term Debt	39	71	81	102	110	88	61	475
Capital Employed	2388	2958	3626	4084	4484	5110	4594	5760
Avg. Capital Employed	2167	2673	3292	3855	4284	4797	4852	5177
Debt, %	1.5	2.1	2.3	2.4	2.5	2.1	1.5	5.2
Earnings—Reported	383	432	547	489	516	644	816	800
—Adjusted	459	579	709	494	448	707	-423	835
Rate of Return, Adjusted, %	21.2	21.7	21.3	12.8	10.5	14.7	-8.7	16.1
Dividends	30.1	40.8	51.3	56.5	56.3	59.2	65.6	83.2
Dividend Payout, %	6.6	7.0	7.2	11.5	12.6	8.4	-15.5	10.0
Number of Shares	250.7	254.9	256.5	256.9	256.1	257.3	234.2	231.0
Price/Earnings	14.6	24.0	17.7	18.0	20.2	22.6	16.2	12.2

	1982-86	1985-89
Avg. Rate of Return, %	17.5	9.1
Avg. Capital Growth, %/yr.	15.8	7.1

following low, most likely, and high estimates for the critical variables:

Hewlett-Packard Performance Estimates
March, 1987

	Low	Most Likely	High
Rate of Return, %			
Initial	14	16	18
Long-Run	9	12	13
Half-Life, years	5	7	9
Capital Growth, %/yr.			
Initial	14	18	20
Long-Run	6	9	12
Half-Life, years	5	7	9
P/E Ratio			
Long-Run	10	13	15
Half-Life, years	5	7	9

Values of the other variables are taken from the analysis of Hewlett-Packard Chapter 10:

Capital Employed, millions	4,484
Shares Outstanding, millions	256
Growth of Shares Outstanding %/yr.	1.8
Debt, %	2
Stock Price, March 1987, $/share	57.25

Analyzing Hewlett-Packard using the unsteady-state model with all of the variables at their most likely values gives a rate of return of 6.1 percent and a maximum allowable price for this investor of $51.36 per share. A 6.1 percent return is less than this investor's 7 percent opportunity cost. The market price of $57.25 per share is higher than the $51.36 maximum this investor should pay. Hewlett-Packard is overpriced and is not a good investment for this investor.

Figure 15-1 shows the results of Monte Carlo analysis of 200 random outcomes. The expected rate of return is the average of the 200 outcomes and is read at the mid-point of the distribution. The expected return is 5.4 percent, which is below the 6.1 percent return calculated with all of the variables at their most likely values. The expected return is less than this point estimate because this investor judged there was a greater likelihood the critical variables would be below, rather than above, the most likely estimates. The maximum allowable price drops to $47.88 per share. Figure 15-1 shows there is only a 35 percent chance of equaling or exceeding the 6.1 percent return with all of the variables at their most likely values. Read the chance of losing money, that is, of earning a return less than this investor's 7 percent opportunity cost, from Fig. 15-1 as 81 percent.

Hewlett-Packard is an excellent company, as you saw in Chapter 10. It was one of the better companies of the computer group. This investor is right to conclude, however, that in March 1987 the stock was overpriced for him. The investor re-evaluates Hewlett-

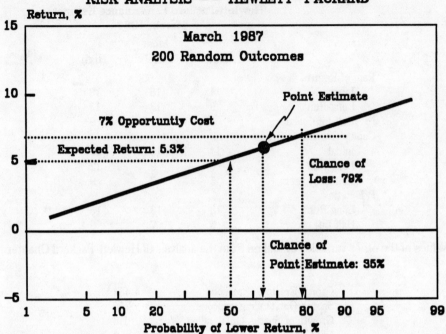

Fig. 15-1

RISK ANALYSIS -- HEWLETT-PACKARD

Packard in November 1989. He has three more years of data to work with, and revises his estimates as follows:

Hewlett-Packard Performance Estimates
November, 1989

	Low	Most Likely	High
Rate of Return, %			
Initial	12	16	17
Long-Run	9	12	13
Half-Life, years	5	7	9
Capital Growth, %/yr.			
Initial	11	15	20
Long-Run	6	9	12
Half-Life, years	5	7	9
P/E Ratio			
Long-Run	9	12	14
Half-Life, years	5	7	9
Capital Employed, millions		5,760	
Shares Outstanding, millions		231	
Growth of Shares Outstanding, %/yr.		-0.5	
Debt, %		4	
Stock Price, November 1989, $/share		42.25	

Fig. 15-2

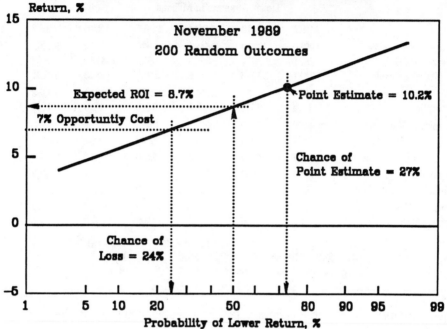

RISK ANALYSIS -- HEWLETT-PACKARD

November 1989
200 Random Outcomes

Expected ROI = 8.7%

Point Estimate = 10.2%

7% Opportuniiy Cost

Chance of
Point Estimate = 27%

Chance of
Loss = 24%

Return, %

Probability of Lower Return, %

The obvious changes are updated values for the price of Hewlett-Packard's stock, capital employed, and number of shares outstanding. But the investor also lowers his estimate of Hewlett-Packard's growth rate and long-run price/earnings ratio as well as extending the uncertainty band around Hewlett-Packard's initial rate of return.

The point estimate, with all values at their most likely levels, shows a 10.2 percent rate of return and a maximum allowable price of $61 per share. Figure 15-2 shows the results of risk analysis with 200 random outcomes. The expected return drops to 8.7 percent and the maximum allowable price drops to $53 per share. There is only a 27 percent chance of reaching the point-estimate return of 10.2 percent. There is a 24 percent chance of losing money by earning less than this investor's 7 percent opportunity cost.

Despite the lower growth and long-run price/earnings estimates, the stock has dropped enough in price since March of 1987 to make Hewlett-Packard a more attractive investment. The expected return of 8.7 percent is higher than this investor's 7 percent opportunity cost. Whether this investor will now invest in Hewlett-Packard depends on his willingness to accept a 24 percent risk of loss and on his other alternative investments.

A BLUE-CHIP COMPANY

A blue-chip company is mature and stable. It has a long record of profitability and dividends. Blue-chip stocks ought to be less risky than growth stocks. IBM is an excellent

TABLE 15-2
IBM

Dollar Amounts in Millions

	1982	1983	1984	1985	1986	1987	1988	E1989
Stockholder Equity	19960	23219	26489	31990	34374	38263	39509	41500
Long-Term Debt	2851	2674	3269	3955	4169	3858	8518	8650
Capital Employed	22811	25893	29758	35945	38543	42121	48027	50159
Avg. Capital Employed	21821	24352	27826	32852	37244	40332	45074	49089
Debt, %	12.6	11.3	10.7	11.0	10.9	10.0	13.7	17.5
Earnings—Reported	4409	5485	6582	6555	4789	5258	5824	5985
—Adjusted	3871	5525	5782	8209	5053	6517	3842	4734
Rate of Return, Adjusted, %	17.7	22.7	20.8	25.0	13.6	16.2	8.5	9.6
Dividends	2072	2266	2512	2708	2669	2628	2596	2743
Dividend Payout, %	53.5	41.0	43.4	33.0	52.8	40.3	67.6	57.9
Number of Shares	602	611	613	615	607	597	590	580
Price/Earnings	9.4	12.7	10.8	12.3	18.0	16.6	11.9	9.5

	1982–86	1985–89
Avg. Rate of Return, %	20.0	14.6
Avg. Capital Growth, %/yr.	13.8	8.9

blue-chip stock to consider. It compared favorably to other computer stocks in the analysis of that industry in Chapter 10.

Table 15-2 details IBM's performance since 1976. The table is developed just like the corresponding table for Hewlett-Packard in Chapter 10. IBM has an excellent record. An investor examining these results in March of 1987 would have found an adjusted rate of return averaging 20 percent over the prior five years. Capital growth averaged 13.8 percent per year. IBM carried only 11 percent debt in its capital structure. IBM suffered from the slowdown in the computer industry in 1986, however. The adjusted rate of return dropped from 25 percent in 1985 to 13.6 percent in 1986, and the capital growth dropped from 19 percent to 7 percent per year.

Our investor must examine IBM's performance, and develop his own estimates of how IBM might perform in the future. He will also have to develop low and high estimates of the critical variables in order to examine risk using the Monte Carlo method.

Suppose our investor analyzes the data through 1986 in Table 15-2, concludes that IBM will recover from the 1986 computer industry slowdown, and makes the following projections:

IBM Performance Estimates
March, 1987

	Low	Most Likely	High
Rate of Return, %			
Initial	15	17	18
Long-Run	8	10	12
Half-Life, years	7	10	12

IBM Performance Estimates
March, 1987

	Low	Most Likely	High
Rate of Return, %			
Initial	15	17	18
Long-Run	8	10	12
Half-Life, years	7	10	12
Capital Growth, %/yr.			
Initial	10	12	13
Long-Run	6	8	12
Half-Life, years	7	10	12
P/E Ratio			
Long-Run	8	13	15
Half-Life, years	7	10	12
Capital Employed, millions		38,543	
Shares Outstanding, millions		607	
Growth Shares Outstanding, %/yr.		0.3	
Debt, %		11	
Stock Price, March 1987, $/share		150.75	

This evaluation, with all of the variables at their most likely values, gives a rate of return of 7.4 percent and a maximum allowable price of $157 per share. Figure 15-3 shows the distribution of rates of return from 200 random outcomes. The expected

Fig. 15-3

RISK ANALYSIS --IBM

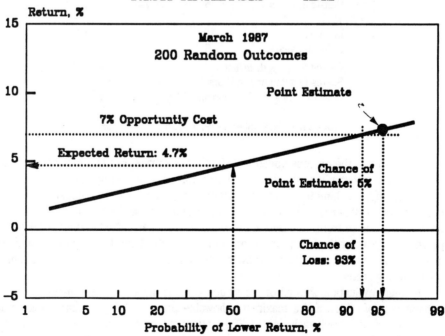

return, read at the midpoint of the distribution, is only 4.7 percent and the maximum allowable price is only $117 per share. There is only a 6 percent chance of earning the 7.4 percent return calculated with all of the variables at their most likely values. There is a 93 percent chance of losing money—of earning a return less than this investor's 7 percent opportunity cost.

This example demonstrates the value of risk analysis. The point estimate, with all of the variables at their most likely values, indicated that IBM was marginally attractive. When the investor projected that some of the critical variables would more than likely fall below the most likely value than above, however, the risk analysis showed the stock to be unattractive.

IBM was not attractive for this investor in March of 1987. IBM is an excellent company and the dominant firm in the computer industry, but investors had bid its price too high to make IBM an attractive investment for him. The investor re-evaluated IBM in November 1989 and revised his estimates as follows:

IBM Performance Estimates
November, 1989

	Low	Most Likely	High
Rate of Return, %			
Initial	8.5	9.5	15
Long-Run	7	8	10
Half-Life, years	5	7	10
Capital Growth, %/yr.			
Initial	8	9	12
Long-Run	7	8	10
Half-Life, years	5	7	10
P/E Ratio			
Long-Run	10	12	13
Half-Life, years	5	7	10
Capital Employed, millions		50,150	
Shares Outstanding, millions		580	
Growth of Shares Outstanding, %/yr.		−0.5	
Debt, %		18	
Stock Price, November 1989, $/share		98	

In addition to the obvious updates of IBM's stock price, capital employed, and number of shares outstanding, this investor notes that IBM's average adjusted return has been dropping, reaching 9.6 percent in 1989. He estimates IBM's initial return at 9.5 percent, with a 10 percent chance that the return might be as high as 15 percent. Capital growth also slowed from 13.8 percent during the five-year period ending in 1986 to 8.9 percent per year for the five-year period ending in 1989. Therefore, he lowered his estimates of IBM's rate of return and growth. He also lowered his estimate of the long-run price/earnings ratio.

A single evaluation with all of the values at their most likely estimates gives a 6.9 percent rate of return and a maximum allowable price of $97 per share. Figure 15-4 shows the results of risk analysis with 200 random outcomes. The expected return rises

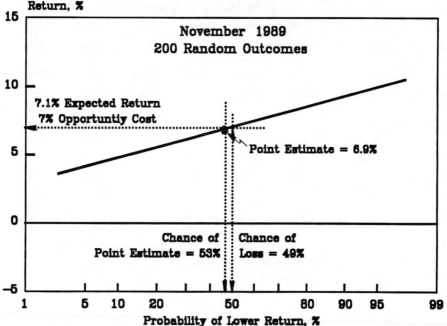

Fig. 15-4
RISK ANALYSIS --IBM

to 7.1 percent and the maximum allowable price rises to $99 per share. There is a 55 percent chance of reaching the point estimate 6.9 percent return. There is a 49 percent chance of losing money by earning less than this investor's 7 percent opportunity cost.

IBM's lower price in November 1989 makes IBM a marginally attractive investment for this investor. The expected return of 7.1 percent is practically identical to this investor's 7 percent opportunity cost. The $99 per share maximum allowable price is just above the $98 market price. Whether this investor buys IBM depends on how he balances a 49 percent risk of loss against a 51 percent chance of bettering his 7 percent opportunity cost.

HOT INDUSTRIES

In the continual search for companies about to surge in profits and growth, one industry after another captures the attention of investors. The prospects of that industry are touted, and there is a buying surge in stocks of favored companies. The industry retains its favored status for a period of time, after which it is replaced by another new hot industry. The pharmaceutical industry was a hot industry in 1987. This industry spends over 8 percent of sales revenue on research, and the research pays off. The FDA approved 20 new drugs in 1986. There is also a growing interest in biotechnology for developing new drugs. The industry has historically earned high rates of return. Merck is one of the most successful pharmaceuticals. With reported earnings increasing sharply in 1986, Merck appears to be a good choice for participating in pharmaceuticals.

Merck's historical performance can be seen in Table 15-3. An investor examining

TABLE 15-3
Merck

Dollar Amounts in Millions

	1982	1983	1984	1985	1986	1987	1988	E1989
Stockholder Equity	2204	2435	2544	2634	2569	2117	2856	3650
Long-Term Debt	337	386	179	171	168	167	143	100
Capital Employed	2541	2821	2723	2805	2737	2284	2999	3750
Avg. Capital Employed	2392	2681	2772	2764	2771	2510	2642	3374
Debt, %	12.1	13.5	10.2	6.3	6.1	6.7	5.9	3.6
Earnings—Reported	415	451	493	540	676	906	1207	1505
—Adjusted	411	440	325	313	193	−129	1247	1443
Rate of Return, Adjusted, %	17.2	16.4	11.7	11.3	7.0	−5.1	47.2	42.8
Dividends	208	209	216	223	258	323	508	648
Dividend Payout, %	50.8	47.4	66.5	71.3	133.7	−250.6	40.7	45.0
Number of Shares	444	444	433	421	409	394	397	395
Price/Earnings	13.7	14.9	13.2	14.5	19.8	25.2	18.0	20.2

	1982–86	1985–89
Avg. Rate of Return, %	12.7	20.6
Avg. Capital Growth, %/yr.	1.4	6.7

Merck in March of 1987 would have found a highly profitable company. The adjusted rate of return averaged 17.8 percent over the prior 10 years, but dropped to 12.7 percent over the prior five years. Merck carries only 6 percent debt in its capital structure, one-sixth of the Standard & Poor's 500 average. Capital growth has been weak, however. Growth had averaged only 1.4 percent per year for the prior five-year period and 7.9 percent per year for the prior 10-year period.

Merck's attraction is the high return it earns, and the prospects of higher returns from new drugs. After studying the performance record in Table 15-3, this investor might make the following projections for Merck:

Merck Performance Estimates
March, 1987

	Low	Most Likely	High
Rate of Return, %			
Initial	15	17	19
Long-Run	9	12	16
Half-Life, years	6	10	12
Capital Growth, %/yr.			
Initial	3	5	6
Long-Run	4	8	10
Half-Life, years	4	5	10
P/E Ratio			
Long-Run	10	14	16
Half-Life, years	7	10	12

Merck Performance Estimates
March 1987

Capital Employed, millions	2,737
Shares Outstanding, millions	136
Growth of Shares Outstanding, %/yr.	−1
Debt, %	6
Stock Price, March 1987, $/share	158.875

The rate of return is projected to begin at 17 percent and decay slowly towards a long-run return of 12 percent with a 10-year half-life. Growth is projected to recover towards the GNP rate of 8 percent per year. The price/earnings ratio drops, primarily because of a projection that the market will drop from the record high of March 1987, but Merck will still remain among the higher price/earnings stocks at the lower long-run price/earnings ratio.

The projections in the previous table indicate a rate of return of 1.9 percent with all variables at their most likely values. Maximum allowable price is only $84 per share, or about half the $159 market price in early 1987. As shown in Fig. 15-5, the expected return, based on 200 random outcomes, is 0 percent. The probability of earning the 1.9 percent return with all of the variables at their most likely values is only 5 percent. The probability of losing money—of earning a return below this investor's 7 percent opportunity cost—is 99+ percent. With these assumptions, Merck is not attractive for this investor.

Fig. 15-5

RISK ANALYSIS −− MERCK

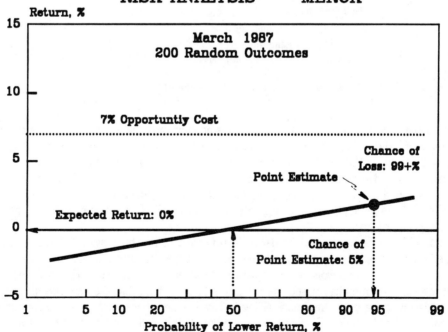

Instead of the gradual erosion this investor expected in early 1987, Merck turned in an extraordinary performance. Success with new drugs raised Merck's adjusted rate of return to 50 percent in 1988 and an estimated 44 percent in 1989. Growth jumped to 27 percent in 1988 and an estimated 22 percent in 1989. Finally, after stock splits, Merck's stock was up 45 percent and was selling for $77 per share.

A prudent investor will not project that such outstanding performance will continue unchanged. Suppose this investor projects a current return of 40 percent and a long-run return of 15 percent. He also projects that the return will decay with a five-year half-life. In five years, the return will drop to 27.5 percent. In 10 years, the return will still be 21 percent. He projects that growth will slow from 20 percent to 7 percent per year, also with a five-year half-life:

Merck Performance Estimates
November, 1989

	Low	Most Likely	High
Rate of Return, %			
Initial	35	40	42
Long-Run	10	15	18
Half-Life, years	3	5	7
Capital Growth, %/yr.			
Initial	15	20	22
Long-Run	5	7	9
Half-Life, years	3	5	7
P/E Ratio			
Long-Run	10	14	16
Half-Life, years	3	5	7
Capital Employed, millions		3,750	
Shares Outstanding, millions		397	
Growth Shares Outstanding, %/yr.		−0.5	
Debt, %		5	
Stock Price, November 1989, $/share		77	

A single evaluation with all of the variables at their most-likely values yields a point estimate of 6.0 percent rate of return and a maximum allowable price of $69 per share. Figure 15-6 shows the result of risk analysis with 200 random outcomes. The expected return drops to 4.8 percent, and the maximum allowable price drops to $63 per share. There is only a 36 percent chance of earning the point estimate return of 6.0 percent. There is a 75 percent chance of losing money by earning less than this investor's 7 percent opportunity cost.

Merck's extraordinary performance is reflected in the high price for the stock. Based on this projection of Merck's future performance, the stock is still not attractive for this investor. It is no wonder then, that the disadvantage of stocks in a hot industry is that investor attention has raised the price of stocks so high that they are not likely to earn reasonable returns. Investors willing to pay $77 per share for Merck are counting on continued high profits. They are assuming that Merck will continue its rapid growth,

Fig. 15-6

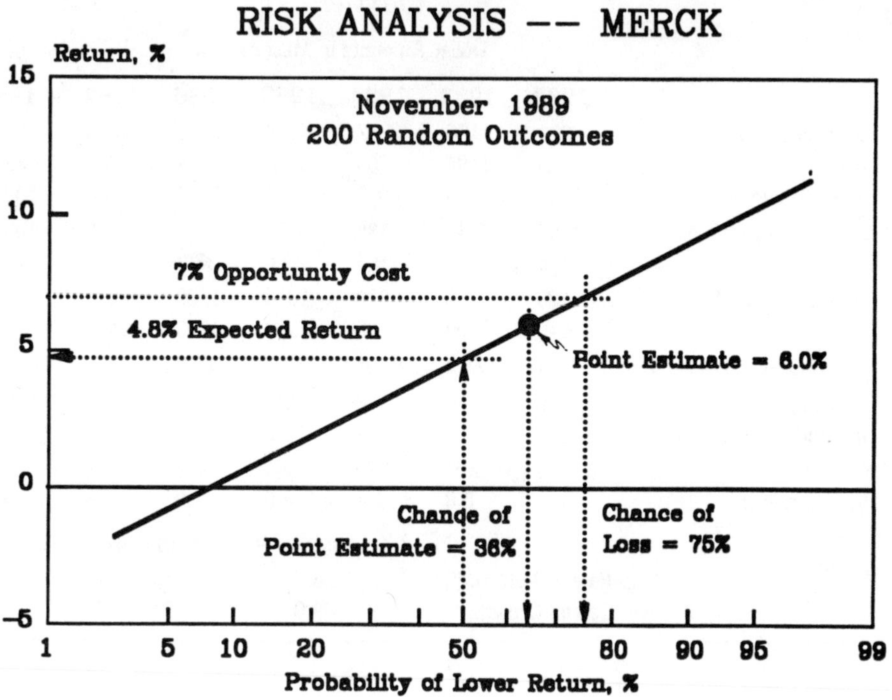

RISK ANALYSIS -- MERCK

Return, %

November 1989
200 Random Outcomes

7% Opportuntly Cost

4.8% Expected Return

Point Estimate = 6.0%

Chance of
Point Estimate = 36%

Chance of
Loss = 75%

Probability of Lower Return, %

and/or that the gradual decline in profitability and price/earnings ratio will be much slower. They might also have lower opportunity costs and lower incremental tax rates.

LOW PRICE/EARNINGS RATIO STOCKS

Although the Standard & Poor's average stock sold at a price/earnings ratio of 20 in March 1987, this ratio is an average. Individual stocks covered a wide range. LTV sold at a price/earnings ratio of 1; NEC Corporation sold at a price/earnings ratio of 81. If the investor is looking for undervalued stocks, he is more likely to find them among stocks selling at low price/earnings ratios. An investor must be cautious, however. There is usually a good reason why such stocks are so inexpensive. Earnings might be declining, the firm might be losing its markets to imports, or the firm might be close to bankruptcy. Obviously the market is not optimistic about the future of those stocks.

Suppose this investor searches the list of low price/earnings ratio stocks looking for a company that might be undervalued, and whose earnings prospects might eventually justify a higher price/earnings ratio. Chrysler might be such a stock. It sold at a price/earnings ratio of 7.3 in early 1987—about 40 percent of the Standard and Poor's average price/earnings ratio. Chrysler's financial performance is shown in Table 15-4.

Chrysler has made a dramatic comeback under Lee Iacocca's direction. Historical data is not too helpful for projecting the future for a firm such as Chrysler, which is recovering from near bankruptcy. Rates of return and capital growth rates rose above 30 percent during Chrysler's recovery. Such outstanding performance might happen during

TABLE 15-4
Chrysler

Dollar Amounts in Millions

	1982	1983	1984	1985	1986	1987	1988	E1989
Stockholder Equity	−330	1126	3282	4166	5281	6503	7582	8280
Long-Term Debt	2189	1104	760	2366	2334	3333	3329	3400
Capital Employed	1859	2230	4042	6532	7615	9836	10911	11680
Avg. Capital Employed	1697	2045	3136	5287	7074	8726	10374	11296
Debt, %	125.6	80.5	29.7	29.6	33.2	32.5	32.1	29.8
Earnings—Reported	170	701	2373	1610	1389	1290	1050	1100
—Adjusted	210	1456	2262	999	1293	1441	1304	974
Rate of Return, Adjusted, %	12.4	71.2	72.1	18.9	18.3	16.5	12.6	8.6
Dividends	0	0	106	115	178	219	225	276
Dividend Payout, %	0	0	4.7	11.5	13.8	15.2	17.3	28.3
Number of Shares	173	261	279	261	222	219	225	230
Price/Earnings	—	5.8	2.4	2.6	4.0	5.8	4.8	4.4

	1982 – 86	1985 – 89
Avg. Rate of Return, %	38.6	15.0
Avg. Capital Growth, %/yr.	39.0	15.2

a year of recovery, but it is almost impossible under normal conditions. Chrysler succeeded in reducing its debt burden from 71 percent of capital employed in 1982 to 33 percent, about the average debt burden of the Standard & Poor's 500 stock average. Chrysler sold at an average price/earnings ratio of only 4.4 in 1986.

Such outstanding performance cannot continue in an industry as mature and as competitive as the automobile industry. Chrysler's rapid growth is bound to slow. Its rate of return is also likely to drop. Our investor concludes that capital growth will eventually drop below the GNP growth, and that the rate of return will drop to about the average return of the Standard & Poor's 500 stock average. He also concludes that the adjustment will be fairly rapid, with a half-life of three years:

Chrysler Performance Estimates
March, 1987

	Low	Most Likely	High
Rate of Return, %			
Initial	13	15	17
Long-Run	6	9	11
Half-Life, years	2	3	5
Capital Growth, %/yr.			
Initial	14	16	17
Long-Run	0	3	6
Half-Life, years	2	3	5

Chrysler Performance Estimates
March, 1987

P/E Ratio

Long-Run	5	8	10
Half Life, years	2	3	5

Capital Employed, millions	7,769
Shares Outstanding, millions	217
Growth of Shares Outstanding, %/yr.	2.0
Debt, %	33
Stock Price, March 1987, $/share	55.50

An evaluation of Chrysler stock, with all of the variables at their most likely values, gives a point estimate of 3.1 percent rate of return and a maximum allowable price of $36.47 per share. Figure 15-7 shows the results of 200 random outcomes. The expected return is 3.0 percent. There is only a 47 percent chance of reaching the 3.1 percent point estimate return. There is a 98 percent chance of losing money on this stock.

Investors expect Chrysler to perform better under Iacocca's leadership, and bid Chrysler's stock up in anticipation of higher earnings. The price is too high in early 1987, however, for the stock to be attractive to this investor.

The auto industry slowdown lowered Chrysler's performance in the fall of 1989. After splitting three for two, however, Chrysler's stocks had dropped 43 percent and

Fig. 15-7

RISK ANALYSIS —— CHRYSLER

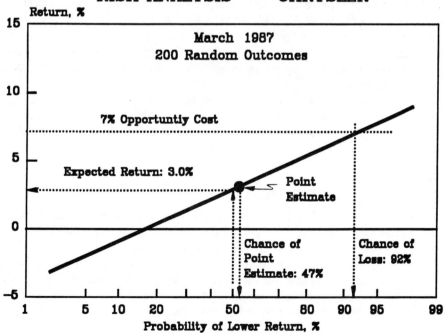

was selling for $21 per share. If the market overreacted, this low price might make Chrysler a reasonable investment. Our investor might lower his estimates for Chrysler as follows:

Chrysler Performance Estimates
November, 1989

	Low	Most Likely	High
Rate of Return, %			
Initial	7.5	8.5	9.5
Long-Run	6	7	8
Half-Life, years	2	3	5
Capital Growth, %/yr.			
Initial	6	8	9
Long-Run	4	5	6
Half-Life, years	2	3	5
P/E Ratio			
Long-Run	3.5	5	8
Half-Life, years	2	3	5
Capital Employed, millions		11,680	
Shares Outstanding, millions		230	
Growth of Shares Outstanding, %/yr.		1	
Debt, %		30	
Stock Price, November 1989, $/share		21.13	

The point estimate, with all of the variables at their most likely values, is a return of 7.9 percent and a maximum allowable price of $23 per share. Figure 15-8 shows the results of risk analysis with 200 random outcomes. The expected return is 10.8 percent. There is an 87 percent chance of earning the 7.9 percent point-estimate return. There is only a 6 percent chance of losing money by earning a return below this investor's 7 percent opportunity cost.

This analysis shows that the market overreacted, and depressed the price of Chrysler's stock too far. Despite the problems of the automobile industry in general, and Chrysler in particular, a low price of $21 per share makes Chrysler a reasonable investment.

EXPERT'S RECOMMENDATIONS

As our investor reads the financial press to learn about the market and the outlook for industries and individual firms, he will find frequent interviews with prominent financial analysts who give their view on where the market is heading. These experts are invariably asked to name the stocks they are recommending to their clients. In one such interview early in 1987, an analyst on the popular television program *Wall Street Week* included Dunkin' Donuts among his recommendations. Our investor might be impressed by the self-assurance of the experts, and consider investing in Dunkin' Donuts. It is still wise, however, to do your own analysis.

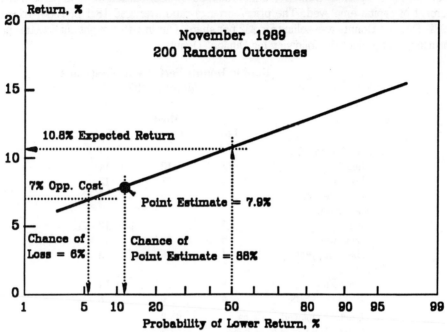

Fig. 15–8

RISK ANALYSIS –– CHRYSLER

Return, %

November 1989
200 Random Outcomes

10.8% Expected Return

7% Opp. Cost

Point Estimate = 7.9%

Chance of
Loss = 6%

Chance of
Point Estimate = 88%

Probability of Lower Return, %

TABLE 15-5
Dunkin' Donuts

Dollar Amounts in Millions

	1982	1983	1984	1985	1986	1987	1988	E1989
Stockholder Equity	38.1	45.0	53.0	62.2	72.6	68.2	72.7	41.5
Long-Term Debt	30.7	27.9	28.7	26.5	23.3	21.1	40.2	80.0
Capital Employed	68.8	72.9	81.7	88.7	95.9	89.3	112.9	121.5
Avg. Capital Employed	67.5	70.9	77.3	85.2	92.3	92.6	101.1	117.2
Debt, %	48.2	41.4	36.6	32.4	27.0	24.0	30.3	51.3
Earnings—Reported	6.7	7.9	9.2	10.6	12.1	13.3	13.5	13.5
—Adjusted	7.9	8.1	9.4	10.9	12.4	−2.3	6.8	−28.9
Rate of Return, Adjusted, %	11.7	11.4	12.2	12.7	13.4	−2.5	6.7	−24.7
Dividends	1.31	1.20	1.43	1.36	1.96	2.08	2.25	2.30
Dividend Payout, %	20.4	14.8	15.1	15.3	15.9	−89.9	33.3	−8.0
Number of Shares	7.00	7.07	7.14	7.20	7.26	6.72	6.43	5.75
Price/Earnings	7.6	13.2	11.7	14.1	18.1	16.2	11.3	18.7

	1982 – 86	1985 – 89
Avg. Rate of Return, %	12.3	1.1
Avg. Capital Growth, %/yr.	8.6	7.9

Dunkin' Donuts performance is detailed in Table 15-5. Dunkin' Donuts average adjusted rate of return for the period was 12.3 percent. Capital grew 8.6 percent per year. During the period, Dunkin' Donuts reduced its debt burden from 48 percent to 27 percent of capital employed. The price/earnings ratio averaged 18.1 in 1986. In early 1987, Dunkin' Donuts was selling for $32 per share. Our investor might analyze this performance and project the following for Dunkin' Donuts:

Dunkin Donuts Performance Estimates
March, 1987

	Low	Most Likely	High
Rate of Return, %			
Initial	12	13	14
Long-Run	8	11	12
Half-Life, years	4	6	8
Capital Growth, %/yr.			
Initial	7	9	12
Long-Run	6	8	10
Half-Life, years	4	6	8
P/E Ratio			
Long-Run	9	12	14
Half-Life, years	4	6	8
Capital Employed, millions		95.9	
Shares Outstanding, millions		7.3	
Growth of Shares Outstanding, %/yr.		0.9	
Debt, %		27	
Stock Price, March 1987, $/share		31.75	

This investor projects that the rate of return will fall from 13 percent to a long-run return of 11 percent. The fall is gradual, with a six-year half-life. He projects growth that will slow slightly from 9 percent to 8 percent per year, about the same growth projected from the GNP. The long-run price/earnings ratio is projected at 12, a reasonable long-run estimate for an average stock.

Based on the most likely values of these variables, an investment in Dunkin' Donuts will earn a return of 4.4 percent. The maximum allowable price for this investor is $23.70 per share. Figure 15-9 shows that the expected return from 200 random outcomes is 3.9 percent. The chance of earning the 4.4 percent return with all of the variables at their most likely values is only 39 percent. The chance of losing money by earning less than this investor's 7 percent opportunity cost is 96 percent. Risk analysis shows a maximum allowable price of $22.81 per share.

Dunkin' Donuts might well have been an excellent choice at the time this expert made his analysis. By the time the expert appears on television and announces his recommendation, however, the stocks he analyzed might have risen enough in price that they are no longer attractive.

Dunkin' Donuts agreed to a $47.25 per share takeover offer by Allied-Lyons PLC in late 1989. Takeover rumors had driven the stock price from $25 per share earlier in the year to $47 in November of 1989. It is too late to buy takeover candidates after such a

Fig. 15-9

RISK ANALYSIS –– DUNKIN DONUTS

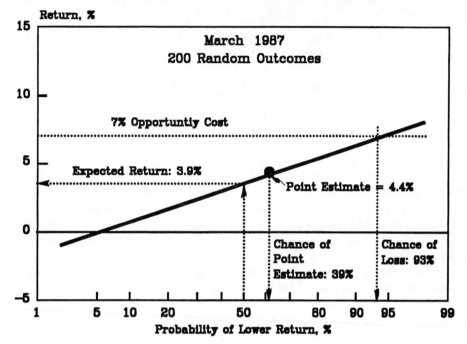

runup in price. Dunkin' Donuts will not be traded after the acquisition, and therefore, was not re-evaluated in November 1989.

BONDS

The list of New York bond prices in the financial pages of the daily newspaper contain a number of bonds that carry high interest rates because they were issued when interest rates were much higher than they were in 1987. Suppose our investor noticed that Commonwealth Edison Company bonds due in 2012 pay $15^3/8$ percent interest. In early 1987, these bonds sold for $116. At that price, the current yield appears to be 13.3 percent, or, for this investor, an after-tax yield of 8.9 percent.

Although Commonwealth Edison had to offer this high interest rate to sell the bonds when they were offered in 1982, they will not be happy paying that interest rate in 1987, when interest rates had fallen to about 6 percent. Therefore, Commonwealth Edison made the bonds callable, so that they could be redeemed by selling new bonds at 1987's lower interest rates.

The investor can find the schedule of call dates and prices in Moody's Utilities Manual. Call dates and prices for industrial bonds are listed in Moody's Industrial Manual. Our investor found that these bonds were issued in August 1982, and are not callable prior to August 1987. After August 1987, the bonds can be called on 40 day's notice prior to each August 14th. The call prices, and the after-tax return the investor could earn buying these bonds for $116 at the beginning of 1987, paying a 1 percent commission, and having these bonds called is:

Call Date	Call Price	After-Tax Return, %
1987	$112.93	2.96
1988	112.41	6.28
1989	111.90	6.95
1990	111.38	7.25
1991	110.86	7.41
1992	110.34	7.52

The returns are low because the high interest earned on these bonds is partly offset by the capital loss when the bonds purchased at $117.16, including commission, are later redeemed at the lower call price. Commonwealth Edison would have to pass two opportunities to call these high-interest bonds before this investor could earn his opportunity cost. Despite the high-interest rate, the call feature makes these bonds a poor investment.

None of the five stocks evaluated, nor the high-interest bond, appear to be better investments for this investor in March 1987 than the 7 percent tax-free bond. This result is not surprising when, in early 1987, stocks were selling at record price/earning ratios. These investments might have been attractive in more normal times when they could have been acquired at a lower price.

Some other investor in different circumstances might evaluate these same securities and find them attractive. Another investor might have a lower opportunity cost or a lower incremental tax rate. Or he might be more optimistic, and project that these companies will earn higher returns, grow faster, and/or that the higher returns and faster growth might decay more slowly. Each investor must make his own projection of the future of these firms, evaluate the investments on the basis of his own projections, and act on the results.

On October 19, 1987, seven months after these securities were analyzed, the stock market crashed, and the Dow-Jones Industrial average fell 508 points in a single day. Why such a drastic fall? The outlook for the stocks in the Dow-Jones average didn't suddenly collapse overnight. Investors had allowed themselves to be carried away by four years of steadily rising stock prices. They believed stock prices would continue rising, and were willing to pay prices well above the stock's basic value. When stocks are overvalued, any sudden drop in the market is likely to ignite a panic as investors try to get out before stocks fall to their true value.

Investors who analyzed stocks using the methods described in this book would not have been caught in the stock market crash. They would have found, like the investor in this chapter, that stocks were overpriced, and would have invested their money elsewhere. The maximum allowable price our investor calculated from 200 random outcomes is compared with market prices in March 1987 and just after the crash of October 19th:

| Stock | Market Price, $/Share | | Maximum Allowable |
	March, 1987	October, 1987	Price, $
Hewlett-Packard	57.25	48	51
IBM	150.75	103	157
Merck	158.88	144	84
Chrysler	37.00*	22*	24*
Dunkin' Donuts	31.75	23	23

*Adjusted for a 3-for-2 stock split in April 1987.

Hewlett-Packard, IBM, and Chrysler had dropped below this investor's estimate of the maximum price he should pay and would have been reasonable investments immediately following the crash. Dunkin' Donuts dropped only to our investor's maximum allowable price. But Merck dropped only from $159 per share to $144 per share. Merck was still 70 percent more expensive than this investor should have paid and remained an overpriced stock.

DIVERSIFICATION

Investing all of your savings in the single stock that appears to offer the highest return subjects you to serious risk if that firm encounters unexpected difficulties. Protect yourself from this risk by diversifying. Invest in a number of firms, in different industries, and by investing in both stocks and other types of securities. Losses in any single investment will then have a much smaller impact on your savings.

Do not use the evaluation methods in this book to locate the single best investment. There is no single best investment. Instead, find a number of investments that appear attractive. Use the methods in this book to locate several attractive investments, and protect yourself by diversifying.

SUMMARY

☐ Begin the process of putting the evaluation methods of this book to work for you by defining your own position. Check your federal and state tax returns and determine your incremental tax rate. Then, review investment opportunities with clearly stated rates of return. Check certificates of deposit, money market funds, Ginnie Mae funds, and tax-free money market and bond funds. Don't overlook interest costs you can save by paying off debts you owe. The highest after-tax return offered by these opportunities becomes your opportunity cost. Review these investment opportunities frequently, because the rates they offer fluctuate, and your opportunity cost will fluctuate accordingly.

☐ With your opportunity cost and incremental tax rate established, examine the possibility of increasing your return by investing in stocks and bonds. Check out companies you think have good growth prospects, work in profitable industries, or ones that might be undervalued. Use the methods outlined in Chapter 10 to measure the basic characteristics of these companies and to compare them with other companies in the same industry, then project the future performance of these companies, and use the calculation forms in Chapter 11 to evaluate each investment.

☐ Compare the rate of return you calculated with your opportunity cost, then compare the maximum allowable price you calculate with the market price of the security. If your analysis shows that any of these investment possibilities offers a higher return than your opportunity cost, use the Monte Carlo method to estimate the risks involved with those securities. Calculate your expected return, and the chance of earning less than your opportunity cost. If the expected return is higher than your opportunity cost, and you find the risk of losing money (of earning a return less than your opportunity cost) fits your willingness to accept risk, then you can invest in that security with a reasonable assurance that the investment will make your wealth grow faster.

16

How to Set Up
Savings Plans

SETTING UP A SHORT-TERM SAVINGS PLAN IS NOT A PROBLEM. IF YOU NEED $1,000 six months from now, for example, the plan is obvious. Save ($1,000)/(6 mo.), or $166.67 per month. Setting up a long-term savings plan, such as a retirement plan, is more difficult. Your savings gradually grow with time and earn interest on a growing investment base for varying time periods. A dollar you invest today earns interest for the full savings period. A dollar you invest later earns less because it is invested a shorter time. Monthly savings are likely to grow as your salary grows. The inflation rate is a reasonable minimum for a savings growth rate. You might be able to save at a somewhat higher rate. Inflation raises the cost of the goal you are saving for. All of these factors complicate the problem of saving. The calculation forms in this chapter can show you how to set up a savings plan and account for these factors.

Savings plans involve two time periods. The first is a savings period. During this period, you invest savings each month. The savings grow and reach some target at the end of the period. The second period is the pay-off period. You invest the sum accumulated during the savings period. Each month, you withdraw enough to pay retirement income, college expenses, or the cost of some other goal. You exhaust the amount you saved by the end of the pay-off period.

Setting up a savings plan involves two considerations. The first consideration is to decide on your savings target. How much money will you need to pay college expenses, retirement income, or whatever goal you are saving for? The second consideration is to decide on the monthly savings you need to reach your goal. For a long-term plan, you need to decide both the initial level of savings, and how those monthly savings should grow as your income and capacity to save grows.

TARGET SAVINGS

The calculation form in Table 16-1 will help you find the sum you must accumulate at the end of the savings period. If your goal is income for some period of time, enter the annual income goal in line 1, and the time period in line 2. Enter the annual income in line 1 in today's dollars. The form will adjust for future dollars. You might want the income to grow gradually during the pay-off period, or you might want retirement income to grow at the inflation rate to offset inflation, for example. Enter that growth rate in line 4. Enter the after-tax return you expect to earn from investing your savings in line 5. Enter the inflation rate you expect in line 6. The savings you need to accumulate is the present value of the future stream of income payments. Calculate that present value in line 9.

That value is in today's dollars. You will need to save more to allow for inflation during the savings period. Find the savings you must accumulate in future dollars in line 11.

The rate of return you project in line 5 and the inflation rate you project in line 6 are not nearly as important as the difference between them. The difference between them is your real rate of return. Focus on your real return. A reasonable estimate might be a real after-tax return of 3 percent. If you project inflation at 5 percent per year, then project your return on investments at the 5 percent inflation rate plus the 3 percent real return, or a nominal return of 8 percent.

Example 16-1. George's two-year old son will enter college in 16 years. George decides to set up a savings plan to accumulate enough money to pay for a four-year college program. He figures today's college expenses at $9,000 per year. He expects expenses to grow 5 percent per year. He believes he can earn an 8 percent return after taxes on his investment program. How much money should he accumulate at the time his son is ready to start college?

Use Table 16-1 to find the required savings. Table 16-2 illustrates the solution. Enter the $9,000 annual income requirement in line 1 and the four-year time period in line 2. He has 16 years available to build his savings. Enter 16 years in line 3. Enter the 5 percent per year growth in estimated expenses in line 4 and his 8 percent return in line 5. Enter the 5 percent per year inflation rate in line 6. Calculate a savings requirement of $33,923 in line 9. That sum is in today's dollars. At 5 percent per year inflation, line 10 shows that savings in future dollars must be 2.2255 times greater. Line 11 shows that George's plan must accumulate $75,497 by the time his son is ready for college.

THE SAVINGS PLAN

Once you have decided on your savings target, you must find a schedule of monthly savings that will accumulate to that target over the course of the savings period. The calculation form in Table 16-3 will help you set up that schedule. Enter the savings target in

TABLE 16-1
Calculation Form—The Savings Target

1. Required Income, $/year. If the income is a lump sum, enter it in Line 9. _____
2. Years Income Required _____
3. Years until Income Starts _____
4. Income Growth %/yr. _____
5. Return on Investments, % _____
6. Expected Inflation, %/yr. _____
7. RT: Multiply the difference between Lines 4 and 5 by Line 2 _____
8. Dc Factor at RT = Line 7. If Line 4 is greater than Line 5, use a Gc Factor instead. _____
9. Savings Target, Today's Dollars: Multiply Line 1 by Lines 2 and 8 _____
10. Gi Factor at RT = Line 3 times Line 6 _____
11. Savings Target, Future Dollars: Multiply Line 9 by Line 10 _____

TABLE 16-2
The Savings Target—College Savings Example

1. Required Income, $/year. If the income is a lump sum, skip to Line 9 and enter it.	$9,000
2. Years Income Required	4
3. Years until Income Starts	16
4. Income Growth %/yr.	5
5. Return on Investments, %	8
6. Expected Inflation, %/yr.	5
7. RT: Multiply the difference between Lines 4 and 5 by Line 2	12
8. Dc Factor at RT = Line 7. If Line 4 is greater than Line 5, use a Gc Factor instead.	0.9423
9. Savings Target, Today's Dollars: Multiply Line 1 by Lines 2 and 8	$33,923
10. Gi Factor at RT = Line 3 times Line 6	2.2255
11. Savings Target, Future Dollars: Multiply Line 9 by Line 10	$75,497

TABLE 16-3
Calculation Form—The Savings Schedule

1. Savings Target, $	_____
2. Savings Period, years	_____
3. Growth in Savings, %/yr.	_____
4. Return on Investments, %	_____
5. Di Factor at RT = Line 2 times Line 4	_____
6. RT: Multiply the difference between Lines 3 and 4 by Line 2	_____
7. Dc Factor at RT = Line 6. If Line 3 is greater than Line 4, use a Gc Factor instead.	_____
8. Initial Savings Required, $/mo.: Multiply Line 1 by Line 5, then Divide by 12 and by Lines 2 and 7	_____

---

line 1 and the time available to reach that target in line 2. During an extended savings period, you are likely to save a little more each month. Enter the growth rate of savings in line 3. Enter the nominal after-tax return you expect to earn from your investment program in line 4. Enter Di and Dc discount factors in lines 5 and 7. If you expect the savings growth rate to be higher than your return on investment, use a Gc growth factor in place of the Dc discount factor in line 7. Find the required initial monthly savings in line 8. Savings required in any future month are the initial savings multiplied by a Gi growth factor. Read the Gi factor at the product of the savings growth rate and time.

Example 16-2. Now that he knows his savings target, George is ready to work out a savings plan. George expects that his salary will grow slightly faster than inflation. Therefore, he plans to increase his monthly savings 6 percent per year. He expects to

_____TABLE 16-4_____
The Savings Schedule—College Savings Example

1. Savings Target, $	$75,497
2. Savings Period, years	16
3. Growth in Savings, %/yr.	6
4. Return on Investments, %	8
5. Di Factor at RT = Line 2 times Line 4	0.2780
6. RT: Multiply the difference between Lines 3 and 4 by Line 2	32
7. Dc Factor at RT = Line 6	0.8558
8. Initial Savings Required, $/mo.: Multiply Line 1 by Line 5, then Divide by 12 and by Lines 2 and 7	$127.73

earn an 8 percent after-tax return from his investment program. Where must his monthly savings begin if he has 16 years to reach the $75,497 target established in Example 16-1. What will the required monthly savings grow to in 5, 10, and 15 years?

Table 16-4 shows how to set up the program. Enter the $75,497 target in line 1 and the 16-year savings period in line 2. Enter the 6 percent per year growth in monthly savings in line 3 and the expected 8 percent after-tax return on investment in line 4. Calculate an initial monthly savings of $127.73 in line 8.

George plans to increase his savings at the rate of 6 percent per year. At 6 percent per year growth, Gi growth factors for 5, 10, and 15 years are 1.3499, 1.8221, and 2.4596. Monthly savings in years 5, 10, and 15 are:

$$\text{Savings, year } 5 = (\$127.73) (1.3499) = \$172.42$$
$$\text{Savings, year } 10 = (\$127.73) (1.8221) = \$232.74$$
$$\text{Savings, year } 15 = (\$127.73) (2.4596) = \$314.16$$

The savings target might be a lump sum instead of a series of income payments. A savings plan to buy a new car is an example. If the target is a lump sum, enter that sum in line 9 of Table 16-2.

Example 16-3. Bill expects to buy a new car in five years. Instead of borrowing the money when he buys the car and paying high bank interest rates, he decides to set up a savings plan now to pay for the car. The car he wants cost $11,000 today. He expects 5 percent per year inflation, and expects to increase his monthly savings 6 percent per year. He anticipates an 8 percent after-tax return on his investments. What should his initial monthly savings be?

Table 16-5 can help Bill determine his savings. The $11,000 savings target is a lump sum; enter it in line 9. Enter the five years he has to save that sum in line 3 and the inflation rate in line 6. Line 11 shows he will need $14,124 to buy that car after five years of inflation.

Use Table 16-3 to find the initial monthly savings. Table 16-6 illustrates the calculation. Enter the $14,124 target in line 1, the five-year savings period in line 2, and the 6 percent per year growth in savings in line 3. Enter the 8 percent return on investment in line 4. Calculate that monthly savings must begin at $165.81 in line 8.

TABLE 16-5
The Savings Target—Automobile Example

1. Required Income, $/year. If the income is a lump sum, enter it in Line 9.	
2. Years Income Required	
3. Years until Income Starts	5
4. Income Growth, %/yr.	
5. Return on Investments, %	
6. Expected Inflation, %/yr.	5
7. RT: Multiply the difference between Lines 4 and 5 by Line 2	
8. Dc Factor at RT = Line 7	
9. Savings Target, Today's Dollars: Multiply Line 1 by Lines 2 and 8	$11,000
10. Gi Factor at RT = Line 3 times Line 6	1.2840
11. Savings Target, Future Dollars: Multiply Line 9 by Line 10	$14,124

TABLE 16-6
The Savings Schedule—Automobile Example

1. Savings Target, $	$14,124
2. Savings Period, years	5
3. Growth in Savings, %/yr.	6
4. Return on Investments, %	8
5. Di Factor at RT = Line 2 times Line 4	0.6703
6. RT: Multiply the difference between Lines 3 and 4 by Line 2	10
7. Dc Factor at RT = Line 6	0.9516
8. Initial Savings Required, $/mo.: Multiply Line 1 by Line 5, then Divide by 12 and by Lines 2 and 7	$165.81

If Bill did not set up this plan, and financed his new car purchase instead, he would have had monthly car payments of $244 for a five-year auto loan. This example illustrates the value of setting up your own savings plan to finance car purchases instead of borrowing the money through your dealer or through your bank.

RETIREMENT PLANS

Inflation has a major effect when the savings plan extends over a long period, such as a retirement plan. Beginning the plan early is important. The longer you postpone a retirement plan, the more you have to save each month to meet a target level of retirement income. You can reduce the required monthly savings by making your investment program more effective and earning a higher return on investment.

Example 16-4. Bob has just started his working career. He has 45 years to save before he retires at age 65. He hopes to have $30,000 of retirement income (in today's dollars) in addition to Social Security. To ensure against running out of money while he is still alive, he plans on saving enough to maintain that level of retirement income for 25 years, or until age 90. The retirement income will have to increase 5 percent per year to offset inflation. He believes he can earn an 8 percent after-tax return from his investment program. He expects his salary to grow slightly faster than an inflation rate of 5 percent per year. Therefore, he believes he can increase his monthly savings during the savings period at the rate of 6 percent per year. How much must he accumulate at retirement to finance this plan? What must his initial monthly savings be?

Use Table 16-1 to work out the savings target. Table 16-7 shows the calculation. Enter the $30,000 income requirement in line 1 and the 25-year income period in line 2. He has 45 years to build savings; enter that time in line 3. Enter his income growth, return on investment, and inflation rate in the next three lines. Line 9 shows a savings target of $527,625 in today's dollars. Because of 5 percent per year inflation over a 45-year period, line 11 shows that he will have to accumulate $5,005,948 in future inflated dollars.

Use Table 16-3 to find the initial monthly savings. Table 16-8 shows the calculation. Enter the $5 million savings target in line 1 and the 45-year savings period in line 2. Enter the savings growth rate and the return on investment in lines 3 and 4. Line 8 shows that Bob must begin saving $383.80 per month now to finance this plan. Bob plans to increase his savings at the rate of 6 percent per year. Therefore, future monthly savings will be the initial savings multiplied by a $Gi_{6,T}$ growth factor. Future monthly savings are:

Year	$Gi_{6,T}$	Savings, $/mo.
10	1.8221	699.33
20	3.3201	1,274.26
30	6.0496	2,321.85
40	11.0232	4,230.70

_____TABLE 16-7_____
The Savings Target—Retirement Example

1. Required Income, $/year. If the income is a lump sum, enter it in Line 9.	$30,000
2. Years Income Required	25
3. Years until Income Starts	45
4. Income Growth, %/yr.	5
5. Return on Investments, %	8
6. Expected Inflation, %/yr.	5
7. RT: Multiply the difference between Lines 4 and 5 by Line 2	75
8. Dc Factor at RT = Line 7. If Line 4 is greater than Line 5, use a Gc Factor instead.	0.7035
9. Savings Target, Today's Dollars: Multiply Line 1 by Lines 2 and 8	$527,625
10. Gi Factor at RT = Line 3 times Line 6	9.4877
11. Savings Target, Future Dollars: Multiply Line 9 by Line 1	$5,005,948

TABLE 16-8
The Savings Schedule—Retirement Example

1. Savings Target, $	$5,005,948
2. Savings Period, years	45
3. Growth in Savings, %/yr.	6
4. Return on Investments, %	8
5. Di Factor at RT = Line 2 times Line 4	0.0273
6. RT: Multiply the difference between Lines 3 and 4 by Line 2	90
7. Dc Factor at RT = Line 6	0.6594
8. Initial Savings Required, $/mo.: Multiply Line 1 by Line 5, then Divide by 12 and by Lines 2 and 7	$383.80

The future monthly savings might seem staggering today. As inflation proceeds, however, Bob's income and the general price level will gradually rise. Bob will gradually become accustomed to the higher prices. When these future times arrive, savings rates that appear staggering now will seem normal then. If Bob postpones this plan until he is in a better position to afford it, the required monthly savings will increase substantially.

The disadvantage of setting up a retirement plan this way is that you need to provide income until, say, age 90 to ensure income for the rest of your life. Otherwise, you risk running out of money before you die.

An alternate way to provide retirement income is to buy an annuity from an insurance company. An annuity is a promise to pay a monthly sum of money for life in return for an initial payment. The insurance company calculates the cost of the annuity on the basis of paying a monthly income for your life expectancy, which is currently 14.2 years for a man aged 65, and 18.5 years for a woman the same age. Instead of needing a sum that pays monthly income for 30 years, the insurance company needs only a sum that

---

TABLE 16-9
The Savings Target—Shorter Savings Period

1. Required Income, $/year. If the income is a lump sum, enter it in Line 9.	$63,510
2. Years Income Required	25
3. Years until Income Starts	30
4. Income Growth, %/yr.	5
5. Return on Investments, %	8
6. Expected Inflation, %/yr.	5
7. RT: Multiply the difference between Lines 4 and 5 by Line 2	75
8. Dc Factor at RT = Line 7. If Line 4 is greater than Line 5, use a Gc Factor instead.	0.7035
9. Savings Target, Today's Dollars: Multiply Line 1 by Lines 2 and 8	$1,116,982
10. Gi Factor at RT = Line 3 times Line 6	4.4817
11. Savings Target, Future Dollars: Multiply Line 9 by Line 1	$5,005,978

---

provides monthly income for 14.2 to 18.5 years, plus an extra amount to cover expenses, provide a margin of safety, and generate a profit.

Example 16-5. Suppose Bob postpones this plan for 5, 10, or 15 years. He will then have only 40, 35, or 30 years to accumulate savings. How does the shorter savings period affect the amount he must accumulate at retirement and his initial monthly savings?

Table 16-9 works out the savings target for the 30-year savings period. His initial retirement target of $30,000 annual income is no longer adequate. There has been 15 years of inflation since he set that target. The same target, after allowing for inflation, is now $63,510. However, that need is now only 30 instead of 45 years away. The 15 years of inflation since he set the target are offset by 15 fewer years of inflation until he needs the money. His target in future dollars remains at $5,005,978.

Table 16-10 determines the initial savings rate for the 30-year savings period. Line 8 shows that the initial monthly savings requirement jumps to $1,678—quadruple the requirement at a 45-year savings period. The results at the four savings periods are:

Savings Period, yrs.	Initial Savings, $/mo.
45	$ 383.80
40	618.20
35	1,007.61
30	1,677.16

Savings plans are much easier to finance if you make your savings program more effective and raise your return on investment. Even small changes are important.

Example 16-6. Bob tightens his control over his investment program and raises his after-tax return from 8 percent to 10 percent. How much does the higher return lower the amount he must accumulate at retirement and the required monthly savings?

Table 16-11 shows how the higher return lowers the amount he must accumulate at retirement. Line 11 shows that his savings target in future dollars drops 19 percent, from $5 million to $4 million. Table 16-12 shows the drop in the initial amount he must save each month. The initial savings rate drops in half, from $383.80 to $180.05.

This example demonstrates the need to make your investment program as effective as possible. Analyze your investment opportunities by the methods described in this

TABLE 16-10
The Savings Schedule—Shorter Savings Period

1. Savings Target, $	5,005,978
2. Savings Period, years	30
3. Growth in Savings, %/yr.	6
4. Return on Investments, %	8
5. Di Factor at RT = Line 2 times Line 4	0.0907
6. RT: Multiply the difference between Lines 3 and 4 by Line 2	60
7. Dc Factor at RT = Line 6	0.7520
8. Initial Savings Required, $/mo.: Multiply Line 1 by Line 5, then Divide by 12 and by Lines 2 and 7	$1,677.16

TABLE 16-11
The Savings Target—Higher Return on Investment

1. Required Income, $/year. If the income is a lump sum, skip to Line 9 and enter it.	$30,000
2. Years Income Required	25
3. Years until Income Starts	45
4. Income Growth, %/yr.	5
5. Return on Investments, %	10
6. Expected Inflation, %/yr.	5
7. RT: Multiply the difference between Lines 4 and 5 by Line 2	125
8. Dc Factor at RT = Line 7. If Line 4 is greater than Line 5, use a Gc Factor instead.	0.5708
9. Savings Target, Future Dollars: Multiply Line 1 by Lines 2 and 8	$428,100
10. Gi Factor at RT = Line 3 times Line 6	9.4877
11. Savings Target, Today's Dollars: Multiply Line 9 by Line 10	$4,061,684

TABLE 16-12
The Savings Schedule—Higher Return on Investment

1. Savings Target, $	$4,061,684
2. Savings Period, years	45
3. Growth in Savings, %/yr.	6
4. Return on Investments, %	10
5. Di Factor at RT = Line 2 times Line 4	0.0111
6. RT: Multiply the difference between Lines 3 and 4 by Line 2	180
7. Dc Factor at RT = Line 6	0.4637
8. Initial Savings Required, $/mo.: Multiply Line 1 by Line 5, then Divide by 12 and by Lines 2 and 7	$180.05

book. It will help steer you to securities with higher yields, and improve the effectiveness of your savings program.

These examples show how difficult it is to save money for a comfortable retirement. The critical factors are obvious. Begin a savings plan as soon as possible. Analyze investment opportunities carefully, and choose those with the highest yields at the level of risk you are comfortable with.

Experiment with combinations of monthly retirement income, real rates of return, and real savings growth rates until you find a combination you are able to afford. Repeat the calculation from time to time as you revise your estimates of the real return you can earn and the amount you can save, and adjust your savings plan accordingly.

SUMMARY

☐ Long-term savings plans are complicated. You earn interest on a constantly changing investment base. Monthly savings grow with time. Each month's savings earns interest for a different time period. Inflation adds to the problem.

☐ Calculation forms make finding the savings target and the initial monthly savings required simple. Examples demonstrate how to save for a college education, a new car, and for retirement.

☐ Saving for retirement and college requires large monthly savings. The examples demonstrate how important it is to begin your savings program early and to make your investment program as effective as possible. Beginning your savings program early and making your investment program effective, substantially reduces the required monthly payments.

17

Some Final Words

THIS CHAPTER CONCLUDES OUR STUDY OF HOW TO GAIN CONTROL OVER YOUR INVESTMENT program and make it more effective. You now know the state-of-the-art methods modern corporations use to evaluate investment opportunities and understand the basic idea of discounting and discounted cash flow analysis. You should feel comfortable applying discounted cash flow analysis to any problem involving cash flows, and calculating the rate of return you should expect and the maximum price you should pay. There is nothing mysterious about the analysis.

You also know more about analyzing securities than most stock brokers do. The next time your broker calls to recommend a stock, you will not be at his mercy. Ask him to send his current analysis of the firm, and its financial record for the past 10 years. Analyze that record by the methods described in Chapter 10. Compare the firm with others in the same industry. Forecast the returns the firm is likely to earn, how fast it is likely to grow, the dividends you are likely to receive, and the stock price when you eventually sell. If the firm has unusually rapid growth, or an unusually high rate of return, allow for both growth and return to decay gradually. If your initial evaluation appears promising, follow up with a Monte Carlo analysis to get a feel for the risk involved. You can then make your own informed decision whether to invest in that security.

This book has not covered every imaginable security. It has, however, analyzed major securities in enough detail so that you should have no difficulty applying the methods to any security not covered in this book. The essential step is estimating the size and timing of all the cash flows you will either spend or receive. Make sure you understand the fees involved, because fees can have a major impact on the return you will earn, particularly if you hold a security for only a short time. A Ginnie Mae fund paying 9.05 percent interest in early 1987 involved a 4 percent fee collected when the shares were eventually sold. If you invested in that fund, held the shares for one year, and then sold, the 4 percent fee would have reduced the 9.05 percent interest rate to a net return of only 5.15 percent. Invest in securities you will feel comfortable holding for a number of years to reduce the impact of fees and commissions. Consider using a discount broker. Once you have estimated the probable pattern of cash flows, the rest of the analysis is a mechanical operation involving calculation forms and elementary arithmetic.

Be aware of the loads mutual funds charge, as well as their redemption fees, operating expenses, and 12b-1 expenses. Include these expenses in your analysis. Don't invest in a mutual fund solely on how the fund performed in the last year or two. Look at a longer record, preferably 10 years. Include years when the market dropped, and see how well the fund maintained its value during those down years.

The critical step in evaluating any security is projecting the future cash flows you expect from that investment. In some cases, you will be very confident about your projections. There is little uncertainty in projecting the cash you will receive from a federally-insured certificate of deposit. You are promised specific interest payments at definite times. There are no fees. Interest from a bank savings account is less certain because of the numerous ways the bank can decide on the amount of your savings that qualifies for interest payments. A bond held to maturity promises a definite schedule of interest payments. But if you sell the bond before it matures, the future selling price will be uncertain.

Projecting the cash you will receive from investing in stock is much more uncertain. Your projections of dividends and the stock price when you eventually sell are bound to be in error. Don't be overly concerned about making precise forecasts. The managers of the firm you are considering often make poor earnings forecasts, even though they have access to detailed internal cost and marketing data. Financial analysts predict confidently, even though they have less information than the firm's managers. Your understanding of the firm is even less complete. Make the most reasonable projections you can. Remember, you are not trying to calculate the expected rate of return to the second decimal place. You are trying to calculate whether the expected return is likely to be higher than your opportunity cost, a much easier problem. The likely range of errors when estimating the rate of return from stocks can be broad, as the Monte Carlo examples in this book show.

The analysis developed in this book pinpoints the critical elements on which you should focus. Projecting the firm's rate of return is the most critical element. Capital growth is less critical. If the firm grows more slowly than you projected, you should receive more dividends than you had projected. The increased dividends tend to compensate for the slower growth. The future price/earnings ratio is also critical. The future price/earnings ratio depends primarily on future interest rates and on how investors view the firm's prospects at that future time.

Solid, well-run companies tend to follow reasonably stable growth patterns. They are not likely to collapse overnight. Rate of return and capital growth tend to follow historic trends. Your forecasts are likely to be more reasonable if you invest in such firms.

The alternate to a rational forecast is a hunch. A forecast based on the corporate growth model of Chapter 6, and focusing on rate of return, capital growth, and future price/earnings ratios will be much better than a hunch. Even so, recognize that your forecast, no matter how carefully made, will be uncertain. Allow for this uncertainty by doing a Monte Carlo risk analysis. Risk analysis with even a small number of trials will give you a much better feel for whether you should invest in that stock or in some other security.

The primary goal of this book is to tune the analysis of securities to your specific circumstances—to your specific incremental tax rate and opportunity cost. Read again how our hypothetical investor determined his incremental tax rate and opportunity cost in the beginning of Chapter 11. Go through that procedure for your own situation. Examine your federal and state tax returns, and determine the tax rate you will pay on your last dollar of income. Remember that changes in your income or in the tax code might change your incremental tax rate. When such changes occur, change your incremental tax rate accordingly.

Track the yields offered on money market funds, certificates of deposit, and tax-free securities. These securities are likely to be the alternate investments that determine your opportunity costs. These yields change frequently. Yields are reported in the financial section of your newspaper, *The Wall Street Journal*, *Barrons*, and *Money* magazine. Monitor them, and adjust your opportunity costs as yields on these investments fluctuate. Don't overlook the possibility that paying credit card debt or prepaying mortgages might be the best alternate use of your money, and might determine your opportunity cost.

Inflation and taxes take a toll on investment income. Your real return might be negative on bank savings accounts and certificates of deposit. Read Example 9-1 in Chapter 9 again to review how inflation and taxes reduce the returns from these investments, and might result in negative real rates of return. Remember that, to earn a real return, you must earn an after-tax return greater than the anticipated inflation rate.

Small changes in the rate of return are more important than they appear on the surface, particularly after you take taxes and inflation into account. Gains in your real rate of return can be much more significant than gains in your nominal return suggest, as shown for an investor with a 37 percent incremental tax rate and 5 percent per year inflation:

Nominal Return, %		Real
Before Taxes	After Taxes	Return, %
9	5.67	0.67
10	6.30	1.30
11	6.93	1.93

The 1 percentage point gain from 9 percent to 10 percent return is only an 11 percent gain in nominal return, but it is a 94 percent gain in real return. The gain from 10 percent to 11 percent is only a 10 percent gain in nominal return, but it is a 48 percent gain in real return. Calculate rates of return as carefully as you can, and pursue even small gains in nominal returns, because they might result in significant gains in real returns.

Changes in interest rates change the value of all securities. Changes in interest rates change investor's opportunity costs, and therefore, the discount rate investors use to calculate the present value of future dividends, interest payments, and the ultimate redemption price of the security. The higher discount rate makes the present value of securities, and therefore, the current market price, go down. The reverse happens when interest rates go down. The investor's discount rate goes down. This lower discount rate then makes the present value of securities go up.

Stocks fluctuate in value as interest rates change just as bonds do, and for the same reason. As interest rates change, investors adjust the discount rate they use to calculate the present value of future dividends and the eventual sale of the stock. Stocks are subject to additional fluctuations as investors change their forecasts of future earnings and growth. Changes in interest rates and in investor's forecasts of future dividends and stock prices are reflected in the price/earnings ratio investors are willing to pay for a stock.

Swings in interest rates create investment opportunities. When interest rates peak and begin heading downward, future dividends and stock prices will be discounted less heavily, and the price of stocks will go up. That is the time to invest in stocks and bonds. When interest rates bottom out and begin to head up, the reverse happens. Future dividends and stock prices are discounted more heavily, and the price of stocks fall. This is the time to take profits in stocks and bonds, and invest in securities where the principal is safe, such as a money market fund or a certificate of deposit. The problem is that forecasting interest rates, and turning points in interest rates, is extremely difficult.

Take advantage of all of the opportunities you can to escape or defer taxes. If your employer offers a 401k plan, invest as much money as the plan allows. An IRA might be attractive, particularly if you can deduct the investment from your taxable income. Check the IRA calculation forms in Chapter 8 to see whether an IRA is justified in your situation.

Understanding the impact inflation has on the savings needed to finance a comfortable retirement or a college education is a sobering experience. Because of inflation, you must save what might appear an impossible sum of money to educate your children and enjoy a reasonable life-style during retirement. Accumulating that sum requires substantial monthly savings, which must grow steadily during your working career. The task is much easier if you can earn a higher return on your investments. With the understanding of security analysis this book provides, you should be able to make your savings program more effective, and make retirement easier to finance.

Appendix A Tables

RT	0	1	2	3	4	5	6	7	8	9
0	1.0000	1.0101	1.0202	1.0305	1.0408	1.0513	1.0618	1.0725	1.0833	1.0942
10	1.1052	1.1163	1.1275	1.1388	1.1503	1.1618	1.1735	1.1853	1.1972	1.2092
20	1.2214	1.2337	1.2461	1.2586	1.2712	1.2840	1.2969	1.3100	1.3231	1.3364
30	1.3499	1.3634	1.3771	1.3910	1.4049	1.4191	1.4333	1.4477	1.4623	1.4770
40	1.4918	1.5068	1.5220	1.5373	1.5527	1.5683	1.5841	1.6000	1.6161	1.6323
50	1.6487	1.6653	1.6820	1.6989	1.7160	1.7333	1.7507	1.7683	1.7860	1.8040
60	1.8221	1.8404	1.8589	1.8776	1.8965	1.9155	1.9348	1.9542	1.9739	1.9937
70	2.0138	2.0340	2.0544	2.0751	2.0959	2.1170	2.1383	2.1598	2.1815	2.2034
80	2.2255	2.2479	2.2705	2.2933	2.3164	2.3396	2.3632	2.3869	2.4109	2.4351
90	2.4596	2.4843	2.5093	2.5345	2.5600	2.5857	2.6117	2.6379	2.6645	2.6912
100	2.7183	2.7456	2.7732	2.8011	2.8292	2.8577	2.8864	2.9154	2.9447	2.9743
110	3.0042	3.0344	3.0649	3.0957	3.1268	3.1582	3.1899	3.2220	3.2544	3.2871
120	3.3201	3.3535	3.3872	3.4212	3.4556	3.4903	3.5254	3.5609	3.5966	3.6328
130	3.6693	3.7062	3.7434	3.7810	3.8190	3.8574	3.8962	3.9354	3.9749	4.0149
140	4.0552	4.0960	4.1371	4.1787	4.2207	4.2631	4.3060	4.3492	4.3929	4.4371
150	4.4817	4.5267	4.5722	4.6182	4.6646	4.7115	4.7588	4.8066	4.8550	4.9037
160	4.9530	5.0028	5.0531	5.1039	5.1552	5.2070	5.2593	5.3122	5.3656	5.4195
170	5.4739	5.5290	5.5845	5.6407	5.6973	5.7546	5.8124	5.8709	5.9299	5.9895
180	6.0496	6.1104	6.1719	6.2339	6.2965	6.3598	6.4237	6.4883	6.5535	6.6194
190	6.6859	6.7531	6.8210	6.8895	6.9588	7.0287	7.0993	7.1707	7.2427	7.3155
200	7.3891	7.4633	7.5383	7.6141	7.6906	7.7679	7.8460	7.9248	8.0045	8.0849
210	8.1662	8.2482	8.3311	8.4149	8.4994	8.5849	8.6711	8.7583	8.8463	8.9352
220	9.0250	9.1157	9.2073	9.2999	9.3933	9.4877	9.5831	9.6794	9.7767	9.8749
230	9.9742	10.0744	10.1757	10.2779	10.3812	10.4856	10.5910	10.6974	10.8049	10.9135
240	11.0232	11.1340	11.2459	11.3589	11.4730	11.5883	11.7048	11.8224	11.9413	12.0613
250	12.1825	12.3049	12.4286	12.5535	12.6797	12.8071	12.9358	13.0658	13.1971	13.3298
260	13.4637	13.5990	13.7357	13.8738	14.0132	14.1540	14.2963	14.4400	14.5851	14.7317
270	14.8797	15.0293	15.1803	15.3329	15.4870	15.6426	15.7998	15.9586	16.1190	16.2810
280	16.4446	16.6099	16.7769	16.9455	17.1158	17.2878	17.4615	17.6370	17.8143	17.9933
290	18.1741	18.3568	18.5413	18.7276	18.9158	19.1060	19.2980	19.4919	19.6878	19.8857
300	20.0855	20.2874	20.4913	20.6972	20.9052	21.1153	21.3276	21.5419	21.7584	21.9771
310	22.1979	22.4210	22.6464	22.8740	23.1039	23.3361	23.5706	23.8075	24.0468	24.2884
320	24.5325	24.7791	25.0281	25.2797	25.5337	25.7903	26.0495	26.3113	26.5758	26.8429
330	27.1126	27.3851	27.6603	27.9383	28.2191	28.5027	28.7892	29.0785	29.3708	29.6660
340	29.9641	30.2652	30.5694	30.8766	31.1870	31.5004	31.8170	32.1367	32.4597	32.7859
350	33.1155	33.4483	33.7844	34.1240	34.4669	34.8133	35.1632	35.5166	35.8735	36.2341
360	36.5982	36.9661	37.3376	37.7128	38.0918	38.4747	38.8613	39.2519	39.6464	40.0448
370	40.4473	40.8538	41.2644	41.6791	42.0980	42.5211	42.9484	43.3801	43.8160	44.2564
380	44.7012	45.1504	45.6042	46.0625	46.5255	46.9931	47.4654	47.9424	48.4242	48.9109
390	49.4024	49.8989	50.4004	50.9070	51.4186	51.9354	52.4573	52.9845	53.5170	54.0549
400	54.598	60.340	66.686	73.700	81.451	90.017	99.484	109.947	121.510	134.290
500	148.413	164.022	181.272	200.337	221.406	244.692	270.426	298.867	330.300	365.037
600	403.429	445.858	492.749	544.572	601.845	665.142	735.095	812.406	897.847	992.275

TABLE A2

Growth Factors for Continuous Investments

RT	0	1	2	3	4	5	6	7	8	9
0	1.0000	1.0050	1.0101	1.0152	1.0203	1.0254	1.0306	1.0358	1.0411	1.0464
10	1.0517	1.0571	1.0625	1.0679	1.0734	1.0789	1.0844	1.0900	1.0957	1.1013
20	1.1070	1.1128	1.1185	1.1243	1.1302	1.1361	1.1420	1.1480	1.1540	1.1601
30	1.1662	1.1723	1.1785	1.1848	1.1910	1.1973	1.2037	1.2101	1.2165	1.2230
40	1.2296	1.2361	1.2428	1.2494	1.2562	1.2629	1.2697	1.2766	1.2835	1.2904
50	1.2974	1.3045	1.3116	1.3187	1.3259	1.3332	1.3405	1.3478	1.3552	1.3627
60	1.3702	1.3778	1.3854	1.3930	1.4008	1.4085	1.4164	1.4242	1.4322	1.4402
70	1.4482	1.4563	1.4645	1.4727	1.4810	1.4893	1.4977	1.5062	1.5147	1.5233
80	1.5319	1.5406	1.5494	1.5582	1.5671	1.5761	1.5851	1.5942	1.6033	1.6125
90	1.6218	1.6311	1.6405	1.6500	1.6596	1.6692	1.6789	1.6886	1.6984	1.7083
100	1.7183	1.7283	1.7384	1.7486	1.7589	1.7692	1.7796	1.7901	1.8006	1.8113
110	1.8220	1.8328	1.8436	1.8546	1.8656	1.8767	1.8879	1.8991	1.9105	1.9219
120	1.9334	1.9450	1.9567	1.9685	1.9803	1.9923	2.0043	2.0164	2.0286	2.0409
130	2.0533	2.0658	2.0783	2.0910	2.1038	2.1166	2.1296	2.1426	2.1557	2.1690
140	2.1823	2.1957	2.2092	2.2229	2.2366	2.2504	2.2644	2.2784	2.2925	2.3068
150	2.3211	2.3356	2.3501	2.3648	2.3796	2.3945	2.4095	2.4246	2.4398	2.4552
160	2.4706	2.4862	2.5019	2.5177	2.5336	2.5497	2.5658	2.5821	2.5985	2.6151
170	2.6317	2.6485	2.6654	2.6825	2.6996	2.7169	2.7343	2.7519	2.7696	2.7874
180	2.8054	2.8235	2.8417	2.8600	2.8786	2.8972	2.9160	2.9349	2.9540	2.9732
190	2.9926	3.0121	3.0317	3.0516	3.0715	3.0916	3.1119	3.1323	3.1529	3.1736
200	3.1945	3.2156	3.2368	3.2582	3.2797	3.3014	3.3233	3.3453	3.3675	3.3899
210	3.4125	3.4352	3.4581	3.4812	3.5044	3.5278	3.5515	3.5752	3.5992	3.6234
220	3.6477	3.6723	3.6970	3.7219	3.7470	3.7723	3.7978	3.8235	3.8494	3.8755
230	3.9018	3.9283	3.9550	3.9819	4.0091	4.0364	4.0640	4.0917	4.1197	4.1479
240	4.1763	4.2050	4.2338	4.2629	4.2922	4.3218	4.3515	4.3816	4.4118	4.4423
250	4.4730	4.5040	4.5352	4.5666	4.5983	4.6302	4.6624	4.6949	4.7276	4.7605
260	4.7937	4.8272	4.8610	4.8950	4.9292	4.9638	4.9986	5.0337	5.0691	5.1047
270	5.1406	5.1769	5.2134	5.2501	5.2872	5.3246	5.3623	5.4002	5.4385	5.4771
280	5.5159	5.5551	5.5946	5.6344	5.6746	5.7150	5.7558	5.7969	5.8383	5.8800
290	5.9221	5.9645	6.0073	6.0504	6.0938	6.1376	6.1817	6.2262	6.2711	6.3163
300	6.3618	6.4078	6.4541	6.5007	6.5478	6.5952	6.6430	6.6912	6.7397	6.7887
310	6.8380	6.8878	6.9379	6.9885	7.0394	7.0908	7.1426	7.1948	7.2474	7.3004
320	7.3539	7.4078	7.4621	7.5169	7.5721	7.6278	7.6839	7.7405	7.7975	7.8550
330	7.9129	7.9713	8.0302	8.0896	8.1494	8.2098	8.2706	8.3319	8.3937	8.4560
340	8.5189	8.5822	8.6460	8.7104	8.7753	8.8407	8.9066	8.9731	9.0402	9.1077
350	9.1758	9.2445	9.3138	9.3836	9.4539	9.5249	9.5964	9.6685	9.7412	9.8145
360	9.8884	9.9629	10.0380	10.1137	10.1901	10.2670	10.3446	10.4229	10.5017	10.5813
370	10.6614	10.7423	10.8238	10.9059	10.9888	11.0723	11.1565	11.2414	11.3270	11.4133
380	11.5003	11.5880	11.6765	11.7657	11.8556	11.9462	12.0377	12.1298	12.2227	12.3164
390	12.4109	12.5061	12.6022	12.6990	12.7966	12.8950	12.9943	13.0943	13.1952	13.2970
400	13.400	14.473	15.640	16.907	18.284	19.782	21.410	23.180	25.106	27.202
500	29.483	31.965	34.668	37.611	40.816	44.308	48.112	52.257	56.776	61.701
600	67.071	72.928	79.314	86.281	93.882	102.176	111.227	121.105	131.889	143.663
700	156.519	170.559	185.893	202.644	220.944	240.939	262.789	286.668	312.769	341.301
800	372.495	406.601	443.896	484.683	529.293	578.091	631.472	689.875	753.777	823.704

TABLE A3

Discount Factors for Instantaneous Cash Flows

RT	0	1	2	3	4	5	6	7	8	9
0	1.0000	0.9900	0.9802	0.9704	0.9608	0.9512	0.9418	0.9324	0.9231	0.9139
10	0.9048	0.8958	0.8869	0.8781	0.8694	0.8607	0.8521	0.8437	0.8353	0.8270
20	0.8187	0.8106	0.8025	0.7945	0.7866	0.7788	0.7711	0.7634	0.7558	0.7483
30	0.7408	0.7334	0.7261	0.7189	0.7118	0.7047	0.6977	0.6907	0.6839	0.6771
40	0.6703	0.6637	0.6570	0.6505	0.6440	0.6376	0.6313	0.6250	0.6188	0.6126
50	0.6065	0.6005	0.5945	0.5886	0.5827	0.5769	0.5712	0.5655	0.5599	0.5543
60	0.5488	0.5434	0.5379	0.5326	0.5273	0.5220	0.5169	0.5117	0.5066	0.5016
70	0.4966	0.4916	0.4868	0.4819	0.4771	0.4724	0.4677	0.4630	0.4584	0.4538
80	0.4493	0.4449	0.4404	0.4360	0.4317	0.4274	0.4232	0.4190	0.4148	0.4107
90	0.4066	0.4025	0.3985	0.3946	0.3906	0.3867	0.3829	0.3791	0.3753	0.3716
100	0.3679	0.3642	0.3606	0.3570	0.3535	0.3499	0.3465	0.3430	0.3396	0.3362
110	0.3329	0.3296	0.3263	0.3230	0.3198	0.3166	0.3135	0.3104	0.3073	0.3042
120	0.3012	0.2982	0.2952	0.2923	0.2894	0.2865	0.2837	0.2808	0.2780	0.2753
130	0.2725	0.2698	0.2671	0.2645	0.2618	0.2592	0.2567	0.2541	0.2516	0.2491
140	0.2466	0.2441	0.2417	0.2393	0.2369	0.2346	0.2322	0.2299	0.2276	0.2254
150	0.2231	0.2209	0.2187	0.2165	0.2144	0.2122	0.2101	0.2080	0.2060	0.2039
160	0.2019	0.1999	0.1979	0.1959	0.1940	0.1920	0.1901	0.1882	0.1864	0.1845
170	0.1827	0.1809	0.1791	0.1773	0.1755	0.1738	0.1720	0.1703	0.1686	0.1670
180	0.1653	0.1637	0.1620	0.1604	0.1588	0.1572	0.1557	0.1541	0.1526	0.1511
190	0.1496	0.1481	0.1466	0.1451	0.1437	0.1423	0.1409	0.1395	0.1381	0.1367
200	0.1353	0.1340	0.1327	0.1313	0.1300	0.1287	0.1275	0.1262	0.1249	0.1237
210	0.1225	0.1212	0.1200	0.1188	0.1177	0.1165	0.1153	0.1142	0.1130	0.1119
220	0.1108	0.1097	0.1086	0.1075	0.1065	0.1054	0.1044	0.1033	0.1023	0.1013
230	0.1003	0.0993	0.0983	0.0973	0.0963	0.0954	0.0944	0.0935	0.0926	0.0916
240	0.0907	0.0898	0.0889	0.0880	0.0872	0.0863	0.0854	0.0846	0.0837	0.0829
250	0.0821	0.0813	0.0805	0.0797	0.0789	0.0781	0.0773	0.0765	0.0758	0.0750
260	0.0743	0.0735	0.0728	0.0721	0.0714	0.0707	0.0699	0.0693	0.0686	0.0679
270	0.0672	0.0665	0.0659	0.0652	0.0646	0.0639	0.0633	0.0627	0.0620	0.0614
280	0.0608	0.0602	0.0596	0.0590	0.0584	0.0578	0.0573	0.0567	0.0561	0.0556
290	0.0550	0.0545	0.0539	0.0534	0.0529	0.0523	0.0518	0.0513	0.0508	0.0503
300	0.0498	0.0493	0.0488	0.0483	0.0478	0.0474	0.0469	0.0464	0.0460	0.0455
310	0.0450	0.0446	0.0442	0.0437	0.0433	0.0429	0.0424	0.0420	0.0416	0.0412
320	0.0408	0.0404	0.0400	0.0396	0.0392	0.0388	0.0384	0.0380	0.0376	0.0373
330	0.0369	0.0365	0.0362	0.0358	0.0354	0.0351	0.0347	0.0344	0.0340	0.0337
340	0.0334	0.0330	0.0327	0.0324	0.0321	0.0317	0.0314	0.0311	0.0308	0.0305
350	0.0302	0.0299	0.0296	0.0293	0.0290	0.0287	0.0284	0.0282	0.0279	0.0276
360	0.0273	0.0271	0.0268	0.0265	0.0263	0.0260	0.0257	0.0255	0.0252	0.0250
370	0.0247	0.0245	0.0242	0.0240	0.0238	0.0235	0.0233	0.0231	0.0228	0.0226
380	0.0224	0.0221	0.0219	0.0217	0.0215	0.0213	0.0211	0.0209	0.0207	0.0204
390	0.0202	0.0200	0.0198	0.0196	0.0194	0.0193	0.0191	0.0189	0.0187	0.0185
400	0.0183	0.0166	0.0150	0.0136	0.0123	0.0111	0.0101	0.0091	0.0082	0.0074
500	0.0067	0.0061	0.0055	0.0050	0.0045	0.0041	0.0037	0.0033	0.0030	0.0027
600	0.0025	0.0022	0.0020	0.0018	0.0017	0.0015	0.0014	0.0012	0.0011	0.0010
700	0.0009	0.0008	0.0007	0.0007	0.0006	0.0006	0.0005	0.0005	0.0004	0.0004
800	0.0003	0.0003	0.0003	0.0002	0.0002	0.0002	0.0002	0.0002	0.0002	0.0001

TABLE A4

Discount Factors for Continuous Cash Flows

RT	0	1	2	3	4	5	6	7	8	9
0	1.0000	0.9950	0.9901	0.9851	0.9803	0.9754	0.9706	0.9658	0.9610	0.9563
10	0.9516	0.9470	0.9423	0.9377	0.9332	0.9286	0.9241	0.9196	0.9152	0.9107
20	0.9063	0.9020	0.8976	0.8933	0.8891	0.8848	0.8806	0.8764	0.8722	0.8681
30	0.8639	0.8598	0.8558	0.8517	0.8477	0.8437	0.8398	0.8359	0.8319	0.8281
40	0.8242	0.8204	0.8166	0.8128	0.8090	0.8053	0.8016	0.7979	0.7942	0.7906
50	0.7869	0.7833	0.7798	0.7762	0.7727	0.7692	0.7657	0.7622	0.7588	0.7554
60	0.7520	0.7486	0.7453	0.7419	0.7386	0.7353	0.7320	0.7288	0.7256	0.7224
70	0.7192	0.7160	0.7128	0.7097	0.7066	0.7035	0.7004	0.6974	0.6944	0.6913
80	0.6883	0.6854	0.6824	0.6795	0.6765	0.6736	0.6707	0.6679	0.6650	0.6622
90	0.6594	0.6566	0.6538	0.6510	0.6483	0.6455	0.6428	0.6401	0.6374	0.6348
100	0.6321	0.6295	0.6269	0.6243	0.6217	0.6191	0.6166	0.6140	0.6115	0.6090
110	0.6065	0.6040	0.6015	0.5991	0.5967	0.5942	0.5918	0.5894	0.5871	0.5847
120	0.5823	0.5800	0.5777	0.5754	0.5731	0.5708	0.5685	0.5663	0.5640	0.5618
130	0.5596	0.5574	0.5552	0.5530	0.5509	0.5487	0.5466	0.5444	0.5423	0.5402
140	0.5381	0.5361	0.5340	0.5320	0.5299	0.5279	0.5259	0.5239	0.5219	0.5199
150	0.5179	0.5160	0.5140	0.5121	0.5101	0.5082	0.5063	0.5044	0.5025	0.5007
160	0.4988	0.4970	0.4951	0.4933	0.4915	0.4897	0.4879	0.4861	0.4843	0.4825
170	0.4808	0.4790	0.4773	0.4756	0.4738	0.4721	0.4704	0.4687	0.4671	0.4654
180	0.4637	0.4621	0.4604	0.4588	0.4572	0.4555	0.4539	0.4523	0.4507	0.4492
190	0.4476	0.4460	0.4445	0.4429	0.4414	0.4399	0.4383	0.4368	0.4353	0.4338
200	0.4323	0.4309	0.4294	0.4279	0.4265	0.4250	0.4236	0.4221	0.4207	0.4193
210	0.4179	0.4165	0.4151	0.4137	0.4123	0.4109	0.4096	0.4082	0.4069	0.4055
220	0.4042	0.4029	0.4015	0.4002	0.3989	0.3976	0.3963	0.3950	0.3937	0.3925
230	0.3912	0.3899	0.3887	0.3874	0.3862	0.3849	0.3837	0.3825	0.3813	0.3801
240	0.3789	0.3777	0.3765	0.3753	0.3741	0.3729	0.3718	0.3706	0.3695	0.3683
250	0.3672	0.3660	0.3649	0.3638	0.3627	0.3615	0.3604	0.3593	0.3582	0.3571
260	0.3560	0.3550	0.3539	0.3528	0.3518	0.3507	0.3496	0.3486	0.3476	0.3465
270	0.3455	0.3445	0.3434	0.3424	0.3414	0.3404	0.3394	0.3384	0.3374	0.3364
280	0.3354	0.3344	0.3335	0.3325	0.3315	0.3306	0.3296	0.3287	0.3277	0.3268
290	0.3259	0.3249	0.3240	0.3231	0.3222	0.3212	0.3203	0.3194	0.3185	0.3176
300	0.3167	0.3158	0.3150	0.3141	0.3132	0.3123	0.3115	0.3106	0.3098	0.3089
310	0.3080	0.3072	0.3064	0.3055	0.3047	0.3039	0.3030	0.3022	0.3014	0.3006
320	0.2998	0.2990	0.2982	0.2974	0.2966	0.2958	0.2950	0.2942	0.2934	0.2926
330	0.2919	0.2911	0.2903	0.2896	0.2888	0.2880	0.2873	0.2865	0.2858	0.2850
340	0.2843	0.2836	0.2828	0.2821	0.2814	0.2807	0.2799	0.2792	0.2785	0.2778
350	0.2771	0.2764	0.2757	0.2750	0.2743	0.2736	0.2729	0.2722	0.2715	0.2709
360	0.2702	0.2695	0.2688	0.2682	0.2675	0.2669	0.2662	0.2655	0.2649	0.2642
370	0.2636	0.2629	0.2623	0.2617	0.2610	0.2604	0.2598	0.2591	0.2585	0.2579
380	0.2573	0.2567	0.2560	0.2554	0.2548	0.2542	0.2536	0.2530	0.2524	0.2518
390	0.2512	0.2506	0.2500	0.2495	0.2489	0.2483	0.2477	0.2471	0.2466	0.2460
400	0.2454	0.2399	0.2345	0.2294	0.2245	0.2198	0.2152	0.2108	0.2066	0.2026
500	0.1987	0.1949	0.1912	0.1877	0.1843	0.1811	0.1779	0.1749	0.1719	0.1690
600	0.1663	0.1636	0.1610	0.1584	0.1560	0.1536	0.1513	0.1491	0.1469	0.1448
700	0.1427	0.1407	0.1388	0.1369	0.1351	0.1333	0.1315	0.1298	0.1282	0.1265
800	0.1250	0.1234	0.1219	0.1205	0.1190	0.1176	0.1163	0.1149	0.1136	0.1123

TABLE A5
t Factors

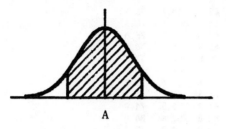 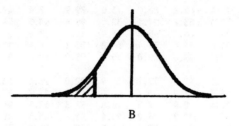

A   B

Probability Scales: Scale A and Scale B shows the probability of a value inside the shaded area in distribution A and B, respectively.

Degrees of Freedom*	Probability, %, Scale A:					
	20	50	80	90	95	99
Scale B:	40	25	10	5	2.5	0.5
1	0.325	1.000	3.078	6.314	12.706	63.657
2	0.289	0.816	1.886	2.920	4.303	9.925
3	0.277	0.765	1.338	2.353	3.182	5.841
4	0.271	0.741	1.533	2.132	2.776	4.604
5	0.267	0.727	1.476	2.015	2.571	4.032
6	0.265	0.718	1.440	1.943	2.447	3.707
7	0.263	0.711	1.415	1.897	2.365	3.499
8	0.262	0.706	1.397	1.860	2.306	3.355
9	0.261	0.703	1.383	1.833	2.262	3.250
10	0.260	0.700	1.372	1.812	2.228	3.169
11	0.260	0.697	1.363	1.796	2.201	3.106
12	0.259	0.695	1.356	1.782	2.179	3.055
13	0.259	0.694	1.350	1.771	2.160	3.012
14	0.258	0.692	1.345	1.761	2.145	2.977
15	0.258	0.691	1.341	1.753	2.131	2.947
20	0.257	0.687	1.325	1.725	2.086	2.787
25	0.256	0.684	1.316	1.708	2.060	2.845
30	0.256	0.683	1.310	1.397	2.042	2.750
60	0.254	0.679	1.296	1.371	2.000	2.660
oo	0.253	0.674	1.282	1.345	1.960	2.576

*Degrees of freedom for the examples in this book are one less than the number of observations.

Biometrika Tables for Statisticians, Vol. 1, Third Edition (1966), by permission of the Biometrika Trustees.

TABLE A6
A Thousand Random Numbers

12.1	65.2	86.9	73.0	79.9	7.4	49.0	45.5	10.7	95.1
70.4	53.2	97.1	32.1	95.6	93.5	53.5	56.4	67.1	70.3
74.1	66.7	45.4	33.4	15.7	73.6	54.3	42.6	5.5	76.8
51.4	56.4	74.1	66.2	23.1	46.4	12.9	48.5	5.5	36.3
57.1	99.0	29.0	65.8	93.9	38.0	89.0	79.8	94.7	32.3
41.3	42.5	73.2	21.9	22.0	76.4	68.3	71.6	93.4	26.2
51.7	47.2	13.7	48.4	60.9	17.7	32.9	24.5	57.0	81.2
12.4	0.9	7.3	16.8	71.3	52.5	93.3	61.2	55.5	71.9
43.5	10.2	34.2	83.4	91.2	45.3	19.4	82.2	57.4	84.9
11.4	98.1	58.2	61.5	69.5	85.2	38.2	22.8	6.7	35.3
27.9	58.5	10.4	17.4	26.8	51.4	87.8	41.5	10.8	54.9
35.7	47.9	65.6	93.4	36.6	21.1	43.9	89.8	78.1	28.9
48.7	16.7	99.0	86.3	40.7	72.8	59.3	45.0	71.5	84.8
35.2	7.0	41.2	33.5	40.0	63.9	81.2	6.2	69.1	60.9
62.2	72.1	70.2	86.0	26.6	84.9	38.9	83.8	46.8	8.7
38.8	94.7	7.7	70.1	46.8	18.9	14.8	34.2	23.7	5.9
26.5	6.6	9.0	67.6	12.6	59.5	41.9	18.5	36.3	84.0
6.0	38.9	63.0	66.0	99.7	64.3	92.1	87.8	31.9	99.5
15.5	55.1	42.1	57.6	0.2	48.3	45.4	24.2	96.2	98.9
3.3	46.0	68.9	91.4	18.9	45.4	57.6	89.6	56.8	59.4
57.7	88.2	88.9	3.4	28.8	89.7	64.7	60.8	27.7	5.3
6.2	96.4	65.7	82.1	28.6	95.9	91.8	54.3	85.4	30.1
0.4	19.9	38.9	43.4	64.2	42.3	55.3	68.4	91.9	76.7
25.1	64.6	10.9	21.8	8.6	82.8	75.4	96.3	5.9	53.7
99.1	40.5	52.4	2.5	13.0	42.7	39.0	87.7	48.0	91.3
57.5	64.9	43.2	50.4	70.9	76.4	78.1	62.5	8.9	64.8
31.1	74.2	87.7	12.4	61.5	88.0	55.7	5.0	18.3	39.0
64.0	21.2	71.9	96.5	61.1	46.1	73.0	90.2	13.8	11.0
34.6	62.3	52.2	56.6	40.1	43.6	40.1	22.9	76.2	55.1
70.3	62.6	90.8	35.0	85.0	80.8	75.3	89.8	20.8	98.3
73.1	70.9	79.5	41.3	11.7	76.4	23.0	55.3	61.4	77.7
93.8	44.0	17.0	70.7	60.3	33.4	6.7	52.5	87.1	61.1
24.2	23.3	30.3	90.1	86.7	12.4	57.7	47.9	17.8	30.4
94.5	90.7	55.4	45.1	93.0	92.2	84.2	83.5	28.6	58.1
93.7	58.3	19.4	64.8	61.0	19.3	72.3	23.4	58.7	30.2
52.4	69.2	87.5	70.0	79.3	75.3	34.3	59.5	46.5	91.9
54.7	12.9	67.4	10.3	81.0	14.7	45.3	52.0	54.9	20.7
68.6	82.8	85.6	85.1	31.5	51.6	32.2	11.5	78.8	54.8
11.7	30.0	76.8	25.3	32.0	98.5	8.0	46.4	49.4	29.3
91.9	90.9	51.6	40.5	30.2	85.4	65.3	32.9	76.9	98.9
89.5	91.3	33.7	57.3	52.7	11.2	70.5	82.4	96.1	50.2
70.5	55.6	81.3	4.9	0.7	7.5	23.2	11.9	7.0	31.5
47.5	75.0	34.7	23.1	74.1	16.2	73.5	44.0	24.2	52.7
28.4	10.9	53.7	98.3	14.4	9.9	10.7	89.8	77.1	35.4
18.5	38.7	38.0	54.0	83.2	8.0	65.0	93.9	26.7	13.3
67.0	58.7	44.3	49.7	15.3	66.5	87.8	43.2	87.9	14.2
73.0	27.4	40.5	66.2	12.9	44.9	1.4	68.7	75.2	74.0
91.9	88.7	65.0	80.1	72.0	78.1	33.0	92.5	10.1	62.6
8.1	5.9	78.6	56.1	55.3	6.6	74.5	99.3	58.3	24.7
64.1	24.2	27.6	10.0	53.8	42.9	33.0	34.2	85.2	61.8

Table A6. (continued)
A Thousand Random Numbers

61.7	16.9	55.6	20.5	1.1	77.4	63.0	56.0	46.3	11.5
76.7	91.9	33.2	92.7	32.5	51.9	96.3	98.8	52.9	99.6
51.4	63.7	92.6	2.1	3.5	53.7	8.9	19.2	79.4	69.3
56.6	17.3	86.0	71.6	8.8	8.9	92.5	33.9	1.7	15.9
38.6	18.2	5.5	59.7	67.4	76.9	19.1	74.2	82.8	79.4
91.0	45.5	32.6	63.3	64.1	76.0	16.3	11.6	46.5	73.1
17.9	53.4	6.2	63.4	63.6	91.3	92.1	31.9	4.8	52.5
78.7	85.9	25.8	65.5	37.0	44.2	76.5	61.6	29.2	51.1
30.4	1.5	29.6	15.2	67.5	26.8	69.3	74.1	81.6	36.7
7.1	82.8	14.0	89.5	24.5	28.1	10.2	29.1	46.1	67.8
3.7	36.6	84.6	94.1	23.3	6.8	11.9	23.6	26.0	50.0
53.4	10.7	54.8	18.3	9.2	86.8	21.7	57.2	98.7	24.4
15.2	82.3	31.4	26.4	33.3	80.9	2.2	39.7	41.4	38.1
11.4	94.5	54.7	89.1	10.1	68.6	46.8	95.0	70.8	76.0
81.6	45.1	82.3	81.2	71.7	82.8	70.4	38.3	61.0	57.6
42.9	55.2	32.6	1.5	60.1	82.1	41.6	30.5	30.0	26.2
72.7	71.5	28.7	90.4	23.6	13.2	45.8	37.6	12.0	83.4
54.4	79.4	8.9	50.1	6.6	90.7	96.5	48.2	54.0	48.0
50.8	31.2	92.6	94.4	49.4	47.3	33.7	27.9	4.3	41.7
98.4	15.7	20.0	82.3	38.7	33.5	75.9	12.0	82.3	29.2
34.3	25.0	3.2	12.1	73.5	68.1	16.8	67.3	45.1	67.7
0.4	94.0	56.9	81.1	38.5	70.3	81.3	73.0	92.9	42.0
87.2	17.4	98.1	36.4	98.7	23.7	81.8	1.8	77.2	88.7
10.2	71.4	29.6	73.0	57.8	52.2	41.1	2.3	3.6	39.1
32.9	94.3	50.4	54.3	44.9	10.4	71.1	11.0	43.8	31.6
78.2	2.5	55.9	60.7	19.6	16.4	24.5	48.8	98.8	73.7
93.2	46.4	20.1	92.5	13.4	80.4	59.0	77.7	77.3	55.7
57.6	34.3	75.6	81.2	44.6	7.2	80.3	22.2	81.1	44.5
52.7	76.2	30.4	87.5	76.0	75.0	53.7	83.8	13.0	10.8
30.3	27.0	89.5	88.2	2.8	20.6	1.3	0.5	47.4	66.8
47.7	31.5	69.4	81.0	88.8	81.5	23.6	30.6	28.9	19.7
59.0	99.1	23.5	60.1	90.0	75.2	13.0	63.1	91.0	66.8
79.9	62.7	16.9	40.1	31.7	17.2	48.7	83.7	8.9	86.4
63.5	97.6	17.9	32.8	29.7	7.3	88.2	48.4	28.0	2.8
56.2	6.0	95.6	2.9	71.9	36.2	97.7	43.7	32.8	28.4
22.0	93.5	40.7	57.7	99.2	91.0	85.5	36.6	48.6	10.1
52.0	91.1	47.9	48.3	53.5	62.8	29.1	41.4	89.4	34.9
98.4	1.9	27.8	84.3	81.5	83.9	13.5	57.8	94.1	71.1
0.8	73.8	37.4	91.9	11.2	49.0	17.9	57.9	16.4	49.5
93.0	27.8	46.0	67.8	41.4	97.0	20.2	24.5	58.2	11.3
8.0	94.1	75.4	6.0	9.4	57.5	7.1	70.3	63.9	77.9
19.9	35.6	82.6	2.6	27.9	90.3	6.8	89.5	13.6	18.8
90.1	58.9	72.6	64.9	6.6	69.7	84.5	21.7	83.7	21.1
7.7	45.2	59.6	79.3	99.8	93.3	66.7	29.0	63.3	90.2
38.7	49.7	15.5	15.2	44.0	17.8	84.0	16.8	43.3	32.6
26.8	51.9	72.3	68.1	78.1	49.6	49.5	49.8	17.9	0.7
9.4	55.7	68.1	71.2	59.9	43.5	12.1	41.8	65.1	1.7
40.6	71.7	53.6	26.4	21.8	88.0	50.6	22.6	96.3	99.4
36.3	31.2	98.3	35.3	28.5	80.2	99.9	10.0	90.3	61.2
82.2	12.0	63.2	31.5	30.1	17.4	24.5	39.9	52.9	29.6

Appendix B
Using Graph Paper

FINANCIAL DATA IS NORMALLY PRESENTED IN TABLES EVEN THOUGH IT IS HARD TO analyze in tabular form. The important data is often buried in a mass of less important data, which makes relationships hard to see. The story data has to tell is much easier to understand if you plot the data on graph paper. Use tables to store data, but use graph paper to plot and analyze data. Four types of graph paper—arithmetic, semilogarithmic, log-log, and probability—are useful for analyzing financial data.

ARITHMETIC GRAPH PAPER

Arithmetic paper is the simplest and most common type of graph paper. Both the vertical and horizontal axes are scaled arithmetically, and it is useful for simple plots where absolute changes in the quantities being examined are important. A sample of arithmetic graph paper is shown in Fig. B-1. Percentage changes are usually more important in financial analysis, so graph paper with one or both axes scaled logarithmically is usually more informative.

SEMILOGARITHMIC GRAPH PAPER

Semilogarithmic graph paper has one axis (usually the vertical axis) scaled logarithmically. Logarithmic scales are used when percentage changes in the quantities being examined are important. Equal percentage changes plot as equal distances on logarithmic scales. The distance from 2 to 4 on a logarithmic scale is the same as the distance from 4 to 8—both distances represent a doubling in value.

A one dollar increase in the price of a stock from $1 to $2 per share is important because it represents a doubling in that stock's value. But the same one dollar change from $100 to $101 per share is trivial, because it represents only a 1 percent increase in value. Logarithmic scales put these changes in perspective. The one dollar change from $1 to $2 per share will appear much larger than the one dollar change from $100 to $101 per share.

A sample of semilogarithmic paper is shown in Fig. B-2. The sample shown has two log cycles on the vertical axis. Semilog paper is also available with a single cycle, and with three, four, and more cycles on the vertical axis. The top division of each cycle is always 10 times larger than the bottom division. The bottom division can be set at any power of 10, such as 0.01, 1, 100, etc. If the bottom line in Fig. B-2 is set at 0.01, for example, the upper division of the first cycle is 10 times larger, or 0.1. The upper division of the top cycle is larger by another factor of 10, or 1.0.

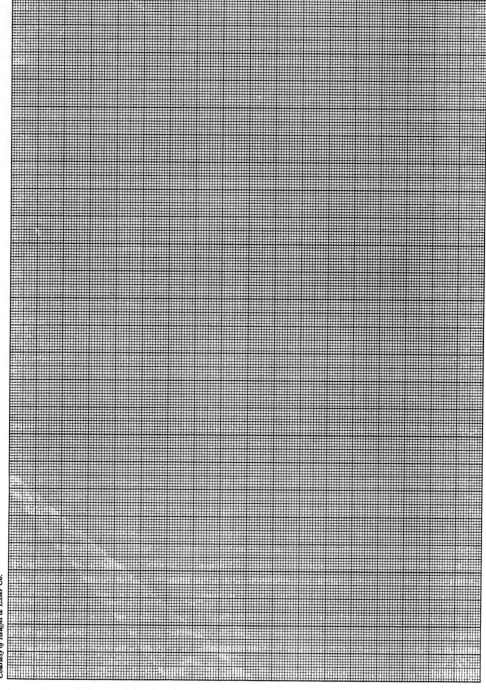

Fig. B-1. *Arithmetic graph paper.*

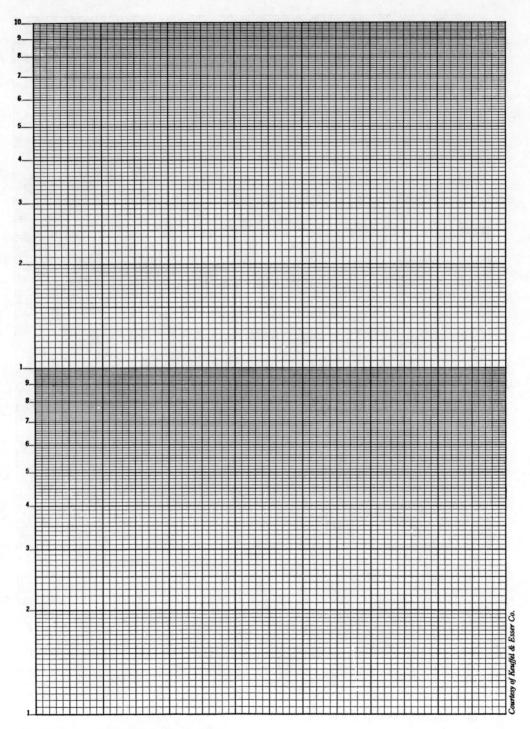

Fig. B-2. *Semilogarithmic graph paper.*

Logarithmic scales can also be adjusted by multiplying or dividing (but not by adding or subtracting) by a constant. Suppose you were plotting a series of earnings that started at $0.57 and ended at $2.80 per share. Two-cycle paper would be required if the log scale were not adjusted. Plotting would begin at $0.57 in the bottom cycle, and end at $2.80 in the upper cycle. If the log scale were multiplied by five, the bottom of the cycle would start at $0.50 and the top of that cycle would end at $5.00. Earnings could then be drawn on single-cycle paper. Single-cycle paper might be preferred over two-cycle paper because vertical movments of the data are twice as large. Note the changes in shading on the logarithmic scale. The changes in shading indicate changes in the way distances between major scale divisions are subdivided. Be careful when plotting on logarithmic scales. You must be certain you understand the value of the interval between grid lines in the region where you are plotting.

Semilog graph paper is particularly useful for analyzing growth rates. Any quantity that grows at a constant percentage rate plots as a straight line against time on semilog paper. The slope of the line measures the growth rate. If the growth rate is gradually decaying, the data will plot as a curve. The growth rate at any point is the slope of a straight line drawn tangent to the curve at that point.

Growth rates are best calculated by plotting the data on semilog paper and measuring the slope of the best straight line drawn through the data. The procedure for calculating growth rates from semilog plots is illustrated in Fig. B-3, which repeats the plot of Hewlett-Packard's earnings from Fig. 11-2. Growth rate is calculated as follows:

1. Line up a transparent straightedge through the data and, by eye, draw the best straight line you can through the data. If the data plots as a curve rather than a straight line, draw the best curved line through the data, then draw a straight line tangent to the curve at the point where you want to measure the growth rate. Extend the line well beyond the data in both directions.

2. Locate a point at each end of the straight line drawn in step 1, and read the coordinates of each point. Call the values you read at times t_1 and t_2, V_1 and V_2, respectively.

3. The growth rate in percent per year is:
$$g = 100 \ln(V_2/V_1)/(t_2-t_1) \qquad \text{(B-1)}$$

4. Alternatively, recognize that V_2/V_1 is a growth factor. Look up that factor in Appendix Table A1 and read the gT product that growth factor corresponds to. The growth rate is:
$$g = gT/(t_2-t_1) \qquad \text{(B-2)}$$
The growth rate will be identical to the growth rate calculated in step 3. If the quantity is decaying instead of growing, the ratio V_2/V_1 will be a discount factor instead of a growth factor. Look up the corresponding RT product in Appendix Table A3 and calculate the decay rate from:
$$g = RT/(t_2-t_1) \qquad \text{(B-3)}$$

Example B-1. Calculate the percentage growth rate of Hewlett-Packard's earnings from 1976 through 1980 from the semilog earnings plot in Fig. B-3.

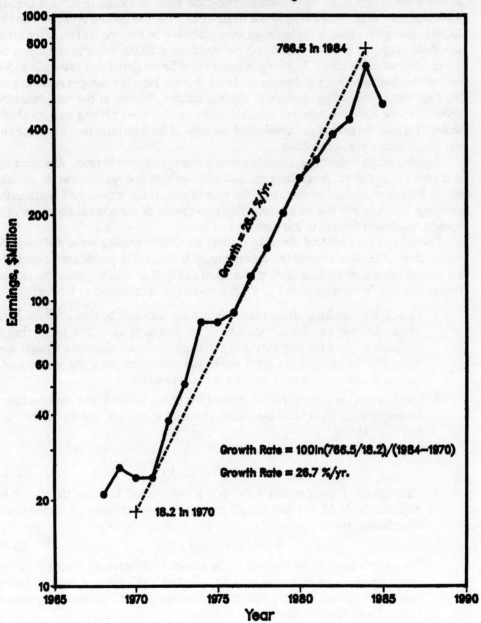

Fig. B-3.
Growth Rate—
Hewlett-Packard Earnings

Determine the growth rate by drawing the best straight line you can through the five data points from 1976 through 1980, as shown in Fig. B-3. Extend the line past the data at both ends for leverage. Read the coordinates of this line as $18.2 million in 1970 at the lower end of the line and $766.5 million in 1984 at the upper end. Calculate the growth rate from Equation (B-1):

$$g = 100 \ln(766.5/18.2)/(1984 - 1970)$$
$$g = 100 \ln(42.12)/(14) = 26.7 \ \%/yr.$$

Note that the growth along this line from $18.2 million to $766.5 million in earnings corresponds to a growth factor of 42.12. Read from Appendix Table A-1 that a growth factor of 42.12 occurs at a gT product of 374. The growth rate over this 14-year period can be calculated from the gT product:

$$g = 374/14 = 26.7 \ \%/yr.$$

This growth rate agrees exactly with the rate calculated from the slope of the line drawn in Fig. B-3.

The best straight line that can be drawn through any data segment is known as a least-squares line. If your calculator is able to do linear regression, you can calculate a least-squares growth rate for the straight-line segment of your data. Follow the instructions for linear regression in your calculator manual. To calculate a least-squares growth rate, you need a regression of the logarithm of earnings (or sales, capital employed, etc.) against time. Convert earnings to ln(earnings), and then enter ln(earnings) into your calculator's regression program. The growth rate is the coefficient of time, and is in decimal form.

Plot the data before you calculate the least-squares growth rate on your calculator. Least-squares growth rates are reliable only for data that plots as reasonable straight lines. Plotting the data identifies time segments for which the data follows a straight line.

LOG-LOG GRAPH PAPER

Log-log graph paper has both axes scaled logarithmically. A sample of two-cycle by two-cycle paper is shown in Fig. B-4. Log-log paper is also available with one, three, four, and more log cycles on each scale. Log-log paper is usually better for plotting data such as sales, earnings, and dividends. These cash flows move the same distance to the right each year on semilog paper, regardless of whether that year was one of economic boom or one of economic bust. Sales, earnings, and dividends do not grow because time passes, but because the economy grows during that time. Plotting the logarithm of sales, earnings, and dividends against the logarithm of some measure of economic activity, such as the GNP, is a more meaningful way to analyze data because it reflects the level of economic activity in each year.

The slope of a straight line through the data on log-log paper is a growth multiple. Growth multiples express growth as a multiple of economic growth. Growth multiples are calculated just like growth rates are calculated on semilog paper. Plot the data on log-log paper, and draw the best straight line through the data. Extend the line well beyond the data on both sides for leverage. Read a value (V_1) at a measure of the economy (E_1)

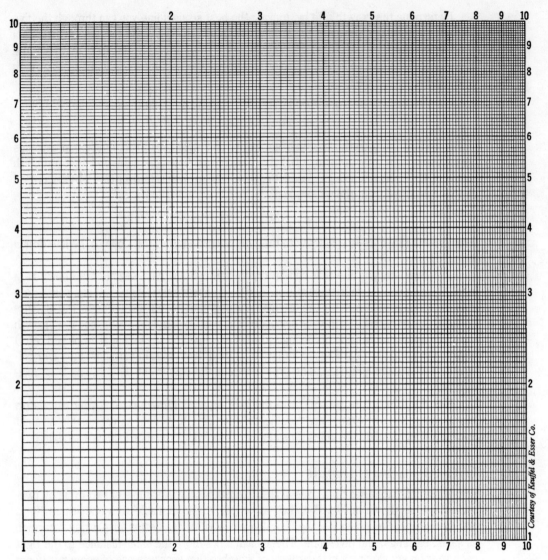

Fig. B-4. *Log-log graph paper.*

at the left end of the line, and a second value (V_2) at a measure of the economy (E_2) at the right end of the line. The growth multiple is:

$$\text{Growth Multiple} = \ln(V_2/V_1)/\ln(E_2/E_1) \qquad \text{(B-4)}$$

Example B-2. Measure a growth multiple for Hewlett-Packard's earnings. Hewlett-Packard's earnings are plotted against the GNP on log coordinates in Fig. B-5, which repeats Fig. 11-3. Draw the best straight line, by eye, through the data, and extend the line well beyond the data on both sides. Read earnings of $16.3 million at a GNP of $884 billion at the left of the line, and earnings of $750 million at a GNP of $4,331 billion at

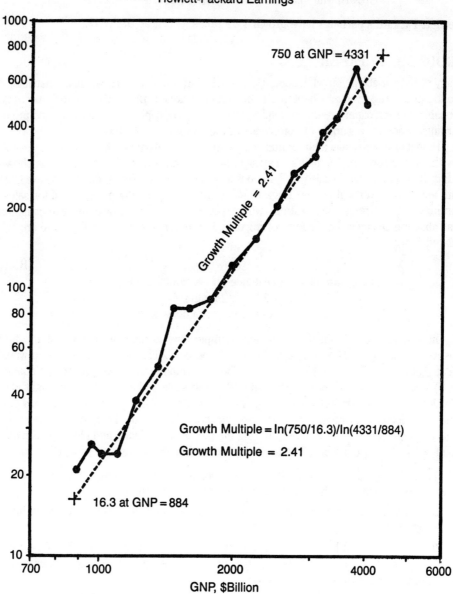

Fig. B-5.
Growth Multiple—
Hewlett-Packard Earnings

750 at GNP = 4331

Growth Multiple = 2.41

Growth Multiple = ln(750/16.3)/ln(4331/884)

Growth Multiple = 2.41

16.3 at GNP = 884

GNP, $Billion

the right end. The growth multiple is:

$$\text{Growth Multiple} = \ln(750/16.3)/\ln(4{,}331/884) = 2.41$$

Hewlett-Packard's earnings have grown 2.41 times as fast as the GNP.

PROBABILITY PAPER

Many of the variables you will encounter in analyzing securities are normally distributed around an average value. Chapter 10 showed how helpful the normal distribution and probability graph paper are for examining rates of return, capital growth rates, and price/earnings ratios for a sample of companies in the computer industry.

Probability paper has a horizontal scale especially constructed so that quantities follow the normal distribution plot as a straight line. A sample of probability paper is shown in Fig. B-6. The vertical scale on Fig. B-6 is arithmetic. Probability paper is also available with logarithmic vertical scales. Logarithmic scales are generally more useful for sales, earnings, and price/earnings ratios, where percentage changes are more meaningful than absolute changes. Points for plotting data on the horizontal probability scale are calculated from:

$$x = 100(n - 0.5)/N \qquad (B=5)$$

where x = Distance on horizontal scale
  n = Observation number
  N = Total number of observations

In a sample of 12 observations, for example, the horizontal position of the first observation would be (100) $(1-0.5)/12$, or 4.2 percent. The second observation would be at (100) $(2-0.5)/12$, or 12.5 percent. The horizontal scale is symmetrical; Equation (B-5) locates two points, one on the left end of the scale and a second at the right end. The location symmetrical to the first point at 4.2 percent is at $100-4.2$, or 95.8 percent. The location symmetrical to the second point is at $100-12.5$, or 87.5 percent. This treatment is equivalent to considering the plot as a bar chart, and plotting each data point at the center of its bar. The following steps simplify plotting on probability paper:

1. Calculate values along the horizontal probability scale from Equation (B-5). Draw a tick mark at each calculated point along the horizontal scale.

2. Draw tick marks along the vertical scale locating the values of the quantity being plotted.

3. By eye, draw a horizontal line from the top tick mark on the vertical scale and a vertical line from the left-most tick mark on the horizontal scale. Draw a data point where these two lines cross.

4. Proceed in the same way to match each tick mark on the vertical scale with a corresponding tick mark on the horizontal scale, and draw a data point.

Probability plots are particularly useful in identifying firms with unusual results. If no firm in an industry is unusual, the data will scatter in the normal way around the average value for the industry. A variable such as the rate of return will plot as a reasonably straight line on probability paper. The firm with the highest return will have only the return one should expect for a random sample of firms. If one firm has an outstanding

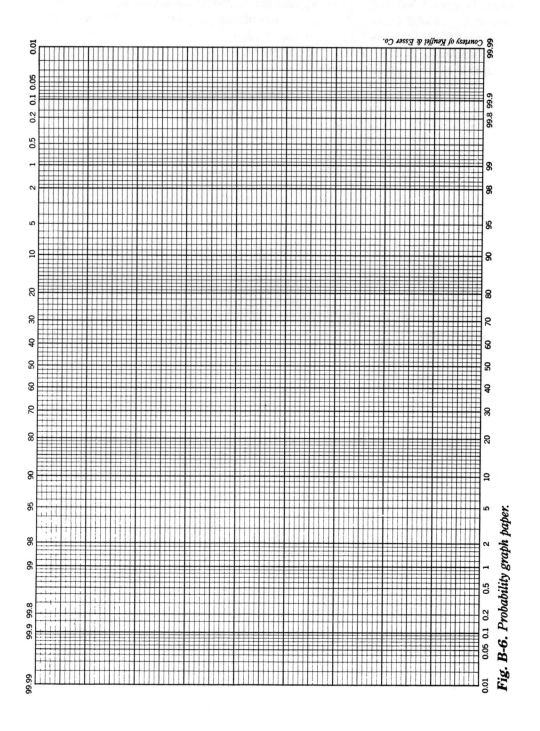

Fig. B-6. Probability graph paper.

Courtesy of Keuffel & Esser Co.

return, however, it will lie above a straight line drawn through the data for all firms in that industry on probability paper. If a firm has an unusually poor return, that firm will plot below the straight line drawn through the other firms.

Example B-3. In 1986, a sample of nine chemical companies paid the following percentages of earnings out as dividends:

Company	Dividend Payout, %
Celanese	28.6
Dow	49.1
Du Pont	48.0
Essex	54.5
Hercules	49.0
Monsanto	55.0
Olin	58.6
Rohm & Haas	31.7
Union Carbide	120.0

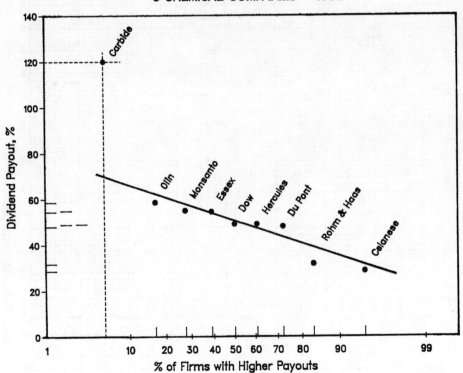

Fig. 8–7
DIVIDEND PAYOUT
9 CHEMICAL COMPANIES – 1986

Plot the distribution on probability graph paper and determine if any firm had an unusually high or an unusually low dividend payout. Draw the vertical dividend payout scale from 0 to 140 percent payout, and make a tick mark for each payout listed in the table above. Now, calculate locations on the horizontal probability scale from Equation (B-5). Because of the symmetry of the scale, each calculation locates two points.

Points	Locations on Probability Scale, %
1, 9	5.6, 94.4
2, 8	16.7, 83.3
3, 7	27.8, 72.2
4, 6	38.9, 61.1
5	50.0

Make tick marks along the horizontal scale at each location calculated above. Finally, plot data points at the intersections of horizontal lines drawn through each tick mark on the vertical scale with the corresponding vertical lines through each tick mark on the horizontal scale. Figure B-7 illustrates the process. The two dashed lines show how to locate the first data point corresponding to the top tick mark on the vertical scale and the leftmost tick mark on the horizontal scale.

Except for Union Carbide, the data points line up reasonably well on a straight line and, therefore, are normally distributed. Union Carbide's dividend payout of 120 percent is significantly higher than one should expect from a sample of chemical companies. The probability plot shows that, excluding Union Carbide, the average dividend payout was 47 percent. Ninety percent of chemical companies had dividend payouts from 29 percent to 65 percent.

Index

Other Bestsellers of Related Interest

FRANK CAPPIELLO'S NEW GUIDE TO FINDING THE NEXT SUPERSTOCK—Frank Cappiello
"Frank Cappiello is one of America's most brilliant analysts...he has few peers as a super stock picker."
Louis Rukeyser

Investors today still marvel at the huge profits made in superstocks of the past such as Xerox, IBM, and Hewlett Packard. For savvy investors, such opportunities still exist. In this new guide, Frank Cappiello reveals his own successful approach to uncovering the superstocks of the future. He shows readers how to sift through the thousands of available stocks and pick out the few that are poised for hypergrowth. 208 pages, 102 illustrations. Book No. 30041, $12.95 paperback, $18.95 hardcover.

UNDERSTANDING WALL STREET—2nd Edition—Jeffery B. Little and Lucien Rhodes
*"An excellent introduction to stock market *intracacies"*
—American Library Association Booklist

This bestselling guide to understand and investing on Wall Street has been completely updated to reflect the most current developments in the stock market. The substantial growth of mutual funds, the emergence of index options, the sweeping new tax bill, and how to keep making money after the market reaches record highs and lows are a few of the things explained in this long awaited revision. 240 pages, 18 illustrations. Book No. 30020, $9.95 paperback, $19.95 hardcover.

THE ARTHUR YOUNG GUIDE TO RAISING VENTURE CAPITAL—G. Steven Burrill and Craig T. Norback

This book equips entrepreneurs with the necessary know-how to obtain venture capital. Complex issues involved in securing funds and negotiating deals are thoroughly and factually addressed. And a directory of venture capital firms in the U.S. and Canada provides you with immediate access to potential investors. 272 pages. Book No. 30014, $24.95 hardcover

SWISS BANK ACCOUNTS: A Personal Guide to Ownership, Benefits, and Use—Michael Arthur Jones

There's a real misconception about Swiss bank accounts: everyone thinks they're only for rich people and criminals. This book is a complete guide to the *uses and benefits* of Swiss bank accounts, by a respected professor of finance and authority on the subject. It's a practical manual that shows readers how to choose, open, use, and maintain an account. All procedures are highlighted with sample forms, documents, and even sample correspondence. 230 pages. Book No. 30046, $21.95 hardcover.

TAX-CUTTING TACTICS FOR INVESTORS: Legal Loopholes For The 1990s—Denise Lamaute

Denise Lamaute describes in layman's terms how to use your home and other real estate as a hedge against taxes, build tax-free wealth with government bonds and other securities, avoid the alternative minimum tax, minimize taxable gain and maximize capital losses, and capitalized on tax-free exchange of assets. Other key topics include: retirement investment, viable tax shelters, tax-smart recordkeeping, deductible borrowing, deductions and credits, and more. 208 pages. Book No. 30048, $14.95 paperback, $29.95 hardcover.

NO-LOADS: Mutual Fund Profits Using Technical Analysis—James E. Kearis

Experts agree that no-load mutual funds—professionally managed funds with no sales charges or commission fees—are the best way for small investors to make big gains in the stock market. Here, James E. Kearis illustrates a three-step plan that involves selecting a reliable newsletter, choosing a good no-load fund, and then tracking your investments by using the technical analysis methods that Kearis illustrates. For as little as $35 a year and 30 minutes a week, you can enjoy the profits of shrewd investing. 216 pages, illustrations. Book No. 30036, $19.95 hardcover.

THE NO-NONSENSE LANDLORD—Richard H. Jorgensen

This is a realistic, no-*hype guide to making money in real estate. Here Richard Jorgensen presents his proven methods of shrewd financing and management—methods that even seasoned landlords will find invaluable. You'll find helpful expert advice on: selecting good tenants, making low-cost repairs, and handling complaints. 204 pages, illustrations. Book No. 30032, $22.95 hardcover.

FIGHT THE IRS AND WIN! A Self-Defense Guide for Taxpayers—Cliff Roberson

With this practical guide you can obtain the best results possible—protect your individual and property rights—in any dispute with the IRS. The outstanding feature of this book is that it takes complicated IRS operations and provides the average taxpayer with advice on how to protect himself in IRS controversies. It is the taxpayer's self-defense book. 224 pages. Book No. 30021, $12.95 paperback, $24.95 hardcover.

AVOIDING PROBATE: Tamper-Proof Estate Planning—Cliff Roberson

Discover how to hand down everything you own to anyone you choose without interference from courts, creditors, relatives, or the IRS. In these easy-to-read planning guide, attorney Cliff Roberson shows how you can avoid the horrors of probate court. Sample wills and trust agreements and checklists in every chapter make planning each step easy. *Avoiding Probate* covers: living trusts, life insurance, specific property, wills, family business, valuing your estate, estate taxes, and more. 263 pages. Book No. 30074, $14.95 paperback, $29.95 hardcover.

THE PERSONAL TAX ADVISOR: Understanding The New Tax Law—Cliff Roberson, LLM, Ph.D

"...condense(s) the three-volume, 2,800 page (tax) law into language all taxpayers can comprehend."

—**Country Journal**

How will the new tax law affect your tax return this filing season? Any reform is certain to mean a change in the way your taxes are prepared. Buy you don't have to be an accountant or a lawyer to understand the new tax laws. 176 pages. Book No. 30134, $12.95 paperback.

Prices Subject to Change Without Notice.

Look for These and Other TAB Books at Your Local Bookstore

To Order Call Toll Free 1-800-822-8158
(in PA, AK, and Canada call 717-794-2191)

or write to TAB BOOKS, Blue Ridge Summit, PA 17294-0840.

Title	Product No.	Quantity	Price

☐ Check or money order made payable to TAB BOOKS

Charge my ☐ VISA ☐ MasterCard ☐ American Express

Acct. No. _____ Exp. _____

Signature: _____

Name: _____

Address: _____

City: _____

State: _____ Zip: _____

Subtotal $ _____

Postage and Handling
($3.00 in U.S., $5.00 outside U.S.) $ _____

Add applicable state
and local sales tax $ _____

TOTAL $ _____

TAB BOOKS catalog free with purchase; otherwise send $1.00 in check or money order and receive $1.00 credit on your next purchase.

Orders outside U.S. must pay with international money order in U.S. dollars.

TAB Guarantee: If for any reason you are not satisfied with the book(s) you order, simply return it (them) within 15 days and receive a full refund.　　　　　　　　　　　　　　　　　**BC**

Winning Investment Strategies:
Using Security Analysis to Build Wealth

If you would like to enhance your capacity to analyze and evaluate stocks, bonds, mutual funds, Ginnie Maes, CDs, and IRAs, you should definitely consider ordering the companion software disk and documentation booklet for *Winning Investment Strategies* (Liberty book No. 3509). The program and booklet allow users to evaluate stocks, bonds, and mutual funds, and to develop forecasts needed to determine when to sell and when to buy stocks. The program extends the user's reach—you will be able to analyze many more securities by computer than by hand—and risk analysis will be much more effective. With this program, you can examine up to 1,000 random outcomes by computer compared to five or so outcomes by hand.

This software is guaranteed free of manufacturer's defects. If you have any problems, return the disk within 30 days, and we'll send you a new one.

Available on 5¼″ disk requring 360K at $49.95, plus $2.50 shipping and handling. You need an IBM PC or compatible and DOS version 2.0 or newer.

See page 305 for a Special Companion Disk Offer

Yes, I'm interested. Send me:

_____ copies 5¹/₄" disk requiring 360K   (#6741S), $49.95 . . . . $ _____

_____ TAB BOOKS catalog (free with purchase; otherwise send $1.00
in check or money order, credited to your first purchase) . . . . $ _____

Shipping & Handling: $2.50 per disk in U.S. $ _____
($5.00 per disk outside U.S.) $ _____

Please add applicable state and local sales tax $ _____

TOTAL $ _____

☐ Check or money order enclosed made payable to TAB BOOKS

Charge my   ☐ VISA   ☐ MasterCard   ☐ American Express

Acct No. _____ Exp. Date _____

Signature _____

Name _____

Address _____

City _____ State _____ Zip _____

TOLL-FREE ORDERING: 1-800-822-8158
(in PA, AK, and Canada call 1-717-794-2191)

or write to TAB BOOKS, Blue Ridge Summit, PA, 17294-0840

Prices subject to change. Orders outside the U.S. must be paid in international money order in U.S. dollars.

TAB 3509